Assessment Centers and Managerial Performance

ORGANIZATIONAL AND OCCUPATIONAL PSYCHOLOGY

Series Editor: PETER WARR
MRC Social and Applied Psychology Unit, Department of Psychology,
The University, Sheffield, England

Theodore D. Weinshall
Managerial Communication: Concepts, Approaches and Techniques, 1979

Chris Argyris
Inner Contradictions of Rigorous Research, 1980

Charles J. de Wolff, Sylvia Shimmin, and Maurice de Montmollin
Conflicts and Contradictions: Work Psychology in Europe, 1981

Nigel Nicholson, Gil Ursell, and Paul Blyton
The Dynamics of White Collar Unionism, 1981

Dean G. Pruitt
Negotiation Behavior, 1981

Richard T. Mowday, Lyman W. Porter, and Richard M. Steers
Employee–Organization Linkages: The Psychology of Commitment,
Absenteeism, and Turnover, 1982

Richard A. Guzzo (Editor)
Improving Group Decision Making in Organizations: Approaches from
Theory and Research, 1982

George C. Thornton III and William C. Byham
Assessment Centers and Managerial Performance, 1982

In preparation

Rudi Klauss and Bernard Bass
Interpersonal Communication in Organizations,1982

Assessment Centers and Managerial Performance

George C. Thornton III

Department of Psychology
Colorado State University
Fort Collins, Colorado

William C. Byham

Development Dimensions International
Pittsburgh, Pennsylvania

ACADEMIC PRESS 1982
A Subsidiary of Harcourt Brace Jovanovich, Publishers

New York   London
Paris San Diego San Francisco São Paulo Sydney Tokyo Toronto

ACADEMIC PRESS, INC.
111 Fifth Avenue, New York, New York 10003

United Kingdom Edition published by
ACADEMIC PRESS, INC. (LONDON) LTD.
24/28 Oval Road, London NW1 7DX

Library of Congress Cataloging in Publication Data

Thornton, George C.
   Assessment centers and managerial performance.

   (Organizational and occupational psychology)
   Includes index.
   1. Assessment centers (Personnel management procedure)
I. Byham, William C. II. Title. III. Series.
HF5549.5.A78T48   658.4'07125   82-1747
ISBN 0-12-690620-3   AACR2

To Douglas W. Bray
without whose research and insights
there would be no assessment center method

Contents

3

Approaches to Predicting Managerial Effectiveness   61

4

The Content of Assessment:
Defining the Dimension of Managerial Success   95

5

Assessment Center Exercises
and Dimension Ratings 143

6
The Assessment Process 219

7
Criterion Validity of Overall Assessment Center Judgments 251

8
Contributions to Management Development 321

9
Unique Uses of Assessment Center Methodology 345

10

Assessment Centers and the Courts 371

11

Past, Present, and Future 391

References 415

Preface

In our opinion, assessment centers are one of the two or three major developments in the field of personnel psychology in the last 25 years. More research has supported this technique of managerial assessment than any other practice in the field of industrial–organizational psychology. Whereas previous books have discussed the use of assessment centers in one organization or have had a decidedly practical orientation, this book is theoretical and analytical. We believe that much can be learned by an examination of the assessment experience.

The purposes of this book are (a) to trace the historical development of multiple assessment procedures with emphasis on those advances relevant to assessment centers; (b) to critique all of the published and unpublished research on assessment centers; (c) to integrate assessment center procedures into several theories of measurement and human judgment; and (d) to present new models of job analysis, the nature of managerial work, work-sampling assessment techniques, and the process of human judgment based on the assessment center experience.

For the past 15 years the authors have been actively engaged in managerial assessment activities. During this time both of us have been employed in private industry, academia, and consulting practice. The book presents a critical evaluation from these various perspectives of assessment center theory, research, technology, and practice. We have not attempted to present a "how-to-do-it" manual for assessment center practitioners. Rather we have reviewed the assessment center literature with an eye toward what the best theory and research have to contribute to the practical business of management assessment.

Our discussion of assessment theory, research, and practice is intended for anyone interested in the development, application, or evaluation of managerial assessment and development programs. The primary audiences are industrial–organizational psychologists and personnel and development managers. In addition, clinical psychologists, vocational guidance counselors, training and development specialists, and managerial consultants will find major sections of the book relevant to their specialty areas.

We first saw a need for a book on assessment centers in 1970. At that time the initial wave of practice and predictive validity research had been carried out in a few pioneering organizations. Major portions of the manuscript were completed by 1974. Then it became apparent that a second wave of research and application was under way in a much larger number of organizations. Researchers were investigating longer range predictive accuracy for multiple criteria, comparing predictive validity of assessment centers and other assessment methods, exploring the human judgment processes of assessors, and studying various administrative and ethical issues. Practitioners were developing new assessment center technologies, using assessment centers for new purposes, and adapting the techniques to meet various administrative demands. Completion of this book awaited the release of many of those studies. Although many other research studies are currently under way, a summary and an integration are clearly needed at this time.

Many people played a prominent role in the completion of this book. First, we acknowledge our numerous colleagues at American Telephone & Telegraph who have been a constant source of inspiration and resources. Their willingness to share ideas and research findings clearly demonstrates that they are models of professional collegial relationships. Second, we wish to thank the many other people who privately communicated unpublished data to us.

The early work on this manuscript was completed while the first author was a Fellow at the Battelle Seattle Research Centers. We gratefully acknowledge the secretarial, library research, and editorial support services provided during this period.

Our various secretaries and assistants over the years deserve special praise, especially Beth Telgenhoff at Colorado State University and Thelma Neubauer at Development Dimensions International. They and many others attempted to translate our ragged writings into a more intelligible manuscript. Any faults or deficiencies which remain are, of course, our responsiblity.

Finally, we wish to thank our respective families—Louise, Charles, Julia, and Lara and Carolyn, Tacy, and Carter—for their patience and support throughout the years. They "live with" assessment centers nearly as much as we do.

1
The Importance of Management Assessment

A variety of methods has been developed to describe, evaluate, and predict management effectiveness. Social science researchers and management practitioners have devised numerous objective and subjective means to obtain information about management behavior. This book is devoted to one of these methods: the assessment center and a comparison of its role to other approaches in the selection, promotion, training, and development of managers. The book will deal primarily with assessment of supervisors and managers, but nonmanagement applications of assessment centers will be discussed where appropriate.

An assessment center is a comprehensive, standardized procedure in which multiple assessment techniques such as situational exercises and job simulations (i.e., business games, discussion groups, reports, and presentations) are used to evaluate individual employees for various purposes. A number of trained management evaluators, who are not in a direct supervisory capacity over the participants, conduct the assessment and make recommendations regarding the management potential and developmental needs of the participants. The results of the assessment are communicated to higher management and can be used for personnel decisions involving such things as promotions, transfers, and career planning. When the results are communicated to the participants, they form the basis for self-insight and development planning.

Behavioral scientists who carry out research in industry, as well as personnel administrators and managers who work in organizations, devote a significant portion of their time to the research, evaluation, and development of managerial performance. Considerable time and effort in any organization go into the recruitment, interviewing, selection, orientation, development, supervision, and appraisal of managerial personnel. Prior to the 1950s there was a preponderance of research on lower level, non-supervisory employees. Over the past 3 decades, substantial research in industrial–organizational psychology has been devoted to the systematic study of factors related to managerial behavior and effectiveness.

Problems of Management Assessment

Why has the evaluation of management behavior been so difficult? There are several reasons, most of which center around difficulties in precisely defining the job of manager. In addition to the obvious differences of requirements for supervisors, middle managers, and executives, there are also subtle but real differences within levels. Some management positions are mainly administrative, with a heavy load of paper work; other positions require a large amount of personal contact to coordinate the work of subordinates; still others involve extensive negotiation with persons outside the organization. No one job description deals effectively with the complexity of all sets of requirements. Management jobs are difficult to analyze because of the long-term cycle of activities (e.g., budgets and performance appraisals are usually prepared only once a year). Furthermore, a manager seldom does the same thing repeatedly in the same way. This further complicates the observation and measurement of jobs. Often we do not know what types of organizational and environmental demands will be placed on the manager nor do we know the relevance of the evaluative information we have about an individual to those job demands. However, job analyses and judgment research for assessment centers have contributed to basic understanding of managerial jobs. Chapter 4 will deal with job analysis research and the attempt of assessment centers to define job requirements of managers. Chapter 5 and 6 will cover the ability to predict the effectiveness of managers relative to the job requirements.

Judgments of competence to perform in a future management position are usually based on one of five sources of information: (a) evaluation of job success and potential by current supervisors; (b) results from traditional paper-and-pencil tests; (c) clinical evaluations by psychologists and related professionals; (d) background interviews; and (e) observations in job simulations in an assessment center. Each of these approaches has strengths that can be utilized in a coordinated program for the prediction of management potential; each also has weaknesses. For example, to equate performance effectiveness in a lower level job with effectiveness in a higher level position where the demands and abilities are different is a tenuous assumption. Such assumptions lead to the situation where a person rises to the level of his incompetence as popularized in "The Peter Principle."

Judgments by supervisors regarding a person's potential success may be biased in many ways, including lack of knowledge of higher level job demands and lack of opportunity to observe the person in situations relevant to the higher level job (Adams & Fyffe, 1969). Problems with the clinical interview center mostly around lack of knowledge of job demands and the maximum potential validity inherent in the procedures. It is difficult for an outsider to know the job requirements and situational pressures in an organization. Abstract diagnoses of adjustment usually do not serve well in the prediction of managerial behavior.

The use of traditional paper-and-pencil tests has proved valid in a number of excellent research studies (Campbell, Dunnette, Lawler, & Weick, 1970) and will remain a valuable method. However, the general public's increasing resistance to such tests (because of their sometimes low face validity and intrusion on personal privacy) and the growing demands for evidence of validity and fairness (Equal Employment Opportunity Commission, Civil Service Commission, Dept. of Labor, and Dept. of Justice, 1978) have led to a search for alternative methods of assessment (Byham & Bobin, 1972). It will be argued here that the assessment center approach, using simulations of actual managerial behavior, has features that avoid the problems involved in other approaches although it should be emphasized that an organization could benefit at times from using any one of the five approaches listed earlier. One purpose of this book is to review the evidence regarding the appropriate use of alternative methods and to evaluate the role assessment centers play in relation to other approaches. Much of this discussion is contained in Chapter 3.

Description of an Assessment Center

An *assessment center* is a procedure (not a location) that uses multiple assessment techniques to evaluate employees for a variety of manpower purposes and decisions. Most frequently, the approach has been applied to individuals being considered for selection, promotion, placement, or special training and development in management. The original industrial centers developed by American Telephone and Telegraph (AT&T) involved line personnel being considered for promotion to first-level supervision. Since then, the technique has been applied to the identification of individuals for many positions (e.g., middle managers, top executives, sales people, and management trainees). The wide variety of uses of assessment center methodology is covered in Chapter 9.

Assessment centers have their greatest value when the participant is aspiring to a job significantly different from the position held. The simulation of job requirements for the new position provides an opportunity to evaluate skills that is not available from observation of performance on the current job. The technique has also proven effective for seemingly similar jobs where greater reliability or objectivity of observation is required.

Individuals are usually assessed in a group. Group assessment affords opportunities to observe peer interactions and aids the efficiency of observation. Anywhere from 1 to 12 people might be observed in a program. For illustrative purposes, we will describe a common arrangement of six assessees, three assessors, and one program administrator.

Staff members of the assessment center may consist entirely of trained management personnel, all professional psychologists, or a combination of both. The low ratio of assessees to assessors (typically 2:1) is important to the assessment center process because it allows close contact and observation of the participant and makes multiple evaluations possible. Management personnel who serve as assessors are usually two or more levels above the participants in the organization hierarchy, trained for the task of assessment, and not in a direct supervisory capacity over the participants.

Industrial assessment centers employ a number of assessment techniques to ensure complete coverage of management abilities. Management games, leaderless group discussions, role-playing exercises, and other simulation techniques are used most frequently, but a few organizations also use a background interview or tests. The job simulations allow the participant to engage in joblike mangerial situations and display job-relevant behaviors: administrative decision making, discussions in small groups, and one-to-one interactions with employees. Chapter 5 reviews in detail the types of exercises used in assessment centers and summarizes the evidence of their reliability and validity. At that point, we will discuss issues related to interrater agreement, stability of measurement of complex behavior, and the predictive and constructive validity of assessment center techniques and dimension ratings. We will show that the evidence supports the use of multiple techniques and multiple dimension ratings.

The tasks of observing complex social behavior, integrating the information, and making predictions is difficult; therefore, most assessment center programs include extensive training for the management assessors. Their ability to make accurate prediction is borne out in the literature reviewed in Chapter 7 and is supported by findings from other multiple assessment procedures summarized by Cronbach (1970) and Taft (1955, 1959). The process of integrating the assessment information and making predictions in an assessment center is quite systematic. Assessors report behavioral observations and dimension ratings for each exercise and then make independent ratings of overall dimension performance. The assessors then reach consensus on dimension ratings and finally make predictions of management success. The process of integrating the assessment information and making predictions in an assessment center is analyzed in depth in Chapter 6 and discussed in the context of the controversy over clinical versus actuarial prediction (Holt, 1970, 1975; Sawyer, 1966). The literature on decision making and the human judgment process is evaluated in conjunction with the assessment center process.

Although most assessment centers are designed to predict management capabilities, they are also used for the development of participants. Participation in the exercises may be a learning experience per se and may provide personal insights into managerial competence. Feedback of results in the form of oral and written reports to the participant and immediate supervisor may clarify developmental needs. In some cases, time is spent following the assessment period for management development and self-analysis activities such as viewing oneself in videotapes of exercises or reviewing decisions made in the "in-basket exercise"—an exercise developed to simulate the administrative tasks of a manager's job. The role of assessment centers in management development and the related research in this area are summarized in Chapter 8.

The Assessment Process

Managerial assessment centers emerged from a rich tradition of multiple assessment programs developed in the 1940s and 1950s. This history is reviewed in Chapter 2. Multiple assessment procedures can be distinguished from other personality measurement procedures, such as tests and clinical interviews, in several ways: Multiple assessment techniques including job simulation exercises, multiple assessors, subjective and objective data gathering, behavioral orientation, judgmental methods of combining the information gathered, concern for the whole person, and prediction of adequacy of performance on a criterion.

Personality measurement does not necessarily involve a large number of assessment techniques. Clinical assessment of personality is often based on nothing more than in-depth interviewing and possibly some psychometric testing. However, assessment center programs are distinguished by the use of multiple techniques. These programs are usually lengthy, requiring up to three days of participant activities.

Assessment differs from psychometric prediction in both the measurement techniques utilized and the process of making the prediction. Pure psychometric prediction involves the more objective or mechanical forms of measurement such as paper-and-pencil tests, questionnaires, and the use of quantified background information. The assessment approach may also use these techniques but it also uses more subjective techniques such as interviews, observations, projective tests, and performance exercises, or situational exercises. Group discussions, games, and other simulations are examples of exercises that require the subject to perform in a situation approximating the real-life situation. Particularly important in this approach is the focus on relevant behaviors displayed by the assessee; of less or no importance are the traits that presumably underlie these behaviors.

The process of making predictions of future behavior is quite different in assessment than it is in the psychometric approach. The latter combines the data from tests and predicts behavior on the basis of the best statistical relationship among the variables. The variables are multiplied by weights and combined to maximize the correlation between an overall predicted score and the criterion. In assessment centers, the overall prediction is made after subjective consideration of the assessment data and judgmental combination of the variables. Precise weights are not given to each variable; instead, various inputs are given more or less importance depending on the assessors' evalution of their relevance to the job in question.

Management assessment centers are designed to avoid the disadvantages of two extreme approaches to measurement. At the one extreme, some paper-and-pencil tests require only very limited (and often trivial) behaviors and measure narrowly defined traits. At the other extreme, some personality assessment programs have been concerned with such broad characteristics as "general adjustment" or "effectiveness."

In contrast, the assessment center process has made a significant modification in these approaches and now emphasizes, first, the observation of an individual's competencies on several separate behaviorally defined dimensions related to job behavior, then a prediction of overall job success. In the next section, we describe this sequence in more detail.

Another feature of assessment is its evaluative nature. The objective of most assessment is to identify the behaviors that are predictive of adequate performance in some specified situation. The assumption is that there is some means of evaluating the effectiveness of performance in the situation and that certain skills, knowledge, and abilities will lead to superior performance. Assessment then evaluates these dimensions and makes predictions. The evaluative component of assessment distinguishes it from the purely descriptive work in other personality measurement. Fiske and Pearson (1970) point out that personality assessment is a specific component of personality measurement in general.

Many personality researchers argue that it is impossible to measure "personality" and one should rather strive to measure traits which reflect major dimensions of personality (Edwards & Abbott, 1973). According to Cronbach (1970), the postulate that persons possess traits is built on three premises:

1. Behavior is consistent: A person tends to show the same habitual reaction over a range of similar situations.
2. People vary in the degree or frequency of any type of behavior.
3. Personalities have some stability.

The assessment center approach also assumes that people possess relatively enduring characteristics that influence their behavior in various settings, but it largely avoids the controversy about traits and whether behavior is determined by person or situation variables (Mischel, 1968, 1973) by emphasizing behavioral observation in work sample and job simulation measurement techniques. It focuses on job-related skills, abilities, and other characteristics (e.g., problem analysis skills, ability to plan and organize work, resistance to stress as it affects ability to make decisions under pressure, and interpersonal approaches to the leadership of individuals and groups).

Chapter 4 will point out how research on assessment centers has contributed to the understanding of the important characteristics of managerial abilities. By studying the structure of assessment ratings on a number of scales of observed behavior, researchers have identified a set of common themes or factors of behavioral observations. From these we have acquired new insights into managerial behavior on the job.

Judgment Models

The assessment center process can be depicted in three stages. Stage 1 covers the observations and ratings in exercises. Stage 2 includes the reporting of exercise information and the derivation of dimension ratings in the staff discussion. Stage 3 encompasses the integration of dimension ratings to form a final overall assessment rating.

Figure 1.1 presents a model of the assessment process for one in-dividual who is observed in a program consisting of three assessors, five performance dimensions, and four assessment exercises. Stage 1 takes place during and immediately after each exercise when observations and dimension ratings are made independently by an assessor. In the hypo-thetical example, Assessor A observed the analysis exercise and rated the person 5 on Decision Making, 4 on Oral Communication, and 4 on Written Communication. (Assume the rating scale runs from 1 low to 5 high.) Assessor A also observed and rated performance in the interview simula-tion; in this exercise, two additional dimensions were rated—Leader-ship and Use of Delegation. Assessor B was the primary observer of this person in the leaderless group discussion, although the other two assessors would be present watching other discussants. Assessor C rated the individual's in-basket performance on all five dimensions.

The figure shows that Written Communication was observed twice—in the in-basket and analysis exercise, but all other dimensions were assessed three or more times. It is desirable to have several "readings" on each dimension as assessors are not asked to evaluate dimensions irrelevant to an exercise. For example, Written Communica-tion cannot be observed in a group discussion.

Stages 2 and 3 take place in the staff discussion when all information is integrated by the assessors. Dimension ratings are derived in Stage 2. Assessors report observations and ratings from the exercises; then each assessor independently records his or her preliminary dimension ratings. Usually, these ratings are displayed on newsprint, a "flip chart," or blackboard for easy examination. In the example, there was clear agree-ment on Oral Communication (all 3s) and Use of Delegation (all 2s). Assessor B rated the person lower than others on Written Communica-tion, and A rated low on Leadership. The assessors disagreed widely on Decision Making, possibly because of lack of clarity of the dimension.

During the ensuing discussion, the assessment team, guided by a pro-gram administrator, arrives at the final dimension ratings. These ratings are consensus judgments, not averages. Many times the team can easily arrive at the final dimension ratings (e.g., 3 for Oral Communication and 2 for Use of Delegation). At other times, lengthy discussion is necessary. Considering Written Communication, the staff would try to understand why Assessor B gave a 2. In this instance, discussion led to the higher rating. In contrast, subsequent discussion led the other assessors to con-cur with Assessor A's lower rating for Leadership even though initially both scored the assessee above average. The final dimension rating on Decision Making ended up being unlike any one of the preliminary ratings.

In Stage 3, the staff arrives at the overall assessment rating. This might be defined "probability of success if hired," "promotability," or "likelihood of attaining middle management." At this stage, preliminary ratings are made independently, posted for examination, and finally consolidated in a consensus discussion. An overall assessment rating is appropriate for selection and promotion programs but when assessment is done for diagnostic purposes, Stage 3 may be omitted.

Figure 1.2 presents the assessment process from the assessors' points of view. This model depicts the contributions to assessment ratings at each stage, including relevant factors shown above the dotted lines and irrelevant "contaminants" below the line. For example, Assessor A's ratings of Decision Making from the analysis exercise is partly a function of relevant, "decision-making" behaviors shown in the exercise plus observations relevant to other dimensions. The assessee's true level of decision making may be something quite different from the exercise rating given by A.

At Stage 2, the primary observers report behavioral observations and ratings for each exercise. Assessor B's dimension ratings for the first exercise would be a function of A's input, direct observations B may have made of relevant behavior (e.g., observations in a group discussion, direct examination of in-basket responses, perusal of written analysis), and contaminants.

Preliminary dimension ratings are formulated by each assessor after hearing all exercise reports. The dimension rating for Decision Making should be a function of reported behaviors exhibiting problem analysis and judgment and ratings on this dimension from all exercises. Assessors are trained to weigh more heavily the exercises that give "stronger" readings on a dimension (e.g., the in-basket is a good measure of delegation skills) and that more closely parallel job activities. An artificially high rating on a dimension may occur if an assessor considers irrelevant behavior (e.g., high verbal fluency may be credited for Leadership). Once the preliminary dimension ratings are posted, they form the basis for the final dimension ratings. Contaminants can still enter at this stage; for example, an assessor may report some new observation picked up in informal interactions outside the assessment center. The likelihood of these extraneous inputs having an influence on the ratings is minimized by careful monitoring by the program administrator and other assessors.

It is not until final, summary dimension ratings are derived by consensus that Stage 3 is carried out. Each assessor examines the final dimension ratings and records his or her independent overall assessment rating. Assessors are encouraged to consider all dimension ratings and to in-

Exercises (Primary observer)	Stage 1 Dimension rating by exercise			Stage 2 Dimension ratings considering the data				Stage 3 Overall assessment ratings			
	Assessors			Preliminary Assessors			Final	Preliminary Assessors			Final
	A	B	C	A	B	C		A	B	C	
Analysis exercise (Assessor A)											
Decision Making	5										
Oral Communication	4										
Written Communication	4			DM: 5	3	1	2				
Leaderless group discussion (Assessor B)											
Decision Making	3										
Oral Communication	3										
Leadership	4			OC: 3	3	3	3				

Interview simulation
(Assessor A)

		L:	2	4	4	2		2	3	2		2
Decision Making	3											
Oral Communication	3	Del:	2	2	2							
Leadership	2											
Use of Delegation	2											

In-basket
(Assessor C)

		WC:	5	2	5	5
Decision Making	1					
Oral Communication	2					
Leadership	5					
Use of Delegation	2					
Written Communication	5					

Figure 1.1. Assessment model for an individual assessee (3 assessors, 5 dimensions, 4 exercises).

Stage 1

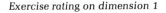

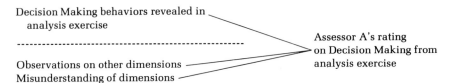

Exercise rating on dimension 1

Decision Making behaviors revealed in
  analysis exercise

Observations on other dimensions
Misunderstanding of dimensions

Assessor A's rating
on Decision Making from
analysis exercise

(Repeated for other dimensions)

Stage 2

Dimension ratings from exercise 1

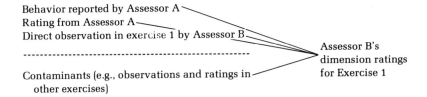

Behavior reported by Assessor A
Rating from Assessor A
Direct observation in exercise 1 by Assessor B

Contaminants (e.g., observations and ratings in
  other exercises)

Assessor B's
dimension ratings
for Exercise 1

Preliminary dimension rating 1

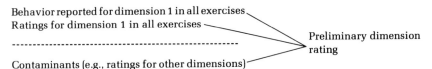

Behavior reported for dimension 1 in all exercises
Ratings for dimension 1 in all exercises

Contaminants (e.g., ratings for other dimensions)

Preliminary dimension
rating

Figure 1.2. Judgment model for individual assessors at various stages of the assessment
center process.

tegrate the information in the manner that best reflects job demands. No
mechanical or statistical formulas are used. A contaminant at this stage
might be some personal information known by one assessor; for example,
the fact that a candidate for promotion was recently divorced and is considering a move to another city. The final overall assessment rating is
determined by consensus. The recommendation to hire or not hire an applicant should be based on the three assessor ratings, but subjective
judgments can play a contaminating role if the administrator does not
guide the group. In reality, once the dimension ratings are agreed upon,

Final dimension rating 1

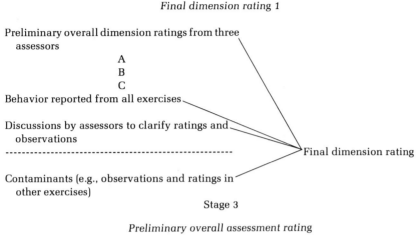

Preliminary overall dimension ratings from three
   assessors

A
B
C

Behavior reported from all exercises

Discussions by assessors to clarify ratings and
   observations

--- Final dimension rating

Contaminants (e.g., observations and ratings in
   other exercises)

Stage 3

Preliminary overall assessment rating

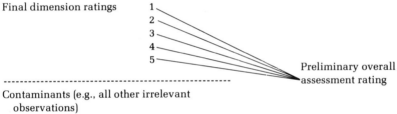

Final dimension ratings
1
2
3
4
5

Preliminary overall
assessment rating

Contaminants (e.g., all other irrelevant
   observations)

Final overall assessment rating

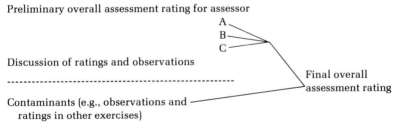

Preliminary overall assessment rating for assessor

A
B
C

Discussion of ratings and observations

Final overall
assessment rating

Contaminants (e.g., observations and
   ratings in other exercises)

Figure 1.2. (*continued*)

assessors usually closely agree on the overall assessment rating and there
is little chance that extraneous information will bias a decision.

Inappropriate Use of the Term *Assessment Center*

Now that we have defined several distinguishing features of the assessment center process, it will help to state what an assessment center is *not.*
Quoting from the *Standards and Ethical Considerations for Assessment*

Center Operations (Task Force, 1980; copy may be found in *The Personnel Administrator*, February 1980, pp. 35–38), prepared and endorsed by a task force of industrial practitioners and academic researchers:

> The following kinds of activities *do not* constitute an assessment center:
> 1. Panel interviews or a series of sequential interviews as the sole technique.
> 2. Reliance on a specific technique (regardless of whether a simulation or not) as the sole basis for evaluation.
> 3. Using only a test battery composed of a number of pencil-and-paper measures, regardless of whether the judgments are made by a statistical or judgmental pooling of scores.
> 4. Single assessor assessment (often referred to as individual assessment) measurement by one individual using a variety of techniques such as pencil-and-paper tests, interviews, personality measures, or simulation.
> 5. The use of several simulations with more than one assessor where there is no pooling of data, that is, each assessor prepares a report on performance in an exercise, and the individual reports (unintegrated) are used as the final product of the center.
> 6. A physical location labeled as an "assessment center" which does not conform to the requirements noted above [p. 5–6].

The term *assessment center* is occasionally used in a way that does not conform to the *Standards*. An example of this misuse appears in an article entitled "Internal Assessment Center: An Organization Development Approach to Selecting Supervisors" (Cowan & Kurtz, 1976). The selection program included two panel interviews by representatives of employees and managers, an interview and testing by an outside consultant, and an interview by the director of the division under study. Two main ingredients were lacking: (a) the assessment procedures included no job simulation activities; and (b) the various interviewers did not meet to systematically discuss and integrate the information gathered. Rather, the director told the panelists from the beginning that he was not asking them to participate but to give advice and to provide him with information. After the interviews, the panelists' evaluations were given to the director who made his own decision. The report contains no data but concludes with the assertion that "this point was definitely proven. *A government manager can successfully run his own assessment center* [Cowan & Kurtz, 1976, p. 23]."

Two points of concern are raised. First, the program did not confirm with the generally accepted practices of assessment centers. Second, no research data were reported to substantiate that participants, employees, or managers were satisfied with the procedure or that the interviewers' rating had reliability or validity. No data substantiated that the program had any predictive validity or relationship to job performance.

Impact of Evaluation on Managers

Social commentators have observed that we are witnessing increasing and more intrusive forms of evaluation in our society. They point out that we are intensely scrutinized for entry into schools, jobs, clubs, and organizations; for credit checks and loan applications; by census takers; and for many other facets of our everyday lives. Objections to these evaluations range from the charge that they are ineffective or biased to the claim that selection per se is morally wrong. The most prevalent objection is that evaluation procedures unduly invade privacy, especially in such matters as the investigation of attitudes toward religion, sexual practices, and family life. Where such matters may be central to the problem being studied (e.g., in the clinical diagnosis of an individual's pathology) there is relatively little objection to such lines of inquiry. On the other hand, where the questions are irrelevant or where an individual's rights to privacy or confidentiality cannot be adequately protected, evaluation should not be intrusive.

How intrusive are assessment centers? Since more than 90% of all operating assessment centers do not contain a background interview, the more objectionable intrusions into a person's past are excluded. Where a background interview is conducted, it is usually a behavioral interview dealing exclusively with job-related activities. Personality tests are also rare in assessment centers, so this source of intrusion is usually eliminated.

The real question is whether participants see participation in the exercises as an intrusion. Since assessment centers use only job-related forms of assessment, they are less susceptible to the criticism that the information being gathered is irrelevant. The exercises have a high degree of "face validity," that is they look as if they are measuring what they are supposed to measure and are, therefore, more acceptable to the personnel who participate in them. Kraut (1972) and Dodd (1977) provided extensive data demonstrating participant acceptance.

Participants believe that the assessment program measures important managerial qualities, that assessment information is useful, and that the program is effective in promoting self-development. In addition, when various samples were asked if they would recommend that a friend volunteer for the program, 53 to 82% said, "certainly," and virtually all the others said, "probably." Assessor and management attitudes are also quite positive.

Evaluation is a regular part of any employment relationship. A supervisor continually makes decisions regarding his or her subordinates involving performance appraisal, promotion, salary raises, disciplinary decisions, demotion, firing, etc. Since evaluation is necessary, it is better done in a systematic, reliable, and valid way rather than in an unsystematic way susceptible to bias. If we know how to make better personal evaluations, we have an obligation to use these techniques.

Today's evidence suggests that the impact of assessment centers is positive. In addition to favorable participant attitudes, there is evidence that turnover decreases when an assessment center is instituted (Ague, 1971) and an assessment center can be used as an organizational development technique to improve supervisor–subordinate relations among managers (Lupton, 1973).

Assessment Centers and Equal Employment Opportunity

A major concern about any technique that is used to make employment decisions is whether it is valid and fair for protected classes of minorities and women. Tests, interviews, background information, and application blanks along with assessment centers must all be used in such a way as to avoid or minimize adverse impact on the employment of minority groups. A critical step is the validation process where it is demonstrated that a selection instrument is job related. This can be successfully done by showing that the behaviors called for in the instrument are a significant and meaningful sample of on-the-job behaviors. Simple face validity is not enough, but where thorough studies of instrument content are compared with job analyses of on-the-job behavior, content-validity evidence is satisfactory. In addition criterion-validity studies of the statistical relationship of instrument behavior and job behavior should be conducted—separately for minority groups, women, and majority groups, if feasible.

The evidence reviewed in Chapters 5 and 7 strongly suggests that assessment centers are job related and predictive of managerial success. The approach has features that make it particularly appropriate for affirmative action programs and, in fact, some organizations are using assessment centers as a means of identifying minorities and women who have the potential for rapid advancement into management and other positions (Boehm & Hoyle, 1977; Bray, 1971a; Jaffee, Cohen, & Cherry, 1972; Moses & Boehm, 1975). An example is the monumental 1973 consent agreement between American Telephone and Telegraph and the U.S. Department of Labor (Hoyle, 1975). The assessment center was accepted as the method by which women would be evaluated for placement in AT&T's accelerated management development program. Nearly 1700 women were assessed and 42% were recommended as having high potential for advancement.

Furthermore, it appears that assessment centers have a minimal adverse impact on protected classes (Chapters 6 and 10). It is one of the fairest predictors available.

In assessment centers, the prediction of potential is based on observation of behavior directly relevant to the job. Overt performance rather than abstract traits is observed and measured. The individual's chances are not left to the whim of a single, possibly biased, supervisor. The progress of minorities, often short-time employees, may be blocked under the seniority system and the restrictions of the jobs in which they are placed. The assessment center gives each individual an equal opportunity to demonstrate capabilities for more advanced jobs.

Orientation of the Book

We stress that this book deals with only one set of personnel procedures dealing with only a segment of management and personnel problems. It is concerned with upward mobility: making predictions of success in managerial positions at succeedingly higher levels in an organization. Even in the cases where assessment centers are used for developmental purposes, that is to assess training needs or to initiate or enhance management development, the orientation is toward upward movement into managerial positions.

At one level, this book is a summary of the past research on assessment centers. It brings together in one source all the published and many of the unpublished relevant studies. These are summarized and evaluated under several major topic headings related to internal and external validity, the evaluation of individual assessment exercises, etc. Major deficiencies of this research are pointed out and further research needs are identified.

At another level, this book is concerned with an analysis of the interrelation of empirical research and psychological theory. This is a two-way street. The development and execution of assessment centers have been based on a number of well-established, theoretical principles. We will show how application of additional psychological theories can enhance the effectiveness of assessment centers. This does not suggest that assessment centers have simply been a matter of "using psychology" to solve practical problems. It is clear that the experience and research findings from assessment centers contribute to a number of areas of general psychology.

A second area of theoretical contribution is better understanding of human judgment and prediction. There have been sharp attacks on clinical or judgmental approaches to evaluation and even some calls for the abolition of such approaches. The fact remains that human judgments are made and will continue to be made on matters of great importance. The assessment center literature demonstrates that accurate judgments can be made when judges are trained, when they have the opportunity to make observations of relevant behaviors, and when the judgmental process is structured in certain ways.

2
History of
Assessment Programs

The previous chapter distinguished assessment centers from other methods of measurement and assessment approaches. Assessment centers are characterized by multiple assessment techniques, multiple assessors, situational tests, and a particular structured procedure for making observations, judgments, and predictions about managerial behavior. This chapter describes a number of early assessment programs, including the earliest assessment centers that completely fit all the characteristics outlined in the preceding chapter, and other developments in the field of assessment which have relevance to current management assessment centers. The purpose of each assessment program was to make practical evaluations of personnel and predictions for complex job assignments. This chapter covers assessment techniques developed by the Germans, British, Americans, Australians, and Canadians prior to, during, and just after World War II. It concludes with a description of the program of American Telephone and Telegraph, which became and still remains the model for industrial applications.

Common Problems in Assessment Programs

In the early 1900s, simple performance tests were used to measure individual differences in behavior and, in some cases, they were used to predict job performance. The major features of current assessment center programs were already clearly visible in the efforts to select German military officers in the 1930s. The features became clearer with each successive assessment program; subsequent programs capitalized on both the successes and the failures of earlier ones. A review of the developmental history of assessment programs reveals a common set of problems with which each group of psychologists dealt. The outline of these problems was apparent in the earliest attempts to use situational and performance-measurement techniques for the prediction of effectiveness in work settings. As the historical review of the evolution of modern day assessment centers proceeds, the reader will note the following common themes:

1. *Identification of characteristics to be measured:* How to determine characteristics, problems in definitions, validity, and interrelationship of characteristics
2. *Types of assessment techniques:* Selection of various exercises, interrelationship of exercises, relationship of exercises to actual work settings
3. *Assessment processes:* Methods by which observations are made, data are recorded, and information is integrated
4. *Evidence of validity:* Reliability of judgments, relationship of program to job behavior, relationship of components of assessment center to job behavior
5. *Operations of the programs:* Need for trained assessors, professional versus nonprofessional assessors, length of program, setting

History of Performance Tests

Since situational tests are one of the distinguishing features of assessment centers, the historical review begins with an examination of performance tests in early psychological testing. Traditionally, the term *performance test* has referred to nonverbal tests requiring some form of behavioral response (Cronbach, 1970). This simple definition is not adequate because all tests require some form of behavior, even if it is no more than a simple hand signal from the examinee. Performance test responses may be such behaviors as speaking, writing, drawing, movement of the hands and body, adjustment of dials, or handling tools and equipment.

In contrast to paper-and-pencil tests, performance tests present more *complex stimuli* to the examinee and require more *complex behavioral responses.* Test materials and setting are often more complex. However, stimulus complexity must be considered a continuum with no clear separation of the simple from the complex. At one end, the task may be nothing more than a single word presented visually or orally, and at the other end the task and setting may be as complex as a management decision-making problem to be solved by a group of participants in a simulated business organization.

The term *situational test* usually refers to complex performance tests carried out in realistic or lifelike settings. Such tests usually presuppose no single solution, often require overt behaviors, and often include interaction between two or more persons.

Most of the early psychological measuring instruments were performance tests in the sense that they required overt behavior on the part of the examinee (Cronbach, 1970; DuBois, 1970). Whether the person was memorizing syllables, tracing a maze, or answering questions about practical problems, active participation was involved. In contrast, the development of objective paper-and-pencil tests caused a shift from overt behavioral responses to responses recorded on an answer sheet. It is an enlightening experience to review earlier measurement efforts and find that they often more closely resembled performance tests than paper-and-pencil tests.

Historically, systematic measurement of individual differences in human characteristics probably began with Sir Frances Galton in the late 1800s. Galton developed a wide variety of measuring tools to pursue his scientific studies of human abilities. For our purposes, we are most interested in his tests of more complex behavior. Thousands of men and women were tested by Galton for breathing capacity, strength of arm pull and hand squeeze, discrimination of pitch and color, and steadiness of hand. Galton pioneered in the development of techniques to provide objective measurement of human abilities. The fact that he was measuring trivial facets of human intellectual functioning was misdirected—that he launched the practice of objective measurement of overt behavior was important. Cattell continued in the Galton tradition and expanded the measurement techniques to include over 50 tests. He also perpetuated the search for psychomotor and sensory abilities underlying intellectual functioning. But these tests failed to correlate with other significant indices of intelligence, and it remained for subsequent investigators to redirect the measurement efforts (DuBois, 1970). This early period has been characterized as a "search, explicit or implicit, for a means to measure 'intellect,' often conceived as the sum of psychological processes, such as sensation, attention, perception, association, and memory [DuBois, 1970, p. 28]."

The major advance toward redirection came from Binet who assembled a set of items to diagnose mental retardation among children. His unique contribution was the design of items to measure broad problem-solving ability, judgment, and learning skills. For our purposes, it is important to recognize that these test items required the subject to engage in complex, overt behavior. That this behavior was verbal does not negate the significance of performance tests in contrast to subsequent paper-and-pencil tests.

A variety of nonverbal performance tests was developed in the early 1900s. Form boards (a wooden base with recesses of various shapes into which the examinee places appropriate objects) were used by Woodworth to study race differences, by Knox to test mental deficiency among immigrants, and by Pintner and Patterson for clinical use (DuBois, 1970).

During this early period, performance tests were used in special cases to assess aptitude for jobs. Link used card-sorting and cancellation tests to select skilled inspectors and a typing test for gaugers; Dodge developed a device for naval gun pointers; Thurstone used auditory testing for selection of telegraphers; and Henmon found certain performance tests could predict flying ability. In other settings, performance and mechanical tests were found to be effective for assessment of clinical positions, mechanical jobs, and assembly tasks (DuBois, 1970).

Efforts along these lines then stopped or remained undeveloped for many years. A great rush to develop efficient paper-and-pencil tests which could be administered efficiently to groups of people followed the creative advances by Otis, Yerkes, Bingham, and others during World War I. The advances in statistical methodology reinforced the search for efficiency of measurement by aiding the development of multiple aptitude test batteries. Such tests were designed to measure a series of separate intellectual traits.

The next significant development in performance testing of managers came with Frederiksen's work on the in-basket exercise. The in-basket exercise was first developed for the United States Air Force in 1953 by a research team at Educational Testing Service to measure curriculum effectiveness at the Air College in such areas as the ability to organize discrete pieces of information, to discover the problem in a complex situation, to anticipate events that may arise because of problems, and to arrive at decisions based on many types of considerations (Frederiksen, Saunders, & Wand, 1957). The introduction of the in-basket opened up many avenues for assessment of new administrative and managerial dimensions. In addition, it stimulated development of new types of exercises such as written analyses and written reports.

Summary of performance tests.   The performance tests of the early 1900s served as a basis for the subsequent development of more complex measures of managerial behaviors. The early test developers struggled to devise measures of variables relevant to everyday life and work experiences. Problems with observation, scoring, and judgment were not solved. For these and other reasons, psychometric efforts during the 1930s and 1940s turned to paper-and-pencil testing. The history of situational tests of leadership and managerial abilities resides in the military assessment programs to be described here.

German Selection Programs

Early applications of the multiple assessment approach were developed for selection of army, air force, and naval officers by German military psychologists. From the beginning of the buildup of the German armed forces after World War I, psychologists were involved in the selection, training, organization, and morale building of the military. By 1929, major advances had been made in the areas of selection and training; and by the late 1930s, a very advanced multiple-assessment procedure for officer selection had been set up. These military procedures were based on techniques developed in psychological laboratories and testing stations for postal and railway administration, a school of commercial aviation, a labor-exchange agency, the Bureau of Statistics, and various police departments (Farago, 1942).

Ansbacher (1941) and Farago (1942) provided an extensive, if at times cursory, review of German military psychology from about 1920 to 1941. They described the work of psychologists in the areas of social psychology of military organizations, special aptitude testing, studies of characterology (personality), ethics and training, morale, propaganda, the psychology of combat, and the conduct of war. Farago (1942) described stringent selection and training standards for military psychologists including the requirement for a PhD in psychology, the evaluation of aptitude and personality characteristics, and three years of training as selection officers. The internship in clinical assessment included an additional three months in the central headquarters of the military psychology agency. During the latter stages of the war, the standards for selection and training were lowered considerably for aviation psychologists (Fitts, 1946).

Although the German assessment procedures have been criticized for methodological weaknesses, many innovations served as models for subsequent British and U.S. assessment efforts. Some of the early advances of German officer selection follow.

The main task of the German military psychologists and the part of their work most relevant to management assessment centers was the selection of future officers. Assessment procedures were built on the guiding principles of holistic and naturalistic evaluation. *Holism* refers to the notion that the components of an entity exist in an orderly arrangement or structure, that the whole is not dependent on the nature of individual parts, and that a whole cannot be understood by examining isolated parts. Holistic observation consists of studying component parts as they relate to the whole. By contrast, an atomistic or molecular approach consists of studying individual phenomena in isolation without regard to how they function in combination in the total unit. Many of these ideas are akin to Gestalt and systems theories. Applied to leadership assessment, these philosophical principles meant that the total personality rather than separate abilities of potential officers were to be assessed. To obtain an accurate evaluation of personality, the German personnel psychologists believed that scientific and practical knowledge should be combined.

Naturalistic evaluation meant that observation of behavior should take place in natural, everyday situations. Intellectual abilities and personality characteristics should be examined using tasks of a realistic and serious nature rather than abstract tests. Assessors were given broad latitude in using different techniques to obtain qualitative evaluations of samples of behavior, and the judgments of several assessors were pooled to attain objectivity.

The German psychologists conceived of leadership as an inherited ability to accept and carry out authority delegated from selected national leaders (Farago, 1942). The characteristics of a good leader were:

1. *Positive will:* A habit of voluntary response to the command of the superior leader
2. *Determination:* The creation of means to achieve the goal and the achievement of a goal
3. *Operative thinking:* Planning and executing a preconceived action
4. *Mental elasticity:* The ability to live up to any situation in order to accomplish a goal
5. *Mathematical thinking*
6. *Character:* Integrity, selflessness, idealism

From these conceptions of personality and leadership, a variety of unique assessment techniques was developed. Intellectual abilities were assessed by ordinary verbal and performance tests, by creative and practical writing tasks, and by objective arrangement and sorting tasks. Vernon and Parry (1949) reported one exercise in which a film was shown and candidates were asked to observe and describe what they saw. Personality functioning (character and temperament) was assessed by a choice reaction test in which the subject had to learn to match hand and foot reactions to 600 visual and auditory stimuli presented in the 20-min test.

> During the test, the subject is observed, and the observations are noted in detail. His adaptation to the situation, the performance itself, and the total behavior may be described. Each of these categories is subdivided into three or four parts relating to such topics as security of conduct, efficiency of movements, facial expressions, etc. [Ansbacher, 1941, p. 382].

Initiative, willpower, and physical performance were observed in the command series exercise. The person was given elaborate instructions for carrying out a series of assignments over a complex and strenuous obstacle course. To note his reactions under stress, he was criticized severely for mistakes. Other samples of leadership behavior were observed in tasks that put the subject in command of a group of soldiers. He then had to accomplish some task or explain a problem to them. Facial expressions, speech patterns, and handwriting samples were observed. In-depth interviews probed life history, schooling, and attitudes. In addition, the air force employed a series of perceptual ability and sensorimotor coordination tests. A comprehensive description of the officer-testing methods used by the German army is provided by Martin (1941).

The assessment procedure lasted two or three days and was conducted by two officers (one a colonel, who made the final decision), one physician, and three psychologists. This board prepared an advisory report on each applicant, which was not binding on the superior officer. Ansbacher (1941) reported that the judgments of the board were validated against ratings during training, but he provided no details or references. Farago (1942) speculated that large-scale validation was not undertaken "probably because some of the charlatans of German army psychology were fearful of results [p. 62]."

What can be learned from the German military assessment program? The officer assessment programs were among the first attempts to use both multiple assessment techniques and multiple assessors to evaluate complex behavior. All subsequent assessment efforts have been built on these two principles of evaluation and were acknowledged by Taft (1959) to be the central features of all assessment center programs. The Germans also were among the first to attempt holistic measurement in contrast to trait measurement, which characterized most other personality measurement of the time. Finally, they attempted to obtain behavioral samples of intellectual and personality manifestations rather than to rely only on paper-and-pencil tests or verbal responses as the basic data for observation.

A number of limitations can be noted. The simulations were crude and lacked consistency from one application to another. The attempt to use handwriting and facial expressions for the assessment of leadership skills was misplaced, but nonetheless the aim of observing covert behavior was a great advancement. Administration was not standardized and observations were not recorded systematically. Probably the greatest limitation was the attempt to assess the overall character of leaders.

Fitts (1946) reported that in 1942 the entire officer assessment program was discontinued and replaced by a procedure involving interviews and examination of background records. It is unclear why this abrupt change occurred, but certain methodological weaknesses in the program can be observed. Ansbacher (1941) reported no clear job analysis that identified the critical characteristics of a successful officer. Psychologists relied heavily on case studies of successful officers, many of which were taken from popular literature. The characteristics being assessed were abstract and not clearly job related. Furthermore, the assessment exercises, although they involved overt behavior, were not close simulations of military leadership behaviors. Most exercises were individual rather than group exercises, and even the group exercises did not allow free interaction of individuals so that leadership could be observed. Ansbacher (1951) reported that leaderless group discussions were used from 1925 to about 1935 in the army, but were then dropped without explanation. The navy continued to use group discussions. Jennings (1949) observed that the German situational tests allowed neither spontaneity of behavior for the individual nor personal interaction in a group. She said the German tasks were more like performance intelligence tests in which the roles were prescribed with a predetermined goal as the correct solution. In each case, the exercises involved a highly structured task.

Jennings's (1949) point about spontaneity is telling, and in subsequent programs exercises that allowed leadership to emerge from a more unstructured situation were used. The British (Harris, 1949) and American (OSS, 1948) programs used leaderless tasks and discussion groups which allowed spontaneous behavior expressing an individual's characteristic pattern of reactions.

Jennings also suggested a broader hypothesis that the status of the individual in society can be understood by examining the methods used in evaluating and processing military personnel. In contrast to German assessment exercises which did not allow individual expression, British and American assessment permitted wider behavior choices. This is an interesting hypothesis, but Jennings (1949) provided only these few supportive examples. In defense of the German program, it must be said that the psychologists were more interested in how the applicant went about solving the problem than whether he got the correct solution.

The holistic approach adopted by the Germans and later modified by the British and Americans may have overemphasized global assessment of the total person. Although it is a decided improvement over atomistic trait concepts, holistic assessment tends to overlook the pattern of behavioral differences in any individual. Each person is a combination of strengths and weaknesses—a fact that is acknowledged and diagnosed in modern management assessment centers. Current assessment center procedures may be seeking some middle ground between atomistic trait evaluation and global, holistic assessment.

Political problems may have also befallen the German officer selection programs. Fitts (1946) provided some insights into the political events of 1942 in Germany. He speculated that return to the use of subjective assessment techniques may have been due to "the belief that there were qualities of the German mind and character which set the race above other national groups, qualities which could not be analyzed or studied scientifically [p. 153]." It may be that such an attitude extended to the decision not to conduct research on the reliability and validity of the assessment process. Lacking validation evidence, it would have been difficult to resist political arguments for dropping the program under pressure of a fast-worsening war situation.

The political subtleties of the time are not known, but Fitts (1946) speculated that opposition came from two sources that opposed the utilization of a democratic method of decision making. The Prussians wanted officers selected on the basis of family background and heritage; the Nazis wanted them selected on the basis of participation in Party Youth Camps. Both may have seen assessment as an encroachment on their rights to make promotions.

Contributions of German programs. The German military psychologists launched the multiple assessment of leadership capabilities. Many features of current management assessment center programs can be traced to this source including multiple assessors, complex situational tests, and a desire to measure characteristics more complex than atomistic traits.

British War Office Selection Boards

The British War Office Selection Boards (WOSBs) were developed to meet the pressing need of identifying potential officers for the British Army during World War II. Until the summer of 1942, officers were selected on the basis of a 20-min interview from candidates who had graduated from certain prominent schools that offered officer training programs. The selection panel relied on intuitive judgments based on information irrelevant to officer performance. The failure of this method to select successful officers, opposition from Parliament, allegations that the method was biased in favor of men from narrow segments of society, and the need to increase the number and quality of officers led to the development of the WOSBs, patterned initially after the German assessment program (Eysenck, 1953; Vernon & Parry, 1949).

Sir Andrew Thorne, a former military attaché at Berlin, had observed the German psychologists' selection program. In 1941, Thorne encouraged two psychiatrists to set up a similar program in the Scottish Command. The initial boards included psychiatric interviews, intelligence tests, and situational tests very similar to the German models. The initial trial was judged successful. The boards met with much acceptance and were greatly expanded. By the end of the war, over 140,000 candidates had been evaluated, of which 60,000 individuals had been selected for training. Harris (1949) and Vernon and Parry (1949) provided a thorough description of the operations of the WOSBs from 1942 to 1946.

The War Office, operating numerous individual boards throughout the country under the new method, assessed potential officers in the 3-day or 4-day program. Groups of eight candidates were assessed by means of a three-phase process involving group exercises in Phase 1, individual psychological and psychiatric testing and interviewing in Phase 2, and a second round of group exercises in Phase 3. In a final board evaluation, each candidate was rated on 17 variables reflecting perceived potential in a number of leadership areas.

The WOSB assessment procedures in Phases 1 and 3 were built on the rationale that group situations provide the best opportunity for leadership testing. Since much military leadership is effected in a group, it made sense to test leadership by controlling the stresses put on a group and by observing how members reacted to those stresses. Harris (1949) summarized: "In short, in the WOSB technique of officer selection, one observes a man *in* a group task in order to determine his group effectiveness (in a particular field): One selects and *tests* him *in* a group *for* a group [p. 11]."

Various group tasks were used by the WOSB including indoor and outdoor exercises, discussion problems, physical activities, and tasks with different levels of stress. Early in the operation of the WOSB, the situational tests were largely drawn from the German program. It became clear that these exercises were limited: Physical prowess was too important in the athletic games and the obstacle course; previous experience played a large role in the leadership command tasks; in general, the German exercises were unstructured and unscorable. Therefore, in 1943,

Bion (1946) revised these exercises and made some of the most original contributions to the WOSBs (Vernon & Parry, 1949).

A number of more realistic problem-solving tasks were devised. In most cases, eight individuals were given a problem to solve, but no leader was designated. The tasks were devised so that group cooperation was required for success. An individual could demonstrate leadership only if he could work within the group to gain their confidence and common efforts. The tasks were designed to reveal the ability to form and maintain effective personal relationships.

Furthermore, each exercise was designed to reveal strengths and weaknesses on predetermined leadership qualities. For example, the leaderless group discussion provided opportunities for assessment of the quality of interpersonal relations, whereas the ability to develop the group into an effective work team could be assessed by the stress group task which involved moving heavy objects over a difficult outdoor course.

Individual exercises were used to assess other leadership qualities. Candidates were asked to give 5-min speeches describing either their job or hobbies as indications of oral presentation ability and breadth of interest.

Eight brief stress interviews, involving role playing by pairs of candidates, were conducted to observe the men's approach to stressful situations and to assess their tact in dealing with difficult personnel problems.

Prior to Phase 2, the observer team met briefly to pool its initial observations of the Phase 1 group exercises. This brief session was designed to formulate questions to be asked by various staff members in subsequent interaction with a candidate. This probing was carried out in individual assessment in Phase 2 and in group exercises in Phase 3.

In Phase 2 of the assessment, psychiatrists conducted in-depth interviews of the candidates and a battery of projective tests were given. The staff carried out a broad assessment of psychological adjustment and attempted to focus on specific aspects of personality believed to be important for successful leadership.

A unifying theme in the WOSB program was its clear conception of the leadership characteristics to be assessed. Leadership was defined as the ability to facilitate a group's attainment of goals. A person's effectiveness in a group was seen by Harris (1949) to have three components:

1. *Level of function:* Ability to contribute toward the functional aspect of the common task by planning and organizing the available abilities, materials, and time.
2. *Group cohesiveness:* Ability to bind the group in the direction of the

common task, to relate its members emotionally to each other and
to the task.
3. *Stability:* Ability to stand up to resistances and frustrations without serious impairment of the first two criteria (Harris, 1949,
pp. 10–11).

These three aspects of leadership were assessed in various ways in the
WOSB operations. For example, the observer team focused on these
qualities when observing the complex interaction of the eight-member
groups. In the brief conference between phases of assessment, the
observer team used the aspects of leadership to organize its discussion
and to plan for subsequent probing. In the final board discussion, the
observer team attempted to interpret behavior of candidates in relation to
these qualities. Finally, ratings of group and individual performance
were made on these three aspects of leadership.

The WOSB's assessment team consisted of four or five individuals. The
president was a senior military officer who interviewed all candidates,
periodically observed the situational exercises, and made the final decision on suitability. In some boards, he was assisted by a deputy. The
technical personnel served as his advisors. A psychologist administered
tests and questionnaires and suggested potential problem cases to the
psychiatrist. The psychiatrist conducted an in-depth interview with candidates nominated by the psychologist to assess ability to withstand stress
and other leadership qualities. In the early boards, the psychologist's role
was confined to research and training of other staff; they did not sit on the
final boards until very late in the war period. The main day-to-day administration of the situational exercises was carried out by the military
testing officer (MTO). Each group of eight candidates was assigned an
MTO who spent the entire time with one group. He ran the exercises, ate
with the men, observed their behavior at informal gatherings, and
attended the final board discussion.

Several sources present evidence regarding the reliability and validity
of the WOSBs. Morris (1949) served on the psychological research staff of
the War Office from 1942 to 1946 and provided a summary of research
during that period. Further data are provided by Vernon and Parry
(1949). Reeve (1971) worked from 1946 to 1953 on further analysis of
early data and conducted validation studies on officer selection after the
war.

The WOSBs were consistently found to predict grades in officer training schools with validities in the .20s and .30s. Validities were higher for
candidates from certain schools and for candidates identified and sent to
the program by certain personnel selection officers (field recruiters). In

some cases, the correlations of WOSB grades with training grades were as high as .60 (Vernon & Parry, 1949).

During the transition from the previous interview method of selection to the new WOSB method, several hundred men were being assessed by both methods, thus affording the opportunity to compare their effectiveness. At several officer-training locations, it was found that cadets selected by the WOSB were more likely to be rated above average than cadets selected by the old method (Table 2.1). In another study, WOSB final grades were correlated .30 with training grades. When the final ratings and five other variables (including intelligence scores, other ratings, and background information) were combined in multiple regression and correlated with training, a multiple correlation of .58 was found. This suggests that a more systematic way of dealing with all of the assessment data would have enhanced prediction.

Very little evidence was available to validate WOSB's selections against performance of officers in the field. When the field performance of commissioned officers selected by the old method of interviews was compared with a sample selected by the WOSB, no clear differences were found. But when various pieces of background information were used as moderator variables, some correlations with field performance were obtained. It was found that WOSB final grades were correlated more highly with ratings of field success of younger commanding officers than with older officers (Morris, 1949). These findings suggest that an assessment center procedure may be relatively more effective where candidates for promotion have not had opportunities to demonstrate leadership or managerial abilities. Support for this hypothesis will be found in research by Hinrichs (1978), discussed in Chapter 7.

The WOSB research staff was concerned that differences in standards among the separate boards might exist and their suspicions were confirmed when a group of candidates sent to two different boards received

Table 2.1
Training Results of Officer Cadets Selected by Traditional and by Psychological Methods[a]

		Percentage of cadets earning training program grades		
Board	N	Above average	Average	Below average and fail
Interview	491	22.1	41.3	36.6
Assessment center	721	34.5	40.3	25.2

[a]From *Personnel Selection in the British Forces*, by P. E. Vernon and J. B. Parry. Copyrighted by Hodden & Stroughton Educational (formerly University of London) Press. Reprinted by permission of publisher and P. E. Vernon.

substantially different rejection rates. However, in one large controlled study where common training programs were instituted, it was found that two boards provided comparable evaluations (Morris, 1949). The rejection rates were the same; there was a correlation of .80 between the final grades of the two boards, and almost equally high correlations between comparable pairs of assessors (i.e., psychologists, psychiatrists, and observers). Aside from demonstrating interboard and interjudge reliability, this study demonstrated the value of training assessors with a common program. Persons developing and operating management assessment centers should be aware that although assessors may bring different evaluation standards into the assessment center, training them will lead to better reliability of assessments.

Studies of WOSB ratings after the war and into the 1950s were conducted by Reeve (1971). Consistent validities were found for the prediction of grades in officer training programs although the correlations were only in the .20s and .30s. As was found during the war, the validities were consistently higher for candidates who had graduated from certain schools and who had been recruited by certain personnel selection officers. The practical significance of the correlations as low as those reported here was demonstrated by data showing differences in failure rates for levels of WOSB's ratings. For example, in one study, no one with an assessment rating of B failed, but 6.2% of the Cs and 12.5% of the Ds failed training and were returned to their units.

One potential reason for the low demonstrated correlations was the low variance of final WOSB ratings. Large portions of ratings fell in one or two categories. These data and the differences in ratings across selection boards point out the need to maintain close control over the assessment procedures and quality of staff performance.

Reeve (1971) also studied the comparative validity with a procedure of reviewing candidate dossiers. Predictions by research personnel after examining the personnel records of candidates yielded validities which equaled, or for some reviewers exceeded, the validities of WOSBs. Hinrichs (1978) found a similar result for a comparison of a naturalistic method of reviewing the personnel folder of experienced managers with assessment center ratings.

Contributions of WOSBs. The British military programs made several advances over the German efforts. Still subjective in nature, the assessment was not as holistic as the German approach. Leadership was defined in terms of three well-defined components. The exercises presented more realistic situations to the candidates, including group discussions and physical tasks, and they were designed to reveal different predetermined aspects of leadership. The responsibility for assessment decisions shifted to the military personnel even though the psychologists and psychiatrists administered the program, conducted the psychometric testing in Phase 2, and conducted validation research. The British psychologists initiated the continuing tradition of empirical evaluation of assessment center operations with numerous reliability and validity studies.

Military Assessment in Australia and Canada

The Australian and Canadian assessment programs for the selection of military officers were quite similar to the British War Office Selection Boards (Yan & Slivinski, 1976). In both cases, the British programs served as the models but were modified to serve somewhat different needs in the other countries. Although similar to the WOSBs in terms of overall purpose, staffing, the general types of tests and exercises used, and the processes of gathering and integrating information, both the Australian and Canadian programs had a larger ratio of military assessors and the programs gave more autonomy to these military personnel in regional assessment locations. These adjustments were made because of large geographical distances across the countries and because of national differences in values (Yan & Slivinski, 1976). For example, in Canada, military service was strictly voluntary and the increased autonomy fit democratic and individualistic ideals.

Both the Australian and Canadian programs placed more emphasis on the personal interview than did the British programs. Up to three interviews were included. In Australia, these were conducted by a sergeant from the testing section, a psychologist officer, and a psychiatrist. The order of interviewers in Canada was: personnel selection officer, psychiatrist, and finally a corps representative. In Canada, an extensive effort to develop and standardize an intelligence test for military personnel had been carried out prior to the assessment center operation. Potential assessees were screened with this test and only a select group reached assessment. Other intellectual and personality tests were administered in the program.

An early example of the transfer of assessment center technology to nonmilitary situations was provided by Taft (1948) who adapted the group situation observation method to the selection of executive trainees in an Australian manufacturing plant. The purpose of this study was to apply the method to a younger group (17–19 years) than had been assessed earlier. Two trainees were selected from among 60 applicants. Members of the original group were successively screened by review of written application materials, an orientation and screening interview by the managing director of the company, a vocational guidance interview by Taft, and self-withdrawals. The remaining 14 candidates went through a 10-step, 6-hr set of activities including written self-descriptions, group Rorschach, a leaderless discussion, and a problem situation discussion. The manager and psychologist discussed the candidates, then integrated the analyzed Rorschach responses, and rank ordered the 13 finalists. Comparison of preferences for the candidates after the entire procedure with the rank order after the vocational guidance interview showed that the top two candidates would have been selected by either method, but there were significant changes in rank for other candidates. Taft (1948) concluded that the group method provided new information, useful for selection of young executive trainees.

Contributions of Australian and Canadian programs. Little new in the way of technology or process emerged in these programs, but a significant lesson can be learned from the experience. The robustness of the method was demonstrated. The British program was adopted in these two countries with only minor modifications. Although there were obvious similarities among the cultures, the method met the unique philosophies and needs in Australia and Canada with great success.

British Civil Service Selection Board

Vernon (1950) provided the first evidence of the validity of assessment center procedures in nonmilitary settings. Beginning in 1945, the British Civil Service Commission developed and validated a complex procedure for selecting civil servants for all middle- or high-level domestic and foreign jobs. One feature of the civil service procedures which distinguished their applications of assessment center procedures from others was the multistage testing of assessees. To clear the first hurdle, the candidates had to pass a series of essay and objective tests and an interview. The second hurdle, to be discussed here, included two or three days of assessments by the Civil Service Selection Board (CSSB, often referred to by the sibilant CISSB) at a residential location, and the third phase was the British Civil Service Commission's Final Selection Board (FSB). The FSB conducted a final interview before making the decision to accept or reject a candidate, but relied heavily on the CSSB recommendations.

For the purposes of this book, interest centers on CSSB test procedures and the validity of their final judgments. The CSSB was made up of a battery of eight assessment techniques, including a set of verbal and nonverbal cognitive tests, projective measures of personality, background information, reports from various sources (e.g., teachers, army officers, and former employers), interviews, results of a qualifying examination, and individual and group situational exercises. In the group discussion exercises, the 21 candidates at each session were divided into three leaderless groups of seven to discuss problems resembling those faced by a high-level civil servant. In other simulation exercises, the candidates gave speeches or wrote reports. These exercises dealt with problems encountered in complex government work in an imaginary community. Candidates were briefed on the setting by "a bulky memorandum in civil service style [Eysenck, 1953, p. 158]." Interest was generated by inclusion of realistic problems (social, political, and economic) of the type that confronted British officials.

The staff included two civil service administrators and a psychologist. At the end of the session, they met to share information. Based on background information, interviews, observations in the exercises, and information from peer nominations among the participants, the three staff members independently graded each candidate's potential for success in civil service positions.

The CSSB and FSB rating were found to be valid predictors of grades in a training course (.422 and .456), ratings of work performance in administrative positions (.505 and .563), and evaluations of success in foreign service (.499 and .617). The last two sets of validities are corrected to account for restriction of range in the board ratings for the 20% of the candidates not placed on jobs. These correlations become more impressive when one considers the inadequacies of the criteria used. The criteria at the training school were of questionable value because they were based on only one officer's observations for two weeks. The criterion for administrative effectiveness was the sum of ratings on several separate scales selected by factor analysis. The foreign service criteria were, for the most part, general impressions.

Precise evaluation of the effectiveness of separate assessments is not possible because of the way the information was integrated and the way the data were presented in the report. It appears that each technique contributed to prediction in at least one group of assessees. Vernon (1950) concluded that parts of the qualifying examination (English essay and a general paper), cognitive tests (verbal facility, general information, and verbal intelligence), the discussion, and the interview were most consistently predictive. Arithmetic, spatial orientation, and sentence-completion tests showed mixed results; a paragraph-reading test was consistently poor.

Comparing evaluations by staff members, Vernon (1950) concluded that whereas psychologists may not be superior to the average nonprofessional staff member, "they appeared to be less variable, i.e., their individual (validity) coefficients did not range so widely [p. 92]."

In one of the longest-range studies of assessment center predictions, Anstey (1977) conducted a 30-year follow-up of civil servants assessed from 1945 to 1948. For 301 subjects remaining in the service until 1976, the correlation of the FSB rating and rank attained in the civil service in 1975 was .354. When corrected to reflect the range of ability present in the sample of 2427 evaluated by the FSB, the correlation is .660. Anstey (1977) concluded that:

> These figures are probably the highest validity coefficients that have ever been obtained for high-grade selection in any country. . . . If correlations were carried back further to the total of 3,100 who reached the CSSB, or to the total of 6,000 candidates who took the qualifying examination (QE), the validity coefficients would rise higher. Furthermore, this QE population was itself a highly selected field. . . . Taking those considerations into account, the figure of 0.660 is unlikely to be an overestimate and may well be an underestimate [p. 153].

Several features of the study deserve mention. First, the criteria of promotion after 30 years is quite stringent. Contamination by the assessment center ratings of the second through fifth levels of promotion becomes exceedingly remote. Second, the predictive validity increased with length of service. Third, components of the CSSB appeared to contribute differentially at the high and low end of the scale: On the one hand, persons who did well in the interview were likely to be successful, but a low interview rating was not necessarily predictive; on the other hand, written tests accurately identified poor performers, but high test marks were not always associated with job success. Fourth, the process of integrating the data by discussion was better than simply adding the results from various assessment components. Anstey (1977) provides no data to support this conclusion and the issue remains controversial in modern managerial assessment programs.

Reviewing the WOSB and CSSB procedures, Eysenck (1962) warned that psychologists in charge of selection procedures may be hard-pressed to maintain program integrity over time. Close scrutiny by candidates who are assessed and high-level officials may lead to questions about assessment procedures that do not appear job related. Activities with high "face" validity may not be those with the highest actual validity. Eysenck (1962) warns that compromises with scientifically sound procedures can lead to large reductions in predictive accuracy and the psychologist must resist erosion of sound practices. Assessment center proponents in industry today are developing certification and standardization procedures to preserve the integrity of the process.

Contributions of the British CSSB. The legacy of the CSSB is great. This program was the first to apply the assessment center concept to a "nonmilitary" setting. The nature of the situational tests changed to reflect administrative and managerial responsibilities. Peer ratings and rankings were used more systematically. To deal efficiently with large numbers of candidates, a multistage assessment procedure was implemented in which various components were applied to successively more select groups. Detailed research into the reliability and validity of the process has undoubtedly contributed to the long-standing role the CSSB has played in the selection of British civil servants. Continuing research, questions, and suggestions for the future (Anstey, 1977) may well lead to further advances.

Harvard Psychological Clinic

Murray (1938) reported a clinical and experimental study of 50 men of college age undertaken by the Harvard Psychological Clinic. Among the 27 cited collaborators are Donald W. MacKinnon, Saul Rosenweig, and R. Nevitt Sanford, each of whom made subsequent contribution to personality and organizational assessment. The purpose of the study was to develop a theory of the total person and investigate the effects of various environmental factors and personal needs on the behavior of indivduals.

Of relevance to our historical recounting of assessment center procedures are a number of important conceptual and methodological innovations built into the study based on Murray's view of psychology. He believed that the subject of psychology is the life history of a single person. Any one event or reaction can be understood only in light of the individual's total experiences. To study an individual, one must do a comprehensive analysis of the totality of that person. Such a study must consider the various states of the individuals as they encounter various environmental pressures. Methodologically, Murray felt that judgments of personality should be based, albeit crudely, on the measurement of variables of interest. Such judgments must be grounded in observed facts and behaviors.

A variety of procedures was used to assess the 50 male subjects: interviews, questionnaires, paper-and-pencil tests, projective techniques, conversations, and performance tests. Among the latter were exercises that required the subjects to copy over standardized material (a measure of aspiration), asssemble jigsaw puzzles (repression and ethical standards), and participate in problem-solving discussions and exercises which provided opportunities for behavioral observation of social interactions and reactions to frustrating events.

The research team consisted of a diagnostic council of five judges who conducted the interviews, ran experiments, administered questionnaires, and met to discuss and rate the individual subjects of the study. Many advancements in the development of personality theory emanated from these efforts; but for our purposes, the greatest contributions were in the development of important assessment philosophy and approaches. Murray (1938) noted the following strengths of their method: The procedure was effective because it brought out a great deal of information about each subject that enabled the experimenters to understand the individual's reaction to environmental events. Different aspects of personality constructs could be understood through observation in various controlled situations. Errors of observation and interpretation were minimized because the several observers relied on behavioral observation and challenged each other's interpretations. There was little reliance on highly abstract conceptions and the trained experimenters continually examined their terminology for the personality variables under study by referring to observed facts about the assessment situation and subject responses. Murray (1938) concluded: "If we have made any contribution to personology it is probably to be found in our general plan of action: numerous sessions, of which as many as possible are controlled experiments, conducted by different examiners who work independently until at a final session they meet to exchange their findings and interpretations [p. 705]."

As we shall see in our examination of the assessment procedures utilized by the Office of Strategic Services (OSS) during World War II (1948), many of these principles were incorporated in the program for the practical business of personnel selection. That linkage is not surprising in view of the active role played by Dr. Murray in the OSS assessment program. Murray was one of two consultants brought in in the early weeks of planning; he was active as an assessor in several locations throughout the two years of operation; and he was one of the primary researchers and authors who evaluated and documented OSS assessment efforts (OSS, 1948).

Office of Strategic Services

The pioneering assessment center work of the OSS during World War II formed the basis for many future applications of multiple assessment procedures in the United States. Although multiple assessment procedures had been used for personality research by Murray (1938) several years earlier, the OSS assessment efforts represent the first fully developed multiple assessment programs for selection and placement devised in the United States. Even though the program was short-lived—1943–1945—a number of prominent psychologists and psychiatrists participated as assessors or consultants. Not the least reason for the lasting impact of this program is the very thorough, readable, and enjoyable book, Assessment of Men (1948), written by the OSS assessment staff immediately following the war. The book reports both the proceedings and results of the program.

The purpose of the OSS management program was to develop a set of procedures to evaluate the personalities of candidates for a variety of positions in the OSS. The personnel were being considered for jobs such as secret intelligence agents, saboteurs, propaganda experts, secretaries, and office workers. The intention was to reliably predict effective field operations. Many of the problems confronted are common to any personnel selection situation, but the nature of the OSS field work increased the importance of these problems.

The task of the OSS staff was further complicated by the fact that the personnel would be going to a variety of field settings in several foreign countries and in the United States. In most cases, the assessors knew very little about the jobs or the settings and in the early months they did not even have adequate descriptions of the jobs the candidates would perform. Jobs were continually changing and being created in the field. At any one time it was not possible to assess people being considered for a single job or even for a group of jobs. As a result, a great heterogeneity of persons was present during each assessment period. The heterogeneity extended to jobs previously held, jobs to be filled, nationality, language proficiency, and education level. These problems, among many others, made the assessment program particularly difficult; it may account for the moderate level of demonstrated predictive validity which will be summarized later.

The assessment program that emerged was described as a "multiform organismic system" to reflect the combination of holistic and elementalistic philosophies and to emphasize the large number of subjective and objective procedures used. A minimum of theorizing was done and the staff drew from various sources to devise a practical program which could be quickly implemented—conception to implementation took little over two months (MacKinnon, 1977).

The following steps, outlined for the OSS assessment program, provide an excellent example of the application of a combination of assessment theory and practice. All were not carried out for all candidates and jobs, but they represent a model that the staff attempted to follow.

1. Analyze job(s) for which the candidate is being assessed.
2. On the basis of the first step, list all personality determinants of success and failure in performance on the job, and then select variables to be assessed. (The cluster of variables generally evaluated were: motivation for the assignment, energy and initiative, effective intelligence, emotional stability, social relations, leadership, and security. In addition, the variables of physical ability, observing and reporting, and propaganda skills were assessed where appropriate.)
3. Define a rating scale for each of the personality variables on the selected list as well as one overall variable of job fitness.
4. Design a program of assessment procedures to reveal the strength of selected variables. Include assessment procedures within a social matrix composed of staff and candidates. Select several types of procedures and several procedures of the same type for estimating strength on each variable. Include a number of situational tests in which the candidate is required to function at the same level of integration and under somewhat similar conditions as he or she will be expected to function under in the field.
5. Construct a sufficient formulation of the personality of each assessee before making specific ratings, predictions, and recommendations.
6. Write in nontechnical language personality sketches that predictively describe each assessee as a functioning member of the organization.
7. At the end of the assessment period, hold a staff conference for the purpose of reviewing and correcting the personality sketch and to decide on the rating and recommendations of each assessee.
8. Construct experimental designs to evaluate assessment procedures so that all the data necessary for the solution of strategic problems will be systematically obtained and recorded.

Unfortunately, as mentioned, at the beginning of the process the assessors knew very little about job locations or requirements. None of the professional members had ever been in the jobs, and only a few of the military staff knew anything about them. After several months of operation, things somewhat improved. The assessment center staff got firsthand information in a variety of ways. Returning OSS staff briefed the assessment staff and, occasionally, it was possible for the assessors to visit the foreign field locations.

Assessors were also able to gain some insights from visits to training programs; but a continuing lack of information greatly hampered the implementation of several important steps in the assessment procedure.

Note that the exercises designed to elicit important personality characteristics were not statistically validated before use. The press of time and the difficulty of obtaining an appropriate criterion prevented empirical test validation efforts. A crude form of content validity was used. Revisions of exercises were made on the basis of some statistical analyses and experience. Another important feature of the OSS program was that the assessment techniques did not yield an objective "score" in most cases. The exercises were devised to elicit behavior, after which the assessors made judgments and ratings.

Still another important feature was the living-in arrangement. The main assessment location was a secluded estate outside Washington, D.C., where the staff and candidates spent the entire three days together, working, eating, sleeping, and living. This arrangement afforded the staff many opportunities for informal interactions, brief conversations, and casual yet important observations.

Assessment techniques. The emphasis on situational tests gave the OSS program a unique flavor and fitted closely with the theory that predictions of job performance should be determined largely by exercises simulating the environment where the jobs would be carried out.

The assessment instruments included both objective and subjective (judgmental) techniques. Although the OSS assessment is generally associated with situational, performance-type exercises, the more traditional techniques also played an important role. In fact, as will be pointed out, the interview, among all techniques, was relied upon most heavily.

The objective tests included a biographical data form, the Otis Self-Administering Test of Mental Abilities, a sentence completion test, a health questionnaire, a work conditions survey, a vocabulary test, and a projective questionnaire. Most of these were unscored and were used in an unsystematic way. They served as preliminary data for the interview and assessor discussions and deliberations about the candidate.

The situational tests that have become most well known are the brook and construction exercises, both of which were borrowed from the British army assessment program. In the brook exercise, a group of candidates was presented with the problem of moving a log and rock across a stream on the farm. They were given boards, rope, a pulley, and a barrel. Only through a cooperative effort could the task be accomplished. The objective of the exercise was to give the assessors a chance to observe important characteristics including leadership, energy, effective intelligence, and social relations.

The construction exercise was an individual exercise involving one candidate and two confederates of the staff. The task required the assessee to use pieces of lumber to build a large wooden structure, using a model as an example to follow. Two "farmhands," Kippy and Buster, were available to help. Actually, Kippy and Buster were junior assessors playing predetermined roles. Kippy, passive and sluggish, did nothing unless given explicit orders. Buster, aggressive and forward, rushed into impractical and incorrect solutions. Both confederates interfered with progress and criticized the candidate in many ways. The purpose of the exercise was to study the person's leadership abilities and, more importantly, his or her emotional stability. None of the candidates finished the task; many got angry, bitter, and upset. Many worked on their own; a few simply gave up. Others started over and did the best they could under the circumstances.

Other situational tests were included. In the wall exercise (also adapted from the British army), a group of candidates were to work cooperatively to scale a wall and to transfer materials and personnel across an open space to the top of another wall and down the other side. Sprinkled throughout the assessment period were exercises including a map test, leaderless group discussions, and case preparations. There was also a stress interview with a panel of assessors asking rapid questions and yelling at the candidate.

Overlying the whole program of specific exercises was the requirement of a false cover story for each candidate. Each person assumed a false name and made up a cover story about his or her life and work. Most of the time (except under "X conditions") the candidate was required to stick to this story, some aspects of which could be true, others fabricated. Assessors would try to trick the candidates into revealing themselves at all possible times. "X conditions" allowed the candidates to discuss their own background, jobs, and future plans. These conditions existed during the background interview, when specifically announced by the staff, or when requested by the candidate. In a sense, then, the entire three days comprised a situational test of the person's ingenuity in making up a story and tenacity in maintaining it.

Subsequent analysis of the situational tests (Sadoka, 1952) revealed two major types of exercises: verbal and active. The brook, construction, and obstacle exercises contributed to "active" aspects of ratings on social relations, energy and initiative, and leadership. The debate and discussion groups contributed to the "verbal" aspect of these traits. Factor analysis of ratings of effective intelligence yielded a third dimension measured by individual tests (nonverbal, general intelligence, and comprehension). In summary, Sadoka (1952) concluded that three concepts—abilities, interest and motivation, and social adjustment—were measured by the OSS exercises.

Assessment processes. The staff assigned to observe each exercise made a series of ratings on each individual, but made no record of behaviors observed. Throughout the assessment period, the staff held periodic reviews of candidates' performances and compared impressions and hypotheses. After an individual completed all the exercises, the staff met to present the numerical ratings, review reports about the candidate, render a summary decision of approval or disapproval, and make final ratings on the personality dimensions.

Several procedural aspects of the final assessment discussion should be noted. The initial step of the discussion was the presentation of a personality sketch written by the interviewer. This report could be modified, but it probably influenced subsequent discussion. Reports of exercise performance during the final assessment discussion may have lacked objectivity and independence because of the previous discussions among staff members. At the least, the procedures probably led to contamination across techniques, factor ratings, and assessors. After all the exercises had been discussed, the staff made a final decision regarding suitability for field performance and made recommendations for training and placement considerations. After the decision was rendered, the staff made ratings on the main assessment variables. Current assessment center procedures involve quite a different sequence: behavioral reporting, ratings of dimensions, then a final prediction. Later sections of this book, especially Chapter 6, will describe in detail the assessment process currently being used in managerial assessment centers; several improvements will be seen.

Relationship to job performance. The accuracy of the assessments was checked in several ways including correlations of staff ratings with several types of criteria. Performance appraisals were obtained from commanding officers in the field via interviews conducted by assessment staff members. An overall rating of total performance and a numerical estimate of the reliability of the overall performance rating were obtained. A second set of appraisals was obtained from theater commanders and involved ratings on six factors corresponding to the most important assessment factors, for example, motivation and effective intelligence on the job. In addition, interviews were conducted with formerly assessed persons when they were reassigned to new areas. Ratings were given by interviewers on problems of adjustment on the job, anxiety, psychosomatic complaints, etc. Finally, when the OSS personnel returned to the United States after duty, they were asked to describe the field performance of peers and to supply ratings of their performance.

Numerous criterion problems were noted, including lack of variation, halo effects, low interrater reliability, lack of firsthand knowledge of the field performance, and hesitancy to give ratings. The authors of *Assessment of Men* question the validity of the criterion data because of these and other factors.

The overall effectiveness rating during assessment correlated .45 with the field appraisal by overseas staff. This figure is an average of correlations for results from the two main assessment locations. For unknown reasons, the validity from a 1-day program exceeded the validity for the original 3-day program. When assessment ratings on the separate personality factors were correlated with corresponding ratings from the field, the results were less positive. Only the ratings of effective intelligence showed a significant correlation ($r = .32$).

Since personnel were actually placed in jobs other than the ones for which they were assessed, validation was difficult. As one would expect, analyses for assessments conducted at two locations (S & W) showed higher predictive validities for persons who performed in the jobs for which they were assessed (Table 2.2).

These data are for the returnee criterion, but similar results were obtained for other criteria and other groups of subjects.

Wiggins (1973) conducted a reanalysis of some of the OSS data using a technique to evaluate the outcomes of prediction. In contrast to an examination of only the validity coefficients, this analysis determines the percentage of correct and incorrect decisions. The technique takes into account the number of candidates selected and the base rate of success on the job. As an example, Wiggins used a set of data from Station S where the validity between final assessment ratings and field performance ratings equaled .37, the percent of candidates selected equaled .75, and the base rate equaled .76.

Random selection would have yielded 63% correct decisions, but the OSS procedures yielded 77% correct. The 14% increase is significant for such important assignments. Comparable analyses for selection data at

Table 2.2

Correlations of OSS Assessment Ratings and Field Performance for Persons Placed in Jobs for Which They Were Assessed and for the Total Sample[a]

Assessment location	Appropriate job		All cases	
	r	N	r	N
S	.39	31	.19	93
W	.29	93	.21	173

[a]From OSS Assessment Staff, *Assessment of men: Selection of personnel for the Office of Strategic Services,* New York: Holt, Rinehart & Winston, 1948. Reproduced by permission.

Table 2.3
Correlations of Ratings on Effective Intelligence Obtained from Various
Assessment Techniques with a Criterion of OSS Returnee Ratings[a]

Technique	r	N
Interview	.44	86
Discussion	.44	84
Debate	.43	72
Matrix test	.30	87
Vocabulary test	.38	87
Mechanical comprehension test	.11	86
Judgment task	.44	84
Final rating on effective intelligence	.53	87

[a]From OSS Assessment Staff, *Assessment of men: Selection of personnel for the Office of Strategic Services,* New York: Holt, Rinehart & Winston, 1948. Reproduced by permission.

Station W resulted in even more dramatic evidence of the value of OSS procedures.

Further analyses using the returnee criterion yielded some insight into the validity of different assessment techniques. Correlations of effective intelligence were computed for ratings on this factor using various test techniques and were compared with returnee ratings on the factor. The data in Table 2.3 show that the interview, the leaderless group discussion, the debate, and the judgment task were most predictive of this criterion.

Various analyses of ratings within the assessment period provide insight into which factors were most important to the assessors and which assessment techniques were most influential in shaping overall impressions. When factor ratings and overall ratings were correlated, it was clear that almost all factors contributed a significant amount to the final rating. No analyses are reported to show the unique contribution of each factor, but the highest correlations were obtained for effective intelligence, leadership, social relations, propaganda, and energy.

Table 2.4 summarizes several sets of data showing the correlation of final ratings of several factors with the ratings on those factors as determined from several assessment techniques. It is clear from these data that the interview is the most important method of determining ratings on almost all factors. It is logical that this assessment technique contributed to the ratings on some factors such as social relations, but one would expect that assessors would rely on other techniques in assessing such factors as leadership and emotional stability. Since the assessors were mostly clinical psychologists and psychiatrists, they may have relied too much on the interview because of their background, training, and ex-

Table 2.4
Intercorrelations of Final OSS Variables and Assessment Techniques[a]

Assessment technique	Energy	Effective intelligence	Emotional stability	Social relations	Leadership	Security	Propaganda
Interview	.78	.80	.90	.69	.79	.62	.70
Brook	.67	.39	.44	.50	.68		
Construction	.56			.39	.54		
Assigned leadership	.77	.48		.56	.68		
Obstacle	.41						
Discussion	.55	.67		.52	.64		.69
Debate	.54	.73		.56	.66		.63
Vocabulary		.63					
Stress interview			.46			.44	
Post-stress			.36			.48	
Nonverbal test		.53					
Otis Quick Scoring Test of Mental Ability		.61					
Manchuria Test (writing propaganda)							.83

[a] From OSS Assessment Staff, *Assessment of men: Selection of personnel for the Office of Strategic Services,* New York: Holt, Rinehart & Winston, 1948. Reproduced by permission.

perience. More importantly, the structure of the assessment discussion may have determined the seeming importance of the interview data. The interviewer wrote most of the final report before having any discussion with the other assessors. Assessors who observed the candidate in the various exercises simply reported their numerical ratings and commented on the interviewer's judgment if they thought it was appropriate.

The data show that several assessment techniques contribute significantly to each factor. The assigned leadership problem and the discussion exercise contributed consistently to the factor ratings.

Contributions of OSS studies. Most subsequent multiple assessment efforts in the United States have drawn many of their ideas, methods, and points of view from this program. Improvements and advancements have been made as a result of suggestions concerning its mistakes and inadequacies. *Assessment of Men* reported details of the method and research and provides an excellent point of departure for anyone wishing to undertake an assessment program.

The outline of steps on how to set up and operate an assessment center program is an excellent model. It could be improved by building in some form of test validation for the instruments before their actual operational use. Validation might be conducted by criterion-related or content-oriented methods. This was a luxury that could not be afforded at the time of the OSS studies, and such methods are difficult to implement even today. For the most part, the OSS outline of analyzing the job and situations, selecting multiple techniques to assess important personality factors, and rating behaviors on important factors by several assessors is sound.

The situational and performance exercises marked a significant shift away from primary reliance on paper-and-pencil instruments in previous personality research in the United States. The living-in arrangement enhanced the opportunities for numerous reliable and accurate observations of the assessee's behavior. The situational tests were miniature samples of the job and, as such, revealed the assessee's behavior in realistic tasks. The follow-up research also discovered another effect of using simulations for selection. They created a positive attitude toward the assessment process. The OSS authors reported numerous accounts of the candidates' favorable reactions to the program. While some exercises like interrogation and construction were frustrating and anxiety producing, they were viewed as necessary and relevant. Several candidates reported they were favorably inclined toward the OSS because it took so much time and trouble to carefully select its members.

Although the actual validity results were not all substantial, many were positive and most were encouraging. Considering the numerous problems in doing the assessments and conducting the follow-up research, the results should be viewed favorably. Wiggins's (1973) reanalysis suggests very strongly that in terms of improvement of selection the OSS procedures led to a higher proportion of successful candidates and a lower proportion of misclassified rejects (i.e., people who would have been successful if they had been selected for service).

Veterans Administration Clinical Psychology Studies

Soon after World War II, the U.S. Veterans Administration (V.A.) undertook a large-scale program to support the training of clinical psychologists (Kelly & Fiske, 1951). Traineeships were awarded to students for graduate studies in universities throughout the United States. A 5-year research project was launched to evaluate several means of selecting the candidates most likely to benefit from these traineeships, by succeeding both in school and in the profession. The project was large in scope and involved many subjects and a wide variety of predictors and criteria. The V.A. project staff tried from the beginning to identify important dimensions of the clinical psychologist's professional performance and to develop good criterion measures on the dimensions. The evaluation research was designed to yield information regarding the relative effectiveness of clinical and objective approaches to assessment.

The research design of the V.A. studies limits their applicability to selection programs. The first group of persons assessed (in 1947) had already been accepted into clinical psychology programs and thus their behavior in the testing situations may not have been representative of behavior of applicants to the programs. The next sample were actual applicants, but they were tested in 32 testing centers and the data were analyzed at a separate location. The standards used by these various centers may not have been the same.

The predictor battery included intellectual, interest, and personality tests; clinical interviews; and individual, two-person, and group situational exercises. A large number of predictors were used because there was not enough prior research evidence to show which ones would be more effective in filling similar types of jobs. More than one test of each type was used, and at least two interviews were conducted. To record observations during situational exercises, rating scales were developed to record: (a) descriptions of behavior; (b) evaluation of the appropriateness of behavior; and (c) predictions of subsequent clinical performance based on the observations.

The V.A. situational tests included a leaderless group discussion; a group performance test in which candidates had to move heavy cement blocks around the yard to form predetermined objects; a simulation task in which the assessee played a superintendent interviewing a teacher regarding rumors about sexual conduct; and an individual exercise in which, without speaking, the assessee acted out interpretations of a poem and several words. Kelly and Fiske (1951) gave little justification for these exercises, and it is hard to see their relevance. Certainly they were much more obscure in relation to the job than those used in the OSS study. The strength of situational tests is that they are usually simulations of parts of the job or small samples of important tasks. More realistic situational tasks could have been devised. The general lack of validity of the situational tests may be due to the lack of prior job analyses. Unfortunately, criterion development was conducted after the assessment program. It would have been far more effective to have studied the job requirements of clinical psychologists prior to devising the assessment techniques and conducting the evaluation of candidates.

The criteria were measured in both traditional and innovative ways. Completion of training, performance on an objective achievement examination, and ratings of performance by teachers and supervisors were the commonly used methods. A case study was devised to test trainee ability to predict behavior of a patient and was used as a measure of diagnostic competence. Therapeutic competence was measured by the researchers in three ways: (a) a test of the trainee's ability to predict patients' diagnostic test responses; (b) a score derived from the evaluations of the trainee's notes taken on therapy progress; and (c) judgments of tapes of the trainee's therapeutic work with patients. In addition, a composite rating of therapy competence was made. (Research competence was another variable, but the measures of this were not adequate. The study extended only into the last year or two of graduate training, at which time little evidence of research competence could be obtained.)

As baseline data for evaluating validity of predictors, the validity of university professors' predictions were computed. These correlations were relatively high (i.e., .50s–.60s). However, the authors (Kelly & Fiske, 1951) tended to discount these figures for several reasons: (a) the raters were members of the same departments where the students would train and, thus, they would know the training situation better than future selection officials; (b) there may have been criterion contamination in which case the correlations were artifically high because the predictions influenced the performance appraisals; and (c) the high-assessed trainees may have gotten preferential training.

The second and third criticisms seem reasonable, but the first is not. The reality of most graduate selection programs is that persons reviewing applications would know the training requirements. These results, coupled with the lower correlations for tests that will be examined next, suggest very strongly that assessors should be persons who know the situation into which assessees may be placed.

Masses of data were collected and much of it is reported in the Kelly and Fiske report with regard to the validity of the objective tests and ratings. One of the strengths of both the study and the report itself is the thorough analysis of various research questions. In contrast, the OSS report presents only scanty data analyses for evaluation of its work.

Some of the most important insights into the project can be obtained by examining the validity of ratings based on various sources and amounts of information. In one sequence of ratings, the assessor started with only the file of credentials. The median validity of ratings based on this information was .22 in relation to several criteria. Table 2.5 presents the sequence in which items of information became available. After each new set of information, ratings were made again. It is apparent that these validities are not as high as the university predictions ($r = .50$–$.60$), and that the validities do not increase appreciably when new information is added to the credentials. The largest increment came when the psychologists had access to objective test data. After that, the biographical and projective tests add very little.

A big surprise to the authors of the V.A. report was the small contribution made by the interview results. Since the majority of evaluators were clinical psychologists skilled in interviewing techniques, the assessment interviews were probably carried out very well. However, the data clearly show that the interview results added very little valid information above that obtained from the file and tests.

The objective tests were not combined into a multiple-prediction scheme, so it is not possible to say how valid the group of tests alone were. Examination of the validity of individual tests for predicting the various criteria showed that the Miller Analogies Test (a high-level verbal reasoning test) was the most effective for both criteria of academic achievement and clinical skills. The Strong Vocational Interest Blank was the second most effective test of the various criteria. All criteria were predicted by some tests, but the criteria associated with clinical skills were less well predicted.

The assessment ratings given by the staff showed significant validities, but the results were confusing. When the final (pooled) overall suitability

Table 2.5

Validities of Ratings Based on Various Amounts and Types of Information Available to Assessor[a]

Ratings based on	Median validity for several criteria[b]
1. Credential file	.22
2. (1) and objective tests	.29
3. (2) and biographical inventory	.28
4. (3) and projective results	.30
5. (4) and interview results	.31
6. (5) and situational tests	.33
7. (6) and final individual ratings	.32

[a] Adapted from *The prediction of performance in clinical psychology* by E. L. Kelley and D. W. Fiske. Copyright 1951 by University of Michigan Press. Reprinted by permission.

[b] Data for different raters are presented in report.

rating was correlated with various criteria, the correlations were in the middle and high .30s. This indicates that the staff's overall impression of the trainees correlated well with the subsequent ratings of clinical competence, supervisory competence, and professional interpersonal relations. Evidence that the assessors and/or the persons providing the criterion data were responding to some generalized impressions of the trainees is found in the correlations of the several trait ratings. There are high correlations on each trait between the assessor and criterion ratings; in addition, there are high correlations of one trait in assessment and another trait's criterion rating. For example, the assessment of academic performance correlates .46 with criterion ratings of academic performance and .45 with clinical competence. Thus, there was a large amount of halo present in either or both the assessment ratings and the criterion ratings.

Summary of V.A. studies. Even though the V.A. studies were not concerned with management jobs in business settings and contained many design flaws, they were an important predecessor to the industrial applications of multiple assessment programs. They involved a broad sample of subjects from many institutions and yielded some important results. The criterion measurement was extensive albeit restricted to training performance.

The research design allowed comparative analysis of the effectiveness of different assessment techniques. As a result, many of the clinical techniques, including the interview and the Minnesota Multiphase Personality Inventory (MMPI), were found to have little predictive value. Interestingly, situational exercises did not prove to be valuable, but this may have been because they were not simulations of important aspects of the job. One major limitation of the study was that no criterion data reflected actual behavior after completion of training. It is quite possible that performance in training is not highly correlated with performance on the job; thus, predictors of the training criteria and the subsequent on-the-job criteria may differ.

Other Programs

To complete the review of other assessment efforts, brief mention will be made of a number of other programs which took place in the 1950s. These programs are included because of specific contributions made by each effort, even though they did not directly affect the development of early management assessment centers. These programs are described

because each program struggled with some degree of success with one or more of the problem areas identified at the beginning of this chapter. Thus their experience provides potential guidance for further advancement of assessment center programs.

INSTITUTE FOR PERSONALITY ASSESSMENT AND RESEARCH

Following World War II, a number of psychologists who participated in the OSS assessment program set up the Institute for Personality Assessment and Research (IPAR) at the University of California at Berkeley. The purpose of IPAR was to conduct basic research on personality structure and functioning of normal adults (IPAR, 1970). The Institute used an all-inclusive empirical approach to identify assessment techniques and procedures which differentiated more effective from less effective individuals in various occupational fields. A wide variety of tests, questionnaires, self-report inventories, situational exercises, observational rating scales, and the like were used to measure individual differences. A part of the assessment included living-in arrangements which provided opportunity for informal observations. Over the years, IPAR assessed a wide variety of occupational groups including artists, air force officers, architects, managers, writers, etc.

The work at IPAR made two significant contributions to assessment methodology. First, in contrast to the earlier assessment programs, IPAR began each assessment effort with a thorough analysis of the criteria of success in the occupation under study. The purpose of these analyses was to identify the characteristics of effective performance in that field and to serve as a basis for the selection of assessment techniques. In place of the holistic approach of the German, British, and OSS assessment programs, IPAR derived a set of characteristics underlying effectiveness in each occupation. These characteristics served as central variables in the selection of assessment techniques, the scoring of these instruments, and the rating of performance of participants at the living-in sessions. The work of IPAR is most noted for its studies of creativity (Barron, 1954, 1965).

The second major contribution of IPAR's work lies in the empirical approach to assessment research. A wide variety of assessment techniques were used and each was correlated with the criteria identified. The results provide a comprehensive and detailed view of the most effective predictors in each case. Of course, this is not a parsimonious approach, but it does allow the distinction between more and less effective assessment tools. The approach also affirms the necessity of determining the empirical relationship between assessment techniques and measures of job performance.

There are several limitations of the IPAR work that restrict its

usefulness for understanding and improving management assessment centers. First, IPAR was interested in understanding personality structure, not in predicting effective job performance. Thus the results of these studies are of limited relevance to the situation where we want to identify those individuals most likely to succeed in an occupational field. Second, the IPAR procedures did not include an assessment discussion session in which all data were integrated in a systematic manner. Each assessment variable was evaluated separately and remained so. In some cases, the staff pooled their ratings on variables, but there was no final discussion in which various observers compared observations and resolved discrepancies.

Finally, we note that the assessment staff was composed entirely of professional psychologists. Even with systematic criterion analyses, we must question the staff's ability to understand thoroughly the job requirements in many occupations. One of the strengths of managerial assessment procedures is that higher level managers, intimately familiar with the job and organization, serve as assessors.

STERN, STEIN, AND BLOOM STUDIES

New directions in job analyses are suggested by studies conducted by Stern, Stein, and Bloom (1956). They conducted a particularly thorough analysis of the situational demands and role requirements of the job in their studies. Murray's (1938) concept of *press* was used to describe the influence these organizational factors have on behavior. The term *press* refers to the effect or power a situation may have on a person. The press may be beneficial or harmful and the strength of the press may be small or large. Stern *et al.* (1956) used these notions to analyze the situational demands in educational and vocational training programs. Examples of important demands in educational organizations are: (a) the significant goals and purposes of the institution which define tasks, activities, and criteria for success; (b) cognitive requirements of intellectual attainment; (c) affective requirements including attitudes and values; (d) institutional roles that prescribe relationships, for example, between students and teacher; (e) the reward and penalty system. It is essential to analyze the psychological conditions underlying successful performance in the situation as it is defined by these and other organizational presses. According to Stern *et al.* (1956), assessment can be effective only if it is built on an understanding of such environmental presses.

MENNINGER STUDIES

Holt and Luborsky (1958) make an important distinction between naïve and sophisticated clinical prediction models in their 10-yr study of

assessment of psychiatric residents at the Menninger School of Psychiatry. In the naïve clinical approach, qualitative and intuitive judgments are made at each stage of the assessment program, including analysis of the job, gathering of the data, and integrating them into a prediction; and "there is no prior study of the criterion or of the possible relation of the predictive data to it [Holt & Luborsky, 1958, p. 105]." In contrast, the sophisticated clinical approach utilizes qualitative data, such as interviews and projectives, in an organized and scientific way. The data are gathered and analyzed systematically. Furthermore, "all the refinements of design that the actuarial tradition has furnished are employed, including job analysis, pilot studies, item analysis, and successive cross-validation. Quantification statistics are used wherever helpful [Holt & Luborsky, 1958, p. 105]." In this approach, the clinician continues to gather and process data, but in the framework of a more precise assessment process.

The distinction between the naïve and sophisticated approaches is important because it points the way toward an integration of the actuarial and clinical approaches to assessment. Whereas the clinical interviewer and data processor may provide "rich" information about individual cases, the actuarial paradigm may place necessary constraints to guide the process to a more systematic and accurate decision. Chapter 6 undertakes a more thorough discussion of the broader issues of assessment processes, but for now it can be suggested that the success which management assessment centers enjoy is largely due to the application of the principles suggested by Holt and Luborsky (1958). Whereas assessment centers are based on judgments that can be broadly termed clinical, the tests and exercises are usually chosen after careful job analysis, the various sources of data are gathered and presented independently, and predictions are made for well-known job situations.

Recapitulation

This brief and selective review of the history of multiple assessment and assessment center procedures has revealed the contributions made by successive programs. Early development of performance tests provided the basis for constructing situational tests of leadership behaviors. The German psychologists emphasized the holistic (rather than elementalistic) measurement of leadership and the need for behavioral observations. The British developed a better social-psychological definition of leadership and used better group testing procedures, such as leaderless discussion techniques. The British conducted the first validation studies

and provided the first evidence of predictive validity. The OSS developed the most elaborate situational exercises and better observation procedures. An empirical test validation procedure was outlined, but predictive studies could not be carried out because of enormous criterion measurement problems. The Michigan V.A. clinical psychology studies extended multiple assessment procedures to new applications and provided data on the relative merit of different assessment techniques. Other early programs led to further advances. Better job analysis and criterion analysis procedures were developed in the IPAR and Stern *et al.* programs. The Menninger selection programs pointed the way toward a better blending of clinical observation and actuarial methodologies. These and other advances culminated in the first program of assessment centers for managers in the United States with the Management Progress Study at American Telephone and Telegraph.

The First Industrial Application: AT&T Management Progress Study

The American Telephone and Telegraph Company's Management Progress Study (MPS) represents a hallmark in the history of multiple assessment procedures. It was at once the culmination of years of previous assessment research and practice in military and industrial settings and the beginning of creative innovations and extensions of earlier procedures dealing with management personnel. Probably no other personnel research study in American industry has been so well conceived and executed over so long a period of time. The study is unique in several respects: It is a study of both individual characteristics of young managers and characteristics of the organizational settings in which they work; it is a longitudinal study of the development of over 400 managers; and the data have not been used for operational purposes in the company.

There have been few longitudinal studies for adult development. According to Bray (1964b), the Management Progress Study was instituted as a long-range research study of psychological development of adulthood. When we consider the significance of work to an adult's life, it seems essential to study developmental processes in the context of work. For Bray:

> The expression of the abilities and motivation developed during the early years of life takes place importantly for most males in the world of work. Because of the individual and social importance of successful work behavior, vast amounts of effort go into the search by individuals for the work role in which they can be most effective and rewarded. . . . Its [the Management Pro-

gress Study] purpose is very general—to learn more than is now known about
the characteristics and growth of men as they become, or try to become, the
middle and upper managers of a large concern [Bray, 1964b, pp. 419–420].

The Management Progress Study deals with the individual and
organizational characteristics that lead to success as a manager. For our
purposes, we will concentrate on the aspects of the study that deal with
the assessment of personal characteristics associated with success.
Detailed reports of the organizational determiners of success in the MPS
can be found in Berlew and Hall (1966), Bray, Campbell, and Grant
(1974).

Support for the Management Progress Study has come from the top
levels of AT&T. Kappel (1960), then president of AT&T, affirmed that
although the study was designed to improve recruiting and early training
of management personnel, it was from the beginning conceived of as long-
range study with no expectation of immediate pay-offs. In addition, he affirmed that information from the original data would be used only by the
AT&T corporate researchers (it was for many years filed with an
organization outside AT&T) and would not affect the participants'
careers. This arrangement facilitated cooperation of the subjects and en-
sured that tests and appraisals would not affect career decisions about
the participants. Although specific information about the participants in
the study was not used, practical applications of the assessment
methodology were forthcoming much sooner than Kappel or the research
team anticipated.

SAMPLE

The study evaluated 422 men. Two-thirds were recent college
graduates, assessed soon after employment with one of six Bell System
companies. The remainder were noncollege graduates who were originally hired as nonmanagement personnel but had moved into management positions relatively early in their careers. The men were assessed in
groups of 12 over a 4-year period between 1956 and 1960.

MANAGEMENT CHARACTERISTICS ASSESSED

Operating within a fairly stable business environment in a relatively
conservative industry, the researchers had the advantage of being able to
select a set of characteristics of successful performance that was not
likely to change drastically in the future. Based on a review of management literature and the judgments of Bell System personnel men, 25
characteristics of successful managers were selected (Bray & Grant,

1966). These characteristics included managerial functions (e.g., Organizing, Planning, Decision Making); interpersonal relations (e.g., Communications Skills, Personal Impression, Sensitivity); general abilities (Intellectual Ability, Adaptability); and values and attitudes (work-related and social). It should be noted that the dimensions were not chosen on the basis of empirical job analysis of Bell management positions. Nevertheless, many of the dimensions remain in use by many assessment centers.

The assessees were rated on each of the variables and on the likelihood of being promoted to middle management in 10 or fewer years. Factor analyses of the rating variables yielded 11 factors for the noncollege sample (see Table 2.6). Many factors of the college and noncollege samples were similar. A large general factor for the noncollege sample separated into three factors for the college group. As a result of analyses and rationale reported later, seven factors were used in subsequent reporting (Bray et al., 1974).

ASSESSMENT TECHNIQUES

Based on the identification of the original 25 management characteristics, several assessment techniques were selected. A 2-hr interview covered background, personal objectives, social values, and interests. An in-basket exercise required the individual to write letters, call meetings, and otherwise deal with 25 items which might be found in a

Table 2.6
Characteristics Assessed in the Management Progress Study[a]

Factor		Identification
I		General effectiveness
II	(College graduates only)	General effectiveness
III	(College graduates only)	Passive dependency
IV		Administrative skills
V		Interpersonal skills
VI		Control of feelings
VII		Intellectual ability
VIII		Work-oriented motivation
IX		Passivity
X		Dependency
XI	(College graduates only)	Noncomformity

[a] Adapted from "The assessment center in the measurement of potential for business management" by D. W. Bray and D. L. Grant, *Psychological Monographs*, 1966, *80* (17, Whole No. 625). Copyright 1966 by the American Psychological Association. Reprinted by permission.

telephone company manager's in-basket. In a business game, six participants worked together to buy parts and manufacture a product. In a six-person leaderless group discussion, each of the participants tried to get his foreman promoted to a higher level job.

Projective tests included the Rotter Incomplete Sentences, the Business Incomplete Sentences Test, six cards of the Thematic Apperception Test (TAT), and a self-descriptive Q-sort. In addition, other paper-and-pencil tests were administered: School and College Ability Test (SCAT), Test of Critical Thinking, Contemporary Affairs Test, Edwards Personal Preference Schedule, Guilford–Martin Inventory of Factors GAMIN, Opinion Questionnaire, Survey of Attitudes Toward Life, and a personal history questionnaire; and each subject wrote a short autobiographical essay.

ASSESSORS

The assessors were professionally trained persons, usually industrial or clinical psychologists; some were Bell staff, some were university faculty or consultants. Later in the assessment efforts, line managers from Bell companies participated as assessors. None were superiors of assessed participants. The composition of the assessment staff is important since the most recent applications of the method have used non-professional assessors almost exclusively (Bender, 1973; Byham, 1978a).

STAFF OBSERVATIONS AND EVALUATIONS

Throughout the 3.5 days of assessments, extensive written reports and ratings were recorded following each assessment technique. The leaderless group discussion and business game were observed by two staff members. Each observer made notes summarizing the activities of each participant and made independent ratings and rankings of the participants' overall contribution to the solution of the problem. In addition, peer ratings and rankings were recorded following each group exercise. More extensive summaries of the interview discussions (Grant & Bray, 1969) and the projective responses (Grant, Katkovsky, & Bray, 1967) were made.

In most cases, each staff member specialized in summarizing and presenting the results of one of the assessment techniques. For example, one assessor reported on the in-basket performance of all participants whereas another, usually a clinically trained psychologist, summarized all the projective responses. Following all assessments, the staff met to review and integrate the observations. Each participant was discussed extensively: His background, his interview and test results, and observations of his performance in the individual and group exercises were reported. After all information was presented, each assessor independently rated the participants on the 25 characteristics. These ratings were then discussed, and the staff had an opportunity to alter their ratings. For research purposes, the average of the final scale ratings was obtained and recorded. Two final ratings were made by the staff: Ratings of "Yes" or "No" indicated whether the staff predicted the candidate *would* make middle management and whether he *should* make middle management in 10 years or less. If the staff came to an even split of yes–no votes, the candidate was placed in a "?" category.

Later, the qualitative and quantitative information was summarized in a narrative report of each participant's performance at the assessment center. Feedback of results was not given to the participants, their superiors, or any other company managers in order to minimize the effect of assessment on the individual's progress in the company.

SUMMARY

Seldom is such a "pure" study conducted in industry. Dr. Douglas W. Bray, who conceived and led the research study, the research staff who participated in the research, and executives who endorsed the arrangements should be complimented! Studies of this type bring true advances in knowledge of the psychology of work. Basic research in chemistry, physics, engineering, and "hard sciences" is commonplace in American industry; basic research in social sciences is unusual. The many personnel advances coming from the Management Progress Study are good evidence of the payoff that can come from social science research. Details of the validity studies coming from the Management Progress Study and related programs of AT&T will be provided in Chapters 5 and 7. In summary, it was found that the overall assessment rating accurately predicted the actual progress individuals made in the company over the following several years (Bray *et al.*, 1974; Bray & Grant, 1966). The unique contribution of using separate assessment exercises (e.g., projectives, interviews, leaderless group discussions) was established. For now, it can be said that the fruits of diligent labor seem to have been productive for this organization and others.

3
Approaches to Predicting Managerial Effectiveness

This chapter describes and compares five approaches to predicting managerial effectiveness: (a) supervisors' ratings of potential; (b) psychometric testing and other paper-and-pencil measurements; (c) clinical evaluations by psychologists and related professionals; (d) background interviews; and (e) assessment centers. The strengths and weaknesses of each approach will be discussed in terms of practical considerations, attitudes of persons being evaluated and of their superiors, and the accuracy of the predictions. Each approach will be evaluated by an analysis of the processes and potential errors involved and by an examination of existing research.

This method of inquiry is not meant to suggest that any organization does or should use only one of these approaches. Obviously, the problems of management evaluation vary so considerably that a variety as well as a combination of approaches must be utilized (Albrook, 1969). It is not the purpose of this chapter to prescribe the best applications of alternative approaches; rather, we present a summary of the effectiveness of these approaches and compare them.

The classification of management appraisal techniques is somewhat artificial. Within each category diversity exists. Supervisory evaluation procedures differ in form, content, and complexity; tests of intelligence, interests, and personality differ in length, format, scoring procedures, and validity; clinical procedures differ from one psychologist to another; and assessment centers differ in terms of length, exercises used, and types of assessors. Generalization about an approach may not apply to specific instances, but enough similarity exists within classes to warrant tentative conclusions.

There are several other less frequently used methods of management evaluation which are not reviewed in this chapter: biographical information blanks, peer evaluations, ratings by subordinates, and self-ratings.

As a frame of reference for evaluating strengths and weaknesses, the second part of the chapter presents a model of prediction errors. The model suggests that alternative prediction approaches are susceptible to different amounts and types of error. This model helps identify sources of error and can lead to the selection of an appropriate combination of procedures.

Points of Comparison

Table 3.1 compares five approaches to predicting managerial effectiveness. The points of comparison are described in this section. The body of the table includes the authors' judgments about each consideration based on current research literature, industrial practices, our personal experiences with the approaches, and discussions with managers. A plus indicates a strong point of the method in comparison with other methods; a minus indicates a relative weakness. Both signs may be used, for example, plus–minus means that in our judgment, the technique is generally strong on this point, but there are certain weaknesses.

Practical considerations. Personnel procedures differ in their ease of implementation and operation. To design and implement some programs, little time or planning is needed from point of conception to full use in the organization; furthermore, relatively little expertise may be needed to set up the initial trial program. However, other programs require extensive planning and may require the consultation of experts outside the organization. Some procedures require coordination among units and functions in the organizations. In large and geographically dispersed organizations, the operational validity (Byham, 1971) of programs is often hard to maintain. Related to these issues are cost considerations. Complex programs requiring high-level professional skills or a large amount of managerial time are usually costly. The time of both the evaluators providing the estimates of potential and the persons being evaluated must be considered. Of course, cost considerations must be compared with benefits derived from the methods. The amount of training the evaluators require varies considerably—but some training is necessary for all of the approaches. Usually, a few days of training is

Table 3.1
Comparison of Methods of Predicting Managerial Effectiveness

	Method of prediction				
Points of comparison	Superior's rating of potential	Paper-and-pencil testing	Clinical evaluation	Background interview	Assessment centers
Practical considerations					
Ease of implementation	+	−	+	+	−
Ease of operation	+	+	+	+	−
Cost of operation	+	+	−	+	−
Amount of time to train evaluators	+	−	+	−	−
Reactions of participants					
Reactions of persons being evaluated					
Acceptance	+ −	−	−	+ −	+
Understanding of system	+ −	−	−	+ −	+
Reactions of superiors					
Acceptance	+	−	−	+	+ −
Control by immediate supervisor	+	−	−	+	− +
Measurement considerations					
Standardization	−	+	−	−	+
Objectivity	+ −	+	−	+ −	+
Reliability	+ −	+ −	−	+ −	+
Content validity	+ −	+ −	−	+ −	+
Predictive validity	?	+ −	−	+ −	+
Acceptability to EEOC	+	−	?	+ −	+

enough to enable supervisors to provide valid and reliable performance appraisals whereas more extensive training is required of assessors. Although the notions of how much training is required to adequately carry out the form of evaluation are generally accepted, it should be recognized that these required levels of training are not often provided in practice.

Attitudes of participants and others. It is important that the people being evaluated understand the system, know how the data are derived and used, and find the procedures credible and acceptable. Employees must have assurance that their personal privacy is protected. Their superiors must understand and accept the procedures, including whether or not they maintain control over promotion decisions. Recent innovations in management and administrative procedures have removed many of the decision-making responsibilities from foremen and supervisors. To the extent that decisions about personnel matters are made by others, the supervisor may feel additional erosion of authority. The reactions of other people in the organization, including middle-level managers and executives, are also relevant. If a personnel practice is not perceived to be cost effective and fair, it will not receive continued support.

Measurement considerations. Drawing heavily on the psychological measurement literature, several questions are raised regarding the accuracy of predictions. The data may be dichotomous recommendations to promote or not promote, estimates of probability of success, or continuous scores on tests. In any case, these results may be treated as numerical data and their quality evaluated.

A measurement technique is *standardized* if all persons are evaluated in the same way. The measurement procedure, the physical setting, the opportunity for achievement, the surrounding environment, and many other conditions must be controlled and held constant for all examinees. The objective of such standardization is to control all factors other than the characteristic being measured.

Objectivity refers to the condition in which human judgment plays a small role in measurement. Physical measurements of height and weight by means of instruments can be very objective. A measurement procedure is subjective if differences in human observation and judgment lead to different scores for the same event. Subjectivity can arise on the basis of biases, errors, and idiosyncrasies of the observers.

Closely related to this consideration is the notion of *reliability*. Interrater agreement is one form of reliability, but reliability also refers to other indications of accuracy or stability of measurement. A measurement procedure is reliable if the same individual gets the same score at two points in time, assuming the individual does not change in the interim period. Reliability is also demonstrated when two equivalent measures yield the same score. Parallel forms of a test, separate observers, superiors with equal knowledge of an employee, or alternate interviewers are examples of "equivalent measurement procedures" which should result in comparable scores. Some degree of reliability is essential for adequate prediction, but reliability alone is not sufficient.

Evidence of *validity* must be presented for each measurement technique. What constitutes validity depends upon the purposes of measurement. If the test user wishes to interpret test performance as a sample of behavior representative of behavior in a larger performance domain, then evidence of content validity must be presented. For predictive validity, there must be evidence that scores at one point in time are related to criterion measures of performance or success at a later time. When a test allegedly measures abstract traits (e.g., intelligence or anxiety), a systematic body of research must demonstrate the constructs underlying test performance. Predictive and content validity are particularly important in assessing managerial effectiveness. A method of assessing management potential is valid if it accurately identifies individuals who later are successful at their jobs (predictive validity). A method of assessing management potential is also valid if the measuring procedure is job related. In this case, we may ask whether the technique gives the persons being evaluated the opportunity to demonstrate capability to display effective managerial behaviors associated with higher positions.

Acceptability to the EEOC. In discussing acceptability to the EEOC we have considered relevant court cases, speeches by EEOC representatives, the EEOC's own selection procedures, and our experiences as consultants and expert witnesses in employment. We recognize that the EEOC takes no official stance on the adequacy of any personnel decision-making procedure and examines the actual use of the method and its effects on the employment opportunities of members of various protected classes. Therefore, this section will include our interpretation of the EEOC's past practices and the likelihood of future actions.

A Comparison of Several Industrial Practices

SUPERVISORY EVALUATIONS

The most common method of assessing managerial abilities is evaluation by the immediate supervisor. Almost all organizations rely in some part on information from the supervisor in making promotion decisions. In most organizations, supervisory evaluations are formed through informal, personal observation. Usually these are unrepresentative, unrecorded, unsystematic, and subject to the vagaries of human memory.

Some companies develop systematic procedures for gathering and recording performance information. An outstanding example is the Performance Management System at Corning Glass Works (Beer, Ruh, Dawson, McCaa, & Kavanagh, 1978). However, Campbell *et al.* (1970) reported that even though every organization in their survey of companies most active in personnel research said merit was important for promotion, only half had a formal performance appraisal system to gather and record evaluations. Some estimates (Gruenfeld, 1975) suggest that 60–80% of organizations have a formal appraisal system for management potential, but these probably exist more frequently for lower levels of supervison rather than for middle managers and higher executive levels.

In most cases, only the immediate supervisor evaluates the performance of a given employee. Occasionally, the supervisor consults with other persons to gather appraisal information, but for the most part, the evaluation is given by a single person. The problems created by relying on only one source of information will be explained later.

In addition to evaluating managerial potential, performance appraisals are carried out for a variety of purposes including salary determination, motivation of employees, and identification of training needs. Tiffin and McCormick (1965) say that the main purpose of a performance appraisal is to aid in administrative promotion decisions but they continue:

> There is, however, an important distinction to be made in using appraisal for this purpose. Such ratings should differentiate between the *performance* of the individual *on his present job,* and his potentiality for performance on a *higher level* job. The ability to perform effectively on one job does not necessarily give assurance of an employee's potentialities for greater responsibilities. These potentialities need to be evaluated separately [p. 224–225].

Unfortunately, nowhere in the text do the authors present suggestions on how these potentialities might be evaluated. In practice, confusion often arises because supervisors are asked to provide assessments of both performance and potential. Seldom is there a clear separation of these considerations.

The situation is further complicated by the fact that, in actual practice, a manager two or three levels above the candidate makes the promotion decision. The second-level supervisor bases the decision partly on the immediate supervisor's recommendation, but *mainly* on his or her own observations and evaluations of potential. The second-level supervisor's information about the employee's performance and demonstrated potential is even less complete than that of the immediate supervisor.

Practical considerations. It appears that the major attraction of using supervisory judgments as a means of identifying potential is low cost, ease of operation, and organizational acceptance. Small expenditures of time and money are needed to initiate and sustain the program. Even though training has been proven absolutely essential to the operation of a successful appraisal program, most organizations do not provide even minimal training in how to accurately identify persons with high potential. Of course the benefits of choosing the right person for the job must be weighed against the costs of selecting a potential failure or overlooking a potential success. Thus, the seemingly small operational costs of this type of management promotion system (without training of raters) may be an understatement of the true costs, some of which are hidden. A good system with managers trained in behavioral observation, recording, and rating may cost more in implementation but may have substantially higher payback in terms of effective employees. Other methods of increasing the reliability and validity of the methods that will be described add to the costs but appear worth it in terms of the return on investment.

Reactions of participants. Generally, the people being evaluated and their supervisors react favorably to the concept of using supervisors' judgments for making advancement recommendations. At the same time, they often report a lack of knowledge about their organization's specific programs and the standards being used for making decisions. Research has shown that subordinates often do not know the criteria superiors use in making personnel decisions (Heisler, 1978; Heisler & Gremmill, 1978; Jolson, 1974). Supervisors like the method because they retain control over this very important, status-enhancing personnel decision. While supervisors often dislike the responsibility of making promotion recommendations because by choosing one person, they must reject others, they would rather make the decision than allow others to do it. Because advancement is often the only means of increasing prestige and income, opportunity for promotion is an important incentive in many work settings. As a result, supervisors wish to retain control of advancement to motivate employees and to reward outstanding performance. Unfortunately, this process can make promotion a function of past achievement and not a function of estimated success on the higher level job.

Measurement considerations. A considerable number of measurement problems are involved in a supervisor's appraisal of potential. The first is that supervisors observe employees performing in very unstandardized work situations. As a result, judgments of potential are based on different amounts and kinds of information. One subordinate has a series of easy tasks and the supervisor has an opportunity to observe him or her closely. Another subordinate, located some place physically distant, may solve more complicated tasks, but the supervisor seldom observes him or her in action. Who will get promoted? Probably the one who has been observed more frequently by the supervisor. The supervisor feels more confident in the better known subordinate. From the point of view of the subordinates, this procedure is unfair because of the unstandardized situations used to observe potential for success in higher level jobs.

Some organizations like Prudential Life Insurance, Housing and Urban Development (HUD), and Department of Health and Human Services are training their managers to overcome these problems. Rather than relying on data they happen to observe, managers in these organizations are trained to "engineer" performance observation opportunities, that is, to set up situations where subordinate supervisors and managers can show the skills they have in a setting where they can be observed.

The lack of objectivity in ratings is well documented. Many problems lie in the rating forms; others are a function of the raters (Cronbach, 1970; Cummings & Schwab, 1973; McCormick & Tiffin, 1974; Whisler & Harper, 1962). Rating scales are notoriously ambiguous; definitions of the characteristics being judged and the meaning of levels on the rating scales are vague. Evaluators ascribe their own meanings to them, and these may differ widely. Various types of biases can affect ratings (e.g., leniency, central tendency, and halo effects). Wide individual differences in these biases have been noted among raters. The important thing to note about these problems is that the scores are more a function of the rating scale used or the judgment of the assessor than they are of the person being assessed.

Again, the solutions to many of these problems are known. Dimensions can be carefully defined and managers can be taught the meaning of definitions and trained to observe behavior and classify the behavior into these dimensions. Knowing the meaning of rating scales they can develop high reliability. The problem is that most organizations are not willing to go to the lengths necessary to improve ratings.

A promising technique to increase objectivity is the coached rating. A representative of the personnel department meets with a manager, asking questions to force him or her to substantiate ratings. Areas of weak data are uncovered and plans to increase the frequency of observations in those areas are made. The technique is applied in two ways: (a) the personnel representative merely acts as a resource or sounding board for the manager as the manager completes the rating form; and (b) the personnel representative completes the form, thus forcing the manager to "sell" his evaluation by citing behavioral evidence. Although some large organizations such as the Chevrolet Division of General Motors (McIntyre, 1975) and McDonald's are using these procedures, they are still relatively rare.

Interrater agreement on the three commonly used kinds of rating scales is low. Raters tend to disagree most when rating personality traits such as perseverance, interpersonal skills, and values. They tend to agree more often when rating behaviorally observable characteristics. When the judgments of several competent raters are averaged (Bayroff, Haggerty, & Rundquist, 1954), some of these problems can be overcome. This suggests that information from several raters should be sought instead of relying on only the immediate supervisor, even though he or she may be the most well-informed source of information. A staff person who seeks and gives information to the employee, a superior in a department who uses information generated by the employee, and persons outside the organization may have valuable descriptive and evaluative performance information. The act of comparing and contrasting data may also have positive effects. Such data sources are seldom used.

Our main concern is the validity of supervisors' ratings of potential. How well can supervisors predict success on higher level jobs? This question should be easy to answer, but a thorough literature search reveals little or no data on this monumental problem! We believe that high validities are theoretically possible for those situations where the present job overlaps in functions, responsibilities, or requirements with future jobs, assuming well-developed forms and proper training. We find it difficult to accept the validity as "self-evident" just because organizations function with management personnel promoted with this method.

Acceptability to EEOC. It is our impression that performance appraisals are a generally accepted method of obtaining information for promotion of personnel to management positions. There have been numerous EEOC cases involving paper-and-pencil tests but only a few notable court cases that have ruled against an organization's performance appraisal practices (Schneier, 1978; Thompson, Klasson, & Lubben, 1979; *Fisher* v. *Procter & Gamble,* 1980). It is clear that performance appraisals must be validated in the same way as tests, but the EEOC has not attacked appraisals with the same force. In our experience, performance appraisal methods are not scrutinized as carefully as testing practices during a compliance review.

PSYCHOLOGICAL TESTING

Psychological testing is probably the most controversial method of identifying management potential. On the one hand, advocates can point to tests' high level of objectivity and to some clear-cut research findings that show relationships with job success. They can contrast this objectivity with the serious subjectivity involved in most supervisory evaluations and the paucity of scientific evidence to support clinical evaluations. On the other hand, opponents of testing have arguments of equal strength. They say that testing is an artificial way to evaluate a person, that it does not consider some of the important forces that influence work in a real-life setting. They contend that constructs such as intelligence and personality characteristics explain only a small part of managerial effectiveness. At a more emotional level, they argue that tests are not acceptable because they usually do not appear to effectively measure managerial potential and, furthermore, they may involve an undue invasion of privacy. Some companies report unpleasant experiences with tests and tell of a negative company image created through the misuse of tests.

How frequently are tests used? While data do not exist that would allow a clear-cut answer to the question, it appears that approximately one-third of all organizations use test information for evaluating managerial potential. Tests are used more frequently for promotion to first-level supervison and less frequently at the middle management and executive levels. Ward (1968) found that 36% of the firms he surveyed used tests for evaluating supervisors and managers for promotion. Campbell et al. (1970) found that about 40% of the 36 industrial and government agencies interviewed used some form of intelligence or personality test for promotion decisions. It should be stressed that Campbell et al. (1970) visited organizations that had been nominated as the most active in research on managerial effectiveness; hence, the authors acknowledged that this was not a representative sample of American business and is therefore probably an overestimate of use in other organizations. Even within this sample of companies using tests relatively frequently, Campbell et al. (1970) found that promotions were based primarily on the amount of experience and performance evaluation. Tests and interviews were less important. Consideration of factors influencing the choice of tests versus alternative methods of making promotion decisions may help explain why objective and valid tests are infrequently used.

Practical considerations encouraging the use of tests. The unwary executive or personnel manager finds it deceptively easy to use tests for managerial evaluation. A series of tests purporting to measure factors essential to managerial success can be selected and used with relative ease. The resulting test information will probably give the decision makers new information and will be perceived as useful. Unfortunately, however, this practice is often problematic. With experience, managers find that the many tests are unrelated to subsequent managerial success; they find the information can be obtained in other ways; and in the case of personality tests, they often find the scores are hard to interpret.

Practical considerations discouraging the use of tests. In reality, it is very difficult to design and validate an effective testing program. First, the technical aspects of test validation must be carried out: One must provide a thorough job analysis to identify critical job elements, design or choose an appropriate test battery, and substantiate the job relatedness of the tests. The validity of some tests (e.g., reading, math, blueprint reading) can be established through content validity, but the validity of most paper-and-pencil tests must be established by a statistical relationship with a performance criterion. Of equal importance is the operational validity (Byham, 1971) of the test. Procedures and policies must be established so that the test is administered, scored, and interpreted in an accurate manner. The persons who receive the results and make decisions on the basis of the results must be trained appropriately. All of these factors affect the overall utility of the test.

In addition to the above requirements, certain legal considerations increase the difficulties of setting up a testing program. Recent concerns over potential racial discrimination have led government agencies (EEOC et al., 1978) to issue a set of requirements that codify many of the professional standards of test validation research. They require that if a company's selection procedure has an adverse impact on the selection of minorities or women, the test user must validate the test according to standards of accepted professional practice of high quality industrial psychological research. As a result, many organizations have chosen to cease testing because they have not established the validity of their selection instruments. One important requirement contained in the EEOC guidelines is that a test must not only be valid, but also that it must not discriminate unfairly against minorities and women. To conform to these requirements for test validation requires an extra level of competence and research effort that many organizations do not have. In summary, while the ostensive costs of testing in terms of materials and time in actual operation are low, the developmental costs and cost of skilled professional effort may be high.

Reactions of participants. Another strong deterrent to the use of tests as aids to promotion decisions is the negative reactions of both assessees and the supervisors who use the data. Many persons do not see the relevance of the tests to the job being considered. The tests—especially general mental ability tests and personality questionnaires—do not have face validity, that is, the tests do not appear to measure what they are supposed to measure. A distinction should be made between the management's attitude toward testing nonsupervisory personnel and their attitude toward testing at management levels. Several surveys (Tiffin & Prevratil, 1956; Stagner, 1946; Thornton, 1969) have shown that although managers believe industrial psychologists and personnel selection procedures can make a contribution to organizational effectiveness, they are less in favor of applying them to managers. At the top executive levels, tests are virtually never used (Glickman, Hahn, Fleishman, & Baxter, 1968).

Measurement considerations. Tests of cognitive abilities and aptitudes stand up well on the critical questions of standardization and objectivity. All candidates for promotion are evaluated in the same way and the scores are not a function of different subjective standards. For most tests, the reliability of measurement is high. Tests of personality and interests are less reliable. Projective tests such as inkblot interpretations and incomplete sentences are more subjective than paper-and-pencil tests. Only under special conditions can reliable scores be obtained from projectives (McClelland, Atkinson, Clark & Lowell, 1953; Grant et al., 1967; McClelland & Winter, 1969).

General surveys of the validity of tests for managerial personnel are summarized here:

1. A small number of organizations have carried out extensive research programs demonstrating adequate predictive validity of tests for managerial effectiveness. The two best known programs were conducted by Sears Roebuck (Bentz, 1967) and Exxon (Laurent, 1962, 1970; Social Science Research Division, SONJ, 1961).
2. Tests of general mental ability are related to managerial success, especially at the lower levels of foremen and supervisors (Dunnette, 1967; Korman, 1968).
3. Personality tests can make valid contributions to the prediction of managerial effectiveness if they are carefully chosen, validated, and interpreted by skilled psychologists (Campbell et al., 1970; Ghiselli, 1966; Guion, 1965). Past research evidence gives little indication of which tests are likely to be valid for which jobs (Guion & Gottier, 1965).
4. Projective devices have not demonstrated general validity (Kinslinger, 1966), but certain tests (Korman, 1968) offer promise, especially if they are scored in relation to some predetermined set of scales which are clearly job related (Grant et al., 1967).

More data on the validity and reliability of tests are provided in Chapter 5.

Acceptability to EEOC. Of all the methods we review, paper-and-pencil tests appear to be the least acceptable to the EEOC. Tests are scrutinized quite closely in compliance reviews and literally thousands of suits have been brought against testing practices. If an organization shows underrepresentation of protected classes and it uses tests, the organization will surely be asked to produce evidence for the job relatedness of the tests.

CLINICAL EVALUATION

The clinical evaluation method uses an outside consultant, usually a psychologist, to provide a psychological profile of the person who is being considered for selection or promotion. *Clinical* is used in a broad, generic sense to refer to the overall evaluation of the psychological functioning of an individual. Clinical evaluation usually includes a description of the person's general adjustment patterns, the characteristic modes of behavior, outstanding personality traits, and the most distinguishing values and beliefs of the individual. The psychologist may try to explain the etiology of the individual's personality by reference to significant events in his or her early life and education.

The objective of clinical appraisal is to arrive at an understanding of the unique combination of intellectual, emotional, and motivational characteristics of the person being examined. One point of view (Belinsky, 1964) suggests that the strength of the clinical approach is its focus on the person rather than on the job. Once a psychologist has a good understanding of the person, a variety of questions about that individual can be answered. It may develop that the assessee is more suited for another job rather than the one for which he or she is being considered. Such insights may be overlooked when the focus is on the job. Looking at the individual *versus* the job is important because it emphasizes the maximal utilization of a person's talents. The orientation is akin to the vocational guidance model which seeks to place people in the occupations for which they are best suited. Clinical evaluation emphasizes the unique strengths and weaknesses of each individual. In contrast, the selection model seeks to find the best person for a given job.

The foregoing does not imply that the clinical appraisal is made without reference to job requirements or the organizational context. Usually, the psychologist insists on knowing something about the nature of the organizational climate, the personality of the chief executive and other important persons, and the peculiar time pressures and demands of the job. All of these considerations and many more would affect the recommendations included in the psychological appraisal (Belinsky, 1964; Glaser, 1958; Guion, 1965). Many consulting firms, specializing in providing this type of service, insist on first working closely with top executives in the organization in order to understand the nature of the work environment. Only then do they feel comfortable making recommendations about potential candidates for positions in the management ranks.

Clinical appraisals usually include some form of prediction about the future work performance of the candidate. This prediction may be in the form of a specific recommendation to hire or not to hire the candidate or to promote or not to promote a lower level employee. The conclusion may be cast in terms of probability of success in a given job. More often, the clinical report describes the types of behavior that might be expected from the candidate in various work situations under different job demands. The report may have a developmental orientation (Belinsky,

1964) in which the consultant points out the types of situations in which the candidate is likely to progress and to grow.

The clinical evaluation is usually based on an examination of psychological test responses and a clinical interview. A wide variety of tests is used by psychologists, but most clinicians would probably use at least one test of intellectual ability and one of personality or interests. In contrast to the psychometric testing approach described earlier in which the tests are statistically correlated with job performance criteria or the tests are samples of parts of the job content, the clinician uses the test to get to know the person better. Test results, subjectively integrated into background information and information obtained from the interview, provide an overall picture of the person's personality.

A sample of the clinical method is the in-depth interview. Depending on the training, style, and experience of the interviewer, the clinical interview takes many forms, ranging from structured to unstructured, relaxed to stressed, directive to nondirective. The interview usually covers the general developmental history of the candidate including education, work history, significant life experiences, current interests and hobbies, and future aspirations.

Practical considerations. It is relatively easy to obtain clinical evaluations. Many consulting firms specialize in providing psychological assessment of managers and potential managers. An organization can retain a consultant to evaluate any number of potential promotees and can obtain the results in a short time. Some consulting firms work on a retainer to provide continuing services, whereas others charge a fixed fee for each report. The cost of obtaining such services outside the organization is relatively low if the organization is small or medium-size, thus needing only periodic assessments. A few organizations such as ITT require a large number of clinical evaluations each year and find it more economical to develop an internal capability to provide these services. Clinical evaluations are highly skilled activities requiring a person with considerable specialized training.

Reactions of participants. The reactions of candidates and managers are probably summed up by the many jokes referring to "visits to the shrink." Participants generally view clinical appraisal with suspicion. A paradoxical pattern of reactions can be noted. On the one hand, people believe that psychologists have extraordinary powers to look deep within their psyches and learn things the individuals do not wish to reveal. Psychologists are reputed to be able to understand why people do the things they do and to predict future behavior. On the other hand, managers often see psychologists as academics and professionals in white coats far removed from the real world of practical problems facing most managers in business. Certainly, most people do not understand the theories or methods of psychologists. As a result, many candidates for promotions react negatively to being evaluated by a clinical psychologist because they do not see the relevance of this procedure to future job success and question the credibility of the psychologist. Line managers may object because they are losing another of their prerogatives in influencing promotion decisions.

Measurement considerations. The most severe criticisms of the clinical approach are in the area of measurement considerations. Psychologists use so many different kinds of interviews and combinations of tests that the method is almost completely unstandardized. Furthermore, the method is admittedly subjective, based on a personal relationship between the clinical interviewer and the assessee. These two weaknesses of the approach are largely responsible for the lack of reliability and validity demonstrated. Miner (1970a) examined a series of studies on the predictive validity of psychological evaluations prepared by several psychologists for a large management consulting organization. The studies showed that psychologists differed markedly in the percentage of favorable reports prepared. The percentage of candidates recommended by the psychologists ranged from 69 to 25 %. Furthermore, there were differences between psychological firms supplying the evaluations.

Differences in styles of reporting and a tendency for equivocal statements place a great burden on the managers who must make decisions based on the reports. Studies (DeNelsky & McKee, 1969; Dicken & Black, 1965) have shown that assessors have difficulties making accurate predictions based on reading narrative reports prepared from clinical appraisals. Dicken and Black (1965) found that ratings based on narrative clinical reports were valid only for certain criteria in one sample, but not valid in another sample. Furthermore, ratings based on examination of basic test data yielded higher validities than ratings based on examination of the summary clinical reports.

DeNelsky and McKee (1969) asked judges to read preemployment psychological assessment reports and to predict overall effectiveness. Although the composite ratings for seven judges correlated significantly with field ratings of 32 overseas government employees, the judges differed greatly in their individual abilities to predict success; only three judges were able to do so with sufficient accuracy, and only one judge's accuracy exceeded the predictive accuracy of the composite.

Taken together, the Dicken and Black (1965) and DeNelsky and McKee (1969) studies suggest that narrative clinical evaluations can be interpreted with some degree of accuracy under special circumstances, but there are special problems that limit their usefulness. In both studies the judges were psychologists who would probably "read between the lines" of the reports more ably and who would make more accurate inferences than nonprofessionals. But even these well-trained professionals had difficulty summarizing and integrating the complex observations from interviews and test responses. The Dicken and Black (1965) study suggested that much information was lost in the process of writing the report.

What is the validity of clinical appraisals? Research literature is lamentably scanty given the extensive use of clinical appraisals. Only three studies were available for evaluating the validity of clinical predictions of management success in relation to subsequent job performance. The first provided minimal support and the other two showed negative results.

Hilton, Bolin, Parker, Taylor, and Walker (1955) evaluated the predictive validity of the Personal Audit Program of the Personnel Research Institute for men assessed in 1951 and 1952. Two psychologists reviewed the test and interview data on file for 100 cases and rated each person on sociability, organizational ability, drive, overall performance, and potential for advancement. Criterion ratings on the same five areas were obtained from on-the-job supervisors two or three years after appraisal. Correlations between corresponding predictor and criterion ratings were statistically significant but small (median $r = .28$). Correlations of a given predictor scale with other predictor and criterion scales were also often significant, indicating halo effects and lack of discriminant validity. Finally, the predictive validity coefficients may be overestimates due to criterion contamination through knowledge of appraisal predictions.

Miner (1970a) described a series of five studies of consulting success in international management consulting firms. Recommendations for hiring by numerous psychologists of the consulting firms were correlated with a variety of success criteria. The reliability of criteria such as tenure, increase in compensation, ratings by superiors, and level in the organization were established. There was no severe restriction of range in predictor or criterion data. The results showed no relationship between psychological evaluations and job success in any study. Miner (1970a) raised issues that may explain the lack of validity in this study, but concluded, "In summary, this series of studies raises serious questions with regard to psychological evaluation procedures as they are currently used in their natural habitat [p. 404]."

However, in contrast to the total lack of validity of clinical evaluations, Miner (1970b) found that executive and personnel administrator interviews and personality tests (Miner, 1971) demonstrated some validity. In the case of interviews, it was found that personnel administrators were more accurate than executives in evaluating such key areas as mental ability, self-confidence, and promotional potential. Nevertheless, extreme caution is urged because many results showed no correlation and, in one case, negative correlation between executive predictions and subsequent consulting success. The test validities were also spotty. The Tomkins–Horn Picture Arrangement Test (PAT) (a general personality test) and the Miner Sentence Completion Scales (MSCS) (a measure of managerial motivation) were correlated with several criteria of success in consulting work. A few scales of the PAT demonstrated validity for more than one sample in the United States, but not for foreign office samples. Miner found that consultant–assessees tended to stress planning and thinking rather than doing, they seemed drawn to authority figures, they did not want to be alone when away from work, they preferred physically close relationships, and they moved toward supportive relationships. The MSCS failed to show validity for these subjects. Because of small samples and inconsistent results, Miner (1971) may have overgeneralized from these results.

This series of articles by Miner (1970a, 1970b, and 1971) provides a unique opportunity to compare the effectiveness of three different approaches to predicting success for the same sample, the same criteria, and the same work settings. While neither the clinical evaluations, the interviews, nor the personality tests demonstrated overwhelming validity, it is clear that the clinical appraisals were least accurate.

The other set of studies that deserves attention resulted from a research program at Western Reserve University (Campbell, 1962; Campbell, Otis, Liske, & Prien, 1962; Hogue, Otis, & Prien, 1962; Huse, 1962; Otis, Campbell, & Prien, 1962; Prien, 1962; Prien & Liske, 1962). The assessment process involved two psychological interviews and a battery of projective and objective psychological tests of personality and intellectual factors. Based on an examination of these data, a psychologist rated each candidate on eight scales: sociability, persuasiveness, supervisory ability, ability to handle complex problems, originality, planning, drive, and overall effectiveness. Similar scales were filled out by immediate and second-level supervisors after the person had been on the job. In addition, each supervisor provided a summary rating that reflected the promotion "action" intended for that individual. Four sets of results were presented for people in sales and nonsales jobs rated by first- and second-level supervisors. The overall effectiveness ratings by the psychologists correlated significantly with the first-level supervisor ratings for nonsales personnel only. No more than four of the eight correlations between corresponding predictor and criterion scales were significant for any set of results. When the psychologists' ratings on the eight scales were correlated with the "action" criterion for the four sets of data, only 4 of 32 correlations were significant. Furthermore, many predictor ratings correlated significantly with "inappropriate" criterion scales, that is, ratings on performance areas not hypothesized to be functionally related. Campbell *et al.*'s (1962) conclusion that "there is general agreement between the supervisors' evaluations and the psychologists' evaluations [p. 65]," seems based on scattered correlations of marginal practical significance. The fact that there are over four times as many inappropriate versus appropriate correlations suggests a lack of discriminant validity.

Acceptability to EEOC. There is little evidence of whether or not the EEOC considers the clinical method acceptable. Evaluations by outside agencies are certainly covered by the testing guidelines and if minorities appear to be disproportionately excluded by the procedure, the organization will be asked to produce validity evidence. It is difficult to predict whether or not clinical appraisals will be the subject of future EEOC action.

BACKGROUND INTERVIEW

The background interview is used extensively to make personnel employment decisions. It may be used by itself or as a part of a more complex set of information gathering methods. Our summary of the strengths and weaknesses of the interview suggest much diversity of opinion. On the one hand, past research and experience have shown that the typical employment or selection interview is fraught with problems. On the other hand, it is hard to conceive of an organization selecting or promoting a candidate to a managerial position without an interview. Recent research on the interview process and interviewer training suggest that if done properly, the interview can make a meaningful contribution to management evaluation.

Practical considerations. Along with supervisors' evaluations, the background interview shares the practical advantages of low cost and ease of implementation and operation. For the interview to be conducted correctly, the hiring managers must be trained to conduct reliable interviews. Although managers may be experienced with performance appraisal or other types of interviews, they usually need extensive training to understand the meaning of relevant dimensions to be evaluated, and to learn techniques to gather behavioral data, the process of classifying behavior into dimensions, and how to make objective hiring decisions.

Reactions of participants. The interview has high face validity. Most people consider it quite appropriate to be interviewed by someone in the hiring department. At the same time, candidates frequently do not understand the criteria used for making promotion decisions. Supervisors generally react favorably to this method because their control is high.

Measurement considerations. Numerous reviews of the research on the employment interview have been written; although we will not attempt to repeat them here, we will summarize much of that literature in Chapter 5. For now we will simply point out a number of potential psychometric concerns that have been raised and point to some new directions for job-related interviews. Even with extensive interviewer training, standardization of measurement may still be lacking because each different interviewer must explore the unique background and experience of the individual candidate. Although the interview has a number of features that make it inherently subjective, objectivity in the interpretation and classification of behavior can be enhanced by adequate training. Previous research has shown high consistency of interviewers over time, but interrater reliability is typically low. Through extensive training, interviewers can develop a common understanding of dimensions and can learn to classify behavior in similar ways. Of course, the dimensions to be evaluated must be identified through careful job analysis. Given an adequate job analysis, the interviewer can accurately cover job relevant dimensions such as oral communication, job motivation, personal impact, and work standards. The interview is less appropriate for measuring certain managerial dimensions (e.g., planning, organizing, delegating). The best use of the interview seems to be in situations where it can be restricted to cover only certain dimensions. Thus, the interview would not be expected to have complete content validity for all job performance domains. The evidence regarding the predictive validity of the interview cannot be summarized concisely. Previous reviewers have typically concluded that predictive validity is questionable, but can be attained when standardized interviewing practices are followed. We agree and further emphasize that, where possible, the interview should be restricted to the evaluation of limited and selected dimensions of job performance.

Acceptability to the EEOC. Until recently, most employment litigation over selection procedures has involved alleged discrimination from the use of tests. On the basis of the number of cases brought by EEOC officials, it would appear that the agency is more concerned about tests than about interviews. In the past 5 years, a few cases involving the interview have been tried in court. In a recent review of these cases and in research related to the potentially discriminatory elements of the interview, Arvey (1979) concluded that even though few lawsuits have yet been resolved, the interview is as vulnerable as paper-and-pencil tests. When the organization is hiring or promoting a small percentage of minorities and uses a procedure that includes the interview, it will have to produce evidence of the reliability and validity of the interview. We will probably see many more cases in the future that involve alleged discrimination from the interview.

Interviews and assessment centers. Although the background interview was a part of the original assessment battery at the AT&T Management Progress Study and continues to be a regular part of the operational assessment programs in the Bell System and some other organizations, the vast majority of organizations do not use the interview in their assessment centers. There are several reasons why most modern assessment center programs do not include a background interview. First, the interview is not a job simulation or work sampling technique. Assessors have a difficult time integrating the background information with behavioral observations from the exercises. Second, until recently the research on interviewing has raised serious questions about the reliability, validity, and discrimination of the selection interview as it is typically conducted (Arvey, 1979). However, new approaches to behavioral interviewing offer promise for more job-related interviewing. Third, the interview should be a separate and distinct part of a total personnel system. It, along with other predictors, should be integrated into a decision about promotability or training needs. Finally, interviews are a good way of involving the manager who has a job opening.

ASSESSMENT CENTERS

This section will be brief because we have described assessment centers earlier and the remainder of this book deals with accuracy of the assessment center procedure. At this time, we will comment only on some of the cost considerations and the reactions of participants. Most assessment centers operating in the United States are based on rather extensive job analyses. This increases the initial cost of the center relative to other assessment procedures only because such a thorough job analysis is not common with the other approaches to management evaluation. In fact, a similar job analysis should be conducted for all procedures.

Practical considerations. Exercise development may be costly, but most organizations use commercially available exercises. A company wishing to develop its own exercises must do a considerable amount of research both in formulating the exercises and in writing and perfecting participant and assessor directions, observation forms, and guidelines for observation. As many as 30 tryouts of an exercise are often necessary before problems are eliminated and the exercise is ready to use. Commercially available exercises are relatively inexpensive, usually costing between $3 and $4 per individual assessed for each exercise. Complicated exercises such as the in-basket may cost $10 to $15.

In addition to costs of the job analysis and assessment exercises, the most significant preassessment-center cost is assessor training. The assessment center staff must be trained in observing behavior, writing reports, and in assessment center procedures (Byham, 1977b). Most organizations spend from 3 days to 1 week preparing their staff; a few spend much longer; and some spend almost no time at all. Most organizations train a large number of managers so that the burden of assessment does not fall too heavily on any one subgroup of individuals. This initially increases training costs, but the investment is returned by other benefits of assessor training (see Chapter 7).

Aside from cost of the exercises, operational cost of an assessment center can be quite high. Participants must be taken off the job for 1 to 3 days and assessors from 3 to 5 days. In addition, an administrator usually devotes twice the amount of time spent by assessors in preparing for the center, writing up assessment reports, and informing participants of results. Published costs per candidate for on-going operations vary considerably because of a great variance of what is counted in the cost (e.g., some centers count assessor time, others consider this a part of their personal management development). Some published costs are: AT&T—$500 for all expenses excluding assessor and participant time (Bray, 1964a), IRS—$275 (Di Costanzo & Andretta, 1970), NCR—$500 to $600 (Sloane, 1971).

One of the best studies of actual costs was done by the South African Mutual Life Assurance Society which kept exact costs of everything related to their assessment program including staff and participant time, travel, facilities (rather elaborate accommodations), and all exercise costs. Their participant cost was $700 per candidate for a 3-day middle-management program.

Participant reactions. The attitudes of people toward assessment centers have been studied by several organizations. Dodd (1977) summarized much of this research from AT&T, IBM, Public Service Commission of Canada, and the IRS. In addition, other studies have been conducted at the U.S. Civil Service Commission (Baker & Martin, 1974), S. C. Johnson & Son (Shankster & Cordea, 1976), and American Airlines (1980). Kraut (1973) reported confirming results from participants in several foreign countries. Using a slightly modified version of Dodd's (1977) outline, we have summarized the attitude research below. Table 3.2 presents Dodd's data.

1. *Preassessment:* Participants find out about the program dimensions and exercises from printed material, their supervisor, and former participants; and 20–37% believe that some participants have information that gives them undue advantage. From 52 to 88% believe that participation is voluntary, and well over half want to attend the program.

2. *Assessment exercises:* From 58 to 93% of the participants believe that the program measures important managerial qualities. The group discussion, game, in-basket, and oral presentation all get high marks in at least one study. Participant reactions are a function of level of assessment performance, quality of feedback on performance, the purpose of the program, and subsequent use of the data in the organization. Up to 41% report that their performance in assessment was different from "real life" situations, but less than 15% report undue stress in the program.

3. *Feedback:* 80–85% report that they understand the feedback given, but anywhere from 10 to 30% believe the assessment did not accurately identify strengths and weaknesses.

4. *Use of results:* When asked whether assessment center results should be used for promotion decisions, 75–100% of the respondents said Yes. Larger portions say the results should be used for identifying developmental needs.

5. *Overall endorsement:* A final, summary question reveals that 75–90% would participate again and up to 100% would recommend the program to a friend. Level of endorsement is somewhat higher among participants who benefited from the program (i.e., were promoted, received special training, etc.) but endorsement was high in all groups.

Management attitudes toward assessment centers are also quite favorable. Table 3.3 presents results from selected questions in a survey of former assessors and other managers at IBM (Dodd, 1977). The majority reported that the assessment center measured qualities necessary for management (at least to a moderate extent) and was a useful management tool. Participation as an assessor improved most manager's estimation of the program. At least one-third of the managers had seen a great improvement in their subordinate's performance since assessment and over two-thirds of the former assessors felt they were now better able to judge the long-range potential of their own subordinates. In other studies (Baker & Martin, 1974; Byham, 1977b; Thornton, 1977), assessors reported an im-

Table 3.2
Summarized Attitudes toward Assessment Centers (in percent)[a]

	Favorable range		Unfavorable range	
	Low	High	Low	High
Adequacy and helpfulness of information provided about center	84	87	10	11
Others have inside info	14	63	5	53
Desire to attend	50	70	5	10
Pressure to attend or voluntary	52	88	9	32
Content				
Relevance and face validity	30	93	0	28
Compared to development or other connected activity	35	86	5	30
Performance versus others	78	91	0	30
Behavior fidelity	49	59	28	41
Stress from external sources	60	80	0	14
Feedback				
Accuracy	50	83	5	30
Understanding	80	87	0	19
Diagnostic value	29	86	10	19
Use of data				
For selection	18	100	19	46
For development	64	94	19	24
Overall endorsements				
Would repeat	73	88	5	16
Would recommend to friend	74	100	0	14

[a] From "Attitudes toward assessment center programs" by W. E. Dodd. In J. L. Moses & W. C. Byham (Eds.), *Applying the Assessment Center Method.* Copyright 1977 by Pergamon Press, Ltd. Reprinted by permission.

provement in their ability to evaluate subordinates and conduct performance appraisals. Negative reactions to assessment centers came from the immediate supervisor if he or she was left out of the decision-making process or if it appeared he or she would lose control of developmental follow-up activities.

From these results, it would appear that candidates perceive assessment centers to be valid procedures for evaluating management potential and that they should be used for promotion decisions. Bray (1961) suggested that if there was a great deal of negative reaction, the line management in operating units of AT&T would complain to corporate staff, but few such objections have been heard.

Reactions from immediate supervisors are more mixed. The more the immediate supervisor loses control over decision making on promotions,

Table 3.3

Attitudes of Former Assessors ($N = 180$) and Other Managers ($N = 309$) toward Aspects of Assessment Center Programs (in percent)[a]

Does assessment measure qualities necessary for management?				
	Not at all	Not very much	Moderate extent	Great extent	To a very great extent
Former assessors	0	5	57	35	3
Other managers	0	10	61	25	4

Have you seen any change in subordinate's job performance since (assessment)?				
	Great deterio- ration	Slight deterio- ration	No change	Great im- prove- ment	Very great improve- ment
Former assessors	0	5	51	41	2
Other managers	1	5	61	33	0

To what extent would you urge promotable employees to attend (an assessment center)?				
	Not at all	Little extent	Some extent	Great extent	To a very great extent
Former assessors	2	5	14	43	37
Other managers	4	3	22	42	29

To what extent is the (assessment center) useful as a management tool?				
Former assessors	1	7	39	34	20
Other managers	1	8	46	34	11

Has (assessor) experience facilitated your judging the long-term potential of your own subordinates?

Former assessors	3	11	39	34	13

Has (assessor) experience improved your estimation of the worth of the (assessment) program?

Former assessors	1	2	23	35	39

[a] From "Attitudes toward Assessment Center Programs" by W. E. Dodd. In J. L. Moses & W. C. Byham (Eds.), *Applying the Assessment Center Method*. Copyright 1977 by Pergamon Press, Ltd. Reprinted by permission.

the more negative reactions are to be expected. If assessment center recommendations have heavy weight in promotion decisions, the supervisor may feel loss of control. But, if management personnel are involved as assessors (even if they do not assess their subordinates) or if supervisors have a part in the interpretation of data from the total promotional system, they respond more positively.

Acceptability to the EEOC. The EEOC seems quite favorably disposed toward the assessment center process. An assessment center was used in 1977 as one part of a complex managerial evaluation system to aid in the reorganization of that agency. A few law suits have been brought against organizations using assessment centers, but none have involved the EEOC. In most cases, the assessment center process was accepted by the court and in no case was the organization ordered to discontinue the assessment center program. A more extensive review of these cases is included in Chapter 10.

A Model for Identifying Errors of Prediction

To aid in the consideration of various methods of managerial evaluation, we have adapted a model for identifying sources of error in prediction originally presented by Cronbach (1970). His model of assessment identifies stages of criterion development and stages of various assessment procedures. More importantly, the model enumerates the potential sources of error at each stage. We have modified Cronbach's model to make it more appropriate for personnel evaluation and have added the assessment center procedure. See Figure 3.1.

The criterion to be predicted is presented in the lower right-hand corner. A criterion is ideally a function of the factors displayed in boxes: (1f) actual abilities, (2f) behavior on the job, (3f) and the supervisor's reports. In reality, errors may be associated with each stage of deriving the criterion. Differences in intervening experiences (e.g., early challenging assignments, amount and quality of training) may affect abilities. Differences in job assignments, quality of subordinates, or constraints imposed by the immediate supervisor can affect behavior displayed on the job. Supervisors may have different opportunities to observe job behavior. Finally, the values of the supervisor may color criterion ratings.

It would appear that these errors are common to the validation of each assessment procedure. When this model is applied to an analysis of various methods of evaluating management potential, some of these errors in criterion development are minimized. For example, when middle-level managers are used as assessors, they are able to interpret the appropriateness of assessment behavior to job performance.

Of primary importance is the left-hand side of the figure. Five methods of managerial evaluation are outlined, corresponding roughly to clinical evaluation, the assessment center, the immediate supervisor's evaluation, and testing methods. One objective of personnel assessment is to maximize the effectiveness of criterion prediction, and use of Figure 3.1 would maximize a correlation of *predicted* criterion ratings (6a, 6b, 6c, 6d, or 6e) with *actual* criterion merit rating on the new job (6f) by recognizing and eliminating the different numbers and types of errors associated with the four procedures.

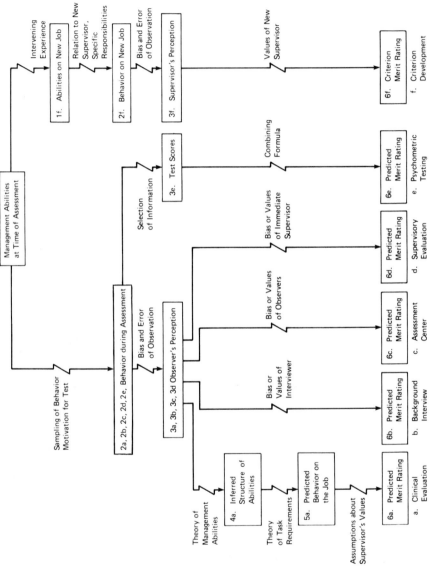

Figure 3.1. Stages and sources of error in evaluation and criterion development. Adaptation of Figure 19.1 (p. 681) from *Essentials of Psychological Testing*, 3rd Edition by Lee J. Cronbach. Copyright 1949 by Harper & Row, Publishers, Inc. Copyright © 1960, 1970 by Lee J. Cronbach. Reprinted by permission of the publisher and author.

It would be inappropriate to simply count the number of potential errors as a means of comparing the methods. Sources of error vary in magnitude, seriousness, and consequence, and whether the error actually materializes is a function of the quality of the specific evaluation program being studied. The value of the model is that it helps explain the different types of error and, hopefully, leads to their solutions.

CLINICAL EVALUATIONS

The clinical approach affords little opportunity for adequate behavioral sampling. The interview is solely verbal and the candidate is unable to display many of the abilities required of managers. (These same criticisms will be raised with regard to the narrow range of abilities covered by tests). The motivation of the assessee may not be appropriate for the clinical interview. If the candidate views the interview as threatening or intrusive, various defense mechanisms may be displayed. Observer errors and biases may also be prominent. The clinical interviewer is often an outsider with only a modest understanding of organizational and job requirements.

Larger problems arise from the conceptual processes involved in clinical inferences. As noted in our initial description of the clinical approach, the clinician tries to understand the person in terms of some conceptual theory of personality dynamics. This process involves making inferences about the structure of abilities and personality of a successful manager in the target job and predicting the candidate's behavior on that job. Potential errors derive from the inaccuracy or inadequacy of these theories.

It might be asked if these theories are really necessary or if they may even interfere with prediction. Research suggests that the clinician's use of some theory of personality structure actually detracts from predictive accuracy. Taft (1955), summarizing the research on the ability to judge people, concluded that nonpsychologists appear to be capable of judging others more accurately than psychologists. He suggested that there are two distinct types of judgment: (a) analytical judgment which entails the ability to formulate inferences and conceptualizations about the person; and (b) nonanalytical judgment which requires only a prediction of the person's overall future behavior. These abilities may be unrelated or even negatively related to each other and analytical skills may interfere with predictive accuracy. Fancher (1967) tested this hypothesis by asking psychologists to predict behavioral events after reading case studies and to write conceptual descriptions of the client's personality. Subsequent comparison of these descriptions with more complete case material provided an estimate of the validity of the conceptualizations. There was a negative correlation between predictive accuracy and conceptual validity; that is, the judges who were more accurate at making predictions tended to write the least valid conceptualizations. Furthermore, there were indications that training in psychology was positively related to the analytical ability to conceptualize personality, but negatively correlated with the accuracy of prediction.

BACKGROUND INTERVIEW

There are several potential sources of error in the process of a manager predicting success after a background interview. Like the clinical interview, the background interview can sample only a limited number and range of behaviors. Many interpersonal, administrative, and decision-making behaviors are difficult to observe in the interview. The interviewee is probably motivated to display optimal behavior, but the process is limited to self-report of previous activities. The interviewer may not ask the right questions to obtain information about job-relevant experiences and may not have the skills needed to accurately observe and listen to the interviewee. Thus many relevant behaviors and statements may go unheeded.

In contrast to the clinical evaluator, the middle manager will probably not be using an explicit theory of management ability of task requirements in his or her interpretation of interview observations. However, the middle manager will have personal beliefs about the types of appropriate behaviors. These implicit theories of personality and implicit theories of management may not be accurate representations of the new job requirements. The interviewer's biases and values may coincide with those of supervisors in the new job situation only to the extent that he or she is familiar with the new job.

Many of these errors can be overcome by providing adequate descriptions of job requirements and by training the interviewers to ask questions and interpret answers properly.

ASSESSMENT CENTERS

Assessment center procedures tend to minimize a number of the sources of error. In contrast to interviews and tests which usually measure narrow traits, behavior simulations in assessment centers are broad behavioral measures. The exercises tap supervisory, managerial, and decision-making skills. Assessment exercises have high face validity and participants are motivated to do well. Through training and the use of observation forms, the staff's observations are focused on a broad range of specific behaviors. Biases and errors of observers are minimized through the discussion of observed behavior in the integration session where differences in observations are resolved. Using assessors who are organizationally two or three levels above the assessees assures that the observers are familiar with the range of behaviors required on the job.

SUPERVISORY EVALUATIONS

A serious source of error stemming from supervisory evaluations concerns behavior sampling. The behaviors displayed in carrying out the current job may not reveal the management abilities required for the new job. For example, a sales person carries out few of the duties of a sales manager.

Many supervisors have little opportunity to actually observe the behavior of their subordinates. Rather, they observe the effects of the behavior. A manager who delegates a report to a subordinate does not observe how the subordinate goes about getting the information and writing the report but only looks at the end result. Likewise, many managers are evaluated relative to profit and personnel indices rather than to how these indices were achieved. Such evaluations may not always be predictive. For instance, we know of a manager evaluated by his superiors as being very high in administrative ability because of the high quality and accuracy of reports developed by his department. When the manager was promoted, it was discovered that, actually, his administrative skills were extremely low. An investigation of the previous ratings indicated that the high quality reports were not developed by the manager, but by a secretary who happened to be highly skilled in these areas.

Other supervisors achieve short-run productivity and gains by cutting the labor force; in the long run this may cause labor unrest. If only the end result over a short time period is considered, the individual may be promoted and cause even larger problems at a higher level.

Another potential source of error is observational error and bias. Figure 3.1 suggests that the supervisor's perception (3d) may be an inaccurate and distorted description of the person's actual behavior on the job (2d). For example, supervisors have preconceptions of the kinds of people who should be in certain jobs and the ways in which the jobs should be carried out. These attitudes and many more probably influence the perception of job behavior.

The next source of error concerns how immediate supervisors predict how a subordinate will perform on a new job (6d), sometimes a job very different from their own. For example, one supervisor has certain preconceptions of how his job should be performed and since he has been fairly successful, he views the potential of others in light of his own modes of behavior. He may have little perspective on the alternative ways in which his own job can be carried out or how other jobs should be done. His own boss, or someone two steps above the candidate, has more experience with different supervisors in the target positions. The higher level manager has seen people come and go in the position. He or she has seen how different behavioral strategies can work or fail.

The model opens up many research areas. For example, it is quite possible that perceptions of on-the-job behavior (3d) may be more highly predictive of measures of behavior on the new job (3f) and, thus, more truly valid than is the case for correlations between predicted (6d) and actual (6f) merit ratings.

TESTING

In the testing approach observer errors are reduced, but several other problems become more serious. The person may not be motivated to demonstrate typical or true behavior patterns if he believes testing is an inappropriate means of evaluating job potential. Such problems can be minimized by proper orientation. A more serious source of error is inadequate behavioral sampling. Test scores may be reliable, but they often measure unrepresentative behaviors simply because most tests entail only simple paper-and-pencil responses and any testing program must limit the number of tests given. Therefore, it is quite possible that test behaviors (2e) are not a representative sample of job behavior (2f). Finally, the formula for combining the test scores into a composite prediction of success may be in error. Usually the combining formula is derived by statistical procedures such as multiple regression; the formula determines the weight or relative importance for each test in the combination. These weights are determined by analysis of the relationship of individual tests to the criterion and the relationships among the tests themselves. Analyses are carried out on a set of test and criterion data for a sample of employees. The relationships and weights, therefore, may be a function of characteristics peculiar to this sample at this particular time; thus they are not generalizable to other samples at other times. Methodological procedures for checking the stability of results (e.g., cross-validation) exist and should be applied routinely. Unfortunately, this is often not done. As a result, statistical procedures often give a false sense of security. Because a procedure is objective and reliable it is very easy to assume it is also valid.

Summary

In comparison with other approaches to the evaluation of management personnel, the assessment center method shows several clear advantages. It is highly acceptable to participants and managers, and its psychometric properties are quite sound. Potential sources of error in measurement and prediction have been minimized by use of multiple management assessors and job sample procedures for observation of relevant work behaviors. Assessment centers are not easy to implement or maintain and they are not inexpensive. However, their value has been demonstrated by utility analyses. For example, Cascio and Silbey (1979) have shown that assessment centers are cost effective over a wide range of assumptions of cost, validity of the ordinary selection procedure, and selection ratio if variation in criterion performance is significant.

Each of the other management evaluation approaches discussed in this chapter has its proper place in personnel administration. The assessment center approach is particularly effective when candidates have little opportunity to demonstrate relevant behaviors on their current jobs or supervisors cannot observe these behaviors and cannot make adequate predictions of future success. Assessment centers are generally applied where there are many participants, but they have been implemented in small organizations quite successfully (McConnell, 1969). Supervisors' evaluations and potential predictions are particularly appropriate when worker behavior can be observed and when the present and potential jobs are similar. Paper-and-pencil testing can make a contribution when there are large numbers of candidates for selection or promotion and when the organization has the resources to conduct adequate test validation studies. Korman (1968) recommends psychometric approaches in stable conditions where criterion behaviors are known and judgmental methods in situations where criterion behavior is relatively dynamic and unknown. Clinical evaluations by outside consultants are most appropriate when a few highly individualized job placements must be made.

For any of these methods to work well, they must be set up, implemented, monitored, and evaluated with professional skill. Each has potential for contribution, but each can be detrimental if handled poorly. Supervisory evaluations are deceptively simple, and frequently supervisors are not given adequate training or reward for correct use. Test validity must be reevaluated periodically and test security must be maintained. Clinical interviewers must be constantly updated on organizational changes. Quality control over assessment center operations must be maintained to ensure consistent administrative procedures. Professional care and standards must be maintained for each of the methods.

Management evaluation procedures might be used in combination with each other or as multiple hurdles. Table 3.4 illustrates how different methods might be used to assess management potential among candidates for a position as branch manager in a bank. Each method is designed to measure some, but not all, dimensions and almost all dimensions are measured by more than one method. The coordination of these assignments allows each method to measure what it is most capable of measuring and also ensures that multiple measurements are made for the most relevant dimensions.

Management evaluation methods can also be made in sequence with each other. Appraisal by supervisors might be used to eliminate the clearly incompetent individuals. In large organizations, tests can be used

Table 3.4

Coverage of Dimensions by a Three-Part Promotion System for the Position of Bank Branch Manager

	Assessment center	Interview	Performance appraisal
Oral Communications	X	X	X
Oral Presentations	X		
Job Motivation		X	
Work Standards			X
Energy			X
Initiative	X	X	X
Sensitivity	X		X
Leadership	X		
Adaptability	X	X	X
Independence	X		X
Problem Analysis	X		X
Judgment	X		X
Creativity		X	X
Decisiveness			X
Planning and Organizing	X		X
Delegation	X		
Management Control	X	X	
Financial Analytical Ability	X		X
Organizational Sensitivity	X		
Extra-Organizational Sensitivity	X		

to screen people without the necessary basic intellectual or personal abilities prior to the use of more extensive selection procedures. Assessment center reports can be combined with tests or clinical interview reports to provide predictive information. These predictive data can be further combined with supervisory evaluations and a background interview. A more extensive discussion of the way these diverse sources of information can be combined in an integrated personnel system is provided by Byham (1979a).

4

The Content of Assessment: Defining the Dimensions of Managerial Success

Management jobs are complex, unstructured, and often ill-defined; some would argue that management is undefinable. While not subscribing to such a pessimistic view, we recognize that efforts to define managerial competence are difficult. In this chapter, we discuss previous attempts to define management jobs and conclude that broad generic definitions of management have been unsuccessful. Then we show how the task has been carried out in the development of many assessment centers. For assessment centers, *management* has been defined as a set of observable behaviors clustered into a number of categories or dimensions. In this context, job analysis of a single job level in a single company becomes a more manageable task.

Three Levels of Managerial Jobs

Managerial jobs can be roughly divided into three levels: supervisory, middle management, and executive. In this book we are using the term *supervision* to refer to the first level of management. Supervisors are directly responsible for the persons who do the actual work—those who assemble products, sell merchandise, and provide services.

Supervisors occupy a unique position in the management hierarchy because they are the only ones who direct workers; all other managers direct supervisors or other managers. A promotion to supervision represents the greatest change in the job hierarchy—job duties, pay differences, role requirements, and reference groups.

Middle management encompasses a wide range of managerial jobs whose boundaries vary with the organization, usually including all those levels between the first level and the vice presidents of the organization. Middle management job titles include department manager, district and regional manager, plant superintendent, department head, and division chief. Middle management often extends to the top manager of a specific manufacturing plant or store at a given geographic location and its chief task is to accomplish prescribed organizational objectives through other people. Although the shift from supervision to management represents another significant change in job duties, it is not as great a change as the move to supervision. Furthermore, subsequent moves upward in the ranks of middle management entail smaller increases in responsibility or changes in duties.

The next major shift is the move from middle management to the executive ranks. Executives in any organization represent a very small fraction of management and usually include only the top two or three levels, the president and vice presidents. The top administrative hierarchy has responsibility for operation of the organization, although executives are responsible to the board of directors or some other governing body. In large organizations, the executives are often physically separated from the middle managers. Corporate headquarters are often located apart from all operational units. Offices of top managers and middle managers are often separated when operational and executive functions are in one location.

The shift to executive status is difficult because new executives broaden their area of responsibility and engage in long-range planning and policy formulation. Dealing with outside pressure groups and with stockholders may also become important functions.

ANALYSES OF MANAGEMENT JOBS

This section covers a sample of job analysis studies of supervision and management conducted outside the assessment center context. It does not include all studies, many of which have been summarized elsewhere (Campbell *et al.,* 1970; McCall, Morrison, & Hannan, 1978; Mintzberg, 1973). We have included only the more prominent, seminal, and unique.

Most of the early, empirical job analysis studies of management dealt with first-level supervisors. Subsequent studies considered middle management and executive positions. Later, broader schemes for analyzing various management levels were developed. Comparative studies of more than one level have been done rather infrequently over the years.

Fleishman. In the late 1940s and 1950s, a number of researchers (Fleishman, Harris, & Burtt, 1955; Shartle, 1949; Stogdill & Shartle, 1955a, 1955b) at Ohio State University conducted research into leadership behavior of supervisors. Beginning with over 1800 statements identified by expert judges to cover a wide variety of leadership functions, descriptions of managers in various settings were obtained. Analysis of correlations among the items revealed two major factors. (Two minor factors, production emphasis and social sensitivity, were later dropped because of their insignificance.) The major factors were:

1. *Consideration:* Manager puts subordinates' suggestions into operation; makes subordinates feel at ease, is friendly and can be approached. These attitudes are contrasted to acting without consulting subordinates, treating people without considering their feelings.

2. *Initiating structure:* Manager sees that subordinates are working up to limits, insists foremen follow standard methods, offers new approaches to problems. This behavior is contrasted to letting others do work the way they think best, waiting for subordinates to push new ideas.

Subsequent refinement led to the development of the Leadership Behavior Description Questionnaire which is completed by the subordinate and the Leadership Opinion Questionnaire (Fleishman, 1960) which is completed by the supervisor. The Ohio State leadership studies were important because they were one of the first behavioral approaches to studying management, and they launched the two-dimensional view of supervisory behavior which remains predominant in most management literature.

Flanagan. As a result of extensive studies of critical incidents of effective and ineffective performance among air force officers in administrative positions, Flanagan (1951) identified six broad categories of administrative behavior:

1. *Handling administrative detail:* Understanding instructions, scheduling work, getting information from records
2. *Supervising personnel:* Matching personnel and jobs, delegating authority, giving orders and instructions
3. *Planning and directing action:* Taking responsibility, solving problems, making use of experience
4. *Acceptance of organizational responsibility:* Complying with orders and directives, accepting organizational procedure, subordinating personal interests

5. *Acceptance of personal responsibility:* Attending to duty and details, reporting for appointments, meeting commitments
6. *Proficiency in military occupational specialty:* Possessing fundamental training, improving effectiveness, keeping well informed in specialty

Among a sample of incidents concerning nearly 3000 officers at all levels, the largest percentage dealt with accepting personal responsibility (36%) and demonstrating proficiency in planning and directing action of others (17%). Incidents dealing with administrative details were mentioned least often (7%). For the top 412 officers in the sample (colonels and generals), 40% of the incidents concerned planning and directing others, and 30% dealt with supervising subordinate personnel.

In another study, Flanagan (1951) obtained reports of critical incidents involving effectiveness of research administrators in 20 research laboratories. Eight broad areas were identified and the frequency of types of incidents for middle level and higher level research administrators was found to be about equal:

1. *Formulating problems and hypotheses:* Identifying and exploring problems, defining the problem, setting up hypotheses
2. *Planning and designing the investigation:* Collecting background information, setting up assumptions, identifying and controlling important variables
3. *Conducting the investigation:* Developing methods, materials, or equipment; applying methods and techniques; modifying planned procedures
4. *Interpreting research results:* Evaluating findings, pointing out implications of data
5. *Preparing reports:* Describing and illustrating work, substantiating procedures and findings, organizing the report
6. *Administering research projects:* Selecting and training personnel, dealing with subordinates, planning and coordinating the work of groups
7. *Accepting organizational responsibility:* Performing own work, assisting in the work of others, subordinating personal interests
8. *Accepting personal responsibility:* Adapting to associates, adapting to job demands, meeting personal commitments

Flanagan's work is important because it introduced the "critical incident" method to the study of managerial work. With modifications, the method has been used in numerous assessment center settings. Further refinements are suggested in the job analysis process advocated at the end of this chapter.

Hemphill. A comprehensive job analysis of management positions was reported by Hemphill (1959). Working with five companies in the Executive Study Conference coordinated by the Educational Testing Service, Hemphill identified 575 job elements including activities, responsibilities, demands, restrictions, and characteristics. Each of 93 executives was asked to indicate to what extent these elements were a part of his job.

Statistical analyses were used to identify common groups of job elements. This led to the following 10 dimensions of managerial jobs:

1. *Providing a staff service in nonoperational areas:* Renders various staff services to superiors, gathers information, interviews and selects employees, briefs superiors, checks statements, verifies facts, and makes recommendations

2. *Supervising work:* Plans, organizes, and controls the work of others; has direct contact with workers and with machines; is concerned with the efficient use of equipment, the motivation of subordinates, the efficiency of operation, and the maintenance of a work force

3. *Providing internal business control:* Controls activities and concerns in the areas of cost reduction, maintenance of proper inventories, preparation of budgets, justification of capital expenditures, determination of goals, definition of supervisory responsibilities, payment of salaries, and enforcement of regulations

4. *Defining technical aspects of products and markets:* Defines activities and concerns in technical areas related to products, markets, and customers; develops new business; is aware of activities of competitors and changes in demand for products or services; maintains contacts with customers; consolidates and analyzes data; assists salespeople with important accounts

5. *Participating in human, community, and social affairs:* Works effectively with others; fosters the goodwill of the community toward the company, maintains the respect of important persons, speaks before the public; nominates key personnel for promotion, appraises performance, and selects managers; participates in community affairs, clubs, and civic organizations

6. *Initiating long-range planning:* Engages in systematic long-range thinking and planning. Concerns are broad, oriented toward the future of the company, and extend to industrial relations, development of management, long-range objectives of the organization, solvency of the company, pilot projects, the business activities that the company should engage in, existing or proposed legisla-

tion that might affect the company, and the evaluation of new ideas

7. *Exercising broad power and authority:* Visits the major units of the company each year; makes recommendations on very important matters; keeps informed about the company's performance; makes use of staff people; interprets policy; is concerned with union relations, capital expenditures, and the long-range solvency of the company; has unusual freedom of personal action; and has very high status in this position

8. *Fostering business reputation:* Promotes the reputation of the company's products or services; engages broadly in either or both of two major directions—product quality, public relations; deals with product design and improvement; handles complaints concerning products or services, delivery schedules, and the general goodwill toward the company. Deviations might reflect on the company's reputation

9. *Demanding behavior:* Stringent demands on the personal behavior of the incumbent and unusually high concern with the propriety of behavior, especially in interactions with superiors; particiaptes at the highest staff levels involving analysis of operations, setting objectives, and making decisions

10. *Preserving assets:* Directly associated with the preservation of the physical assets of the company, including capital expenditures, expenditures of large sums in routine operations, taxes, and the loss of company money

Hemphill's work made several contributions, mainly in terms of the diversity of functions, jobs, and organizations studied. The study also provided one of the first standardized questionnaires to study managerial jobs that has been used by other researchers.

Katzell, Barrett, Vann, and Hogan. In a study of 194 middle-level civilian-staff executives of the Department of the Army, Katzell, Barrett, Vann, & Hogan, (1968) obtained descriptions of work behavior using the Executive Position Description Questionnaire (Hemphill, 1959), the Work Analysis Form (Stogdill & Shartle, 1955), and the Performance Style Questionnaire (Barrett, 1961). After elimination of irrelevant and infrequently used terms, 90 items were factored into eight orthogonal dimensions:

1. *Long-range planning:* Plans for future activity, including forecasting trends or events; conducts pilot projects, being concerned with legislation that might affect the organization; establishes long-range objectives for the organization

2. *Staffing:* Personnel activity characterized by involvement in selection, placement, training, and advancement of employees
3. *Technical consultation:* Gathers, consolidates, interprets, and provides others with facts and information
4. *Budgeting:* Prepares and defends budgets, and accounts for expenditures
5. *Shared versus individual responsibility:* Shared pole keeps others informed of present states of affairs; individual pole emphasizes personal responsibility for taking action
6. *Operational versus professional concerns:* Operational pole is concerned with the efficiency of present organizational operations and personal professional development; professional pole is oriented toward advising others on technical matters
7. *Technical versus administrative activity:* Technical pole uses professional tools and techniques, including writing technical reports; administrative pole coordinates activity, communication, and recommendations
8. *Controlling:* Formulates limited plans or specifications in regard to resources and finances of organization, including reducing costs

A ninth variable, time spent with other people, was added because of its intrinsic interest value.

Prien. Noting that Hemphill's (1959) description of management functions may be too general to apply to any one level, Prien (1963) developed criterion dimensions for first-level supervisory positions. In a study of 24 supervisors in one company, he found two second-order factors (work–job orientation and employee orientation) that closely matched the initiating-structure and consideration dimensions from the Fleishman (1953) study. Seven first-order job factors were obtained from a factor analysis of job positions. These factors and a description of their job clusters follow:

1. *Manufacturing process supervision:* Adjusts process operations to facilitate maintenance work; initiates start-up and shutdown procedures
2. *Manufacturing process administration:* Periodically checks quality-control reports; reports and prepares requests for maintenance and repair work
3. *Employee supervision:* Explains and discusses problems with staff personnel; explains personnel policies and procedures
4. *Manpower coordination and administration*

5. *Employee contact and communication:* Provides task instructions for subordinates; discusses quality control with subordinates
6. *Work organization, planning, and preparation:* Prepares yearly vacation schedules; attends operation–coordination meetings
7. *Union-management relations:* Discusses formal first-step grievances with union committee people; discusses misunderstandings with union committee people

Prien's contribution was to redirect interest in supervision and to demonstrate that homogeneous clusters of *positions* can be identified in contrast to most earlier analyses of clusters of job variables.

Dowell and Wexley (1978) extended Prien's analysis of supervisors' jobs in a study of 255 supervisors from 40 plants in a large manufacturing company. Analyses yielded seven factors, four of which correspond to one or more of Prien's factors. The three new factors were maintaining safe/clean work areas, maintaining equipment and machinery, and compiling records and reports.

Comparisons of the importance of and time spent on the seven dimensions across different types of *production technology* (e.g., tire production, industrial products fabrication) revealed few significant differences. Comparisons across departments conducting different *functions* (e.g., processing raw materials, fabrication of components, processing to finished products) revealed several differences in the time spent on the activities, but not in their importance.

Dowell and Wexley (1978) confirm the importance of a number of the earlier job activities identified by Prien and demonstrate the generality of the factors to a much broader sample of production areas and functions.

Mahoney et al., *Haas* et al., and *Penfield.* In a series of related studies, estimates of the amount of time spent in several functional areas of management have been investigated. Mahoney, Jerdee, and Carroll (1965) surveyed 452 managers in a wide variety of industries. Haas, Porat, and Vaughan (1969) questioned 355 officers in a large metropolitan bank. Penfield's (1974) respondents were 204 first- and second-level managers in a public utility. Definitions of the eight functions are given below:

1. *Planning:* Determines goals, policies, and courses of action. Schedules work, budgets, sets up procedures, sets goals or standards, prepares agendas, programs
2. *Investigating:* Collects and prepares information, usually in the form of records, reports, and accounts. Does inventorying, measures output, prepares financial statements, keeps records, performs research and job analysis

3. *Coordinating:* Exchanges information with people in the organization other than subordinates in order to relate and adjust programs;
   advises other departments, expedites, is liaison with other managers, arranges meetings, informs superiors, seeks other departments' cooperation
4. *Evaluating:* Assesses and appraises proposals of reported or
   observed performance; makes employee appraisals; judges output
   records, financial reports; inspects products; approves requests;
   and judges proposals and suggestions
5. *Supervising:* Directs, leads, and develops subordinates; Counsels
   and trains subordinates, explains work rules, assigns work,
   disciplines, handles complaints of subordinates
6. *Staffing:* Maintains the work force of a unit or of several units;
   recruits at colleges, carries out employment interviews, selects
   employees, places employees, promotes employees, transfers
   employees
7. *Negotiating:* Purchases, sells, or contracts for goods or services;
   negotiates taxes, contacts suppliers, deals with sales representatives, handles advertising products, collective bargaining, selling
   to dealers or customers
8. *Representing:* Advances general organizational interests through
   speeches, consultation, and contacts with individuals or groups
   outside the organization; handles community drives, news releases,
   conventions, business club meetings

In the Haas study, staffing was omitted and negotiating and representing were combined. Table 4.1 shows the means and rank order of time
estimates for the three studies.

There is similarity in the Mahoney and Penfield findings with supervising occupying the largest portion of the managers' time, followed by planning, evaluating, and coordinating. Haas found that bank managers spent
the largest percentages of their time negotiating (24%) and supervising
(21%), and about equal amounts of the remainder of their time on the
other four functions. This sample felt that they ideally should be spending
more time planning and less time investigating than was actually the case.
In comparison with the Mahoney sample, the Haas sample of bank
managers spent much more time negotiating (primarily dealing with
customers) and less time planning. The differences would be expected
because many bank managers have no supervisory subordinates.

In all three studies, there was great variation in time estimates for
managers in jobs with similar titles. Thus, it is important to recognize that

Table 4.1

Means and Ranks for Percentage of Time Managers Believe They Actually Spend in Eight Managerial Activities[a]

Activity	Mahoney et al. (1965) (N = 453)		Haas et al. (1969) (N = 355)		Penfield (1974) (N = 204)	
	Mean	Rank	Mean	Rank	Mean	Rank
Supervising	28.4	1	20.7	2	32.6	1
Planning	19.5	2	12.2	6	19.4	2
Evaluating	12.7	4	13.2	3	11.2	3
Coordinating	15.0	3	13.1	4	10.7	4
Investigating	12.6	5	12.8	5	9.9	5
Representing	1.8	8			6.1	6
Negotiating	6.0	6	24.2	1	5.8	7
Staffing	4.1	7			4.1	8

[a]From "Time Allocation Patterns and Effectiveness of Managers" by R. V. Penfield, *Personnel Psychology*, 1974, *27*, 245–255. Copyright 1974 by *Personnel Psychology*. Reprinted by permission.

job titles are often not very informative and that great individual differences exist in the way managers carry out their jobs.

Wofford. Building on his own theory of work behavior, Wofford (1970) generated 183 managerial behavioral items covering six broad categories: security and maintenance, ordered structure, personal interactions, achievement, personal enhancement, and group achievement. Factor analysis of the responses of 136 managers from 85 companies describing supervisory behavior yielded five factors:

1. *Order and group achievement:* Provides careful and thorough planning, organizing and controlling; stimulates high motivation to attain goals; is tactful but firm; employs teamwork
2. *Personal enhancement orientation:* Uses authority and control; obtains compliance through pressure, power, and close control
3. *Personal interaction:* Provides interpersonal relationships; is viewed as a close friend; works closely with subordinates
4. *Security and objectivity:* Is concerned about insecurity feelings of employees (i.e., with security of work, job, and personal life) but maintains an impersonal perspective
5. *Dynamic and achievement oriented:* Reflects air of confidence, delegates authority, encourages people, operates with flair for action

A strength of this study is confirmation of an hypothesized factor structure. The study shows a combination of theorizing on the basis of previous literature and empirical analyses.

The next two studies to be reviewed are particularly sound. They are based on previous research and/or theory of managerial performance; large and diverse samples were included, behavioral or process variables were studied, and factor analysis techniques were used to identify clusters of behaviors.

Tornow and Pinto. Tornow and Pinto (1976) began their research by developing a questionnaire that would be content valid for several different functions and jobs. Over 1000 items were reduced to 505 items and administered in a pretest to 41 diverse managers. These respondents rated whether or not the item applied to their job and its significance (i.e., importance and frequency). Item analyses led to selection of 208 statements that showed relevance, had variance across levels and positions, and discriminated among positions. The responses of a second sample of 433 incumbents were factor analyzed and yielded the following dimensions:

1. *Product, marketing, and financial strategy planning:* Does long-range thinking and planning; has broad concerns for future of company, including business potential, objectives, and solvency
2. *Coordination of other organizational units and personnel:* Coordinates people over whom there is no direct control, handles conflicts, cuts across boundaries
3. *Internal business control:* Reviews and controls manpower and other resources; monitors product and service delivery, quality, and cost
4. *Public and customer relations:* Has general responsibility for reputation of company and concern for promoting company's products, services, and goodwill
5. *Advanced consulting:* Applies technical expertise to special problems
6. *Autonomy of action:* Exercises discretion of handling the job, makes decisions not subject to review, engages in unstructured thinking about abstract problems
7. *Approval of financial commitments:* Approves large financial commitments, makes final decisions that obligate the company
8. *Staff service:* Gathers facts, compiles data, and keeps records for supervisors
9. *Supervision:* Plans, organizes, and controls work of others on a face-to-face, daily basis
10. *Complexity and stress:* Operates under pressure of time and risk
11. *Advanced financial responsibility:* Preserves assets and makes investment decisions

12. *Broad personnel responsibility:* Has responsibility for human resources and policies affecting them

Tornow and Pinto's study is outstanding because of the great care they took to include behavioral variables in their job analysis questionnaire. The result is one of the few standardized job analysis instruments available for studying managerial job dimensions.

Morse and Wagner. In an attempt to develop an instrument to describe both the common and unique features of a broad range of managerial positions, Morse and Wagner (1978) focused on process variables (rather than person or product variables). One hundred and six statements were clustered into nine managerial roles described by Mintzberg (1973): strategic problem solving, resource managing, conflict handling, organizing, information handling, motivating, providing for growth and development, coordinating, and managing the organization's environment. An initial group of 115 managers was asked to rate the effectiveness of a subordinate on each item on a nine-point scale. In addition, the managers were asked to indicate the usefulness of the nine categories, the clarity of the statements, and critical incidents of behavior for each managerial role. A new sample of 406 managers rated subordinates on a revised 96-item questionnaire. Factor analyses yielded six factors accounting for 56% of the common variance:

1. Managing the organization's environment and its resources
2. Organizing and coordinating
3. Information handling
4. Providing for growth and development
5. Motivating and conflict handling
6. Strategic problem solving

This factor structure was replicated (with only slight variation in factor importance) in another sample of over 420 managers who completed a questionnaire containing over 51 final items. The instrument was validated by comparing factor scores for high and low performers in another sample of 231 managers. Significant differences were found for all six factors and overall scores. In addition, significant correlations were found between overall scores and ratings and ranking of performance effectiveness.

It should be emphasized that this study dealt with ratings of performance effectiveness rather than job activities. Nevertheless, it provides confirmation of a number of the factors identified through traditional job analysis. The study is particularly useful because of the large and diverse samples used and because of the replication of results.

COMPARATIVE RESULTS

This chapter has alluded to the pervasive need to analyze managerial jobs at different levels in an organization. One side argues that management jobs at various levels are qualitatively different from each other: They involve different tasks and functions; they require different skills and capabilities; and they require different leadership styles. The other side of the argument holds that while there are minor variations in job requirements, management skills are no different throughout an organization; the same management and leadership principles apply, and the same personal characteristics are required. In essence, "good management is good management." A variation on the second stance argues that there are no *qualitative* differences in management abilities, only *quantitative* differences. That is, as one moves up the management hierarchy, higher levels require increased amounts of certain skills (e.g., decision-making ability), and decreased amounts of other skills (e.g., technical knowledge).

Our position is that both positions hold some truth. Some management skills are required at all levels with only the degree of skill required and the nature of the task changing. However, management skills do differ throughout the organizational hierarchy. Research evidence and observational information support the notion that middle management jobs are different from supervision and that executives are in turn different from middle managers. There is a lack of evidence comparing levels of management but, such as it is, existing comparative research establishes that there are differences.

Nealey and Fiedler (1968) reviewed the literature comparing roles and functions of middle managers to those of lower level and higher level managers. In an attempt to tease out comparisons, they examined expert opinion, material in training programs, and empirical data. In summarizing the opinion of experts, Nealey and Fiedler stated that the supervisor deals with technical aspects of work and the direct supervision of employees on a daily basis. Higher level managers have "broader perspective, greater interpersonal and administrative skill, and the ability to translate broad policy into action in the coordination of different work units [Nealey & Fiedler, 1968, p. 316]."

The content and form of management training programs generally confirms the opinion of experts, but provides few insights into actual differences in management functions and job requirements. Even though the information is vague and the programs are seldom based on sound analysis of needs, some differences by level are suggested. Normally, middle-level programs are designed to give a broad company-wide perspective rather than a narrow functional specialization, but the content of lower level programs is often indistinguishable from those at higher levels. Training in interpersonal relations skills is common at all levels.

Summarizing eight empirical studies of managerial behavior across levels, Nealey and Fiedler concluded that a few differences between levels have been clearly established. One consistent finding is that certain communication patterns change and decision making becomes more complex at higher levels of management. Comparative analyses of job demands revealed some distinctions: First-level supervision involves more time pressure, more direct contact with work, control of material, and greater technical expertise. In contrast, middle-level managers must work through others and must rely on formal power of the position and written communications. Middle managers are involved in cost control, setting standards, and selection and placement of personnel.

Summarizing available research, Nealey and Fiedler (1968) concluded that "the second level of management differs more sharply from the first level than it does from the third or fourth level. [There appears to be] another major break in functions between the divisional and corporate management levels, but there are as yet no empirical studies to test this conjecture [p. 326]." From this point of view it appears that the job of middle management is more different from first level management than it is from higher level management. In other words, within management levels the major shift in role and functions takes place when the supervisor is promoted; relatively fewer shifts take place with subsequent promotions. Nealey and Fiedler concluded, "It seems clear that the most successful first-level supervisor will not always be the most successful second-level supervisor [p. 326]."

If this is correct, it has major implications for the application of assessment centers. As we have said before, assessment centers are most appropriate in situations where performance on the higher level job cannot be predicted from performance on the current job. Where roles, functions, leadership demands, etc., change greatly, we can expect less relationship between performance at adjacent levels. The Nealey and Fiedler research would lead one to think that assessment centers would be most productive in identifying potential for first-level supervision, for movement into middle management, and (less clearly) for movement into top management; and these are precisely the common uses of the methodology.

Hemphill's (1959) study is helpful in pointing out some of the differences in managerial jobs at different hierarchical levels. Insights into such differences can be obtained from analyzing Table 4.2 which shows 10 important job dimensions and what percentage of jobs at three organi-

Table 4.2
Proportions of Positions Which Measure Relatively High on Each of Ten Dimensions[a]

	Management level		
Dimensions	Upper management	Middle management	Beginning management
Staff service	.46	.54	.90
Supervision of work	.21	.54	.62
Business control	.71	.60	.62
Technical products and markets	.29	.54	.71
Human affairs	.55	.41	.19
Planning	.63	.47	.43
Broad power	.55	.35	.14
Business reputation	.46	.39	.52
Personal demands	.46	.23	.19
Preservations of assets	.42	.31	.19

[a] From "Job Descriptions for Executives" by John K. Hemphill, *Harvard Business Review*, (September–October, 1959). Copyright 1959 by the President and Fellows of Harvard College. Reprinted by permission.

zational levels require a large amount of each dimension. Virtually all beginning management jobs are more involved in providing staff services in nonoperational areas (as defined by Hemphill). Lower level management is also more frequently involved in dealing with the technical aspects of products and markets. It should be noted that in Hemphill's study this dimension is rather narrowly concerned with securing, maintaining, and analyzing sales accounts rather than with broad policy decisions regarding markets and new products. It would appear that this dimension characterizes only a segment of lower level jobs in any organization and does not describe supervision of internally oriented departments such as manufacturing.

There are two functions which markedly increase in importance from lower to middle positions: human affairs and broad power. The human affairs dimension is complex, but appears to have at least two components. First, the dimension suggests middle managers are active in community affairs—giving speeches and participating in civic organization. Second, this dimension involves interaction with people and evaluation of their performance for promotion. The more frequent exercise of broad power and authority is reflected in increased opportunity to manage important parts of the business and to make recommendations on major organizational commitments.

Differences between executives and middle managers stand out in several areas. The power and authority to make broadly significant decisions is the most important dimension for upper management jobs and is the dimension that increases most clearly from lower to upper levels. Status, independence, and power are important aspects of this dimension. Personal demands such as increased hours of work and restrictions on personal behavior increase at the upper levels. It is also helpful to note the areas where upper management is least involved. Supervision of work diminishes among executives and dealing with the immediate concerns for markets and products is infrequently required.

Haas *et al.* (1969) compared three management levels in a bank with regard to the percentage of time spent in six broad activities. Even though Table 4.3 shows a striking similarity for most of the areas, differences in patterns of activity existed. Lower level managers spent more time than the others investigating and processing information such as reports and records. Middle-level bank managers spent comparatively more time negotiating with individuals and groups outside the organization; and top-level managers spent relatively more time coordinating information exchanged between departments within the organization. In most organizations, middle- and low-level managers do not spend such a large portion of time relating to persons outside the organization.

Katzell *et al.* (1968) provided some indication of the relationship of role behavior to organizational level within a relatively narrow range of government service (GS) levels 13, 14, and 15. Higher level managers were more involved in long-range planning and administration, but less involved in technical activities and consultation. They also spent more time in personal contact with other people.

Tornow and Pinto (1976) provided some evidence that beginning, mid-

Table 4.3

Average Percentage of Time Bank Managers Report They Actually Spend in Each of Six Activities by Level[a]

	Level of Management		
Activity	Top (N = 52)	Middle (N = 120)	Low (N = 182)
Planning	14	11	12
Investigating	10	12	14
Coordinating	16	12	13
Evaluating	14	13	13
Supervising	18	20	21
Negotiating	24	29	21

[a] From "Actual versus Ideal Time Allocations Reported by Managers: A Study of Managerial Behavior" by J. S. Haas, A. M. Porat, and J. A. Vaughan, *Personnel Psychology*, 1969, *22*, 61–75. Copyright 1969 by *Personnel Psychology*. Reprinted by permission.

dle, and upper levels of management clustered into identifiable groups could be distinguished by patterns or scores on the 13 factors in their management questionnaire. Three clusters corresponded to three levels of management:

1. *Upper management:* High scores on product planning, broad personnel responsibility, autonomy of action, approval of financial commitments
2. *Middle management:* High scores on product and service responsibility, public and customer relations, autonomy of action, coordination of other units
3. *Beginning management:* High scores on staff service, supervision, product and staff responsibility

Three other clusters were defined in terms of functional area:

1. *Marketing:* High scores on public and customer relations, coordination of other units, supervision
2. *Personnel:* High scores on broad personnel responsibility, coordination of other units, staff service
3. *Legal:* High scores on approval of financial commitments, staff service, advanced financial responsibility

PERSONAL CHARACTERISTICS OF MANAGERS

The studies reviewed thus far deal with job analyses of duties, tasks, and responsibilities. They have analyzed *job*-oriented variables in contrast to *worker*-oriented variables (McCormick, 1959). This section summarizes studies of the personal characteristics required for managerial success. Here the literature is quite confusing. On the one hand, there are lengthy lists of traits, literally from A (ambitious) to Z (zealous), that supposedly characterize the effective manager. On the other hand, there is a nihilist position that suggests that leadership is entirely situational and it is fruitless to search for any enduring characteristics among effective leaders.

As a framework for the discussion of personal requirements of managers, we can look at a model proposed by Katz and Kahn (1978). They hypothesized a different set of cognitive and affective abilities for lower, middle, and upper management. Supervisors need technical knowledge, an understanding of rules, and interpersonal skill to use rewards and sanctions equitably. Middle managers need a perspective on subunits in the organization and human relations skills to integrate the formal and informal relationships within the organization. Executives must be able to view the organization as a whole and as one part of a broader environment. Charisma is critical at this level. The characteristics on this list are too general to be of use for most practical purposes. Other research provides more detailed clues.

Leadership traits. Studies of leadership provide evidence of the traits necessary for effective management. Management talent encompasses a far wider range of skills, but many would claim that leadership is essential for all levels of management and may be the "core" of management, comparable to the "g" factor in intelligence.

For the past 30 years, Stogdill has been investigating leadership and summarizing the results of numerous other research studies. One massive review of the literature was completed in 1948 and covered all studies back to 1904. Another review covered all studies during the span from 1948 to 1970. In his *Handbook of Leadership,* Stogdill (1974) summarized these empirical studies of leadership behavior, leader–follower interactions, situational determinants of leadership, theories of leadership, and new directions for research. Three chapters are most relevant to our present topic. One summarizes the leadership trait studies during the early period, another covers more recent trait research, and the third integrates all factor analytic studies of leader descriptions.

Table 4.4 lists the main findings of Stogdill's reviews. To appear on the trait lists, the trait must have shown positive findings in at least 10 studies. To appear on the factor list, the factor must have been present in at least 5 of the 52 studies summarized.

Some clear themes emerge in these three lists. A leader possesses a number of intellectual, cognitive, and administrative skills. The leader also possesses interpersonal skills which enhance leader–follower relationships. Personally, the leader has high levels of energy, initiative, and drive. This complex of attributes enables the effective leader to secure group performance and cohesiveness.

Trait theories of leadership have been supplanted by situational, interactional, and contingency theories (Stogdill, 1974). The recent emphasis in leadership research has been on the characteristics of situations from which different types of leaders emerge, on the characteristics of followers and exchange processes between leaders and followers, and on various other parameters that determine the most appropriate leadership style. At the same time, there is still much value in the study of the personal attributes of the effective leader. Once the situation has been defined in terms of the task, followers, time constraints, etc., effective leadership *in that situation* can still be analyzed in terms of leader characteristics.

Table 4.4
Summary of Stogdill's Review of Leadership Research[a]

Traits: 1904–1947	Traits: 1948–1970	Factor analyses
Capacity: Intelligence, alertness, verbal facility, originality, judgment	*Physical:* Activity, energy	*Skills:* Social and interpersonal, technical and intellectual skills; leadership effectiveness and achievement; social nearness and friendliness; group task supportiveness; and task motivation and application
Achievement: Scholarship, knowledge, athletic accomplishments	*Social background:* Education status	
Responsibility: Dependability, initiative, persistence, aggressiveness, self-confidence, desire to excel	*Intelligence and ability:* Intelligence, fluency of speech, knowledge	*Group relations:* Maintaining cohesive work group, coordination and teamwork, standards of performance
	Personality: Adjustment, assertiveness, ascendance, emotional balance, independence, originality, self-confidence	
Participation: Activity, sociability, cooperation, adaptability, humor		*Personal characteristics:* Willingness to assume responsibility, emotional balance and control, ethical conduct, personal integrity, communicativeness, verbality, ascendance, dominance, personal soundness, good character, physical energy
Status: Socioeconomic position, popularity	*Task-related characteristics:* Achievement, drive and responsibility, task orientation and initiative	
	Social characteristics: Administrative ability, sociability	

[a] From Stogdill, 1974.

Management talent. Ghiselli (1971) has studied a number of traits associated with managerial talent, using a self-report adjective checklist to measure 13 characteristics. The first three are abilities.

1. *Supervisory ability:* The capacity to direct the work of others and to organize and integrate their activities so the goal of the work group can be attained
2. *Intelligence:* A broad domain of cognitive abilities, including judgment, reasoning, and the capacity to deal with ideas, abstractions, and concepts
3. *Initiative:* The ability to begin actions without stimulation and support from others, and the capacity to see courses of action and to discover new means of goal achievement

The next five are personality traits.

4. *Self-assurance:* The extent to which the individual perceives himself or herself to be effective in dealing with problems
5. *Decisiveness:* Seeing that decisions should be made, making rapid decisions, being willing to take action without investigating all possible aspects of a problem
6. *Masculinity–Femininity:* Robustness versus gentleness, activity versus passivity, intellectual versus initiative problem solving
7. *Maturity:* The extent to which an individual's self-image is more like that of older persons rather than younger individuals
8. *Working-class affinity:* The extent to which the individual is likely to be accepted or rejected as a suitable person to be associated with by those of the working class

The last five are motivational traits.

9. *Need for occupational status:* The need to achieve appointments to high-level positions in business and industry such as top management and professions
10. *Need for self-actualization:* The extent to which the person needs and wants to utilize talents to the fullest, to be creative through use of capabilities
11. *Need for power:* The need for control over others, to impose one's ideas on others
12. *Need for high financial reward:* The primacy of an individual's desire for monetary gain from work
13. *Need for job security:* A concern for continuity of employment and protection from adverse forces on the job

Ghiselli (1971) determined the relative importance of these traits to managerial talent by conducting numerous studies of diverse samples of managers over a 15-year period. He was concerned that the trait meet three conditions: *(a)* higher level managers should possess more of the trait than supervisors who in turn should possess more than workers; *(b)* there should be a relationship between the trait and managerial success; and *(c)* the relationship between the trait and success should be higher for managers than supervisors, and lowest for workers. Ghiselli assessed the extent to which the 13 traits met these conditions and quantified the relative contribution of each to managerial talent. Table 4.5 presents the results.

Supervisory ability emerged as the most important trait. Others that

Table 4.5
The Relative Importance of Thirteen Traits of Managerial Talent[a]

Level	Value	Trait	Role
Very important in managerial talent	100	Supervisory ability	Major role
	76	Occupational status	
		Intelligence	
	64	Self-actualization	
	61	Self-assurance	
		Decisiveness	
	54	Need for security	Minor role
	47	Working-class affinity	
	34	Initiative	
	20	Need for high financial reward	Unimportant
	10	Need for power over others	
Plays no part in managerial talent	5	Maturity	
	0	Masculinity–feminity	

[a] Adapted from *Explorations in Managerial Talent* by Edwin E. Ghiselli, Pacific Palisades, Calif., 1971, p. 165. Copyright 1971 by Goodyear Publishing Company. Reprinted by permission.

play a major role include intellectual ability, two personality traits—self-assurance and decisiveness, and two motives—needs for occupational status and self-actualization. Three traits played a relatively minor role. Need for security and working-class affinity were negatively correlated with criteria, indicating that successful managers do not worry about job security or feel a close association with workers. There was a positive relationship between initiative and success. The remaining traits do not meet the conditions although in some cases, a trait may be important.

Reviewing the sum of his studies, Ghiselli (1971) concluded:

> The general properties of managerial talent are a restrained democratic leadership, a creative and effective intelligence, a faith in one's self, and a desire for achievement. The successful manager utilizes democratic procedures when dealing with his subordinates but at the same time keeps himself apart from them so as to maintain an impartial position. He is a very bright person, and his intellect is forceful, practical, and constructive. He recognizes that he possesses these qualities, and so he has the confidence that is so necessary if he is to successfully deal with complex executive and administrative problems. Finally, he is a highly motivated person: one who is fully capable of maintaining his goal of orientation, his goals being quite worthwhile ones [pp. 108–109].

Management knowledge. Different kinds of knowledge may be required as a person moves up the management hierarchy (Ewing, 1964). At lower levels, the manager must have knowledge of methods and techniques that will enable the organization to answer specific production or sales problems. This kind of knowledge is the technical knowledge of the specialized problems faced in achieving the company's current goals. The second level is knowledge of the people, conditions, and trends that make up the organization. This kind of knowledge requires an understanding of the situation or context in which the organization operates. The third level of knowledge, required at the executive level, is the knowledge of alternative goals, policies, and priorities for the organization. The manager must have such information in order to make major decisions regarding changes in products, organizational structure, and long-range plans. An important contribution of this analysis is that it highlights the role that cognitive facts and information play in the functions of all levels of management—functions which often seem emotionally loaded and intuitive.

One definition of executiveship. Campbell *et al.* (1970) reviewed the numerous studies for managers above the level of supervision in order to define the "*construct* of effective executiveship [p. 164]." (These studies deal mainly with middle management: Only one or two of the reviewed studies include any material exclusively relevant to higher level executives.) In summarizing the actuarial studies of managerial effectiveness, Campbell *et al.* (1970) concluded:

> Taken together, these studies provide good evidence that a fairly sizable portion (30 to 50%) of the variance in general managerial effectiveness can be expressed in terms of personal qualities measured by self-response tests and inventories and combined by predetermined rules or statistical equations. The *construct* of effective executiveship that we set out to define . . . includes such factors as high intelligence, good verbal skills, effective judgment in handling managerial situations . . . and organizing skill; disposition toward interpersonal relationships, hard work, being active, and taking risks; and temperamental qualities such as dominance, confidence, straightforwardness, low anxiety, and autonomy [pp. 195–196].

Dimensions in Assessment Centers

Thus far we have reviewed two types of studies of managerial work. The first involved analyses of the tasks, activities, duties, responsibilities, and functions of supervisors, managers, and executives. The second involved studies of personal attributes including knowledge, traits, and personality characteristics associated with success in management positions. Each type of study contributes to a better understanding of managerial work and offers suggestions for managerial assessment. Task analyses provide guidance for the selection and development of assessment center exercises. Trait analyses provide suggestions of the characteristics to be observed in the exercises.

Managerial assessment centers have gone beyond the task and trait approaches to identify behavioral *dimensions* of managerial work. By *dimension* we mean a cluster of behaviors that are specific, observable, and verifiable, and that can be reliably and logically classified together. A list of common assessment dimensions is presented in Appendix A.

Even though the label *dimension* may appear to be very similar to the label *task* or *trait,* dimensions are quite different. In contrast to *task* which states what is accomplished on the job, *dimension* is defined in terms of specific behaviors the person carries out to accomplish the task. For example, a common management function is planning. The dimension Planning is often used in assessment center programs and is defined by behavioral examples such as, "Made a list of meetings with agenda items for his return to the job," "Gave the subordinate a sequence of tasks to complete with target dates to ensure timely completion of the project," and "Anticipated and stated several potential problems that might arise if the recommendation were adopted and gave suggestions for dealing with each problem."

Other common dimensions that look like tasks but are similarly defined with specific behavioral examples are Delegation, Management Control, and Decision Making.

The use of behavior to define dimensions also distinguishes them from traits. Usually traits are thought to be *underlying personality constructs* that determine behavioral consistency across situations. They are assumed to be "causal" variables that define a person's stable and enduring nature at work, at home, or during leisure time. Although some dimension labels may look like traits, they are behaviorally defined and observed and do not require judgments about underlying personality constructs. For example, Sensitivity subsumes such behaviors as, "Asked the person how she would feel if the plan were implemented," "Stated that he thought he understood how the customer felt because a similar thing happened to him," and "Repeated and rephrased what the subordinate suggested to clarify understanding between them." Behavioral examples for a few dimensions are listed in Appendix B.

The following, highly simplified description of how a job analyst goes about defining dimensions may help to clarify the concept. Figure 4.1 shows the behaviors that might be obtained in a job analysis for a specific job or job level. Each letter B indicates a specific behavior. The pluses and minuses indicate whether the obtained behavior was related to job success or lack of success. It is the job of the analyst to find communalities

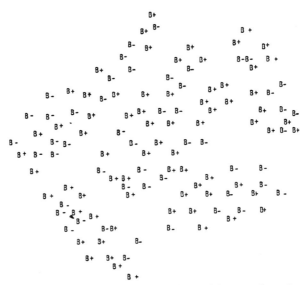

Figure 4.1. Job-related behaviors obtained from a job analysis.

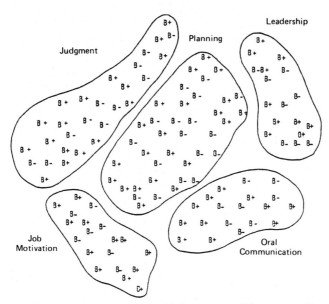

Figure 4.2. Categorization of behaviors into "dimensions."

among the behaviors and to label these communalities. In other words, as illustrated in Figure 4.2, the job analyst draws circles around the behaviors that form logical homogenous clusters. Then the job analyst labels the constellation of behaviors. The analyst can label one constellation as "No. 1," the next as "No. 2," and the next as "No. 3," etc., or the analyst can use descriptive terms. For example, the analyst might group together all the behaviors that have to do with leadership activities and label the constellation *Leadership.* Or the analyst might combine the behaviors that have to do with planning and label them *Planning.*

ILLUSTRATIVE DIMENSIONS

To illustrate the types of dimensions assessed for different purposes, Table 4.6 provides three very different lists. The list for an early identification program is relatively short and consists of dimensions that do not presuppose any specific type of prior experience. This list is appropriate for identifying individuals who will benefit from accelerated training programs. By contrast, the list for promotion purposes is much longer and more diverse. It includes personal dimensions, interpersonal dimensions, administrative dimensions, and communication dimensions. These dimensions provide a more detailed assessment that is appropriate for judging whether a person is likely to be an effective manager. A still different list from a diagnostic development planning program for experienced first- and second-level managers is shown on the right side of Table 4.6. Decision Making is divided into more refined dimensions: Analysis, Judgment, and Decisiveness. Delegation and Management Control are added. There are no "personal" dimensions which are hard to develop. The list has been restricted to dimensions that can be developed in training programs and on-the-job coaching.

Table 4.6
Illustrative Assessment Center Dimensions

Early identification	Promotion	Developmental planning
Communication Skills	Oral communications	Oral Communication
		Oral Presentation
	Written Communication	Written Communication
Energy	Energy	
Job Motivation (obtained from an interview)	Job Motivation (obtained from an interview)	
Career Ambition (obtained from an interview)	Career Ambition (obtained from an interview)	
Initiative	Initiative	Initiative
	Creativity (obtained from an interview)	
Sensitivity	Sensitivity	Sensitivity
Leadership	Leadership	Individual Leadership
		Group Leadership
		Behavioral Flexibility
		Negotiation
	Tolerance for Stress	
Planning and Organizing	Planning and Organizing	Planning and Organizing
	Delegation	Delegation
	Management Control	Management Control
Decision Making	Decision Making	Analysis
		Judgment
		Decisiveness

DIMENSIONS OF SUCCESSFUL MANAGEMENT
AT THREE LEVELS OF DIFFERENT TYPES
OF ORGANIZATIONS

In order to obtain a clearer picture of the types of dimensions required for management success, lists of dimensions assessed in numerous organizations were examined and classified. Jobs were categorized into three levels: first-level supervision, middle management, and top executive. Sufficient cases of first-level positions existed to further classify them into groups representing manufacturing, government and clerical, and sales. The lists for middle management positions were grouped into sales versus manufacturing and office settings, and the top management lists were grouped into sales versus all other positions. Table 4.7 summarizes the findings. An A signifies that the dimension was a requirement for more than 80% of the positions; B signifies that it was required about 50% of the time; and C suggests it was present on about one-third of the lists.

Review of information in the table provides a number of insights into managerial job requirements which in some instances confirm, and in others contradict past research. Extraorganizational Sensitivity and Awareness are important only for top management positions—a finding supported by the research of Dubin and Spray (1964) and Horne and Lupton (1965) which revealed an increase in external contacts at high levels. Stewart (1967) found that middle-level sales managers had business contacts outside their organizations, but most lower level and middle managers have very few contacts with outsiders.

The management skills of Planning and Organizing were found on virtually all lists. This may come as a surprise since most studies have shown that managers have little time for planning and reflection (Carlson, 1951; Mintzberg, 1973; Stewart, 1967). This discrepancy may be explained by the nature of the dimension as it is defined in most assessment programs. Behaviors classified as Planning and Organizing include not only the long-range planning to meet organizational objectives, but also the minute-by-minute actions that are taken to manage one's own time and the time and resources of other people. For example, planning among foremen means knowing what to do to assign people to tasks in order to meet production requirements and how to adjust if an employee is absent or a disciplinary case arises. The nature of Delegation and Control also differs at higher levels. In lower level programs, the first-level supervisor would be expected to assign work and maintain close supervision over work processes, whereas middle managers would formally assign full responsibility for work and use reports and records as control mechanisms.

Interpersonal and supervisory skills are required of all managers who must successfully deal with the wide variety of people the typical foreman and manager must contact, including subordinates, peers, supervisors, and service and staff personnel. The importance of leadership skills is shown by McCall et al.'s findings (1978) that about "26–28 percent of a manager's time was spent with subordinates . . . ; 32 to 46 percent of their contact time was spent with subordinates . . . ; and subordinates represented 60–70 percent of a supervisor's internal contacts [p. 12]."

The abilities to analyze problems, evaluate alternative decisions, and exercise judgment in a rapid (decisive) fashion are considered important in almost all assessment programs—a fact supported by the often replicated findings that managers engage in many types of activities and their work is a rapid succession of brief and fragmented episodes. Interruptions are frequent and the decision-making process may be broken up by pauses to gather more information or obtain input from subordinates (McCall et al., 1978). The common assessment center complex of several relatively brief exercises with rigorous time restrictions is probably justified in light of this discontinuous nature of management jobs. Creativity and Risk Taking are relatively unimportant in lower level jobs, except for sales positions.

That Oral Communication skills are important for virtually all positions should be no surprise, given the universal finding that a manager's job is primarily verbal. Estimates of the amount of time managers spend in verbal communication range from 28 to 80% for first level supervisors, 27 to 82% for middle managers, and 65 to 90% for top executives (McCall et al., 1978). Note that Technical Knowledge diminishes in importance at higher levels. This is consistent with most prior research.

The finding that personal dimensions such as Energy, Motivation for work itself, and Independence are more important for middle and higher levels is supported by the general findings that managers work long hours (McCall et al., 1978). Typical estimates of work weeks are at least 50 hours, with many executives putting in even more time. During work, managers display a high activity level engaging in 200, 300, or up to 500 incidents per day.

A MODEL OF THE COMPONENTS OF A MANAGER'S JOB

Based on an analysis of dimensions reported in the literature (Bender, 1973; Bray & Grant, 1966; McConnell & Parker, 1972; Thomson, 1969; Wollowick & McNamara, 1969) and a review of dimensions assessed in hundreds of organizations where the authors have had personal contact, we have summarized the components of successful management in Figure 4.3. The vertical axis represents level in management that is divided roughly into three categories. The dotted lines suggest less-than-precise distinction between levels. The width of the horizontal bands depicts the homogeneity of success components at that level. The executive levels occur less frequently than other levels. More importantly job requirements are relatively homogeneous. It may be surprising to see the supervision band wider than that of middle management. In terms of number of levels, there are certainly more middle management positions. However, *job requirements* for middle managers are relatively homogeneous. In contrast, supervisory positions are quite heterogeneous. That is, a factory foreman's job may be quite different from a supervisor of research technicians.

Vertical and diagonal slices of the figure represent various success components. These slices represent clusters of dimensions, job requirements, and skills. The categories correspond to those in Table 4.7.

The width of the slice depicts its importance at that level. At the lowest levels of supervision, technical and supervisory dimensions are most important. Management dimensions are occasionally irrelevant, but in many positions they are as important as they are at higher levels. For middle managers, technical dimensions are less critical but managerial skills are universally predominant. The figure shows that supervisory dimen-

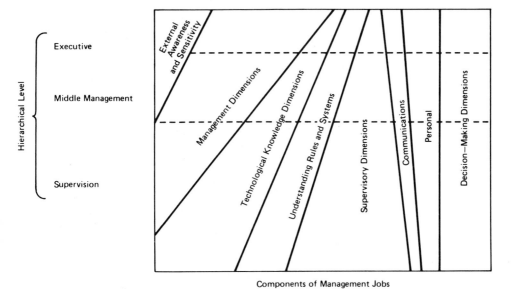

Components of Management Jobs

Figure 4.3. Management requirements vary across organizational levels.

Table 4.7
Incidence of Dimensions in Assessment Centers at Three Levels of Management in Different Types of Organizations[a,b]

	First-level supervision			Middle management		Top management	
	Manufacturing supervisor	Government and clerical	Sales	Manufacturing and office	Sales	All except sales	Sales
Organizational and extra-organizational awareness and sensitivity							
Organizational Sensitivity	C	C		B		A	A
Organizational Awareness						A	A
Extraorganizational Sensitivity					B	B	B
Extraorganizational Awareness						B	B
Management							
Planning and Organization	A	A	A	A	A	A	A
Delegation		C	C	A	A	A	A
Management Control	B	A	A	A	A	A	A
Development of Subordinates		B	A	B	A	A	A
Supervisory							
Sensitivity	A	A	A	A	A	A	A
Individual Leadership	A	A	A	A	A	A	A
Group Leadership		C	B	A	A	A	A
Tenacity			C	B	B	A	A

Decision making						
Analysis	A	A	A	A	A	A
Judgment	A	A	A	A	A	A
Creativity		A	A	C	C	A
Risk Taking		C	C	C	C	A
Decisiveness	A	A	A	A	A	A
Technical knowledge						
Technical and Professional Knowledge	A	C	B	C	C	
Personal						
Energy			B	B	B	A
Range of Interests			B	B	B	A
Initiative	A	B	A	A	A	A
Tolerance for Stress	A	C	A	A	A	A
Adaptability				C		A
Independence		B	B	A	B	A
Motivation	C	B	A	A	A	A
Communications						
Oral Presentation			B	C	A	A
Oral Communication	A	A	A	A	A	A
Written Communication	A	A	B	B	B	B

[a] (A = 80% or more; B = 50–79%; C = 30–49%)
[b] 150 programs summarized

sions are important, although in a few instances middle managers do not supervise other people. Some middle managers are called upon to relate to the external environment, but these dimensions are required for all executives and are what clearly distinguishes the top echelons of an organization from lower levels.

The changing size of the slice shows that the dimensions are more or less important at the three levels in the hierarchy. For example, technical knowledge is less important at higher levels, whereas skills in delegation become more important as one moves up the hierarchy.

What is not represented in the figure is the qualitative nature in certain dimensions at different levels. For example, whereas decision-making dimensions are equally important at all levels, supervisory decisions could be characterized as immediate, short range, low impact, and person oriented in contrast with executive decisions which are long range, high impact, and concerned with the organization's structure and its product or service.

Several comments can be made about assessment centers in relation to the components shown in the model. First, assessment centers are usually designed to measure the management, supervisory, and decision-making dimensions listed. The other areas can usually be evaluated more adequately on the job or through a well-conducted background interview. Furthermore, there is probably little variation in technical skills and in understanding the organization rules among candidates for promotion to a specific job level who are seen in an assessment center.

Job Analysis for Assessment

OBJECTIVES

For purposes of assessment centers, job analysis has two specific objectives. First, the job analysis is designed to identify clusters of job activities that constitute important aspects of the manager's job. These clusters consist of the kinds of things managers actually do during their work day and should include all the important tasks, responsibilities, and interpersonal relationships of the job. An example of one set of activities might be the one-to-one supervisory relationships in which a manager advises, directs, or counsels with a subordinate. Another set of activities might be the group planning meetings attended by manager and peers. It is important to identify these clusters of activities so that simulation exercises that accurately reflect the target job can be devised. The only way we can ensure that the evaluation tasks are job related is to know what the job entails.

A corollary of this first objective is to determine the relative importance of each of the several job areas and the frequency of each activity.
How frequently a manager makes oral presentations outside the company is part of an indication of the importance of that activity to the job
and the weight it should get in assessment. Activities that are most important and that occupy a large portion of a manager's time should be assessed more thoroughly. As a rough guide, the portion of time in certain
assessment activities should match the portion of time in the manager's
work life. If situational exercises are designed to cover a representative
sample of job activities, major strides toward content validity have been
taken.

The second objective of job analysis for assessment purposes is to
determine the dimensions required to carry out the job activities effectively. The process of identifying these characteristics is one of inference
based on careful study of the job activities and critical incidents of success and failure on the job. No single method of deriving a complete set of
human characteristics from job analysis information exists. McCormick
and his students (McCormick, Cunningham, & Thornton, 1967; McCormick, Jeanneret, & Mecham, 1972) developed methods of converting
ratings on a large set of "worker-oriented" job variables into human attribute requirements. These methods have proved helpful for a wide
variety of jobs, but have been applied to managerial jobs on only a limited
basis. Refinements of the McCormick approach could yield greater insights into the important dimensions of managerial jobs. The method of
developing behaviorally anchored rating scales through the Retranslation of Expectations (RE) procedures (Smith & Kendall, 1963) also offers
promise. Although it appears the RE procedure has seldom been used to
identify assessment center dimensions, it has several distinct advantages
for performance appraisal ratings (Schwab, Heneman, & DeCotiis, 1975)
and in one study it provided a firm basis for defining job dimensions,
training assessors, and giving developmental feedback to assessees
(Thornton, 1976). Until recently, the derivation of dimensions to be
assessed has been largely judgmental, but more objective methods are
now being implemented.

NEED TO CONSIDER TOTAL SELECTION–PROMOTION
SYSTEM IN DESIGNING JOB ANALYSIS
AND ASSESSMENT CENTER

Whether used for selection or for diagnosis of development needs,
whether used with internal or external candidates, an assessment center
should seldom stand by itself. In its most effective form it is usually part of
a selection–promotion system. For example, in promoting individuals to

first-level supervisory positions, an organization may have three sources of data—assessment center data, interview data (usually performed by the hiring supervisor or hiring manager), and performance appraisal data. In a selection situation, the system may include multiple interviews, reference checks, health checks, and assessment center data. It is both inappropriate and extremely wasteful to conduct separate job analyses for each portion of the system. The system components need to be integrated so that their contribution can be optimized. When integration does not take place, one finds a situation where the data produced by various elements of the selection system are incompatible; thus, the system is not optimized. A good example is the very common situation where a manager making a promotional decision would get data from the assessment center using a standardized set of dimensions and a one-to-five rating scale. Another set of data from the organization's performance appraisal system may have totally different dimensions and a totally different rating scale, and the manager may have organized his or her selection interviews on a third set of dimensions.

Even more confusion is brought in when another element such as a report from a clinical psychologist is used in the selection decision. When multiple, uncoordinated elements are considered as part of a selection system, the elements are often not given appropriate weight. Thus, the unique impact of certain elements is lost. Also, in this situation, one runs the risk of having one weak link in a system ruin the validity of the entire system. A very common example of this is the nomination procedures used to make decisions about who will attend an assessment center. Many organizations have untrained supervisors make nominations for their assessment center. A great deal of money can be wasted on an assessment center to evaluate unqualified nominees. If the supervisors are not being both accurate and fair in their nominations, the assessment center can produce biased results through no fault of its own.

The solution to the problems noted above is to have an integrated promotion or selection system built around a common set of dimensions defined in the job analysis (Byham, 1979a). With this as a goal, it is important for the job analysis to define the job in its totality without concern about whether or not the dimensions can be accurately assessed using a particular methodology. Of course, with this broader goal in mind, the list of dimensions expands to include areas of professional and technical knowledge and legal constraints, such as the need to have a driver's license or a professional engineering certificate.

Once the list of dimensions has been developed and clearly defined, the most appropriate selection system can be designed. Table 3.4 on page 92 shows an example of a selection subsystem for the promotion of a bank teller to branch manager position which includes an assessment center, selection interview, and a performance appraisal. The choice of which dimensions to seek with the particular selection technique depends on the strength of each technique and the weaknesses of the other techniques relative to a particular dimension.

In the following chapter, we will be concerned with the dimensions that are most validly evaluated in an assessment center. Here we will discuss some general factors that lead to the assignment of various dimensions to selection elements in the particular system illustrated in Table 3.4. The table is meant as an illustration of the kind of thinking that takes place in making these decisions.

1. Oral communication is evaluated by all three techniques because it is easy to evaluate and the person has to talk in each situation.
2. Oral presentation is evaluated only in the assessment center because it is assumed that in the person's normal job, he or she would not make oral presentations. Thus, a performance appraisal would not provide accurate data. A special assessment center exercise requiring oral presentation would be utilized.
3. Job motivation is evaluated only in the interview. Assessment centers without an interview cannot evaluate motivation. Job motivation for a higher level job is difficult to assess by a performance appraisal.
4. Work standards and energy are assessed through a performance appraisal. A person might be able to put on a good "show" during a 2-or 3-day assessment center. The same person might be able to tell a good story in an interview; however, daily observation over a period of time would certainly be a good indication of energy and work standards.
5. Initiative is evaluated by all three techniques because it is an extremely important dimension and can be accurately evaluated in all three techniques.

In order to make judgments such as the ones above, one has to be thoroughly familiar with the selection techniques being considered for the system and have additional information which is obtainable from the job analysis.

Relative importance of the dimensions. The relative importance of the dimensions to the job under consideration must be considered because they will almost never be equally important. For example, it may be found that there are certain groups of manufacturing supervisors for which the ability to make oral presentations before groups is relatively unimportant but the ability to form understanding, empathetic relationships with younger employees from a range of ethnic and cultural backgrounds may be extremely important. Information on the relative importance of dimensions is essential before deciding the amount of emphasis to place on different dimensions in the selection system. The important dimensions should be evaluated by more than one selection element if possible and within the assessment center should be evaluated by more than one assessment center exercise. Redundancy can help ensure accuracy of measurement.

Most job analysis procedures include one of various methods for establishing the relative importance of dimensions, including rating, ranking, or paired comparisons.

Observability of dimensions on the job. An important piece of information to help determine which dimensions can be evaluated by a performance appraisal is an indication of the observability of the dimension in the typical candidate's job. This information is also typically obtained as part of the job analysis procedure.

Trainability of the dimension. If the behaviors identified as important to the job can be acquired in a relatively brief period of time, they should not be assessed in a selection program (EEOC et al., 1978). For a developmental program, only trainable dimensions should be assessed so meaningful feedback and development planning can be done.

EEO concerns. A final but very important element of the development of a selection system based around a job analysis is the need to ensure that the dimensions are being evaluated by the use of the most valid methodology consistent with the need to avoid adverse impact on minorities and women. The EEOC et al.'s (1978) Guidelines require that where adverse impact has been shown, the organization must demonstrate that it has considered alternate methods that are equally valid and less discriminatory.

METHODS OF JOB ANALYSIS

A variety of job analysis methods have been utilized for lower level and technical jobs: observation, interview, job checklists, activity profiles, questionnaires, diaries, written source material, training manuals, etc. (Bass & Barrett, 1972; McCormick & Tiffin, 1974; Prien & Ronan, 1971). Certain features of these methods limit their usefulness for managerial positions. Many facets of management jobs are not amenable to observation because some activities are unobservable, occur infrequently, and must be private. Checklists, profiles, and questionnaires are most appropriate for well-defined and simple jobs. Nealey and Fiedler (1968) found that written source material and descriptions of management development programs are too vague to give insights into job requirements.

The two most common job analysis techniques for evaluating management jobs are incumbent interviews and the retrospective critical incident technique. In most cases they should be used in conjunction with each other.

Incumbent interviews. The reason for the popularity of this technique is obvious. Is there anything more natural than to ask a manager how time is spent, what is important to the job, what difficult decisions must be made, etc.? These interviews range from quite informal discussions to a more formalized interview conducted around a patterned interview form. Sampling issues are extremely important. In a large-scale job analysis where an adequate sample of incumbents cannot be directly interviewed, a specially designed questionnaire can be developed to send to incumbents who were not interviewed.

Critical incident approach. The critical incident approach is one of the basic tools of industrial psychological research. Since its origination and explication by Flanagan in the late 1940s and early 1950s, the method has been used in studies of job analysis, performance appraisal, development of rating scales, personnel selection and training, leadership, etc.

> The critical incident technique consists of a set of procedures for collecting direct observations of human behavior in such a way as to facilitate their potential usefulness in solving practical problems and developing broad psychological principles. The critical incident technique outlines procedures for collecting observed incidents having special significance and meeting systematically defined criteria. By an incident is meant any observable human activity that is sufficiently complete in itself to permit inferences and predictions to be made about the person performing the act. To be critical, an incident must occur in a situation where the purpose or intent of the act seems fairly clear to the observer and where its consequences are sufficiently definite to leave little doubt concerning its effects [Flanagan, 1954a, p. 327].

The original critical incident approach as suggested by Flanagan involved actual observation of behavior as when a manager notes the behavior of a subordinate or the use of diaries by a job incumbent. Both procedures require a high degree of discipline to write down incidents as they happen. The methodology used in most job analyses associated with assessment centers is a variation on the Flanagan technique and might better be described as a "retrospective critical incident approach." Managers above the level of the target job are asked to recall critical incidents illustrating particularly successful or poor performance in the target job. The recall process is facilitated by the use of group brainstorming techniques—several managers sit around the table and share examples. One manager often reminds another manger of a category or incident.

A Model Job Analysis Procedure

The steps of a comprehensive job analysis procedure for the identification of dimensions to be included in a management assessment center are outlined below.

1. *Plan the job analysis:* Before the job analysis can actually start, several factors must be considered. Among these factors are the purpose of the assessment program (e.g., selection, promotion, diagnostic, early identification, etc.), the range and diversity of jobs to be studied, the resources available to conduct the analyses (e.g., number and level of experience of the job analysts), the need to generate evidence supporting a program in compliance with equal employment opportunity guidelines, and the size and geographical dispersion of the job incumbents and their bosses.

2. *Study available job descriptions and past job analyses:* A logical place to start is the material available on the target job and similar jobs. The organization may have job descriptions, descriptions of work tasks, or previous job analyses. Studies may have been conducted for salary administration or for the development of training programs. A survey of professional literature relative to the job category may provide information. For managerial jobs, the previous sections of this chapter can provide a source of dimensions which may be important for the target job.

None of these sources can be considered completely adequate for understanding an individual job. They may provide helpful suggestions for questions to ask and hypothetical dimensions.

3. *Observe individuals performing the job:* Observations on the job will help the analyst who is unfamiliar with the job and will provide a framework for understanding the incumbent and supervisor comments in subsequent steps. Observations allow the analyst to ask questions about job activities often overlooked by the incumbent. Finally, a judge in employment litigation will be favorably impressed if the analyst states that he or she actually observed the job.

It is rarely necessary to make extensive observations. Because the purpose is usually to simply orient the job analyst, one or two days suffices; subsequent steps will provide detailed information. However, if one knows the job analysis is likely to be challenged in court, it is advisable to spend more time observing the job.

4. *Conduct one-to-one interviews with job incumbents:* The purpose of these meetings is to determine the activities comprising the job. Included in the interview are questions about the daily activities, responsibilities, reporting relationships, decision-making authority, problems encountered, and use of time. In each of these areas, the analyst must obtain specific behavioral information about what the job incumbent actually does.

An hour-long patterned interview developed expressly for the job and organization is used to collect the data. The analyst must be trained to use specific questions and techniques to ensure accurate data are obtained. A stratified sample of incumbents representing major clusters of jobs should be interviewed. The percentage of total incumbents interviewed depends on the size and diversity of the population.

5. *Develop a job activity questionnaire based on the incumbent interviews and administer the questionnaire to a wide sample of incumbents:* The questionnaire consists of job activities defined from the incumbent interviews. The respondent is asked to rate the frequency, importance, time, or difficulty of each activity to the target job. Responses are obtained from a large sample of job incumbents not interviewed in Step 4. Responses to the questionnaires are analyzed and all items not meeting a previously defined decision rule concerning the importance or frequency of the activities are dropped.

The remaining items are categorized into job dimensions by the analysts. An iterative process is followed in which the analysts start with a long list of dimensions, perhaps 30, into which activities are categorized and then recategorized in order to derive a list which is as short as possible and still accounts for the majority of the frequent and important behaviors. The job analysts may have to specify totally new dimensions never used in an assessment center or amend the definitions of commonly used dimensions to ensure they truly represent job requirements.

6. *Collect critical incident data from the supervisors of employees in the target job:* Simultaneous to the collection of job activities from job incumbents, critical incidents of job behaviors associated with job success and failure are obtained from supervisors one or two levels above the incumbents. Incidents should be significantly important and have a sizable impact on the organization. The reporters are asked to describe actual,

specific examples of effective or ineffective performance in existing or previous target job incumbents.

Individuals or groups of four to six people at a time are queried by a trained analyst using a patterned interview. The analyst records the retrospective critical incidents or asks the managers to record the incidents on a standardized form which requests such information as the setting, participants, problem, action taken, and the result.

The incidents are typed and scrutinized for job dimensions. As with the categorization of behavioral data obtained from incumbents, the critical incidents are categorized into one of a long list of dimensions, then recategorized in an iterative manner to identify a shorter list of dimensions. Neidig (1977) has shown that three rater groups (psychologists, managers, and students) were able to reliably rate incidents obtained from three different sources (observations in one company and group interviews in two others companies). The judges were able to agree on the assignment of behaviors to dimensional categories and the rank order of dimension importance.

Behaviorally anchored rating scales (BARS) can be developed using the retranslation of expectations procedure (Smith & Kendall, 1963). Although the BARS may not enhance the psychometric properties of ratings using this format (Schwab, Heneman, & DeCotiis, 1975), the procedure may foster acceptance of the dimensions because people in the organization are involved in the process of defining dimensions, selecting illustrative behaviors and incidents, and identifying standards of high and low amounts of the dimension.

7. *Interview subordinates of employees in the target job:* There is some rationale that a job analysis should involve people who report to the job incumbents. A few unique job dimensions may be identified. For example, if you talk with the workers below a first-level supervisor, you often get the dimension Interest in Workers' Safety. There are arguments against involving the subordinates: You may get biased data; the results may be viewed as critical of the supervisor; it is difficult to adequately sample the potential respondents; and seldom do new dimensions emerge from the analyses.

8. *Establish a preliminary list of dimensions based on the data obtained in previous steps:* The lists of dimensions derived earlier are compared. Similar dimensions are noted. It is sometimes necessary to review the raw behavioral evidence (contained in activities and critical incidents) used to name the dimension to determine if the same basic dimensional area is involved or if two separate dimensions are really needed.

The advantage of using both activity data and critical incident data is that each produces a slightly different insight into the job. Thus one should not expect the two techniques to produce exactly the same results. With the exception of the overlaps in dimensions, all dimensions obtained from all of the primary sources are put into the preliminary list. While 80 % of the dimensions may be the same, an important 20 % are different. For example, one rarely gets the dimension Work Standards from incumbent data, but it very frequently is evident in critical incident data. Oral Communication, on the other hand, comes out of incumbent data much more strongly than from critical incident data.

At this point, additional dimensions may be added to the preliminary list even though they had not emerged from the current activities or from retrospective incidents. Higher managers can be asked to describe the kinds of behaviors that they want when a job is changing to meet new organizational or societal demands. This technique can also be applied even though the job is just being created. By systematically pooling the expert judgment of managers designing the new job, it is possible to make a good approximation of the dimensions which will be required when the job actually exists.

9. *Obtain ratings of the importance of the dimensions from incumbents' supervisors:* The preliminary list of dimensions is placed on a questionnaire along with the definitions and illustrative behaviors. Managers one or two levels above the target job are asked to rate the importance of the dimensions, rank order them, or choose the most important among all possible pairs in a paired comparison procedure.

Other types of judgments might also be obtained from the raters. Neidig, Hall, and Baker (1977) asked for two types of information: *(a)* a rating of whether or not the area differentiated superior employees from those barely acceptable; and *(b)* an indication of which dimension is necessary for the completion of a list of tasks comprising the target job. Dimensions were retained that showed high differentiation ratings, were used by a large number of tasks, and could be measured in an assessment center.

If the questionnaire is to aid in the design of a promotion system, the managers may be asked to evaluate the observability of the dimension in the incumbent's current job. Dimensions that are observable at the level expected in the target job may be evaluated through appropriate performance evaluations; dimensions that are not easily observed make prime targets for a behavioral simulation.

10. *Select the final list of dimensions using predetermined decision rules:* Statistical procedures are used to select the final list of dimensions. The decision rules will vary depending on the purpose of the program. For

example, in promotion programs, dimensions are retained if they are rated high in importance, are not observable on the current job, and cannot be trained in a brief orientation to the job (EEOC *et al.*, 1978). In diagnostic development programs, important dimensions may be eliminated if they cannot be developed efficiently by the organization. However, dimensions may be retained even though the organization is not committed to their remediation, simply because the individual might benefit personally from being alerted to certain weaknesses such as annoying mannerisms or low verbal and reading skills. The important point here is to select carefully only those dimensions that match program objectives (Thornton, 1979).

11. *Evaluate incumbent data to determine appropriate selection–promotion exercises:* Statistical procedures are used to analyze the incumbents' activity questionnaire data to determine appropriate exercises. Clusters of important job activities can be simulated with existing types of exercises (e.g., an in-basket or an interview simulation) or a new behavioral simulation may be constructed. The goal of these statistical analyses is to show objectively that *(a)* the major job activities are measured by behavioral simulations (or by other means described in the next step); *(b)* simulations that are used actually cover several significant job activities; and *(c)* the dimensions are being evaluated in situations similar to those that appear on the job. If a job incumbent does not have to analyze data under time stress, then it is inappropriate to have a tightly timed analysis exercise in the assessment center.

12. *Determine the most appropriate selection–development system to predict and enhance the dimensions:* A total selection system is designed based on the job analysis data. In an integrated system, all dimensions will be measured by one or more methods such as behavioral simulations, an objective background interview, a performance evaluation, or a medical examination. The total system is designed to ensure some, but not total, redundancy of measurement (i.e., we do not attempt to measure all dimensions with all methods), to ensure effective utilization of current on-the-job training, and to eliminate adverse impact on protected groups.

13. *Write a detailed report that documents each decision-making step and provides a clear description of the entire process:* The final report contains a description of each step in the job analysis process and shows the flow of data and results from each source, culminating in the final dimensions and exercises. This document will be used by management to evaluate the analysis and by government agencies to determine compliance with selection guidelines. The report must be complete, accurate, and clear because it may be used at some point in the future in a legal proceeding.

COMMENTS ON THE TASK OF JOB ANALYSES

Into how many dimensions should job behavior be divided? How would an analyst know if he or she had too few or too many dimensions? The behaviors obtained in a job analysis can be grouped at various levels of abstraction. A group of behaviors can be labeled Decision Making or that broader dimension can be broken down into Analysis, Judgment, and Decisiveness. Behavior in each of those dimensions can be further broken down (e.g., Judgment can be divided into Creativity, Organizational Sensitivity, Extraorganizational Sensitivity, Risk Taking). The guideline is *practicality*.

Behavior should be broken down to the smallest units that will be useful and no further. Usefulness is most often defined relative to ease of communication of the dimension to the assessee and to management or ease in prescribing an appropriate training program. For example, Oral Communication and Oral Presentation are often separated because very different training prescriptions are appropriate for each diagnosis, whereas Judgment is less likely to be broken down because the available training programs all deal with the more general concept.

Can a job analysis define appropriate leadership styles? For example, will a job analysis determine if an authoritarian or a participative style is more appropriate? Job analyses typically find that no one style is always appropriate. Rather flexibility in the use of styles is the key ingredient. An effective manager uses different styles in different situations and with different types of people. The assessment center exercises are chosen to confront the assessee with a variety of leadership situations (individual and group, competitive and cooperative, assigned leader and leaderless, hostile and friendly) to see if the assessee shows flexibility of style and approach. The ability to handle effectively a number of leadership situations is evaluated rather than the appropriateness of a particular style for a particular situation. The same general approach holds for other situational dimensions such as Delegation and Assertiveness.

Contributions of Assessment Center Research to Understanding Managerial Jobs

In 1968, Korman stated, "Little has been learned from selection research which can contribute to a theory of leadership behavior [p. 319]." Ten years later we can say with some assurance that research on assessment centers has led to a better understanding of managerial effectiveness. Leadership and management are not synonomous but they overlap to a great extent. Job analysis efforts carried out as preliminary steps in the development of assessment centers have led to much clearer understanding of managerial work.

Based on a review of job analysis efforts in managerial assessment centers, we conclude:

1. Managerial jobs can be defined in terms of a set of behavioral dimensions. These behavioral dimensions can be operationally defined as clusters of behaviors observable on the job and in performance tests that simulate important aspects of the job.
2. Managerial jobs can be distinguished from each other in terms of unique sets of dimensions. Jobs at different levels of management and often at the same levels are characterized by different sets of dimensions. The same dimension label (e.g., Analysis) may be manifested in qualitatively different ways for jobs at different hierarchical levels.
3. Managerial jobs must be defined in terms of a relatively large set of dimensions. An exact number cannot be specified, but we do not believe it is adequate to use only two major categories that have been variously labeled task centered (initiating structure, production-oriented) and employee centered (consideration of people, employee-oriented). Ten to fifteen dimensions are required to adequately define managerial jobs for the purposes of assessment programs. For developmental purposes, a longer list of dimensions provides a more thorough diagnosis of reasons for effective and ineffective performance.

We have also learned that selection, promotional, or diagnostic developmental programs should be considered as systems containing several sources of data. The various data sources should be organized around a common set of dimensions and definitions. Assessment centers should focus on dimensions that cannot be evaluated adequately on the basis of current job performance. In developmental programs it is also important to distinguish which dimensions are trainable with a realistic amount of effort from those which are less amenable to development.

Appendix A: Common Managerial Dimensions

Oral Communication: Effective expression in individual or group situations (includes gestures and nonverbal communications)

Oral Presentation: Effective expression when presenting ideas or tasks to an individual or to a group when given time for preparation (includes gestures and nonverbal communication)

Written Communication: Clear expression of ideas in writing and use of good grammatical form

Planning and Organizing: Establishing a course of action for self and/or others to accomplish a specific goal; planning proper assignments of personnel and appropriate allocation of resources

Delegation: Utilizing subordinates effectively; allocating decision making and other responsibilities to the appropriate subordinates

Control: Establishing procedures to monitor and/or regulate processes, tasks, or activities of subordinates and job activities and responsibilities; taking action to monitor the results of delegated assignments or projects

Development of Subordinates: Developing the skills and competencies of subordinates through training and development activities related to current and future jobs

Organizational Sensitivity: Action that indicates an awareness of the impact and the implications of decisions on other components of the organization

Extraorganizational Sensitivity: Action that indicates an awareness of the impact and implications of decisions relevant to societal and governmental factors

Extraorganizational Awareness: Use of knowledge of changing societal and governmental pressures outside the organization to identify potential problems and opportunities

Organizational Awareness: Use of knowledge of changing situations and pressures inside the organization to identify potential organizational problems and opportunities

Sensitivity: Actions that indicate a consideration for the feelings and needs of others

Leadership: Utilization of appropriate interpersonal styles and methods in guiding individuals (subordinates, peers, superiors) or groups toward task accomplishment

Recognition of Employee Safety Needs: Awareness of conditions that affect employees' safety needs and taking action to resolve inadequacies and discrepancies

Analysis: Identifying problems, securing relevant information, relating data from different sources, and identifying possible causes of problems

Judgment: Developing alternative courses of action and making decisions based on logical assumptions that reflect factual information

Creativity: Generating and/or recognizing imaginative solutions and innovations in work-related situations

Risk Taking: Taking or initiating action that involves a deliberate gamble in order to achieve a recognized benefit or advantage

Decisiveness: Readiness to make decisions, render judgments, take action, or commit oneself

Technical and Professional Knowledge: Level of understanding of relevant technical and professional information

Energy: Maintaining a high activity level

Range of Interests: Breadth and diversity of general business related knowledge— well informed

Initiative: Active attempts to influence events to achieve goals; self-starting rather than passive acceptance. Taking action to achieve goals beyond those called for; originating action

Tolerance for Stress: Stability of performance under pressure and/or opposition

Adaptability: Maintaining effectiveness in varying environments, with various tasks, responsibilities, or people

Independence: Taking action in which the dominant influence is one's own convictions rather than the influence of others' opinions

Tenacity: Staying with a position or plan of action until the desired objective is achieved or is no longer reasonably attainable

Job Motivation: The extent to which activities and responsibilities available in the job overlap with activities and responsibilities that result in personal satisfaction

Career Ambition: The expressed desire to advance to higher job levels with active efforts toward self-development for advancement

Integrity: Maintaining social, ethical, and organizational norms in job-related activities

Work Standards: Setting high goals or standards of performance for self, subordinates, others, and organization. Dissatisfied with average performance

Resilience: Handling disappointment and/or rejection while maintaining effectiveness

Practical Learning: Assimilating and applying new, job-related information, taking into consideration rate and complexity

Appendix B: Complete Definitions of Several Behavioral Dimensions

Planning and Organizing: Ability to efficiently establish an appropriate course of action for self and/or others to accomplish a specific goal; make proper assignments of personnel and appropriate use of resources.

Most of the planning and organizing required of a first-level supervisor in the Packaging Division is on a rather short-term basis. This type of planning is quite critical to the successful operation of the plant. A first-line supervisor from the machine shop stated that his first priority every morning was to line his people up for the jobs that needed to be accomplished. It was often necessary to move people around from job to job to make sure the people were experienced in the different types of jobs and to relieve boredom.

One supervisor talked about the changing priorities which occur during the day requiring him to reassign jobs. He said it was quite possible for an operator to work on three jobs during the day and never complete any of them.

A first-line supervisor from the chemical area stated that his first priority when he comes to work is to see if his complete crew is in. If not, he has to switch people from their normal duty stations. He said this was often complicated because of the fact that not everyone under his supervision can perform every job.

The critical incident discussions with the managers also yielded a number of examples where planning and organizing were critical to a supervisor's success. A story about the first-level supervisor who called the scheduling supervisor on Friday night and arranged for a trucker to have all the material moved out very early Monday morning in time for the Monday morning shift would be a good example of effective planning. Another example told about supervisors who have 22 to 25 people who must be scheduled equally over a number of different machines. This requires a very complex recordkeeping system which must be kept up to date on a daily basis. One particular supervisor was very good in doing scheduling, which was at least partially responsible for this person's high level of job performance.

Judgment: Ability to develop alternative solutions to problems, to evaluate courses of action, and to reach logical decisions.

First-line supervisors have to make decisions on a large variety of different topics. Some of these are actual technical decisions having to do with the product and the manufacturing process. It is imperative for the first-level supervisor to know when he should make these types of decisions and when these decisions should be referred to his manager. For instance, a first-level supervisor from the drying area discussed the decision as to whether or not to continue making casing if it is not perfect. He stated that if the casing is not absolutely within specification, it is important he consult his supervisor to see what should be done. He said it often depends upon how badly the customer wants the casing. If the customer is not in a great hurry, then the casing can be thrown out. However, if the customer is in great need, then the manufacturing should continue. The first-level supervisor stated that since he did not have that type of information, it was important that he give these decisions to his manager.

Another major area concerning judgment has to do with setting priorities. A first-level supervisor in the machine shop said that very early in the morning he looks at the jobs to be accomplished for the day and identifies the ones which have to be done immediately and the ones which can be postponed. He said that sometimes he does not know all the variables which impact the decision and contacts the people who are placing the orders if there is a question.

From the first-line supervisor's perspective, a difficult area requiring judgment has to do with personnel problems. Reprimanding an employee seems to be high on the list of the difficult areas under this heading. Although a first-level supervisor cannot fire an employee, it is the responsibility of the first-level supervisor to recommend this if he or she feels it is necessary.

A number of instances of this dimension were generated from the critical incident component of the job analysis procedure. One situation described the relieving of a supervisor. The supervisor who was being relieved, in addition to writing in the log any problems which occurred in his shift, should have also described potential problem situations to the relieving supervisor. In one situation which was described, the supervisor being relieved did not tell the relieving supervisor of a problem they were having with a motor on a piece of equipment. As a result, when the equipment broke down, the supervisor was not prepared to take action.

Another situation was described where a supervisor was transferred. When the new supervisor looked through the overtime records he noticed that one employee had no record of overtime, but had not refused overtime either. When this situation was investigated, the hourly employee said that he had not been asked. Further investigation revealed that the hourly employee had another job at night and had asked the previous supervisor not to request him to take overtime. In this situation, the supervisor had made a bad decision in going against company policy.

5

Assessment Center Exercises and Dimension Ratings

This chapter evaluates the adequacy of assessment center exercises commonly used and the dimension ratings emanating from them. The first part of the chapter describes the exercises most frequently used in managerial assessment centers, summarizes important research involving each exercise category in management assessment centers, and reviews evidence of their reliability and validity in assessment center studies. The section ends with a model for managerial job simulation exercises. The second section discusses the reliability and validity of dimension ratings made by observers during the staff discussion in which information from several exercises is integrated. This section ends with a discussion of the importance of dimension ratings for purposes of prediction and diagnosis.

In the previous chapter, we discussed the selection of dimensions by means of a job analysis. Behaviors associated with successful and less successful job performance are identified through various job analysis techniques, and the most common and important behaviors are grouped together under labels called dimensions. The iterative process of categorizing behaviors by dimensions can usually be applied to the vast majority of important behaviors relative to the job and produces a list of dimensions that covers all elements important to the job. However, this does not mean that all the dimensions developed in the job analysis are appropriate for assessment in an assessment center. Usually, there are other parts of a promotional decision-making system (e.g., performance appraisal data or background interview data) which can provide information on some dimensions. Then one must decide which dimensions to evaluate in the assessment center and which dimensions to evaluate through other means. Of course, this depends on the specific assessment center exercises used and the other personnel evaluation methods to be included in the total system.

The previous chapter also dealt with the identification of categories of assessment center exercises. It described how a job analysis identified the most common and important activities performed by job incumbents and used this information to determine categories of assessment center exercises so that the assessment center exercises mirror the majority of day-to-day activities of individuals performing in the target level job. But, as with the selection of dimensions, other factors must be considered in the selection of specific assessment center exercises. One must consider the ability of the exercise to bring out the target dimensions defined as important, the reliability of the exercise, and the overlap of various possible exercises. Obviously, since the goal is to cover all of the target dimensions for the job, exercises that cover several dimensions and dimensions *not covered in other exercises are more appropriate*. Exercise selection decisions are based on the ability of the exercises to efficiently bring out reliable judgments of behavior. Some exercises take an hour to produce the same one or two observations that can be obtained in 15 min in another exercise.

Another reason for considering the reliability and validity of specific assessment center exercises is the possible use of a construct validity validation methodology. Experience and research with various types of assessment exercises have provided a basis for specifying which exercises provide accurate observations of the defined dimensions in terms of job performance. Thus, although no practitioner has reported the use of construct validity as a method of establishing the validity of an assessment center, it is an appropriate methodology.

Evaluation of Individual Assessment Techniques

In evaluating the contribution of any assessment technique, it is helpful to note these relationships: (a) the reliability of observers' judgments; (b) the correlation of the technique with overall assessment ratings; (c) the correlation of the technique with subsequent criteria of managerial success (e.g., progress in the company or performance ratings); and (d) the unique contribution of the technique over and above other techniques. The last requirement is very important. For the sake of efficiency we do not want to use an elaborate or costly assessment technique if a simple or less expensive one is just as effective. To decide whether a specific component of an assessment center is of value, we need to know if it adds something to prediction or understanding beyond what is obtained from other measurement techniques.

Validation of exercise ratings against the overall assessment rating (b) assumes that the summary index is a relevant, worthy criterion. The overall assessment rating (OAR) is certainly a readily available synthesis of multiple observations by multiple assessors in multiple exercises. To assign the OAR the status of a "criterion" may be premature but, as we shall conclude in Chapter 7, the OAR is highly predictive of several criteria of managerial success. Furthermore, in many situations no better evaluation of managerial behavior exists. Correlations of assessment components with the OAR give insight into the assessors' judgment processes and can lead to revisions in exercises, dimensions, and assessor training.

Examining the validity of individual assessment techniques may not adequately reflect the complex nature of multiple assessments. The synthesis of the assessment data by several assessors during the staff discussion builds on complex interactions of observations which take place over a period of time. Nevertheless, knowledge of the contribution of each technique is of practical and theoretical value.

THINGS TO CONSIDER IN ASSESSMENT CENTER
EXERCISE CATEGORIES

We have defined nine categories of assessment center exercises. These categories represent the vast majority of all exercises used in assessment centers (Crooks, 1977). But this requires the categories to be broad. For example, there are numerous kinds of analysis exercises that fall under the general definition of *analysis exercises*. These range from very simple analysis situations which may take 15 min, such as those confronted by a foreman, to very complicated analysis that may require 4–5 hours of work by a participant. Thus, the reader is cautioned to recognize that in the discussion of the merits of exercises, there are considerable individual differences among exercises within a category.

When considering an exercise for possible inclusion in an assessment center, an organization should:

1. Consider the appropriateness of the exercise for the target job. Does the exercise represent a frequent and important job activity?

2. Consider the ability of the exercise to bring out important job related dimensions defined in a job analysis. The more dimensions brought out, the better the exercise. This involves the notion of probability of observation. Some assessment center exercises are designed to bring out certain dimensions and always do bring out those dimensions. An example would be an exercise in which an individual is asked to write something, and his or her Written Communication is being evaluated. However, other assessment center exercises do not guarantee an observation of a dimension to which they are targeted. For example, a group exercise may be designed to bring out the dimension Persuasiveness. However, the dynamics of a particular group in a particular assessment center may be such that an individual never has to use any persuasive behaviors because every single idea he or she presents is automatically accepted by the group. Thus, the dimension is not observable in that particular situation even though in the majority of groups it is observable. Obviously, the more sure an assessor is of actually observing a dimension in an exercise, the more preferable the exercise.

Another feature is ease of observation. The more an exercise can be designed so that particular observations of behavior can be narrowly defined for assessors, the more reliable is the assessor judgment for the particular dimension.

3. The efficiency of the exercises must be considered. Efficiency deals with a combination of factors including length of the exercise, number of dimensions brought out by a particular exercise, and the expense of the exercise material. Exercises requiring only paper and pencil for instructions and response are much cheaper than exercises requiring role players. Similarly, exercises that require two role players are more expensive than those requiring only one.

4. The validity of the exercise as a whole may be important. If one is considering a construct validity paradigm, then the validity of the exercise in other similar selection situations becomes critically important. Even if one does not try to establish construct validity, these are still important data in that they lend credibility to decisions based on the combination of exercises.

Several writers have suggested that the notion of dimensions be eliminated from an assessment center and that the assessment center be built completely around job-related exercises. They argue that if the person can do each of the job-related exercises and if the job-related exercises account for most job activities, then the person can perform on the job and it is not necessary to go through the intermediary step of categorizing behavior by dimensions. This is discussed in the latter part of this chapter.

SIGNS VERSUS SAMPLES: THE CONCEPT

Wernimont and Campbell (1968) emphasized the importance of using measures of "samples" rather than "signs" of behavior in the prediction of job performance. Signs are tests, questionnaires, biographical information blanks, or other paper-and-pencil instruments that measure general predispositons to behave in certain ways. The actual behavior involved in a sign may be nothing more than a minor physical response of marking a piece of paper or answering a direct question in an interview. Samples are more complex measures that require complex behavioral responses very much like the responses required on the job. The behavior involved in a sample type of test is more consistent with the behavior on the job (Asher & Sciarrino, 1974) and may include writing a complete report or guiding a group toward task accomplishment.

In the next sections we review assessment techniques that represent both types of measurement. Examples of signs include the paper-and-pencil tests of intellect, personality, and knowledge. Examples of work samples include leaderless group discussions, in-baskets, games, written case studies and situations in which the manager interviews a subordinate or client.

We emphasize that work samples are not necessarily complete job simulations or job replicas. A simulation or replica is an exact duplicate of a part of a job placed in another setting; for example, a flight simulator that is a reconstruction of the controls and cockpit of an airplane placed in a training facility. Simulations and replicas possess a high degree of "fidelity" to the job, including identical equipment, materials, rules, and procedures. By contrast, a work sampling procedure is designed to sample behavior relevant to the job requirements without duplicating the actual job situation. For example, in a management assessment center, behaviors relevant to planning, problem analysis, and sensitivity can be elicited by an in-basket exercise, yet it need not replicate the company policies, procedures, and personnel in the actual target job for which candidates are being considered.

It is useful to know frequency of use of various assessment center techniques in operating managerial assessment centers. The following list was developed from a review of approximately 500 centers with which the authors have been associated:

Assessment Exercise	Percentage of frequency of use
In-basket	95
Assigned-role leaderless group discussion	85
Interview simulation	75
Nonassigned-role leaderless group discussion	45
Scheduling (primarily for supervisory positions)	40
Analysis (primarily for higher level positions)	35
Management games	10
Background interview (as part of the assessment center as opposed to being part of a promotion system)	5
Paper-and-pencil tests	
Intellectual	2
Reading	1
Mathematics and arithmetic	1
Personality	1
Projective tests	1

As one reviews the research on assessment center techniques, it is interesting to note the lack of correlation between the frequency with which an assessment center exercise is used in practice and the amount of available research evidence on that use. We know a great deal about paper-and-pencil tests, but they are infrequently used as part of assessment centers. We know relatively little about in-baskets or interview simulation, yet they are very frequently used as part of assessment centers. This may be because knowledge about the pros and cons of a specific technique may have led to decisions not to use them. For example, to the extent that the tests have been proven to be ineffective predictors of future performance, their use would not be justified.

Another contributing factor is the increasing pressure from the U.S. federal government to show the content validity of selection instruments. Content validity is more easily established for certain kinds of exercises than others. Again, paper-and-pencil tests are usually (but not always) more difficult to validate using content validity.

To the extent that the choice of exercises is in direct response to the frequency of job activities, certain exercises automatically arise more frequently than others. A good example is the interview simulation exercise which is becoming much more popular in assessment centers. Of all the assessment centers established in recent years that the authors have observed, almost 100% use interview simulations. This is in direct response to the fact that almost all supervisory–managerial jobs have a very strong one-to-one component. However, other exercises seem to be declining in popularity in response to job content studies. A good example of this trend involves some of the group exercises, particularly for supervisory level jobs, where group activities are less frequently found to be important.

Finally, and perhaps most important, is the growing movement in assessment centers to be more behavioral and less clinical. Paper-and-pencil tests and inputs from projective instruments could be combined with inputs from assessment center exercises as long as the exercises are being evaluated on a clinical level (e.g., the OSS Assessment Centers and even the early AT&T Management Progress Study). Increasingly, assessment centers have turned to a highly behavioral orientation where assessors observe behavior in the exercises, categorize the behavior by dimensions, share their ratings of the dimensions with each other, and back up those ratings with their recorded observed behavior. All decisions are made based on behavioral evidence. Nonbehavioral input signs (e.g., emanating from tests or a clinical interview) do not readily fit in and thus have been very frequently dropped.

PAPER–AND–PENCIL TESTS

As one might expect, a wide variety of tests has been used in assessment centers. In no reported case have tests been used in a strictly psychometric manner by setting up failing scores and the like. Usually the tests are considered during the assessor discussion along with all other data to form the overall evaluation of the participant. Tests are used currently by a number of the original assessment center proponents such as AT&T, Sears, Standard Oil (Ohio), and IBM. Other early test users dropped paper-and-pencil tests with the advent of federal pressure to demonstrate validity of tests. Recent adopters of the assessment center method have tended not to use tests. This is especially true in cases where middle managers are being assessed or where the program operates in an organization not employing an industrial psychologist.

To review all the tests used in managerial assessment and prediction would be an overwhelming task. The purpose of this section is to discuss a representative set of findings, emphasizing the most common conclusions and the most controversial points.

Psychological test is a generic term that refers to a wide variety of techniques for observing and measuring human behavior. This section will review paper-and-pencil tests and projective devices. These techniques require the person to answer questions or make verbal responses which often are not directly related to the job itself. They are aimed at measuring aptitudes, abilities, motivation, and personality characteristics. Later in this chapter, we will discuss what some people call "work sample tests" such as in-baskets and leaderless group discussions, where an assessor must observe and measure behavior. Work samples are "tests" but they require the person to exhibit behaviors very similar to the behaviors of the manager on the job.

To begin at the most general level, Ghiselli's review, *The Validity of Occupational Aptitude Tests* (1966), presents a summary of thousands of studies that have investigated the relationships between tests and performance on all kinds of jobs. Jobs are classified according to two different systems: the General Occupational Classification System (GOC) and the Dictionary of Occupational Titles (DOT). For our purposes, the GOC considers the classification of managerial occupations, including executives and administrators and foremen. Table 5.1 shows the average validity coefficients for these occupations. It will be observed that for executives and administrators, tests of intellectual abilities, perceptual accuracy, and personality traits predict performance with correlations of around

Table 5.1
Validity Coefficients for Managerial Occupations (GOC)[a]

	Proficiency		
	Executives and administrators	Foremen	All managers
Intellectual abilities	.29[e]	.24[f]	.25[g]
Intelligence	.30[e]	.25[f]	.26[f]
Arithmetic	.26[c]	.20[e]	.21[f]
Spatial and mechanical abilities	.18[b]	.23[f]	.23[f]
Spatial relations	.18[b]	.21[e]	.21[e]
Mechanical principles		.24[f]	.24[f]
Perceptual accuracy	.24[c]	.14[c]	.19[c]
Number comparison	.00[b]	.20[b]	.13[c]
Name comparison		.08[b]	.08[b]
Cancellation	.32[c]		.32[c]
Personality traits	.28[e]	.15[f]	.17[g]
Personality	.27[e]	.15[f]	.17[g]
Interest	.31[e]	.15[f]	.22[f]

[a]From *The Validity of Occupational Aptitude Tests* by E. E. Ghiselli. John Wiley & Sons, Inc. Reprinted by permission.
[b]Less than 100 cases.
[c]100 to 499 cases.
[d]500 to 999 cases.
[e]1,000 to 4999 cases.
[f]5,000 to 9999 cases.
[g]10,000 or more cases.

Table 5.2
Validity Coefficients for Managerial and Official Occupations, 0–71 to –99 (DOT)[a]

	Proficiency			
	Retail managers 0–72	Floormen and floor managers 0–75	Inspectors, public service 0–95	Managers and officials 0–97, –98, –99
Intellectual abilities	.50[c]		.42[b]	.28[e]
Intelligence	.50[c]			.28[e]
Arithmetic			.42[b]	.25[c]
Spatial and mechanical abilities				.18[b]
Spatial relations				.18[b]
Perceptual accuracy				.24[c]
Number comparison				.00[b]
Cancellation				.32[c]
Personality traits	.33[b]	.34[c]		.21[e]
Personality	.33[b]	.34[c]		.21[e]
Interest				.44[b]

[a]From *The Validity of Occupational Aptitude Tests* by E. E. Ghiselli. Copyright 1966 by John Wiley & Sons, Inc. Reprinted by permission.
[b]Less than 100 cases.
[c]100 to 499 cases.
[d]500 to 999 cases.
[e]1,000 to 4999 cases.
[f]5,000 to 9999 cases.
[g]10,000 or more cases.

.20 to .30. Ghiselli concluded that, "None of these three types of tests can be considered to be outstanding, but all would seem to have some value in personnel assessments [p. 35]." For foremen, tests of intellectual ability and spatial and mechanical ability correlate on the average .25 with job performance. Tests of perceptual accuracy and personality traits correlate only around .15 with the criteria.

Using the DOT, managerial jobs of concern to us fall into managerial and official occupations, 0–71 to 0–99. Ghiselli found sufficient data to report on retail managers, floormen and floor managers, and managers and officials. Table 5.2 shows the average validity coefficients for these occupations. Performance as a retail manager correlated quite well (.50) with intellectual tests, and moderately well (.33) for personality tests. For floormen and floor managers, Ghiselli reports that personality tests correlate .34. Among the occupations classified as managers and officials, tests of intellectual abilities show the highest correlations (.28), but tests of perceptual accuracy (.24) and personality (.21) show lower validity.

In considering Ghiselli's work, it is important to know that these validities are averages of hundreds of studies involving numerous research designs, specific tests, different criteria, and a variety of methods of analysis. All of these factors, when summarized, would probably tend to lower the indication of relationship. The data show that only a small proportion of criterion variation is accounted for by the tests. However, we would tend to agree with Ghiselli when he states in his preface, "It (the data) is testimony to the fact that occupational behavior is predictable, and that it is possible to develop objective and impartial means to assess aptitudes for different kinds of work [Ghiselli, 1966 p. vi]."

Guion (1965) points out that a vast majority of the applications of testing for selection of managerial personnel have not been well researched. Such problems as job analysis, criterion development, and insufficient numbers of personnel make test validation a difficult task. The result all too often is that the validity of tests, interviews, and other managerial selection devices are taken on faith alone. Despite a number of problems in this area, Guion concludes that, "Managerial selection efforts have been fairly succesful [p. 458]." After reviewing many tests and testing projects in a number of companies, he concludes:

1. Standardized test batteries of nonprojective tests and inventories provide the primary basis for improved managerial selection, whether used alone or in personal appraisals (i.e., clinical evaluations).
2. Intellectual skill must not be overlooked in the enthusiasm for assessing total personality; consistently, measures of mental ability have been among the best predictors.
3. Test data may include projectives where the importance justifies the expense; however, there is no basis for assuming that they can do more than offer supplementary information about motivational patterns.
4. Personal (clinical) appraisals (by a trained psychologist) appear to be moderately valid predictors for generalized situations where test use is likely to be weak. The validity seems to lie in the psychologists' skill and judgment in integrating test data with impressions about the characteristics of specific job situations.
5. In large organizations, where Ns adequate for validation can be found for jobs of the same level and function, test patterns alone—without subjective, clinical judgments—can probably be developed that will offer prediction superior to that possible with appraisers' ratings.

A summary to this point would suggest that paper-and-pencil tests can predict managerial performance criteria with only a moderate level of accuracy. The typical validity coefficients average .30 to .35, indicating that only 10 to 12 percent of criterion variance can be predicted by paper-and-pencil instruments.

A much higher level of predictive accuracy was found in a series of studies of the validity of tests reviewed by Campbell *et al.* (1970). Large-scale, actuarial studies dealing with supervisors, middle-level managers, and executives were reviewed. The review included research programs by Standard Oil Company of New Jersey (Detailed reports of these studies are available in a series of papers authored by their Social Science Research Division, 1961–1964), the Industrial Relations Center at the University of Minnesota, Sears Roebuck, Minneapolis Gas Company, Jewel Tea Company, American Oil Company, North American Aviation, and Lockheed Aviation.

In summary, Campbell *et al.* (1970) state:

> Taken together, these studies provide good evidence that a fairly sizable por-tion (30 to 50 percent) of the variance in general managerial effectiveness can be expressed in terms of personal qualities measured by self-response tests and inventories and combined by predetermined rules or statistical equa-tions. The *construct* of effective executiveship . . . includes such factors as high intelligence, good verbal skills, effective judgment in handling managerial situations . . . and organizing skill; dispositions toward interper-sonal relationships, hard work, being active, and taking risks; and temperamental qualities such as dominance, confidence, straightforward-ness, low anxiety and autonomy [p. 195–196].

The considerable difference in these results and those of Ghiselli and Guion may result from the sample of studies reviewed. Campbell *et al.* (1970) surveyed the practices and research of the largest organizations and those known to be in the forefront of industrial psychology applica-tions at the time. Furthermore, their review of actuarial studies covered only those that met high standards of research quality—large samples, adequate designs, and conditions that do not limit generality of results. The findings from these studies probably illustrate the upper limits of our ability to predict managerial effectiveness from paper-and-pencil tests.

INTELLIGENCE TESTS

Intelligence tests, designed to measure the intellectual or cognitive abilities of a person, may focus on one general ability or they may measure several separate mental abilities (e.g., verbal and numerical abilities). The common core of most intelligence tests is the ability to reason with abstractions such as words, numbers, or other symbols. Ver-bal abilities play a major role in many current tests of intelligence: the meaning of words, identification of synonyms or antonyms, completion of analogies of words, or many other ways of demonstration of reasoning with words.

Considering the broad domain of intelligence, it is clear that the intelligence tests used for managerial assessment measure only a part of the entire spectrum of intellectual activity. Very few of the performance components, such as are revealed by Wechsler's block design or picture arrangement, are measured. The "fluid analytic" abilities (Cronbach, 1970)—spatial mechanical, spatial visualization, etc.—are usually not included. This is probably appropriate considering the job requirements of a manager, but it should be clearly understood that "intelligence" is being defined and measured fairly narrowly by the tests reviewed in this section.

Intellectual tests have played a key role in the selection research programs at major corporations (Campbell *et al.*, 1970). Organizations using a sample of tests with significant criterion validities included:

1 . Standard Oil of New Jersey: Miller Analogies Test, Nonverbal Reasoning Test, Management Judgment Test
2. Industrial Relation Center, University of Minnesota: Wonderlic Personnel Test
3. Sears, Roebuck: American Council of Education Test of Problem-solving and Linguistic Abilities
4. Minneapolis Gas: Wonderlic Personnel Test, Shipley–Hartford Abstraction, Science Research Associates Test—Linguistic and Quantitative Abilities, Differential Aptitude Test—Abstract Reasoning, Spelling, Sentence Usage, Watson–Glaser Critical Thinking, Concept Mastery Test

Even though intellectual ability is an important managerial job requirement, it cannot be assumed that a test of such ability will correlate with a measure of success. Kraut (1969) found little or no correlation between the Concept Mastery Test (CMT), the Ship Destination Test (SDT), and a criterion of managerial mobility reflecting increase in position level after training. While giving a number of possible explanations of the negative results, Kraut points out that the lack of validity may rest with the tests themselves and the traits they measure. Performance on the CMT is largely a function of knowledge of the meanings of words; SDT performance requires arithmetic skills. Perhaps these tests measure specific abilities rather than a general reasoning ability that is important to managerial success. Clearly, this study points out the importance of carefully selecting the tests to be included in an assessment center.

Intellectual tests in assessment centers. Bray and Grant (1966) used three mental ability tests in the Management Progress Study: School and

College Ability Test (SCAT), Critical Thinking in the Social Science Test, and the Contemporary Affairs Test. All three of the tests correlated significantly with the staff prediction of success and with the staff rating on general effectiveness. However, correlations were found to be higher for the noncollege groups, and in all cases there was much variation in assessment center performance which could not be accounted for by the intellectual tests. Since the verbal portion of the SCAT correlated highest with the staff judgments, it was included in further analyses that studied the relative contributions of several assessment techniques. The SCAT was less predictive in the college sample than three situational exercises, but in the noncollege sample it was second most important. Moreover, when the three tests were correlated with the criterion of salary progress, the results were highly variable, with the SCAT verbal showing a significant relationship for four of the seven groups. However, in one of those cases, the correlation was negative. Bray and Grant (1966) give no explanation for this unusual finding. Higher correlations for the noncollege group may be attributable to larger variation in test scores. While we can see that the mental ability tests do contribute to the predictions in the Management Progress Study, it is clear that they do not tell the whole story; and when mental ability test scores are statistically partialed out of the staff judgment ratings, staff judgments still correlate significantly with salary progress. This indicates that the more elaborate assessment process makes additional contributions over what is possible with only the mental tests. Furthermore, although tests contribute to prediction, an acceptable level of accuracy can be obtained without them. For the Management Progress Study then, Bray and Grant (1966) concluded that even though situational tests contribute more to assessment, paper-and-pencil instruments measuring mental ability should be included in the battery of techniques. (See Table 5.3 for summary of results.)

Positive results have been found in a number of other studies at SOHIO, Sears, AT&T, and the Civil Service Commission in Canada. SCAT Verbal and Quantitative scores correlated with a composite criterion of behavioral ratings at SOHIO (Carleton, 1970). Bentz (1971) reported that the Sears Test of Mental Ability Linguistics, Quantitative and Overall scores predicted various ratings of effectiveness during and at the end of a training program for store managers. The magnitude of the correlations increased with more time between the assessment and criteria. The Watson–Glaser Test of Critical Thinking was consistently related to a final ranking of effectiveness in training. Scores on the American College Examination correlated positively with ratings on job performance elements one year after training but scores on the Thurstone Mental Ability Test correlated negatively for another sample. No explanation for the discrepancy is offered.

Table 5.3

Validity of Intellectual Tests in Assessment Centers

Study	Test	College OAR	College Salary progress				Noncollege OAR	Noncollege Salary progress		
Bray and Grant (1966)	SCAT—V	.36	.36,	.51,	.19,	.14	.44	.35,	.30,	− .44
	—Q	.06	.23,	− .04,	.09,	− .28	.29	.44,	.19,	− .10
	—Total	.27	.39,	.32,	.18,	− .03	.41	.45,	.28,	− .30
	Critical Thinking	.31	.26,	− .21,	− .02,	.29	.43	.46,	.36,	− .38
	Contemporary Affairs	.29	.35,	.32,	.32,	.37	.22	.26,	− .09,	− .17
Wollowick and McNamara (1969)	SCAT—Total	.11 managerial progress								
	Otis—Total	.07 managerial progress								

		OAR	Salary	Supervision potential rating
Hinrichs (1969)	SCAT—Q	.03	.03	− .13
	Concept Mastery	.10	.24	.02

		Composite	13 dimension ratings
Carleton (1970)	Miller Analysis	.37	6 scales significant
	SCAT—V	.29	7 scales significant
	—Q	.35	9 scales significant
	Watson–Glaser	.25	6 scales significant
Bentz (1971)	Watson–Glaser	.20s and .30s	Various ratings in training
	Test of Mental Ability		
	American College Examination		

		OAR	Progress
Moses (1972)	SCAT—V	.33	.21
	—Q	.28	.20
	—Total	.33	.18

		OAR White	OAR Black
Huck (1974)	SCAT—V	.40	.27
	—Q	.39	.26
	General information	.41	.42

		Progress
Mitchel (1975)	Miller Analogies	Grand average for 3 samples at different time periods = .08.
	Doppelt Math Reasoning	
	Watson–Glaser	
	Davis Reading	
	SCAT	
	Guilford–Zimmerman Aptitude	

Other research at Sears has been concerned with the role of intellectual tests in its miniassessment program (one day) for screening applicants for training programs for store managers. For one sample, Kohls (1970) found that a summary of test data was related to the final offer made to candidates, although the final-decision maker relied more on rating information from the assessors who saw the candidates in a leaderless group discussion and in two interviews. For another sample of 329 college recruits, Marquardt (1976) found that the mental ability tests predicted 16 of 26 performance measures taken at the end of a one-year training period, including ranking of overall performance. Analyses for subgroups of whites, blacks, men, and women showed that mental abilities tests related to performance for the white, male, and female groups, but not for blacks.

Other positive findings were reported by Moses (1972) and Huck (1974) using AT&T samples. Moses (1972) presented data from a study with the largest sample ($N = 5,943$) over the longest time period on record (4–11 years). The SCAT correlated significantly with both overall assessment ratings and the subsequent management level attained. Correlations are higher with the overall assessment rating.

Huck's (1974) study showed that the SCAT was equally valid for white and black females in his sample. Although the General Information Test showed a significant zero-order correlation, it did enter into the multiple regression equation when the criterion was regressed on the test battery.

Mixed results come from other studies with a predictive validity design. The criterion used by Wollowick and McNamara (1969) was the increase in managerial responsibility after the assessment procedure. It included a consideration of the number of persons supervised, job complexity, and financial and skill responsibilities. Correlations of the SCAT-total (.11) and the Otis (.07) were not significant. In a study by Hinrichs (1969), scores on the Concept Mastery Test (CMT) and the quantitative part of the SCAT were compared with external (relative salary standing), internal (assessment center staff evaluation), and parallel (managerial potential evaluation following review of normal personnel data) criteria. There was essentially no correlation between the mental ability tests and the criteria. This lack of correlation does not mean that there is no relationship between mental ability and success. Since the study is concurrent in design, conclusions are tenuous. Better information would be evidence of the predictive validity of the tests in relation to subsequent criteria of managerial success.

In Mitchel's (1975) study at SOHIO, multiple regression of the OAR on tests and assessor ratings showed that the SCAT-total was the second variable to enter the equation in all three samples. However, the average correlation of all tests with subsequent salary progress was .08.

Summary. Where data are available on the role of intellectual tests in assessment center results, the findings are mixed. Because a wide variety of tests have been used with a number of different managerial levels, it is difficult to generalize about the findings or to make firm statements about the applicability of specific tests. However, intellectual tests have been found predictive of subsequent success in some assessment center studies and the results are such to warrant the recommendation that some test of intellectual ability be included in an assessment center, particularly in selection programs for first level supervisors. Note, however, the problems of establishing the content validity of such tests which may prevent many United States organizations from using them if a criterion related validity cannot be conducted.

PERSONALITY TESTS

Personality and interest tests sometimes measure general "adjustment." More frequently, however, they measure several separate factors such as emotional stability, sociability, and dominance. A common characteristic of these tests is their attempt to tap areas of typical "will do" behavior rather than maximum "can do" performance revealed in ability tests (Cronbach, 1970).

Personality tests were included in the major selection research programs reviewed earlier. Examples of standardized tests demonstrating criterion validity include: Guilford–Zimmerman Temperament Survey, Strong Vocational Interest Blank, California Psychological Inventory, Guilford–Martin Personality Inventories, Allport–Vernon Survey of Values, Kuder Preference Record, and Thurstone Temperament Schedule.

A strong word of caution should be sounded here. In many cases, a limited number of scales from the above tests showed validity, and frequently the correlations are only marginally significant (i.e., $r = .20-.25$). In other cases, specially derived sets of items and unique scoring keys were derived.

Personality tests in assessment centers. In the Management Progress Study, Bray and Grant (1966) used two multiscale tests: The Edwards Personal Preference Schedule (EPPS) and the Guilford–Martin Inventory of Factors (GAMIN). As shown in Table 5.4, only two EPPS scales and one or the five GAMIN scales correlated with the final assessment rating. The results against the progress criterion were mixed for the seven separate groups studied. Greatest success was found in one group in which five scales of the EPPS were significant.

For Hinrichs (1969) the Allport–Vernon–Lindzey Study of Values did not correlate with the concurrent criteria. To a small extent, the Gordon

Personal Preference Schedule did correlate with the internal criterion, and two scales of the same test also predicted the long-range criterion in the Wollowick and McNamara (1969) study.

Over a period of several years, Merrill Lynch Pierce Fenner & Smith administered the California Psychological Inventory to account executives being considered for branch manager positions. No scales on the inventory correlated with dimensions or the overall assessment center rating (Schwartz, 1980).

Carleton (1970) reported the predictive correlations of personality tests against an overall composite criterion and managerial ratings on 13 scales reflecting important managerial characteristics. The Gordon Survey of Interpersonal Values and the Welsh Figure Preference both showed correlation with the overall criterion, but less ability to predict the performance rating scales, even those scales supposedly reflecting noncognitive behaviors.

Studies of the Sears executive assessment centers (Bentz, 1971) show that its Factored Personality Scales has only low and inconsistent correlations with a variety of criteria internal to the program and such variables as supervisor's potential rating, job mobility, and salary progress.

Personality tests appear to be influential in the Sears mini-assessment program for college recruits. A summary of test scores correlated with the final offer made by the decision maker (Kohls, 1970), and Marquardt (1976) found that personality variables predicted (but at a low level) virtually all performance criteria taken at the end of a 1-year training program.

Summary. Personality tests have met with moderate to slight success in assessment centers. This reflects the general lack of success with these tests in other management research. Job analyses certainly show that affective and interpersonal characteristics are important for a manager's job and one would think that personality tests should prove useful in assessment. Their failure probably reflects on the measurement techniques, not the importance of the constructs. Personality tests were used more frequently in early centers but, because of their moderate success and potential invasion of privacy, have fallen into disuse in operational programs. Many of the personality characteristics are probably manifested in behavior in the work sample exercises found in assessment centers.

PROJECTIVE TESTS

Projective techniques can be distinguished from other tests by several characteristics. Ambiguous stimulus materials are used as test items (e.g.,

Table 5.4
Validity of Personality Tests in Assessment Centers

Study	Test	Criterion/validity			
		College		Noncollege	
		OAR two scales	Progress in four groups	OAR two scales	Progress in three groups
Bray and Grant (1966)	EPPS 13 scales	two scales	no more than five scales significant	two scales	no more than three scales significant
	GAMIN 5 scales	one scale	one scale significant	one scale	n.s.
	Attitudes toward Life	n.s.	significant for 1 group	n.s.	n.s.
		OAR	Salary	Potential rating	
Hinrichs (1969)	Study of Values 6 scales	n.s.	n.s.	n.s. except Political (.33)	
	Gordon Personal Preference				
	Ascendency	.43	.10	.29	
	Responsibility	−.19	.08	−.26	
	Emotional stability	−.32	−.06	−.37	

		level
(truncated) McNamara (1969)	Gordon Personal Preference	
	Ascendency	.39
	Sociability	.23
	Gordon Personal Inventory	
	Vigor	.32
Carleton (1970)	Gordon Survey of Interpersonal Values	*Global, composite criterion*
		Ratings on 13 scales
	Conformity	one scale significant
	Leadership	n.s.
	Benevolence	one scale significant
	Welsh Figure Preference	
	Art	.43
	Conformity	– .72
Bentz (1971)	Executive Battery	*Ratings in training; salary*
	Several tests in the Factored Personality Battery	r's in 20s and 30s
Schwartz (1980)	California Psychological Inventory	No correlation with dimension ratings or overall assessment ratings

n.s. = not significant.

161

a picture, an incomplete sentence, or inkblots). The task presented to the person is fairly unstructured (e.g., the examinee is given only very general directions about how to respond and is allowed a wide variety of possible responses). There are no right or wrong answers. Since the tests are usually designed to measure the underlying personality structure and the dynamics that explain why a person behaves in a certain way, the purpose of the testing is often disguised from the examinee.

Because projective tests are somewhat less familiar to most persons than other tests, we will now describe a few that have been used in managerial assessment. The Rorschach Ink Blots are a set of black and white figures (some with colors) that appear similar to a large pool of spilled ink. The assessee is asked what he or she sees in the ink blot and to explain where and why he or she sees it. Another projective device, the Thematic Apperception Test (TAT), includes a set of realistic pictures usually involving one or two persons about to engage in some activity. The subject is asked to explain what is going on, what is the background, and what will happen next. In the Incomplete Sentence Test, the subject is asked to finish a list of incomplete sentences (e.g., "I am . . .," "What I enjoy most . . .," "Men . . .").

Investigators using projective techniques in personnel psychology are often attempting to study the following major questions:

> Whether the test can identify a general personality pattern within a given occupation; whether such a pattern is similar to, or different from, patterns found in other occupations; and whether successful workers can be differentiated from unsuccessful workers on the basis of specific personality characteristics revealed in test performance [Kinslinger, 1966, p. 135].

Kinslinger reviews the literature on the success that has been reported in studying these questions using the following tests: Rorschach, Thematic Apperception Test, Worthington Personal History, Tomkins, Horn Picture Arrangement, and others. Kinslinger found virtually no empirical evidence of the relationship of projectives and criteria such as job success measures, measures of promotion potential, and job satisfaction and adjustment. "Furthermore, many of the studies that have indicated positive findings are of little practical value because of methodological shortcomings such as inadequate criteria or lack of adequate validation, particularly cross-validation [p. 147]." He concludes that the use of projective techniques in practical personnel settings is not warranted.

It may be because of such data that there is a decline in the use of projective techniques in the diagnostic battery of academic clinical psychologists (Thelan, Varble, & Johnson, 1968).

Since the time of Kinslinger's review there have been few other attempts to relate projective techniques to managerial success. Cummins

(1967) reported a successful attempt to differentiate successful managers as evidenced by their being above or below the median salary for their age group. When responses to four TAT pictures were compared for the two criterion groups, it was found that the successful group scored higher on two motives (need for achievement and need for power) but there were no differences on four other motives (affiliation, autonomy, aggression, and deference). There was no cross-validation of the results, and the study was not predictive in design. These and other problems led Cummin to warn against the practical use of the TAT in managerial selection.

The major exception to these negative findings has been the work of McClelland and Boyatzia (1980). They have found long-term relationships between motives derived from projective instruments and management success.

Projectives in assessment centers. In contrast with the general negative results reported by Kinslinger and others, projective techniques have proven useful in one experimental and one on-going assessment center. We hasten to emphasize that projective tests should be used only by professionals who are trained specifically in their use. Since projectives are usually time-consuming to administer, score, and interpret, their use is probably warranted in only a few special cases.

Grant, Katkovsky, and Bray (1967) reported that projective techniques administered as part of the Management Progress Study influence predictions of the assessment center staff and were predictive of a subsequent criterion of salary progress. After reviewing the results of three projective techniques, clinical psychologists rated the managers on nine rating scales for variables such as optimism–pessimism, general adjustment, self-confidence, and leadership. These ratings were found to correlate with various components of the assessment center staff evaluations and the overall staff prediction. The variables measuring leadership and motivation proved more valuable than those measuring adjustment and other personality factors.

Grant *et al.* (1967) concluded that the projective techniques made a significant contribution to the assessment process, but carefully warned against the over-generalization of these results:

> The conditions under which these encouraging results were obtained should be noted. The projective report is a summary report based on three different instruments. This report is in no way a scoring of the projective protocols but is impressionistic in nature. Neither is the report deeply "clinical"; every effort was made to orient it to the motivations relevant to business management. Finally, because four-fifths of the reports were written by one psychologist a question could be raised regarding the replicability of the findings [p. 232].

Further research has recently been conducted on the relationship of TAT protocols for the managers in the Management Progress Study in relation to subsequent management success. Preliminary results suggest that evidence of need for achievement and power evidenced in the protocols is predictive of long-range progress (Bray, 1981).

Finley (1970) reported a study in which 13 psychological predictions based on information from two projective techniques were compared both with the predictive ratings from the entire assessment center staff (after considering all sources of information) and with supervisors' ratings gathered several years later. The projectives did not correlate with supervisors' ratings in as many cases as they did with the assessors' ratings.

Several comments are warranted with regard to this study. It should be recognized that there was contamination of both the assessor ratings and the supervisory ratings by prior knowledge of the projective information; supervisor ratings were further contaminated by knowledge of the assessor ratings at the end of the assessment program. Finally, there was no cross-validation of the results, although replication was present in the form of separate analyses for two different groups of managers.

Other projectives. A variety of other projective techniques have been used occasionally in assessment centers. These include incomplete sentences, Rorschachs, and the Thematic Apperception Test. These are quite infrequent and do not fit with the behavioral orientation of most assessment centers.

Summary. There is not enough research to allow firm conclusions about projective techniques in assessment centers. Considering the lack of success in other management research, high cost, lack of face validity, and the necessity to have projectives administered and scored by professional psychologists, it is unlikely that projective techniques are appropriate for many assessment center programs.

INTERVIEW

The interview may be either a formal or informal discussion between two persons. The level of formality is determined by the amount of structure and planning introduced. In most cases the interviewer has reviewed background information provided by the candidate in a life history form. The interview usually covers education, previous work experience, and other biographical information. In addition, the interviewer may explore preferences for certain activities, hobbies, aspects of job satisfaction and dissatisfaction, career aspirations, and other future goals.

The history of research on interviewing can be divided into two periods. The first, beginning with personnel selection studies in the early 1900s and extending to around 1960, dealt with an evaluation of the overall utility and psychometric properties of the selection interview. The second period began with pivotal studies by Webster around 1960 that focused on the *process* of interviewing. Recently, a resurgence of interest in the selection interview has occurred, and major efforts have been undertaken to untangle the many factors detracting from and contributing to the validity of the interviewing process.

Research in the earlier period was reviewed by Mayfield (1964), Ulrich and Trumbo (1965), and Wright (1969). The findings of these reviews were rather discouraging. It was commonly said that the interview was the most widely used yet the least reliable and valid personnel selection technique. Some of the specific findings are listed below:

1. *Reliability*

   Interrater reliability is low, especially with unstructured interviews.

   Conversely, intrarater reliability of a patterned interview is high; interviewers have a consistent approach and this approach can be modified by training.

2. *Validity*

   Even with high reliability, predictive validity from interviews is low.

   Interviews make little or no contribution to the prediction of job performance over tests.

   The characteristics of intelligence, personal relations skills, and motivation can be evaluated fairly accurately.

   Multiple interviewers can increase validity.

3. *Structure of interview*

   With an unstructured interview, material is covered inconsistently by different interviewers.

   Structured interviews lead to increased interrater reliability.

4. *Use and interpretation of information*

   Even with the same information, interviewers weigh the information differently.

   A decision to hire or not hire is made early in the interview.

   Unfavorable information is more important than favorable.

   Attitudes of the interviewer influence evaluation of information.

   The quality of previous interviewees is important.

The early research on selection interviewing pointed out the fallacies and limitations of the interview as a predictive device, but with few exceptions it did not clarify the processes that led to its ineffectiveness.

Subsequent research has investigated the interviewing process and analyzed the reasons for low reliability and validity.

Recent research on the interviewing process has been extensive and intensive and it would be impossible here to adequately review it all. However, three programs of interviewing research should be mentioned: Mayfield and Carlson at the Life Insurance Agency Management Association (Carlson, 1967a; 1967b, 1968, 1969, 1970, 1971; Carlson & Mayfield, 1967; Mayfield & Carlson, 1966), Hakel and Dunnette at Minnesota and later Hakel at Ohio State (Hakel, 1971; Hakel, Dobmeyer, & Dunnette, 1970; Hakel, Hollman, & Dunnette, 1970; London & Hakel, 1974; Washburn & Hakel, 1973), and Yukl and Wexley at University of Akron (Wexley, Sanders, & Yukl, 1973; Wexley, Yukl, Kovacs, & Sanders, 1972). Other valuable studies have been conducted more recently by Landy (1976), and Landy and Bates (1973).

A portion of this research, summarized below, points out the problems with the traditional selection interview and the need for new forms of interviewing procedures.

1. *Interviewer characteristics*

   Interviewers hold stereotypes of the ideal applicant in relation to general and specific jobs.

   Interviewers have different perceptions of interests of job incumbents.

   Applicant attitudes closest to the interviewer's "ideal" affects the salary offer to the applicant, but not the decision to hire.

2. *Reliability*

   Most disagreements among interviewers are due to unstandardized information rather than to unreliability.

   Given standardized information, reliability can be high.

   Interrater agreement increases under pressure of quotas (e.g., to hire the top 10%).

   Experience doesn't increase reliability but may decrease order effects.

3. *Information available*

   Information that is highly valid, favorable, and reliable influences the hiring decision. In other words, relevant information is used.

   Factual data are more important than appearance data, but the presence of a favorable photograph may be enough information for an interviewer to make a final decision. Interactions exist among type, form, and amount of information.

4. *Form of rating*

   Higher reliability is obtained for hire–no hire decisions than for ratings and rankings.

Scaled rating forms do not eliminate halo in ratings.

Absolute standards for judgment do not reduce order effects.

5. *Context variables*

Quotas affect number of offers.

Order effects play a minor role (1 %–4 % of decision variance) for above and below average applicants and a major role (80 %) for average applicants. Order effects may be less for experienced interviewers.

Order effects can be reduced only by elaborate workshop training sessions (simple warnings and absolute standards for ratings are inadequate).

Research in these areas has led to improvements in the interview process and in the quality of interviewer training. The personnel interview continues to be universally used in personnel selection, including management assessment. Recently, emphasis has been placed on applying many of the principles from the assessment center approach to the interviewing process and on focusing the interview on only those dimensions that can be most effectively measured (Dapra & Byham, 1978). The interview can make a valid contribution to managerial assessment if it is properly embedded in a total system of management evaluation.

Interviewing in an assessment center. As discussed in the previous chapter, the background interview is often an important element in a selection or promotion system. It provides information on a subset of dimensions which is very hard to obtain in any other way. This is combined with other information from other sources such as an assessment center and performance appraisal data in order to make a final decision. However, in some assessment centers, the background interview is an integral part of the assessment center. In that case, the assessors develop a report similar to a report from observations of an assessment center exercise and present that report in the same manner as an exercise report. It consists of a list of dimensions with examples of behavior that support a rating on each of the dimensions. The only difference is that the data come from self-report or background information as opposed to direct observation as in assessment center exercises.

Whether the background interview is conducted separately from the assessment center or as part of the assessment center, the interview typically differs from the traditional selection interview. The selection interviewer usually carries out several functions: He or she gathers information, evaluates the significance of that information and integrates it with other data, and decides to hire or not to hire an applicant. In addition, the interviewer usually provides information to the candidate and "sells" the organization. In contrast, an assessment interview functions primarily as an information-gathering technique. It is a controlled observational situation generating relevant behavioral information from the participant's past. The assessor records both positive and negative behavioral observations and categorizes the behavior by the target dimensions, then rates the designated dimensions using the same scale used in the other parts of the assessment center. Evaluation is present, but the assessor concentrates primarily on data gathering.

The process of a targeted behavioral interview tends to overcome many of the problems detected in research on the interview. Each interview is planned and structured around the dimensions to be assessed. Questions are prepared to pursue behavioral evidence in each individual's past work history that will allow the interviewer to rate selected dimensions. Factual data rather than hypothetical situations are discussed. The same dimensions are covered by all interviewers and form a consistent definition of job requirements. Interviewers are asked not to make summary judgments of overall suitability, but to gather as much information as possible relative to the dimensions. The interviewer usually has more time (1–1.5 hours) and fewer dimensions to evaluate than the typical selection interviewer. The interviewer is not placed under any quotas nor asked to make any comparative judgments among interviewees.

Reliability and validity in assessment centers. The interviewing technique described above can be proven valid using a content validity paradigm. The interview is focused on dimensions established through a job analysis as being job related. The interviewers are trained to seek behavior in the applicant's past similar to behavior established in the job analysis as related to success or failure. Procedural controls are placed on the introduction of nonrelated, nonbehavioral data. The possibility of establishing the content validity of the interview and the possibility of reporting the interview data in the manner directly comparable with data obtained from other assessment center exercises (same dimensions, same ratings scale, same requirement for behavioral support of all ratings) have led to the adoption of this behavioral approach by many organizations using interviews as part of a formalized selection or promotion procedure. Less structured interviews are more common in selection systems which are not formally designed or articulated and have not been built around a set of job-related dimensions.

In spite of its popularity, there is little research into the direct reliability or validity of the technique although research is currently under way. One study that involved the examination of the interview as part of an assessment center procedure was conducted as part of the Management

Progress Study and the procedure has never been replicated. In that study Grant and Bray (1969) found that the interview can make a positive contribution to the assessment and managerial potential (see Table 5.5). Since this study is both controversial and relevant, it warrants detailed description. Assessment interviews were structured around the dimensions and conducted by psychologists as a part of the Management Progress Study at AT&T (Bray, 1964a). Interviewer reports were coded by judges and rated on 18 variables, including such things as Personal Impact, Oral Communication Skills, and Behavior Flexibility. Intercoder reliabilities were generally in the .80s, with only 6 of 36 correlations (18 variables for 2 samples) below .70. Correlations of interview variables with several composite assessment variables based on all assessment techniques showed that the interview made a substantial contribution. The most important interview variables seemed to be Personal Impact–Forcefulness, Oral Communication Skills, Energy, and Needs Advancement. Correlations of interview variables with staff predictions of participant advancement to middle management within 10 years revealed 22 of 36 significant relationships. Finally, 18 of 36 correlations between interview variables and a subsequent criterion of salary progress were significant. The authors clearly acknowledge that these analyses do not show the relative effectiveness of the interview in comparison with other assessment techniques. The study does establish that the interview (in this case, unstructured and carried out by trained professionals) makes a reliable and valid contribution to the assessment of managerial potential.

In a design more closely matching the typical assessment center situation, Slivinski, McCloskey, and Bourgeois (1979) correlated dimension ratings from assessors who had conducted interviews and reviewed

Table 5.5
Validity of Interview in Assessment Centers

Study	Internal validity	External validity
	OAR	*Salary progress*
Grant and Bray (1969)	College: 14 of 18 variables significant	9 of 18 variables significant
	Noncollege: 8 of 18 variables significant	9 of 18 variables significant
Slivinski *et al.* (1979)		*Increase in level*
		6 of 11 variables significant

background information with a criterion of position level increase over 2.5 years. Six of eleven dimensions (including Creativity, Independence, and Oral Communication) were significantly correlated with progress and the interview contributed unique prediction over assessment center ratings. The design allows a direct comparison between the two methods because the interviewers had no assessment information and the assessors had no knowledge of the assessees' personal backgrounds and conducted no interviews with the assessees. The study is not completely appropriate to assessment center interviews because the dimension ratings were derived from interviews by 10-member panels.

Studies by Bray (1973) and Neidig, Hall, and Baker (1978) show that variables such as Work Motivation, Work Standards, and Career Orientation are measured most effectively by the background interview.

Summary. Interviews are currently used in a small portion of assessment center programs. The decline in use is due in part to the different nature of information coming from an interview. Whereas most assessment center exercises provide directly observed behavioral information, the interview provides descriptions of past behavior. When a background interview is used, the information is integrated with dimension discussions along with exercise observations. When an interview is not used in the assessment center program, a separate interview is usually conducted by managers in the hiring department. Subsequently, input from the assessment center, interview, performance appraisal, and other sources are integrated into a final recommendation to hire or promote.

LEADERLESS GROUP DISCUSSION

A leaderless group discussion (LGD) consists of a group of four to eight participants (usually six) who are given a problem to solve and are instructed to arrive at a group decision within a specified period of time. No one is designated the chairperson, but various roles of equal status may be assigned. The problem, usually provided in written form, often requires a written solution signed or endorsed by all participants. The content, number of specific subproblems, and the complexity vary depending on the composition of the group. The problem may involve a relatively simple disciplinary case, or it may be a highly abstracted and value-laden problem regarding corporate social responsibility in such areas as environmental protection or equal employment opportunity. The task may be cooperative or competitive. Competition is often heightened by assigning roles and instructing participants to distribute limited resources. For example, a participant may be asked to obtain a raise for his or her subordinate or to obtain a large share of a budget for his or her department. Observers rate performance on a number of dimensions related to effectiveness in group problem-solving situations and sometimes to the subject matter being discussed.

The LGD simulates certain aspects of a number of situations managers face daily on their jobs. The LGD with no roles assigned is similar to ad hoc committees formed to study company problems, devise a new safety procedure, plan a special program for visitors, implement a new regulation, or generate ideas for new marketing strategies. Assigned-role LGDs contain many of the ingredients of decision-making meetings in which limited resources must be divided equitably. Examples of such discussions are the allocation of budgets to departments, the decision of who will use limited office space, and where temporary or overtime help will be assigned.

Ansbacher (1951) provided a detailed account of the first uses of the LGD technique in German military assessment. He credits the origination of the technique to J. B. Rieffert, director of German military psychology from 1920 to 1931. According to this account, a round-table discussion procedure was used, beginning in 1925, to aid in the selection of officer candidates. The LGD was used in conjunction with three other procedures to obtain samples of problem-solving behavior. Often conducted over the dinner table, it was used to observe behaviors toward peers. Separate branches of the military developed different versions of the technique to suit their own needs. In the army program, the discussion first centered around an evaluation of the assessment procedures, then was shifted to officer qualifications or the importance of a strong army. The assessor played a role in these discussions. The army abandoned the technique in the late 1930s, but it was continued in a modified form by the navy until the end of World War II. Navy psychologists introduced more controversial topics into the discussions in order to observe social skills such as striving for objectivity, conciliation, and compromise. The technique was also used in civilian settings in wartime Germany, and in the succeeding years it was used in nationwide talent searches for manpower in trade, commercial, educational, and artistic occupations (Ansbacher, 1946, 1951).

The leaderless group performance and discussion exercise played an integral role in other early assessment programs. Beginning with the British WOSB and continuing through the American OSS and VA clinical studies, the LGD became a centrally important evaluation tool. Bass (1950, 1954) provided many details of the use of the technique in other locations and organizations including British industry, Australian military and industry, and several U.S. federal and state civil service agencies and private industries after the war. Reliabilities were in the .70s, .80s, and .90s and predictive validities in the .40s and .50s.

Based on a review of research to 1954, Bass offered several hypotheses regarding the LGD technique which have, in the main, been borne out in subsequent studies:

1. The LGD can be used as a technique to observe or evaluate the immediate behavior of participants.
2. Validity is enhanced when real-life problems are presented. One or a small number of LGDs adequately predicts leadership potential.
3. Compared to tests, the LGD is expensive; compared to interviews, it is economical.
4. The LGD provides a technique for assessing general leadership skill, but tailor-made tests may yield higher validities for specific cases.
5. The LGD may not be successful when participants differ widely in rank or experience, or where participation is falsely restricted, verbal skills are too low, or abilities are very homogeneous.
6. Validity will be low when the LGD task is irrelevant.

LGD performance has been correlated with test scores, peer ratings, and ratings of other personality and behavioral variables. From these studies several hypotheses have been advanced regarding the personal characteristics being measured by the LGD:

> Ratings based on LGD performance appear to assess the extent to which an individual initiates structure or is socially bold in ambiguous situations. Esteem, or personal worth, and verbal ability are also involved. On the basis of these studies it may be inferred that there exist three independent sources of variance underlying leaderless group discussion performance: I. Tendency to Initiate Structure, II. Tendency to Be Esteemed or of Value to a Group, III. Ability in Verbal Situations [Bass, 1954, p. 486–487].

According to Cronbach (1970) the LGD measures prominence, group goal facilitation, and sociability.

LGD in assessment centers. A summary of reliability and validity evidence from assessment center research is presented in Table 5.6. For both the college and noncollege groups in the Management Progress Study, Bray and Grant (1966) found that judgments of overall effectiveness in an assigned role (competitive) LGD yielded higher reliabilities and more consistently significant relationships with the OAR and salary progress than the manufacturing game. Interrater agreement for two observers was .75 for both ratings and rankings. Agreement between

Table 5.6
Reliability and Validity of the Leaderless Group Discussion in Assessment Centers

Study	Reliability (type)	Validity/criterion
Bray and Grant (1969)	.75 [c](interrater—ratings)	.60 overall assessment ratings .30, .50, .26, .38 Salary progress in 4 groups
Greenwood and McNamara (1969)	Promotion exercise .66 (interrater—rating) .64 (interrater—ranking) Task force exercise .70 (interrater—rating) .71 (interrater—ranking)	
Wollowick and McNamara (1969)		.25—Promotion, .15—Task force increase in management skills
Bentz (1971) [b]		Mdn = .26 ratings on performance elements Mdn = .42 ratings on performance factors Mdn = .37 global rating
Hinrichs and Haanpera (1974, 1976)	$\overline{X}$ = .41 (internal consistency) [a]	
Grossner (1974)		Mdn r = .46 ratings on eight behavioral criteria
Huck (1974)		.66, .67 OAR, whites and blacks
American Airlines (1976)		.66 OAR, Mdn = .53 25 dimension ratings
Clingenpeel (1979)	.72 (interrater) .69 (interrater)	

[a] Average correlation of the rating of 11 dimensions within the exercise versus the total score for the dimension across all exercises after partialing out the contribution of this exercise from the total.

[b] Bentz (1971) presents detailed data on relationships of numerous group problem solving tasks and rating scales in relation to numerous criterion ratings; the average validities reported here are meant only to be representative.

[c] Reliabilities estimates for all subjects.

observer and peer was somewhat lower (.73 and .69 for ratings and rankings) and between observers and self (.55 and .50) and between peer and self (.51 and .45) even lower. LGD ratings correlated significantly with the final assessment prediction regarding the probability of progressing to middle management in 10 years. For the college sample, the LGD contributed most to the OAR and to four of nine factors among the assessed dimensions dealing with general effectiveness, interpersonal skills, control of feelings, and motivation. For two of four college samples and one noncollege sample the LGD correlated with a criterion of subsequent salary progress 5–8 years after assessment. Other analyses of these data (Bray, 1973) show that the group exercises are most influential in determining assessments of interpersonal skills. Other evidence of key dimensions in the LGD come from Neidig, Martin, and Yates (1978) who found that final skill ratings on Flexibility were determined by the nonassigned role LGD and that ratings of Tenacity, Initiative, and Independence were determined by the assigned role LGD.

Greenwood and McNamara (1967) evaluated the interrater agreement among professional and nonprofessional assessors for programs in six divisions of a large company. After observing participants in an exercise, the assessors rated and ranked the six group members on overall effectiveness in the exercise. Two variations of the LGD were evaluated. The first, more well defined and structured, required the participants to discuss their own candidates for promotions and try to arrive at a fair decision (a competitive situation). The second was less structured: In it the assessees evaluated data and made a recommendation to the president regarding three alternate courses of action (a noncompetitive situation). The results in Table 5.6 suggest that ratings of both exercises are adequately reliable. There were no significant variations in reliability across divisions. Furthermore, there were no consistent differences in mean ratings or reliability estimates for the professional and nonprofessional assessors. Some comparisons between the two groups showed low agreement (e.g., $r = .21$) but, on the whole, the cross-group comparisons were equivalent to the same-group comparisons.

Wollowick and McNamara (1969) found a significant correlation ($r = .25$) of LGD ratings with a criterion of increase in management responsibility three years after assessment, but the manufacturing game and in-basket exercises correlated more highly with this criterion. The LGD did not contribute unique variance when the three exercises were combined in a multiple regression equation.

In 1971 Bentz summarized years of research on the various components of the Sears assessment procedures. He reported correlations of exercise and dimensions ratings with follow-up criteria for several groups of management trainees, middle managers, and executives. This thorough and detailed research established the unique contribution of the LGD, in-basket, and test battery to the prediction of success in management training and job performance. Table 5.6 presents some representative correlations of LGD ratings at time of assessment with a sample of job performance ratings.

Other evidence that the LGD contributes to overall assessment judgments comes from Huck (1974), who found equal contribution to staff predictions for black and white female assessees, and American Airlines (1976) who found that the LGD contributed to 25 dimension ratings. Grossner (1974) found that LGD ratings correlated significantly with eight behavioral ratings by job supervisors.

In a study involving 369 premanagement candidates from eight countries, Hinrichs and Haanpera (1974, 1976) evaluated the internal consistency, reliability, and construct validity of assessment ratings on 14 dimensions observed in six exercises including an assigned role LGD. A special type of internal consistency was measured by finding the average correlation (across eight countries) of a dimension rating from a *single* exercise with the *total dimension score,* after partialing out the effect of that exercise on the total. In other words, these correlations were estimates of the overlap of information about a dimension provided by one exercise with the information about that dimension provided by all other exercises. (Reliability of dimension ratings and construct validity are described later.) For the LGD, an average internal consistency correlation across 14 dimensions was .41. This was the highest average for the six exercises. In summary, dimension ratings from the LGD overlapped with ratings on the same dimension more than did the ratings from other exercises. In a similar vein, Neidig *et al.* (1978) found that the LGD showed only a moderate level of convergent validity when compared to other exercises in the FBI assessment program. The median correlation of dimension ratings from multiple sources was .27.

Changes in the acceptability of LGD. Until 1978, the leaderless group discussion was the single, most popular exercise in assessment centers. The authors did not know of a single assessment center that did not use an assigned-role group discussion. Since 1978, a number of criticisms have been leveled at assigned group exercises, particularly as they relate to equal employment opportunity issues.

The first criticism deals with the lack of representation of the situation in terms of the job activities of individuals in the target job. Many job analyses of lower level positions have found that incumbents are never in a competitive group situation. Further, supervisors may seldom be in meetings of any kind. In the few meetings they do attend, they are often the assigned leader and do not have to wrest this responsibility from others. Thus, the use of the assigned-role group exercise as a method of evaluating leadership can be questioned. What seems to be evaluated is emergent leadership or leadership coupled with initiative rather than the ability to use the leadership that comes with a position. Responding to these criticisms some organizations have eliminated assigned-role group exercises and others have reoriented the assessor's observation task from observation of control of group process to observation of individual interactions within the group context.

A second criticism that has been leveled against the assigned-role group exercise is the possible lack of uniformity of the group to which an individual happens to be assigned. (This criticism may also be relevant to nonassigned-role group exercises and management games.) Any assessor will attest that groups vary. Some groups are highly combative; some groups are very cooperative. The leadership tasks required in these two situations vary. In general, assessors believe that dimension ratings will not be greatly affected by the make-up of a group, but there is no question that leadership and sensitivity can be exhibited more easily in some groups than in others. Thus, the criticism has been raised that the uncontrolled nature of the exercise permits more variation in the evaluation process than would be desired or is found in other assessment center exercises. We know of no assessment center research studies which have established the effects of this variation on dimension ratings or overall assessment ratings of promotability.

Summary. It appears that the overall effectiveness of a LGD can be reliably evaluated and this exercise contributes substantially to the final assessment rating. Furthermore, in four studies it has been found that LGD ratings predict subsequent progress or performance on the job. The majority of LGDs used in this research were assigned-role exercises that call for both cooperative and competitive behaviors. The results may not hold for nonassigned-role formats and, in fact, the Task Force discussion reported by Wollowick and McNamara (1969) did not correlate with a criterion of salary progress. Three potential problems with the LGD should be noted. First, LGD ratings may be influenced by forcefulness and verbal fluency rather than real leadership. Such contamination can be minimized by adequate assessor training. Second, a number of uncontrolled variables (e.g., the activity level, emergence of other strong leaders, and hasty resolution of the problems) may affect performance of some group members. Third, the LGD may not be representative of job activities of many first-level supervisory positions. Nevertheless, the research evidence strongly supports the inclusion of a LGD in middle and top-management programs.

MANAGEMENT GAMES AND LEADERLESS GROUP TASKS

In this set of exercises, a group of individuals is assigned a problem and must work together cooperatively to solve it. The exercise usually involves some physical activity such as buying and selling supplies, assembling some apparatus, or moving materials from one location to another. A competitive element is often introduced in which three, four-person groups try to maximize sales or obtain larger shares of a market. The distinction between games (or leaderless group tasks) and leaderless group discussions is not always clear but games usually involve physical as well as verbal behavior, some organization of effort and division of labor among the team members, the requirement of team work, a sequence of interactions with a dynamic environment, and more complex decision-making processes.

Games or tasks were an important part of early assessment programs. The Brook exercise in the OSS program, the group leaderless exercises of the British WOSB, and the block test in the VA clinical psychologist studies have been described in Chapter 2.

Further evidence of the versatility of these exercises is demonstrated by a series of studies in the selection of supervisors from among groups of native African mine workers (Biesheuvel, 1952). The first-level foreman, called "boss boy" in mine parlance, was a working supervisor very similar to the "straw boss" in the United States. The boss boy served as an intermediary between the European miner and the native mineworker. Mineworkers were recruited from many different areas in Africa and spent up to 18 months at the mines before returning to their native tribes. Most workers were unskilled and inexperienced at first but became more skilled as they returned for a second or third tour of duty (Jacobs, 1957). A diversity of backgrounds and languages was represented and communication was difficult—relying on a composite lingua franca which evolved in the mines.

The recruits were tested and classified into various manual labor jobs or into supervisory positions. All tests were performance tests administered with a minimum of verbal responses. The instructions were given by mime and by silent film. For supervisory selection, a series of leaderless group tasks were presented to groups of six men. The group was told what was required but not how to do it. For example, in one task the six participants were asked to move several pieces of equipment over an 8 ft. wall. In another task the group moved across a 30 ft. distance using several stepping stones and a plank (Hudson & Kruger, 1958).

Several observers were trained to note characteristics of the participants, such as dominance, assertiveness, cooperativeness, and rate them on a three-point scale: superior, average, or inferior. The observations and ratings of leadership behavior were found to be related to success in supervisory training and performance ratings on the job. When recruits were randomly chosen as supervisors, 27–30% were considered unsuitable for the job; when the group tasks were used as a basis for selection, less than 2% were considered unsuccessful. The leadership ratings were significantly related to performance ratings on the job ($r = .43$) and added to the ability to predict success over and above the information from other performance tests used for prediction for manual jobs (Sichel, 1951). In one study (Hudson & Kruger, 1958) it was found that only 2% of a group failed to complete supervisory training among those who were identified as potentially successful by the group tasks, whereas 10% of the test-selected group were unsuccessful.

This application illustrates that leaderless group tasks are appropriate for situations where a wide diversity of background, education, and language skill are present. The tasks provided valuable information regarding people with very little education and no familiarity with tests and other selection procedures.

Games in assessment centers. Because such a wide variety of games is in use, it is difficult to generalize about their makeup. Two games which contain some common features of many others are briefly described:

1. *Conglomerate:* Teams of participants trade shares of company stock in order to gain control of companies and then to merge the companies into conglomerates. To win, a company must plan and organize its activities during three fast-paced trading sessions. Behavior flexibility, interpersonal sensitivity, operation under stress, and leadership are some of the evaluations made by assessors.
2. *The keyboard problem:* Teams of six participants play the role of the board of directors of a small business concern. They buy and sell keys for keyboard consoles used in computer products. Given a selection of keys differing in profit margin, each team must decide how to invest money, organize purchasing, control stock, and sell the product. Assessors watch for indications of emergent leadership, organizational ability, financial acumen, quickness of thinking, and operation under stress. Adaptability is observed when bo-

nus options occur throughout the problem, calling for the drastic redeployment of resources.

Table 5.7 presents evidence of the reliability and validity of games reported in the assessment center literature. Interjudge agreement for ratings in the AT&T manufacturing game were somewhat lower than the LGD ratings. This held for the interassessor comparisons reported in Table 5.7 and for comparisons between assessors and peers (.64 and .59 for ratings and rankings), assessors and self-ratings (.47, .43) and peers and self-ratings (.45 and .38). Ratings from the game correlated significantly with the OAR, but to a lesser extent than the LGD ratings for the college sample. For the noncollege sample the game was the predominant correlate of four factors of assessed dimensions dealing with general effectiveness, interpersonal skills, motivation, and passivity (negative relationship). The significance of this exercise for noncollege graduates is further affirmed from the significant correlations with salary progress. By

Table 5.7
Reliability and Validity of Management Games and Leaderless Group Tasks in Assessment Centers

Study	Reliability (type)	Validity/criterion
		College samples
Bray and Grant (1966)	.60[a] (interrater—ratings) .69 (interrater—rankings)	.41 OAR .51, .41, .14, − .01 Salary progress
		Noncollege samples
		.42 OAR .37, .50, .29 Salary progress
Greenwood and McNamara (1967)	.74 (interrater—rating) .75 (interrater—ranking)	
Wollowick and McNamara (1969)		.28 Change in level
Hinrichs and Haanpera (1974, 1976)	$\overline{X}$ = .31	
Huck (1974)		.59, .64 OAR, whites and blacks
American Airlines (1976)		.55 OAR, Mdn = .38 25 dimension ratings
Grossner (1974)		Mdn r = .59 ratings on four behavioral criteria

[a] Reliability estimates for all subjects.

contrast, in only one of the college samples was the game predictive of the follow-up criterion.

The interrater reliability of ratings from the manufacturing exercise at IBM (Greenwood & McNamara, 1967) was higher than the reliabilities for the LGD. As reported earlier, no differences in reliability were observed across four different divisions of the company or between professional and nonprofessional observers. In a follow-up study of 94 managers (Wollowick & McNamara, 1969), the game ratings correlated with change in mangement level three years after assessment and made a unique contribution to the prediction of this criterion in addition to in-basket ratings.

The internal consistency analyses of Hinrichs and Haanpera (1974, 1976) revealed that dimension ratings from the manufacturing exercise did not correlate to a great extent with ratings on the same dimensions from other exercises. For example, Planning and Organizing in the game does not correlate with the same dimension observed in the in-basket. For some dimensions the degree of overlap with other exercises is much greater than the average ($r = .31$) shown in Table 5.7. These results suggest that the behaviors relevant to any given dimension revealed by the game are quite different from the behaviors relevant to that same dimension as seen in other exercises. Similar results were found by Neidig et al. (1978). Other evidence that the game contributes to overall assessment judgments comes from Huck (1974), who found equal contribution to the staff predictions for black and white female assessees, and American Airlines (1976) who found that the game impacted on 25 dimension ratings. Grossner (1974) found that game ratings correlated significantly with four behavioral ratings by job supervisors.

Summary. From the limited assessment center data reported, it can be concluded that overall effectiveness in games can be reliably rated. Final assessor judgments seem to be influenced by performance in this exercise and this appears consistent with validity in relation to subsequent job progress. Obviously, more such research data are needed, especially since such a variety of games are used. Games may suffer from the problems mentioned for leaderless group discussions and they are often very difficult to observe because participants usually move around the room to accomplish their tasks. If an assessor is assigned to watch more than one participant, the problem becomes compounded as one assigned assessee may be on one side of the room and the other assigned assessee on another. Games often consume much more time than other assessment center exercises, such as LGDs, that also measure leadership. Most games take more than one hour to complete; some of the higher level games take 2.5 or more hours.

In setting up an assessment center, one is often faced with choosing between a cooperative LGD and a cooperative game. Both have advantages as reviewed above. Usually the choice centers on the nature of the leadership to be observed. Games provide the opportunity for assessees to exhibit a forceful "let's get organized and get going" style. Tasks are assigned and reassigned. Clarity and speed of communications are critical. Appeals to "rally 'round the flag" and "let's beat the other team" are used. Cooperative LGDs are much calmer interactions where respect is earned through good ideas and leadership is manifested in persuasiveness of arguments and a feeling for the dynamics of the group to know when to summarize or call for a vote.

IN–BASKET

The in-basket exercise is a partial simulation of administrative tasks of a manager's job. The exercise material consists of a sample of the wide variety of documents which might appear in the typical in-basket on a manager's desk. The participant reads letters, reports, and memoranda; decides how to deal with the material; and then writes responses, schedules meetings, or assigns tasks to other persons. Specific in-basket materials, constructed to realistically portray significant aspects of the job or job level in question, usually vary in urgency, complexity, and significance of impact on the organization. Hemphill *et al.* (1962) attempted to ensure representativeness of an in-basket they constructed by writing items that sampled four content areas (e.g., obtaining and developing personnel and maintaining effective community relations) and three skills (technical, human, and conceptual).

Realism for the assessee is heightened by using different styles and sizes of paper, including typed and handwritten material, and by making a series of comments on a letter as though it were passed among other managers. Some items usually are interrelated to add complexity as well as realism.

Elaborate instructions are given to the participant to prepare for the in-basket. The scene is set so that the participant is working alone (say on Sunday or in the evening) and thus must write all letters and instructions to others instead of using the telephone. Time pressure is created by giving the participant only a limited time (usually two to three hours) before departure for a plane. Descriptions of the organization, its policies, personnel, and past history are provided. The participants are told not to role play or to say what they would do, but rather to actually respond as they would in that position. The responses are the written work completed on the items. Following the completion of the in-basket, participants are sometimes asked to fill out a reason-for-action form, describing what they did with each item and why. The participant may also be asked to complete a report form asking for reactions to the exercise and seeking additional insights into the most pressing problems and the strategy used in completing the exercise. This information plus the actual responses provides insights into the person's approach to problems. After assessors have had an opportunity to review the in-basket, they often conduct an interview to explore reasons for actions and to clear up any questions that have occurred to them relative to the actions.

In-basket exercises have a high degree of face validity, making them highly acceptable to participants. Beyond that, the content, construct, and predictive validity of the exercise have been clearly established in numerous studies. Much of this work has been done by Frederiksen and his colleagues (Crooks, 1968; Frederiksen, 1962, 1966; Frederiksen et al., 1957) at Educational Testing Service (ETS) and in conjunction with other organizations such as the Port of New York Authority (Lopez, 1966), General Electric (Meyer, 1970), and an association of public schools (Hemphill et al., 1962). This research has shown the in-basket exercise measures a number of administrative skills including the ability to set priorities for work to be undertaken, the ability to handle a large amount of work in a relatively short amount of time, cognitive skills of planning and analytical decision making, and certain personality characteristics related to style of dealing with people and problems.

Factor analytic studies (Frederiksen, 1962; Hemphill et al., 1962) of the correlations of large numbers of content and style categories of in-basket responses have suggested several common dimensions of administrative performance being measured in the in-basket. These include complying with suggestions, preparing for action by gathering more information, putting off decisions, directing others, and discussing problems with others. Frederiksen (1962) found three general factors that accounted for most performance variance: preparing for action, amount of work, and seeking guidance. In a subsequent study of the construct validity of the in-basket in relation to psychological test scores, Frederiksen (1966) found certain components of performance related to personality and interest factors. For example:

1. Individuals who take many imaginative courses of action tend to have high ability as measured by a vocabulary test $(r = .41)$.
2. Those who write a great deal tend to get high scores on the *active* scale of the Thurstone Temperament Schedule $(r = .40)$.
3. Those who plan to have many discussions with subordinates tend to

resemble life insurance salespeople in their responses to the Strong Vocational Interest Blank ($r = .37$).
4. Those who frequently give directions and suggestions tend to be in high administrative levels ($r = .38$).
5. Those who tend to prepare for action by becoming informed are likely to resemble presidents of manufacturing concerns rather than policemen in their responses to the SVIB.
6. Those who tend to procrastinate are likely to be of low educational level.
7. Those who tend to supervise work of subordinates are likely to have supervisory duties in their real jobs.

In a study of 79 undergraduates Denning (1980) found that cognitive style (defined as ability to deal effectively with many bits of heterogeneous information) was related to in-basket performance. She correlated in-basket scores with a test of cognitive complexity and cognitive simplicity, and obtained significant relationship with both scales.

None of nine tests from the ETS Kit of Factor-Referenced Cognitive Ability Tests correlated significantly with the overall rating of in-basket performance. Thus, cognitive style appeared to be related to overall in-basket performance in its own right, but differentially from cognitive abilities, which have long been recognized to correlate with some aspects of managerial performance.

In a study of black and white disadvantaged trainees in a government manpower training program, Jaffee et al. (1972) found that whites and blacks performed equally on an in-basket and there was no correlation of in-basket performance and reading skill. However, Russell and Byham (1981) found in two studies that blacks completed fewer in-basket items than whites when held to a tight time limit. They recommend very generous time limits for all candidates if blacks are to be assessed by the in-basket exercise.

Predictive validity of the in-basket has been established in several studies. Lopez (1966) found that several categories of in-basket performance correlated with performance on the job in the Port of New York Authority. Meyer (1970) found that managers scoring high on the in-basket were more likely to rate as above-average performers on the job. He also found that the in-basket exercise was related to two performance ratings of skill in supervision and to planning and administration. The correlations for individual in-basket scoring categories ranged from $-.19$ to $+.35$ with a median of .10 for the supervision factor and .13 for planning and administration. Factor scores reflecting composites of in-basket scores (e.g., preparation for decisions, taking final action, and organizing systematically) tended to correlate more highly. In general the in-basket correlated highly with the planning criterion. Significant correlations were found between in-basket performance and age ($-$ .49), education (.56), managerial experience ($-$ .21), and a general ability test (.42). These findings suggest that in-baskets must be chosen carefully to match the experience and education level of assessees. The finding that experience does not enhance in-basket performance was also found by Bray *et al.* (1974) in reassessment of managers after eight years experience. But Crooks and Slivinski (1971) found significant differences in in-basket scores among four groups with different amounts of management experience.

These and other studies have demonstrated that even though the in-basket is difficult to score and reliability of ratings on specific items and categories are low, dimension ratings from in-baskets show reliability and validity.

In-baskets in assessment centers. In contrast to the psychometric approaches to in-basket scoring used by ETS, in-basket exercises in most assessment centers are used to elicit behavior relevant to the dimensions being assessed. In the usual case, an assessor reviews the actual responses, and the reason-for-action or participant report forms if they are available. The assessor then discusses the in-basket with the participant to clarify his or her understanding of the action taken—not to obtain new data. The assessor categorizes the behaviors into the dimensions being assessed in the assessment center and rates performance on those dimensions. The in-basket has demonstrated predictive validity in assessment centers in seven studies as summarized in Table 5.8.

Bray and Grant (1966) asked assessors to read a narrative report of the assessee's performance on both the in-basket itself and the discussion of reasons for action, then rate the overall in-basket performance on a five-point scale. Interrater agreement between two raters was .92. Mean ratings were correlated with assessment staff evaluations and subsequent criteria. The in-basket contributed a sizable amount to the OAR for both college and noncollege groups. Against an external criterion of salary progress, the in-basket correlated significantly for only one of four college groups and one of three noncollege groups. Wollowick and McNamara (1969) found a correlation of .32 between judged in-basket performance and a criterion of change of position level over a 3-year period. This was the highest correlation for six exercises. Grossner (1974)

Table 5.8
Reliability and Validity of the In-Basket in Assessment Centers

Study	Reliability (type)	Validity/*criterion*
		College samples
Bray and Grant (1966)	.92 (interrater)	.55 *OAR* .35, .32, .32 .37 *Salary progress*
		Noncollege samples
		.51 *OAR* .26, − .09, − .27 *salary progress*
Wollowick and McNamara (1969)		.32 *Change in position level*
Bentz (1971)		.42 *global rating;* .28 *compensation increase* Mdn = .28 *six month store ratings* Mdn = .24 *final store ratings*
Hinrichs and Haanpera (1974, 1976)	.22 (internal consistency)	
Huck (1974)		.69, .51 *OAR*, whites and blacks
Grossner (1974)		Mdn r = .72 *ratings on three behavioral criteria*
Neidig *et al.* (1978)	.19 (internal consistency)	

found sizable correlations between corresponding in-basket and on-the-job dimension ratings.

Bentz (1971) found a number of significant correlations between scores on an in-basket and various performance ratings on the job for three samples of managers. The most impressive finding was a correlation of .42 between total in-basket score and an overall job rating for 51 participants at a staff school. Bentz also found significant correlations between several individual and factor scores on the in-basket and criterion ratings on several dimensions of job performance in a management training setting. Two factors among in-basket scores that yielded consistent validity were Informal Initiation of Structure and Idea Proliferation.

Internal validity studies show the in-basket is an important exercise and contributes uniquely to the overall assessment rating and various dimension ratings. Huck (1974) found that the in-basket was the primary determinant of the OAR for white females and the second most valid predictor for black females. In Huett's (1975) study, dimension ratings from the in-basket were the primary determiners of final ratings on most dimensions.

Internal consistency comparisons (Hinrichs & Haanpera 1974, 1976) of dimension ratings from the in-basket with ratings on the same dimensions from other exercises averaged .22, the lowest figure for all exercises. This indicates the in-basket overlapped the least with other methods of measurement. Similarly, Neidig et al. (1978) found that the in-basket appeared to contribute the most unique information to those skills it was supposed to measure.

Summary. In view of the frequent use of an in-basket in assessment programs (Bender, 1973), it may seem surprising that relatively little data are reported on its reliability and validity in these settings. Three explanations can be given: (a) users may believe the face validity is so high (Meyer, 1970) and empirical validation in other settings is so extensive (Lopez, 1966) that further research is unnecessary; (b) evidence of content validity may be so strong and the amount of time the organization spends in training managers to evaluate in-baskets so great (12–16 hours) that users do not see the need for research; and (c) the time required and the difficulty of evaluating in-baskets (2–5 hours per in-basket) discourage users from undertaking adequate studies. Reviews of research indicate that in-baskets possess adequate psychometric properties to substantiate their use in assessment centers where the job analysis shows that the types of decisions and actions required in an in-basket are required on the job.

New procedures for in-basket evaluation using highly structured patterned interviews appear to offer great hope for cutting down the amount of assessor time required and for increasing the reliability of measurement. Several research studies are under way to evaluate these procedures.

SIGNS VERSUS SAMPLES: THE EVIDENCE

Wernimont and Campbell (1968) emphasized the importance of using measures of samples rather than signs in the prediction of future job behavior. *Signs* are tests, questionnaires, biographical information blanks, etc., used to measure general predispositions to behave in certain ways; *samples* are measures of behavior consistent with on-the-job behavior. Whereas Wernimont and Campbell (1968) suggest that job simulations such as games and in-baskets may prove to be more effective, the literature covered thus far in this chapter suggests that both traditional tests and situational exercises have contributed to the overall assessment rating and have proven valid in predicting subsequent job-related criterion.

By examining the assessment center literature, the evidence for situational exercises and traditional tests may be directly compared, both in partial correlation and by multiple regression analyses. These designs allow some determination of the relative contribution of several factors to the prediction of a given criterion.

The situational exercises were found to make more significant contributions to the prediction of performance criteria in several studies (Bray & Grant, 1966; Hinrichs, 1978; Moses, 1972; Moses & Boehm, 1975; and Wollowick & McNamara, 1969). In the Management Progress Study (Bray & Grant, 1966), it was found that when the ability test was partialed out of the correlation of the overall assessment rating with the criterion, significant variance remained. This suggests that the larger assessment process including situational exercises was measuring something not measured by the ability tests alone. However, Wilson and Tatge (1973) observed that the median correlation for the ability tests was .38 and for staff judgments was .48. They question the real gain from accounting for an additional 9% of the criterion variance (i.e., $.38^2 = .14$ versus $.48^2 = .23$). Similar findings were reported by Meyer (1980) of Jewel Companies, who found that judgments based on a combination of test and interview data correlated with a criterion of job effectiveness .37, while judgments based on exercises only correlated .14. Bray and Grant (1966) concluded that "neither kind of technique could be omitted without loss of important information (p. 21)." In a similar analysis, Bray and Campbell (1968) found a multiple correlation of .33 for four tests with ratings of field performance, in comparison with a zero-order correlation of .51 for the overall assessment rating. Presumably, information from the situational tests was contributing valid information to the assessment process. In addition, Moses (1972) found that ratings made from behavioral observations correlated higher than the SCAT (total) with both the overall assessment rating and with criterion of management level. Furthermore, the multiple correlation of behavioral assessment variables was virtually identical to the multiple correlation for *all* assessment variables in comparison with both the overall assessment rating (.816 versus .824) and the progress criterion (.461 vs. .463). Moses and Boehm (1975) found similar results for a group of 4846 women. The correlation of the OAR and management level (.44) was higher than all dimension ratings from exercises (median $r = .32$), which in turn were higher than correlations for School and College Aptitude Test ($r = .21$).

Although each of the above studies lends some support to the notion that situational tests contribute valuable and unique information, they do not conclusively determine that situational tests are better than paper-and-pencil tests. Moreover, the studies often do not provide evidence about each separate exercise in relation to the criterion because the dimension ratings usually summarize many kinds of information gathered by the assessors from situational exercises, interviews and, in a few cases, informal interactions.

Wollowick and McNamara (1969) provide a better set of data. Zero-order correlation is provided for each test, exercise, and dimension rating; multiple correlations are provided for combinations of tests, exercises, and dimensions are included; and multiple correlations for three types of predictors are provided. Here it was found that tests, dimension ratings, and exercises contributed to the criterion of position level prediction. Table 5.9 shows the individual predictors that contributed most to the multiple R. It is interesting to note that all three types of predictors entered the prediction equation. Table 5.10 shows the multiple Rs for the three types of predictors separately and combined. There is no practical difference among the three sets of variables, but it is clear that a significant increase in variance is accounted for when the three types of predictors are used in combination. These data suggest that while each type of predictor makes a significant and unique contribution to the prediction of criterion variance, no one method demonstrates clear superiority.

Similar conclusions have been drawn from other studies. Huck (1974) found that both behavioral ratings from exercises and test scores contributed to the prediction of management progress of both black and white females. Slivinski et al. (1979) conducted two studies comparing simulations and other testing methods. In the first, there was no difference found between the amount of criterion variance accounted for by a set of five simulations ($R = .25$) and a set of three paper-and-pencil tests

Table 5.9

Stepwise Multiple Prediction of Criterion with Various Types of Predictors[a]

Variables	Type	R
Ascendency	Test	.39
In-basket	Exercise	.46
Administrative ability	Characteristic	.51
Vigor	Test	.56
Manufacturing	Exercise	.59
Interpersonal contact	Characteristic rating	.60
BCD success key	Test	.62

[a] Adapted from "Relationship of the Components of an Assessment Center to Management Success" by H. B. Wollowick and W. J. McNamara, *Journal of Applied Psychology*, 1969, 53, 348–352. Copyright 1969 by the American Psychological Association. Reprinted by permission.

Table 5.10
Multiple Rs and R^2 for the Three Types of
Predictors Separately and Combined [a]

Predictors	R	R^2
Tests (T)	.45	.20
Exercises (E)	.39	.15
Characteristics (C)	.41	.17
T and E	.54	.29
C and E	.52	.27
C and T	.55	.30
T, C, and E	.62	.38

[a] Adapted from "Relationship of the Components of an Assessment Center to Management Success" by H. B. Wollowick and W. J. McNamara, *Journal of Applied Psychology*, 1969, *53*, 348–352. Copyright 1969 by the American Psychological Association. Reprinted by permission.

($R = .30$). Furthermore, each set contributed to the predictive accuracy of the other set ($R = .40$ in both cases). Slivinski *et al.* (1979) concluded that assessment centers "do not eliminate the need for paper-and-pencil testing and vice versa [p. 3]." In the second study, biographical data (e.g., education, age, management experience, and tenure) added significantly to the predictive accuracy of situational exercises and tests.

Summary. The conclusions derived from these analyses must be tentative. Much of the research comes from a small sample of companies who adopted assessment centers in the early years (1955–1965). Their exercises and approaches were very similar to the AT&T model. In contrast to the wide variety of situational exercises now in use, the exercises covered by the reported research are quite narrow. Seldom was more than one exercise of a given type (LGD, game) used. The technology of building simulations has changed and, we hope, improved. More research like that reported here is needed on the newer exercises. Utility of exercises cannot be inferred from the scanty research in the past.

The distinction between sample tests and sign tests is meaningful. Assessment center research suggests that situational and paper-and-pencil tests tap two somewhat different performance domains. There is a relatively low correlation between the different types of instruments, yet both yield reliable and valid measurement. The question of which type of instrument is "better" is unsettled. The data strongly suggest that both traditional tests and situational exercises contribute uniquely to the overall staff judgments of management potential and to subsequent performance and progress criteria in management positions. The utility of various types of exercises, considering time in testing, cost, reactions of participants, and defensibility in court, has not been studied systematically but must also be considered in the selection of assessment methods. In conclusion, it seems highly inappropriate to deprecate either paper-and-pencil or situational testing.

OTHER EXERCISES

A wide variety of other types of assessment techniques has been used in assessment centers. Few statistical studies have been published showing their reliability or criterion-related validity. Their use is based on content validity evidence, assumptions about reliability derived from the amount of assessor training, and evidence of reliability found in similar observation tasks.

Interview simulation. Frequently supervisors and managers must deal with difficult situations on a one-to-one basis with subordinates, peers, or customers. Job analyses of managerial behavior strongly suggest that the most characteristic feature of managerial work is the large number of brief encounters that managers have with a variety of people throughout each day (McCall *et al.,* 1978). These situations can be simulated by having an assessor, administrator, or other trained person role play a similar confrontation with an assessment center participant. The assessor observes how the participant handles the simulated interview and rates behavior on dimensions such as Oral Communication, Sensitivity, Leadership, and Problem Analysis.

This type of exercise can simulate an interview with a problem employee, a formal performance appraisal session, coaching a salesperson on how to improve customer relations, a selection interview, or a phone call from an irate customer.

Interview simulations are conducted not only on a one-to-one basis; a number of organizations have interview simulations where two role players are involved. Usually, this situation is such that one role player is cooperative with the assessee and the other role player is quite hostile. Almost always the players are trained to portray contrasting "personality types." Certainly having two role players is twice as expensive as having one, and the decision on the appropriate number must depend on the type of interactions defined in the job analysis.

The authors are aware of two unpublished studies which included interview simulation exercises among the predictors. In one study, the interview simulation had the highest correlation with the OAR, and in the other study it had the second highest correlation. A measure of observer reliability of the exercise was reported by Russell and Byham (1980). After two days of assessor training, 39 assessors were shown a videotape of an interview simulation and were asked to evaluate the individual on the videotape relative to three designated dimensions (Leadership, Interpersonal Sensitivity, and Oral Communication Skill). The estimate of the reliability of the mean of the 39 judges (as determined through the procedure using analysis of variance outlined in Winer, 1971, pp. 283–289) was .80.

Case study analysis. In this type of exercise, participants are given data on a situation and asked to recommend appropriate courses of action. The ability to sift through data, recognize and document organizational problems, generate alternate solutions, and formulate defensible solutions can be observed. The content of the material may call for such things as financial decisions, new product and marketing strategies, solutions to personnel and job problems in a department, and reorganization of a complex division or agency.

After the analysis phase, participants may be asked to prepare a written report for submission to higher management, to present the findings individually to an assessor who then interviews the participant on use of the data and reasons for recommendations, to present the findings formally to a group of assessors, or to discuss the situation with a group of fellow participants to come up with a single set of recommendations. Different dimensions can be observed in each of the options.

Scheduling exercise. A common job requirement for first-line supervisors is to schedule employees to tasks or machines. Very often the supervisor must schedule and then reschedule based on changes in allocated manpower, unexpected illnesses of employees, etc. This common task is simulated in assessment centers by scheduling exercises. The assessee is given a description of the situation, the number of employees to be scheduled, and any constraints on who can do what. The assessee is given time to make an initial allocation of the personnel. Then, new information is given to the assessee. For example, the product mix may be changed necessitating changes in the assembly line, or three of the people initially scheduled may have phoned in ill. The assessee must reassign his or her employees using this new information. A third cycle of changes may also be introduced. As with all assessment center exercises, the nature of the scheduling experience is determined by the job analysis. The exercises range from the scheduling of route salespeople or repairpeople over a fairly large geographic area to the assignment of workers on two or three assembly lines in a single plant.

Fact-finding. Participants are given a brief description of the immediate circumstances concerning a problem or incident. They then must seek additional information from a resource person and make a decision within a specified time. During the fact-finding phase, the participant must ask direct questions to obtain information from the neutral resource person. All responsibility for structuring and timing the inquiry rests with the participant. After the allotted time, the participant makes a brief oral presentation of his or her decision to the resource person, who then questions the participant to probe adequacy of information obtained, quality of reasoning, persuasiveness, and ability to think and talk under pressure. Selective stress can be placed on the participant to get him or her to change the original decision.

The fact-finding exercise is a variant on the incident process described by Pigors and Pigors (1961). The original procedure was a variant on the Harvard case study method of training managers or prospective managers in practical, analytical thinking.

> [The purpose of the incident process is] to stimulate self-development in a blend of understanding that combines *intellectual ability* (the power to think clearly, incisively, and reasonably about specific facts and also about abstractions); *practical judgments* (the capacity to modify conclusions, arrived at intellectually, so that they meet the test of common sense, including organizational sense); and *social awareness* (the ability to appreciate the force of other people's feelings and the willingness to adjust or implement a decision so that it will be acceptable to persons who are affected by it) [Pigors, 1976, 35–36].

The dimensions mentioned in the above quote and many others can be assessed as individuals carry out the fact-finding exercise with a resource person–assessor.

Examples of situations used in assessment center fact-finding exercises are arbitration over the dismissal of a trainee, reconsideration of a project terminated for budgetary reasons, and diagnosis of a production problem that requires immediate corrective action. In summary, these exercises appear to assess (a) the ability to collect data and analyze problems by asking questions; and (b) the ability to reach a logical decision using information. They may also assess the ability to present a recommendation logically and to defend one's point of view.

Staff meetings. A unique exercise developed for assessment of executive functioning in the federal public service (Slivinski et al., 1979) involves one participant and four subordinate staff who are trained professional actors. For one hour the assessee must question the role players about organizational problems in preparation for a subsequent meeting with the president of the agency. Following presentations by the four subordinates, the participant can make further inquiries, explore differences in view, or direct the staff members.

Presentations. Presentations may be called for after the participant has prepared for a leaderless group discussion, analyzed a case, or conducted a fact-finding interview. In addition, an oral presentation may be made on some specially selected problem (e.g., a critique of an article or company report, the issues surrounding changing work values in our society, or the defense of the company's policy on minority recruiting to a citizen's group). Such exercises have been made to assess special requirements for the target job, such as the requirement to be able to appear as an organizational representative at a press conference to defend organizational policy.

Negotiation. Higher managers frequently find themselves in situations where they must negotiate with subordinates, peers, superiors, or individuals outside the organization. The subject may involve resources, pay, services, or the purchase of equipment or even of a company. These situations are simulated by having an assessor or other trained individual play the other half of the negotiation.

Others. Several other types of situational tests have been used in managerial assessment. Participants may be observed at meal times (Kohls, 1970; McConnell & Parker, 1972), observed in complex organizational simulations (Olmstead, Cleary, Lackey, & Salter, 1973, 1975), or asked to discuss a film involving an employee promotion (McConnell & Parker, 1972).

NEEDED RESEARCH

In Chapter 1 we presented a model of the assessment center process and a set of hypothetical data for one participant. The first part of Figure 1.1 shows the dimension ratings on several exercises. The assessment center literature does *not* contain a systematic body of evidence regarding the adequacy of observation and rating at this stage of the process. More research into the reliability and accuracy of the observation process is clearly needed. Do different assessors perceive the same behavioral events when watching an exercise? If the same assessor were to observe on two different occasions, would he or she make the same observations? Accuracy of observation is also problematic. What systematic omissions or additions do observers make? What is the reliability and validity of assessor ratings of separate dimensions in situational exercises?

In summary, little research has been conducted on the observation and rating processes which take place during Stage 1 of the assessment process depicted in Figures 1.1 and 1.2. Such studies can seldom be done in the context of an operational assessment program because usually only one assessor is observing each assessee. The most feasible place for these studies would be at the end of assessor training or during "refresher" training sessions periodically held by organizations to prepare assessors who were trained several months before actual service in an assessment program.

A MODEL OF TYPES OF ASSESSMENT EXERCISES

Most assessment centers use a relatively narrow set of assessment exercises. For the most part, they have been limited to written exercises (e.g., in-basket or analysis), group discussion activities, and more recently interview simulations. Managerial job analyses have shown that managers engage in a wide variety of different tasks with different types of people and deal with a diversity of content. We acknowledge that assessment techniques in assessment centers have more realism and content validity than traditional paper-and-pencil tests and clinical interviews, but we believe even more diversity would be beneficial.

In an attempt to map out the types of exercises used and to stimulate thinking about potential new exercises, Figure 5.1 was prepared. Assessment exercises are conceived to fall along two axes: the stimulus material presented and response mode required from the participant. The first continuum is defined by the types of stimuli (who and what) encountered by the participant. In some exercises, the assessee is presented only written material (e.g., a test); in others, the assessee is presented questions by the assessor; and in others, the assessee is given a complex set of directions from the administrator or has dialog among other participants. Figure 5.1 presents these various stimulus conditions along a continuum from "standardized" to "unstandardized." Toward the left are those exercises for which very controlled testing conditions exist; toward the right are those exercises for which conditions may vary considerably. The situation an assessee confronts may differ depending on the compositon of the group, the level of cooperation and competition that evolves, and the personality characteristics of individual group members.

The response mode varies among exercises. Some call for clearly structured responses by the participant (e.g., answers on a test or the written response to a single in-basket item). In contrast, the responses called for by a complex game are very unstructured. Not only must the participant

Stimulus material

| Response mode | "Standardized" | | | | Role players (Subordinate, Peer, Boss, Customer) | | Other assessees in: | | "Unstandardized" |
	Written	Videotape	Administrator	Assessor	One role player	Two or more	Assigned roles	Non-assigned roles	Other teams
"Structured" Completion of form	Ability test Personality questionnaire Background information form								
Handwriting	Case study In-basket		In-basket						
Verbal presentation Verbal response to questions	Case study			Fact-finding Background interview Interview after in-basket or analysis	Creative subordinate Irate customer		Analysis/Discussion		
Assessee con-trolled interview	Interview simulation			Fact-finding	Interview simulation				
Group discussion	Case study LGD					Staff meeting	LGD	LGD	Game
Multi-group discussion									Game
Combination of verbal, written and physical behaviors "Unstructured"									Game

Figure 5.1. Model of assessment center exercises.

be able to respond appropriately, he or she must also ascertain whether or not a form of response is appropriate in an ill-defined situation.

Within the figure, we have listed many of the exercises commonly used in managerial assessment centers. Individual exercises are listed in more than one "cell" of the figure if they involve a combination of stimuli presentations or responses called for. The display compels one to come to a strong conclusion. Currently available exercises tap a relatively narrow cross section of potential formats.

In addition to the two dimensions defined above, other parameters of the testing situation must be considered: (a) pressures due to time and seriousness; (b) cooperation versus competition; (c) problem content of exercises including finance, marketing, production, etc.; (d) presence or absence of observer.

The model has significant heuristic value. Examination of the "stimulus material" continuum suggests other procedures for eliciting participant responses. Written material, audio tapes, or videotapes might be used to present standardized material to the participant. He or she could then be asked to report observations made or to respond in an appropriate way. Such techniques are used in microteaching (Ivey & Authier, 1978) and counselor training (Brammer, 1979; Egan, 1975a, 1975b).

Videotape and film simulations are rarely used in assessment centers. The American Management Association has used filmed case studies as a stimulus in its assessment centers. Three applications that show more of the potential of this form of stimulus have been developed by Development Dimensions International. In one exercise designed for selecting school administrators, the assessee is put in the position of a new administrator who has the opportunity to observe a citizens' committee in action (on videotape) prior to assuming the leadership of that committee. Based on his or her observations of the individuals on the committee, the participant is asked to describe methods that could be used to influence each of the members of the group towards a specific goal and to make recommendations on restructuring the committee and making special assignments to individual committee members. The exercise is a way of evaluating group leadership without actually putting a person in a group.

In another exercise designed to evaluate pharmaceutical sales managers, assessees are placed in a role of a sales manager and are shown a videotape of a pharmaceutical sales person selling to a physician. The assessee is encouraged to take notes on the observed behavior and then is asked to conduct a feedback counseling session with the sales person on the tape (role played by an assessor). A similar exercise was developed for school principal selection. Videotapes of teachers in action were shown to assessees who were then asked to evaluate those teachers and feed back that evaluation.

In exercises designed to evaluate managers in police and fire departments, the candidates are allowed to listen to a tape recording providing a series of inputs about a "subordinate." They can stop and discuss a matter with the subordinate (assessor) or let the tape play on to see what happens next. The key manager's decision of when to take action is thus evaluated.

A wider range of "live" stimuli could also be used. For example, multiple role players could be trained to simulate a group of departmental employees called to participate in a problem-solving discussion (Cohen & Sands, 1978).

Examination of the "response" continuum reveals deficiencies in the current group of exercises. Participants might be asked to dictate memos, lead a discussion with an external pressure group, or mediate a dispute between two subordinates.

A review of current exercises suggests that certain combinations of stimulus material and response mode are commonly associated with each other. For example, from written materials the participant produces a written report; an irate employee or customer is dealt with verbally. Other combinations may be generated from the figure. A written performance appraisal or "incident file" might be prepared after the participant observes behavior on a videotape. Participants' analyses of a previous interview simulation or leaderless group discussion exercises might be observed for insights into the participants' understanding of group dynamics or self-awareness.

Some progress is being made in breaking up the standard combinations of stimuli and responses. As part of an assessment center to evaluate vocational rehabilitation counselors, participants provide the assessor with an oral description of actions for each in-basket item rather than writing the item down (Goldberg, Costello, Wiesen, & Popp, 1980). In addition, several high-level assessment centers have offered assessees services of a stenographer or the use of recording equipment to respond to in-baskets.

Often the selection of a response is predicated on the ease with which the data may be collected. Decisions based solely on ease of collection may result in inaccurate and illegal assessment centers. A good example of this was the assessment center devised to select captains in the St. Louis Fire Department (FIRE v. the City of Louis, 1980). One exercise in the assessment center called for the firemen to observe a series of slides of a fire and to make command decisions relative to the handling of the fire. The command decisions were made in writing. One of the arguments of the plaintiffs in the case was that fire captains rarely do anything in writing, and the judge made a special point of citing the inappropriate use of a written response modality in his decision.

Another example of potential exercises suggested by the empty cells of the figure would be a situation in which the participant completes a questionnaire or written summary following an interview situation or group discussion. Bass (1979) reported the use of objective responding in small group exercises as a method in his cross-cultural studies of management values and behavior (Bass & Burger, 1979). While participating in group discussions, the assessees record their preferences, decisions, or values.

A variety of performance or situational activities have been devised for management research and might be adapted for assessment centers. Vroom and Yetton (1973) devised a set of problem situations to study models of participative leadership styles in decision making. One unique feature of these exercises is that they are administered as paper-and-pencil instruments and yet retain the essential features of situational tests. The manager is presented with a description of a case involving some decision-making problem and must choose one of four alternative approaches. These approaches vary in the extent to which the supervisor involves subordinates in the decision-making process. The respondent must make a choice of using one or more alternatives predetermined to be either autocratic or participative. In research studies these exercises have been used to study the factors, such as time pressures and competence of subordinates, that affect the choice of alternative leadership styles.

Vroom and Yetton (1973) cite a number of by-products of their basic research. Among these is the use of the exercises for individual assessment of leadership style. One advantage of such exercises is that they can be administered in groups and do not require extensive administrator or scorer time. The limitation of these exercises is that they do not involve any interpersonal interaction between the leader and follower and they do not allow assessment of the overt behavior or process that a manager uses in carrying out the decision-making process.

Another innovation in assessment center measurement is the development of a set of interrelated exercises by the Canadian Public Service Commission (Slivinski et al., 1979):

> Each participant, in coming to the assessment center, immediately assumes the role of an executive in charge of a particular organizational unit within a newly formed government agency. In this role, the participant then proceeds to engage, over a two and one-half day period, in a series of duties and meetings related to the unit. This begins with work on the in-basket which has accumulated (In-basket Test) followed by a meeting with the executive's

subordinate staff (Staffing Meeting). An opportunity then arises to meet the president of the agency (Meeting with the President), followed by a meeting with representatives of another government agency (Treasury Board Presentation). Finally, the candidate is requested to participate in a group discussion related to the problems being faced by both the organizational unit and the agency as a whole (Task Force Exercise).

The advantages of this procedure are that subsequent exercises can build on previous ones, the tasks are realistic, and the exercises can be made more complex. The participant's understanding of the general situation and the participant's ability to put himself or herself in the role or simulation more fully is increased.

A good example of the benefits of integrating exercises is an assessment center designed for selection of high-level managers for Pepsico International. The three exercises in the assessment center are set in a group of hypothetical foreign countries and involve a highly innovative new product. Almost 15 typed pages are required to provide the necessary background on the countries and the product. The same background and country information is used in all three exercises. The advantage of having the exercises integrated is that the participant only has to read the background information once.

The disadvantage of an integrated set of exercises is that poor performance on an exercise may put an individual at a disadvantage in the next exercise. This need not be the case. In the Pepsico selection system described above, each of the exercises is completely independent of the others. No information gained in one exercise is used in any way in the others.

An increasingly popular development is the abandonment of formal time limits in middle- and high-management assessment centers. In the usual assessment center, the participant has four hours to complete an in-basket, two hours to prepare for an analysis exercise, one hour to prepare for an interview simulation exercise, etc. Under a new format, designed to replicate the flexibility inherent in a manager's actual job, the assessee is given all of the exercises the first morning of the assessment center and is told when each exercise must be completed or when appointments are to be met in which exercise data would interface. The assessee then has the opportunity to spend as much or as little time in preparation for each exercise as desired, and the dimension Judgment can be evaluated relative to decisions in consideration of time allocation.

The fidelity of assessment center techniques could also be improved by employing a wider diversity of simulation exercises. The "band-width–fidelity" issue (Cronbach, 1970) raises its head. Given limited time for observation, some choices must be made. On the one hand, to enhance reliability or "fidelity" of measurement, it is desirable to have relatively long exercises (e.g., a 1-hour leaderless group discussion) and redundancy in measurement (e.g., two different discussions). On the other hand, it may be more beneficial to sample more broadly across the entire "band-width" of the behavioral domain, even at the sacrifice of some reliability. For example, it may be better to substitute a fact-finding exercise for a second LGD. Much of this is speculation and more research is needed. The purpose of this section is to point out the relatively limited nature of exercises in many assessment programs and encourage the use of a wider array of exercise types in the future.

THE IMPORTANCE OF GOOD SIMULATIONS

Job analysis, as we have described it, should result in information useful for the development of assessment exercises that are clearly samples of important activities of the job. Content-valid work samples are important for several reasons:

1. *Accuracy of measurement and prediction:* Content-valid and job-related performance exercises are likely to improve prediction effectiveness.
2. *Enhancement of development:* The exercises serve as training devices for participants and staff.
3. *Orientation of managers:* Realistic job expectations can be transmitted via these exercises.
4. *Face validity and internal public relations:* Any personnel activity must be accepted widely.
5. *Fulfillment of EEO requirements:* A good job analysis that leads to job-related evaluation procedures is required by the Uniform Guidelines (EEOC *et al.,* 1978).

In selecting and building exercises for an assessment center, it is important that each individual exercise sample an important job domain and that the set of exercises cover a wide variety of domains in the job universe. Job analysis information and Figure 5.1 above can help in the construction of job-relevant assessment exercises.

Dimensions Observable in Assessment Exercises

One bit of evidence supporting the content validity of assessment centers is provided in a unique study originally conducted by Byham and Byham (1976) and recently updated with new data. Over 1000 assessment reports in 12 large companies were examined to identify the number of assessors who were able to make a judgment of the participants' skill levels on the basis of behavior observed relevant to each of 25 dimensions. In these programs the assessors were instructed not to rate the dimension if insufficient behavior was observed. Therefore, the assessment reports contain evidence of whether or not the exercise elicited adequate behavior relevant to the dimensions. Table 5.11 presents the findings. A checkmark (✓) means the dimension was observable at least 90% of the time it was sought, a star (*) means the dimension was observable at least 95% of the time, and (X) means the dimension was observable at least 90% of the time it was sought, but in only some of the exercises in the category.

The data in the table are an indication of the standardization of the responses obtained in relation to certain dimensions. Dimensions that *might* be displayed, such as Creativity, do poorly in this analysis because they are not seen every time the exercise is conducted. Data such as these provide a partial basis for selecting exercises and for substantiating the content validity of a program once the dimensions of the job are established.

Inspection of the table supports much of the research reviewed so far in this chapter and contains some surprises. The in-basket is clearly the best exercise for measuring the administrative and decision-making abilities listed near the bottom of the table. The group discussions measure many of the interpersonal skills (e.g., Impact and Leadership) and activity level (e.g., Initiative). The large number of entries for the background interview shows its adaptability and the fact that trained interviewers can obtain information on many dimensions if they do so systematically.

Looking across the rows, we can see that some dimensions are almost universally observable (e.g., Impact, Oral Communications, and Leadership). By contrast, some dimensions are seldom observable except in the background interview (e.g., Creativity). If an organization wishes to assess these latter characteristics by some method other than a background interview, it may need to design new, specific exercises to elicit relevant behavior. If you eliminate the column representing the background interview, it becomes apparent that many of the administrative skills are measured only by the in-basket. Again, this suggests the need to develop new exercises.

One measure of the efficacy of an exercise is the number of dimensions that can be reliably evaluated by an exercise. The more, the better. In some cases, however, an exercise may be included to reveal a single dimension such as Business Creativity or Awareness of Cleanliness. In addition, exercises may be included to give variety or change of pace

Table 5.11
Evidence of Dimensions Observable in Several Assessment Exercises[a]

Categories of exercises

Job-related dimensions	Business game	In-basket and interview	Leaderless group discussion (assigned roles)	Leaderless group discussion (non-assigned roles)	Analysis	Scheduling	Background interview	Fact-finding and decision making	Interview simulation	Written presentation	Analysis/oral presentation
1. Impact	✓	✓	✓	✓			✓		✓		★
2. Oral Communication Skill		✓	★	★	X		✓		★		
3. Oral Presentation Skill			★								★
4. Written Communication Skill		★			✓		✓			★	
5. Creativity					X						
6. Tolerance for Stress					X[b]	X[b]		✓	✓[c]		
7. Work Standards		✓			X					X	
8. Leadership	✓		✓	★			✓		★		
9. Persuasiveness/Sales Ability			✓		✓			✓	X	X	★
10. Sensitivity		★	✓	★					✓		

202

11. Behavioral Flexibility	X	✓	✓				✓	✓		
12. Tenacity	✓	✓	✓				✓	X	✓	
13. Risk Taking	✓	★		X	✓		✓			✓
14. Initiative	✓	✓	✓	★			★	X		
15. Independence		✓					✓	X	X	
16. Planning and Organizing	✓	★			X	★	✓			
17. Delegation		★					✓	X		
18. Managment Control		★					✓	✓		
19. Analysis	✓	★		★	★		✓	✓	X	★
20. Judgment		★	X	★	★		✓	✓		★
21. Decisiveness		★	X	★	★		X	✓		★
22. Development of Subordinates		X					✓	X		
23. Adaptability	✓						✓			
24. Technical Translation		X							★	✓
25. Organizational Sensitivity		X			X		✓	X	X	X

[a] From "Effectiveness of Assessment Center Exercises in Producing Behavior" by R. N. Byham and W. C. Byham, Assessment & Development, March 1976, 9–10. Copyright 1976 by Development Dimensions International. Reprinted by permission.
[b] Time stress.
[c] Interpersonal stress.
★ means observed in 95% of the exercises;
✓ means observed in 90% of exercises;
X means observed in 90% of certain exercises in category, but not all exercises.

in the program or they may be used as a preliminary step for subsequent management training.

Although an exercise may produce behavior that can be categorized under a number of dimensions, an argument can be made for having a smaller number of dimensions evaluated in an exercise, thus focusing exercises specifically on one or two dimensions. Multitrait, multimethod analysis of assessment center data have shown that exercises are more important in determining evaluations than the dimensions. Additionally, a common source of unreliability is the disagreement among assessors about where behavior should be classified. For example, assessors may disagree about whether poor planning in a presentation should be recorded under Planning or Oral Presentation. Often a greater reliability is obtained when a global dimension, such as Decision Making, is used rather than when three unique dimensions such as Analysis, Judgment, and Decisiveness are used. Assessors know that they are observing something to do with decision making but, without substantial training, may be unreliable in their classification of behavior among the three dimensions. Several large-scale assessment centers have used this technique. They are the junior high school principal's examination for the New York City Board of Examiners, the police and fire department examinations for the City of Orlando, and the selection program for United States Army lieutenants. Such a procedure is highly advantageous when the assessment center is used strictly for selection purposes, when a high degree of dimensional reliability is desired, when assessor training cannot be extensive, or where unique methods of assessor training must be used (i.e., United States Army situation). An example of the strategy used in these assessment centers is to ask assessors to evaluate only two dimensions in a group exercise (Oral Communication and Leadership) or two dimensions in a fact-finding exercise (Oral Communication and Analysis). Breadth of observations from the exercises is decreased, but the reliability of each discrete observation is increased.

Reliability and Validity of Dimension Ratings

In the previous section of this chapter, the reliability and criterion validity of *exercise* ratings were examined. That evidence is helpful in evaluating separate exercises for research purposes and for deciding if exercises are contributing anything unique to measurement over and above other exercises. To evaluate such contributions, we examined ratings of overall performance in an exercise. Such ratings may have several distinct disadvantages: (a) exercise behavior is complex and a single rating of overall performance may be difficult; (b) overall performance, whether one "wins or loses," may be irrelevant; (c) halo error (i.e., high intercorrelations among dimension ratings) may be increased if an assessor knows he has to give an overall rating; (d) premature attention to overall effectiveness may lead assessors to overlook specific behavioral observations (i.e., "they may miss the trees for the forest"); (e) for developmental programs, measures of overall success in an exercise are not meaningful. These reasons explain why most assessment programs do not ask observers to judge overall participant effectiveness in exercises.

Whether for selection or developmental purposes, most managerial assessment centers are designed to measure level of functioning on several separate dimensions of managerial success. In this section, we review empirical research literature that examines the reliability and validity of dimension ratings emanating from assessment exercises.

In terms of the judgment model presented in Figures 1.1 and 1.2, the data reviewed here are relevant to Stages 1 and 2 of the assessment process. Data from Stage 1 have been analyzed for internal consistency of judgments about a given dimension as measured by different methods. Agreement among assessors on dimension ratings at Stage 2 after hearing all exercise reports has been evaluated by testing interrater correlations. Validity of final dimension ratings (Stage 2) has been investigated by correlating final dimension ratings with overall assessment ratings and subsequent success criteria (e.g., ratings of overall job performance, ratings on behavioral performance dimensions, and management progress in terms of level attained or salary increases).

Table 5.12 summarizes the results of 23 studies which contain relevant data. Appendix A contains the list of references. Median correlations are presented followed by the number of data points summarized. For research studies with distinct samples (e.g., college versus noncollege, whites versus blacks) several correlations are included in the average.

RELIABILITY

The internal consistency estimates came from reports by Byham (1981a), Hinrichs and Haanpera (1976), Huett (1975), and Neidig et al. (1978). These are measures of the relationships among ratings on the same dimension from different exercises (e.g., Oral Communication rated in the group discussion and game). The reported estimates are fairly low, but it should be recognized that they are a comparison of ratings from different exercises and different raters. Even assuming perfect judge reliability, we would expect to see different oral communications

Table 5.12
Median Reliability and Validity Estimates of Dimension Ratings (indicates number of studies)

Dimensions	Reliability		Validity			
			Internal		External	
	Internal consistency[a]	Interrater	Overall assessment rating	Overall performance rating	Progress[b]	Performance rating on dimension
Management						
Planning and Organizing	.19 (4)	.87 (20)	.73 (8)	.38 (2)		.24 (2)
Delegation	.13	.82	.55 (3)		.23 (7)	.20 (2)
Control	.13	.79 (5)	.57 (2)	.44	.03 (3)	
Administrative	.04		.38 (4)	.34 (3)	.28 (8)	.28 (2)
Decision Making						
Problem Analysis	.23 (3)	.82 (2)	.77 (5)		.13 (3)	.46 (2)
Creativity	.42	.85 (9)	.69 (4)	.30 (2)	.17 (9)	.25 (5)
Judgment	.22 (2)	.86 (2)	.85 (3)		.28 (3)	
Decision Making	.22 (2)	.84 (12)	.70 (6)	.31 (2)	.30 (3)	.20 (4)
Decisiveness	.20 (3)	.71 (3)	.78 (2)		.35 (3)	.19
Risk Taking	.08	.57	.53		.12 (4)	− .22
Communications						
Oral	.34 (4)	.88 (13)	.65 (12)	.32 (2)	.24 (14)	.39 (5)
Presentation	.32 (3)	.80	.68 (3)		.12 (3)	.46 (2)
Written		.84 ( )				

	Col 1	Col 2	Col 3	Col 4	Col 5	Col 6
Interpersonal						
Leadership	.25 (3)	.90 (14)	.84 (7)	.43 (2)	.27 (5)	.36 (2)
Sensitivity	.12 (2)	.73 (2)	.62 (9)	.23 (4)	.21 (3)	.40 (3)
Persuasiveness and Salesmanship	.62	.65	.82 (3)		.31 (4)	
Human Relations and Interpersonal		.43	.65 (7)	.35 (3)	.33 (7)	.27 (5)
Impact		.89	.76 (8)	.20	.32 (9)	.43 (3)
Aggressiveness	.66		.74		.24	
Relations with Authority		.80 (2)	.50		.16	.36
Development of Subordinates			.35 (3)			.67 (2)
Other						
Flexibility	.16	.82 (12)	.67 (5)	.45 (2)	.23 (3)	.18 (3)
Functional Ability		.91 (8)		.41		
Initiative	.15 (3)	.91 (11)	.60 (6)	.23 (6)	.32 (3)	.37
Personal Acceptability		.81	.26 (4)	.30 (2)	.31 (7)	.35
Company Orientation		.80 (18)		.41		
Personal Breadth and Range of Interests		.82 (5)	.46 (3)	.28	.03 (3)	.48 (2)
Self Confidence	.69		.80		.32	
Energy (Drive)	.52	.75 (4)	.58 (8)		.24 (10)	.20
Resistance to Stress and Tolerance of Uncertainty	.19 (3)	.68 (18)	.68 (5)		.23 (11)	.22 (4)
Inner Work Standards	.35 (3)	.61 (3)	.72 (3)		.26 (10)	.22 (2)
Self-Objectivity		.72 (2)			.10 (3)	
Need Advancement and Career Ambition		.84 (2)	.58		.28	.62
Amount of Participation		.93	.58			
Tenacity	.14 (3)	.80 (2)	.58 (2)		.24 (3)	.17
Independence	.19	.69 (2)	.56 (3)		.31 (3)	

[a] Average correlation of dimension ratings across different exercises.
[b] Promotions, management level, increase in salary.

behavior in different exercises. Considering each exercise a test item, we would hypothesize that the set of assessment exercises is heterogeneous. Therefore the low estimates are not necessarily negative evidence.

The interrater reliability estimates are adequate for most dimensions. Agreement among raters is consistently very high (over .80) for Planning and Organizing and Decision-Making skills, Communications Effectiveness, Initiative, Leadership, and selected other variables. Much lower agreement (less than .70) was consistently found for some stylistic dimensions (e.g., Resistance to Stress) and intrapersonal attributes (e.g., Inner-Work Standards and Independence). These data suggest that assessors can rate assessment center performance on most dimensions with a high level of agreement.

In most of these studies, the dimension ratings were obtained after all behavioral observations and exercise reports were given and the candidate had been discussed. At this point in the integration session, most differences in opinion should have been aired and resolved. Schmitt (1977) investigated changes in agreement before and after the discussion among four assessors who assessed 101 participants over a four-month period. Before discussion the median interjudge reliability across 17 dimensions was .67 and the median coefficient alpha (considering the four raters "test items") was .89. After discussion, the corresponding reliability estimates were .82 and .95. Clearly the discussion led to more agreement, but it should also be recognized that the agreement was fairly high at the start.

Most of the studies involved management personnel as assessors yet a few included combinations of managers and psychologists. In an attempt to evaluate any differential effects of rater group, Thomson (1970) compared reliabilities among two staff psychologists and three managers in the SOHIO program. Interrater reliabilities within the groups were comparable (.85 versus .89), mean and standard deviations of ratings by the groups were not significantly different, and the median correlation of dimension ratings from the two groups on 17 dimension was .85.

The previous review of interjudge reliability suggests high reliability for most exercises and dimensions, especially when adequate training has been carried out. To further ensure comparability among assessors, Neidig and Hall (1977) recommend "team balancing," a unique concept which utilizes data generated in training to match three-person teams in operational programs. Seventeen assessors (one assessor was used twice) were given three days of training, which consisted of observing six mock participants. The behavioral observations of two of these mock participants were reviewed in a traditional assessor discussion, followed by independent ratings on seven dimensions. Interjudge reliability was .88, but Neidig and Hall (1977) conducted further analyses of individual assessors. First, a leniency measure, comparing the individual assessor with the mean of all 17 assessors, was computed. Second, they summed difference scores across the seven dimensions to provide a discrepancy score. Teams were formed which yielded equivalent leniency and discrepancy scores. In addition, each team consisted of one female and two males. No validation of the comparison of the teams' judgments during the operational program was possible, but the authors believe team balancing can further enhance the defensibility of assessment center procedures by demonstrating equal rater qualifications across programs.

Another unique method of enhancing reliability of assessor ratings for operational assessment programs has been reported by Russell and Byham (1980). They tested the reliability of assessors during assessor training and eliminated all assessors whose ratings in the designated dimensions were significantly different from those of the other assessors. No comparative data are available, but one would suspect that such a procedure would produce more reliable final judgments.

VALIDITY

More important is the validity evidence. Table 5.12 summarizes the evidence regarding which dimensions contribute the most to the determination of the overall assessment rating. The most impressive feature of these data is the large number of dimensions to have been found to correlate significantly with the final assessment rating. These data, of course, come from a large number of studies; no one study included all the listed variables. Within any single study the same pattern is generally observed (i.e., significant correlations for most variables). These results would suggest that assessors are using a wide variety of data in making their overall rating.

Not all dimensions are weighted equally. Regression analyses have shown that assessors tend to place *more* weight on:

1. Leadership (Moses, 1972; Neidig *et al.*, 1978; Sackett & Hakel, 1979)
2. Planning and Organizing (Moses, 1972; Sackett & Hakel, 1979)
3. Decision-making (Moses, 1972; Hall, 1976; Neidig *et al.*, 1978; Sackett & Hakel, 1979)
4. Persuasiveness (Hinrichs & Haanpera, 1976)
5. Interpersonal Effectiveness (Huck, 1974)
6. Sensitivity (Neidig *et al.*, 1978)
7. Administrative Skills (Huck, 1974)

8. Oral Communication (Hall, 1976)
9. Impact (Mitchel, 1975)
10. Relations with Authority (Mitchel, 1975)
11. Personal Acceptability (Mitchel, 1975)
12. Drive (Mitchel, 1975; Sackett & Hakel, 1979)
13. Behavior Flexibility (Sackett & Hakel, 1979)

and to place *less* weight on:

1. Written Communication (Moses, 1972; Hinrichs & Haanpera, 1976; Sackett & Hakel, 1979)
2. Oral Communication (Moses, 1972)
3. Administrative Skills (Hinrichs & Haanpera, 1976)
4. Human Relations (Hall, 1976)
5. Problem Analysis (Hall, 1976)
6. Reliance on Others (Sackett & Hakel, 1979)
7. Resistance to Stress (Sackett & Hakel, 1979)

The most thorough study of the way in which assessors use assessment information to form overall ratings was conducted by Sackett and Hakel (1979) using archival data accumulated over a 3-year period at AT&T. Dimension ratings and the OAR recorded after the integration discussion were analyzed for 719 individuals assessed by 20 assessors in four teams. Regression analyses of the OAR on 17 dimensions for each individual assessor and assessor team revealed that only five to seven dimensions added significantly to multiple prediction. In reality, three dimensions accounted for the vast majority of variance in the OAR with dimensions four to seven adding only .05 to the multiple correlation. For the total sample, the five most important variables were Leadership, Organizing and Planning, Decision Making, Behavior Flexibility, and Energy. Wide differences in significant dimensions were identified for the individuals and teams. Comparison of the variables entering these regression analyses and clusters of variables emerging from factor analyses (to be discussed below) showed that Leadership variables and one or more of Organizing, Decision Making, Decisiveness always was weighted by the assessors. On the other hand, for 12 of 19 assessors and all teams, at least one interpretable factor did not appear to be weighted in the OAR. Sackett and Hakel (1979) conclude:

> In summary, overall decisions could be modeled accurately using a subset of available dimensions. Despite individual differences, use of a common set of predictors produced only a small decline in predictive power over the use of the optimal predictors for each assessor and assessor team. Two factors common to virtually all assessors were consistently formed to contain dimensions which entered significantly into the regression equation [pp. 131–132].

On the basis of these and other analyses, Sackett and Hakel (1979) question the standard practice of instructing assessors to consider all information when making an overall rating. For several reasons, it should not be inferred (and Sackett and Hakel do not overtly make the inference) that the results suggest a change in these instructions or a reduction in the number of dimensions assessed.

First, the statistical analyses assume and investigate only the *linear* relationships among dimension ratings and OAR. It is possible that nonlinear and configural judgment patterns are present. Second, the study does not address the validity of the dimension ratings in relation to subsequent performance criteria. Third, behavioral information reported and discussed in relation to "unimportant" dimensions may, in fact, contribute to predictive accuracy in the OAR. Fourth, the individual differences in weighted dimensions may be a strength rather than a weakness of the assessment center method by contributing unique points of view that would be squelched if all dimensions were not considered. Finally, dimension ratings themselves are important in developmental and diagnostic programs.

Review of the dimension data points out that each organization must analyze the dimensions of success for the particular job it is assessing. Some skills appear relatively more important in some settings and relatively unimportant in other settings.

Predictive validity of dimension ratings in comparison with criteria following the assessment program leads to similar conclusions. The right hand portion of Table 5.12 lists the relevant data. Overall job performance ratings are predicted ($r > .30$) in at least two studies by a number of management skills (Planning and Organizing, and General Administrative Ability), decision-making abilities (Creativity and Decision Making), Communication Skills, and interpersonal relations (Leadership, Sensitivity, Flexibility, and Human Relations), and other attributes (Initiative and Personal Acceptability). In general, the dimension ratings are less predictive of criteria of management progress, although significant correlations ($r > .30$) were found for some dimensions (e.g., Decision Making, Decisiveness, Persuasiveness, Interpersonal Relations, Initiative, Personal Acceptability, and Independence). Relatively few data back up the entries in the column for the on-the-job dimension ratings. The data which do exist are encouraging (i.e., there are high correlations between assessment center ratings and subsequent dimension ratings by managers who observe individuals on the job). High correlations were found for Problem Analysis, Oral Communication, Leadership, Sensitivity, Impact, and Development of Subordinates in at least two studies. More research is needed in this area.

There is also some evidence that there is close correspondence between the most "predictive" dimensions and the dimensions considered most "important" by the assessors. Moses (1972) and Moses and Boehm (1975) have shown that the rank order of correlations of dimensions with the OAR and correlations of dimensions with management progress are quite similar. Inspection of Table 5.12 leads to similar conclusions. The dimensions that consistently correlate most highly with overall performance are also those which correlate most highly with the OAR. To facilitate this comparison, Table 5.13 shows the dimensions with the largest correlations $(r > .30)$ with job performance. With the exception of administrative skills and personal acceptability, these dimensions are highly correlated with the final assessment rating. It appears that the assessors are using the right information to arrive at the final rating.

FACTOR ANALYSIS STUDIES

In an attempt to understand the construct validity of assessor ratings, a number of studies have used factor analysis to analyze dimension ratings. Beginning with the intercorrelations among dimensions, factor analysis identifies the common features of sets of these dimensions. The results provide some evidence of the major variables that influence assessor perceptions of manager behavior in the assessment exercises.

Table 5.14 summarizes the results of factor analyses in eight studies. It is often difficult to compare factors that emerged in the different studies because of differences in exercises, samples, dimensions, and their definitions. Nevertheless, a number of common factors can be observed. One factor represents a set of Administrative Skills including such dimensions as Planning and Organizing, Decision Making, and Written Communication skill. That Thomson (1969) found no similar factor is not sur-

Table 5.13
Comparison of Internal and External Validity of Dimension Ratings

Dimension	Correlation with overall job performance	Correlation with final assessment rating
Flexibility	.45	.67
Leadership	.43	.84
Planning and Organizing	.38	.73
Human Relations	.35	.65
Administrative	.34	.38
Oral Communication	.32	.65
Decision Making	.31	.70
Creativity	.30	.69
Personal Acceptability	.30	.26

Table 5.14
Summary of Factor Analysis Studies of Dimension Ratings

Factor Label	Bray and Grant (1966)	Thomson (1969)	Hinrichs (1969)	Huck (1974); Huck and Bray (1976)	Schmitt (1977)	Hinrichs and Haanpera (1974)	Sackett and Hakel (1979)	Huett (1975)
Administrative skills	1		2	2	1	2	1	3
Interpersonal skills	2	1, 3		1	2		2	4
Activity			1		3			1
Control of feelings	3		3			1		
Intellectual ability	4			4				
Work-oriented motivation	5	5						
Passivity	6							
Dependency	7							
Nonconformity	8							
Need for structure		2						
Quality of independent thinking		4						
Sensitivity				3		3		4
Independence								
Oral communications							2	1
Written communications							5	5

prising since no SOHIO dimensions or exercises cover administrative skills.

A second common factor seems to encompass a number of interpersonal skills. A wide range of specific dimensions fits this cluster: Human Relations skills, Behavior Flexibility, Personal Impact, Amount and Quality of Participation in a Group, Oral Communication skill, Energy, Forcefulness, and Leadership. Note that in the Huett study, separate communications factors were identified. The Interpersonal Skill factor is not present in the IBM studies (Hinrichs, 1969; Hinrichs & Haanpera, 1974) but again, this can be explained because there are no dimensions that clearly cover interpersonal skills.

A third factor clearly evidenced in four studies was amount of Activity. The related dimensions include Persuasiveness, Aggressiveness, Energy level, Self-Confidence, and Forcefulness. Elements of this factor are embedded in the interpersonal skills factors found in the AT&T studies (Bray & Grant, 1966; Huck, 1974; Huck & Bray, 1976).

No other factor emerges in more than two studies. The variety of factors suggests a diversity and lack of consistency in the dimensions used by various organizations.

Limitations in the reported studies should be noted. Hinrichs (1969) factor analyzed the ratings of only 47 assessees, and Schmitt (1976) analyzed data from only four raters, one of whom did not see the participants in situational exercises.

The Bray and Grant (1966) study analyzed dimension ratings with a hierarchical factoring procedure. Three general factors, possibly reflecting rater "halo," emerged. The first was interpreted to be a reflection of the general picture assessors had of the men with management potential. The factor had high loadings on most of the dimensions listed previously for the administrative and interpersonal factors, plus many other dimensions tapping motivation. In the noncollege sample, the first general factor split into two clusters (i.e., the administrative and other skills and the motivational variables). Factors 1 and 2 accounted for 30% of the total variance in the college sample and Factor 3 accounted for 26% of the variance in the noncollege sample. General effectiveness, as reflected in these factors, had a great influence on the assessor ratings. In addition, "factor scores" derived from the AT&T factors were correlated with salary progress in seven samples. Significant predictions were found for general effectiveness and passivity in four samples; administrative skills, interpersonal skills, and control of feelings in three samples; and intellectual ability and work-oriented motivation in two samples. Such findings support the meaningfulness of the factor structures and the accuracy of staff judgments in identifying relevant clusters of dimensions independent of general impressions.

The report by Hinrichs and Haanpera (1974) summarizes factor analyses of data on 393 individuals from eight countries. The diversity is both a strength and weakness. The first two factors, Activity and Organizing (administrative skills) were found in a majority of countries and we can be confident of their generalizability. An Independence factor occurred in only about half the analyses. Beyond this, there were great differences in the number and composition of factors patterns. The lack of consistency across countries may be attributable to small sample sizes (e.g., 24, 23, and 36) and differences in dimensions rated in some countries.

Sackett and Hakel (1979) factor analyzed the ratings of 20 individual assessors and four assessor teams and used parallel analysis to identify the number of nonrandom factors. Differences in the number and types of factors were observed, with only two consistent factors present (Table 5.14).

The most methodologically sound study was conducted by Huck (1974) using data from Michigan Bell's Personnel Assessment Program. Dimension ratings were analyzed for 241 white and 238 black females assessed over a 5-year period, 1967–1972. Factor analyses of the intercorrelations among the 16 dimensions were conducted for both samples. Four factors with eigenvalues greater than one emerged from both factorial solutions. Coefficients of congruence between comparable factors across the two racial samples were all over .90. Step-wise multiple regression analyses of factor scores and the overall assessment rating revealed that, in both samples, the four factors entered the two regression equations in the same order and produced multiple correlations of .944 for whites and .941 for blacks. Huck (1974) concludes, "In summary, the factor structures, the intercorrelations among the factors, and the contribution of each factor to the Overall Assessment Rating appear to be nearly identical for whites and blacks [p. 60]."

Stability of factor structures over time was found in a unique study by King and Boehm (1980) using data from SOHIO's program in three time periods from 1969 to 1978. Even though the assessors and assessees were different populations in each analysis, factor one always consisted of a set of cognitive ability test scores, factor two included dimensions representing performance style, and factor three included dimensions representing interpersonal style.

Importance of dimension ratings. Dimension ratings are important for both selection and development programs. For diagnostic purposes, the program should yield clear indications of the individual's relative strengths and developmental needs. The assessment exercises must provide convergent and discriminant validity; that is, there must be confirmation of measurement from more than one method and there must be relatively low correlations among dimensions as measured by the various exercises. For selection purposes, the final assessment rating must have validity, but dimension ratings are also important for two reasons. First, accuracy of prediction will be *increased* if valid dimension ratings are examined before a final rating is given. Second, accuracy of prediction may be *decreased* if invalid information is generated or if too much information is presented to the rater.

SUMMARY OF DIMENSION RATINGS

The research reviewed in this section provides a wealth of data to support the accuracy of behavioral observation and dimension ratings in assessment centers. Assessors show high levels of agreement when rating performance on several behavioral dimensions. They use a wide variety of information when formulating an overall assessment judgment. Even more important, the dimension ratings appear to be related to subsequent job performance and progress and to behavioral ratings on comparable criteria on the job. Furthermore, when combining information into the overall assessment rating, assessors weight most heavily the dimension ratings that are the most predictive of job performance. Factor analyses show consistency in clusters of dimensions used in several programs. In general, assessment center research has demonstrated that dimension ratings meet a number of psychometric standards of reliability and validity. What has not been shown is that discriminant validity exists for the dimensions ratings derived from the various exercises. In other words, correlations between ratings of the *same* dimension assessed in *different* exercises are often lower than the correlations between ratings of *different* dimensions within the *same* exercise (Byham, 1981a).

Needed Research

Looking over the evidence presented in this chapter provides clear support for the content validity and construct validity of assessment centers. The exercises cover a wide range of intellectual, administrative, and interpersonal activities. Many behavioral dimensions reflecting managerial, decision-making, and communications skills are measured. What is missing is a body of research showing the particular dimensions which can be accurately observed and reliably rated in each exercise. In other words, the existing data do not tell us much about the construct validity of separate exercises. What is clearly needed are more research studies such as those by Byham (1981a) and Hinrichs and Haanpera (1976) showing the correlations of dimensions ratings from several exercises. Data could be cast in the framework of a multitrait–multimethod matrix (Campbell & Fiske, 1959) and analyzed with analysis of variance techniques proposed by Kavanaugh, MacKinney, and Wolins (1971). The payoffs would be in a better understanding of the convergent and discriminant validity of the exercises.

There is a potential limitation of the proposed design for assessment center data; that is, type of exercise and assessor are highly confounded. For example, as illustrated in Figure 1.1, Assessor A conducts the background interview, Assessor B observes the leaderless group discussion, and Assessor C reviews the in-basket responses. Any correlation of Creativity ratings would be partly a function of the method (exercise) and source (assessor). This criticism is partly mitigated by the standard practice of rotating assessor assignments for different assessees.

Further research is also needed on the question of whether dimension ratings should even be used in assessment centers. It may be more effective to select exercises which simulate a large portion of the job activities and simply rate the overall effectiveness of assessees in these exercises. No research studies have evaluated the comparative reliability and predictive validity of exercise ratings versus dimension ratings.

In summary, more research on the judgment processes in the various stages of assessor judgments is necessary. These studies are relatively easy to do in the framework of assessor training and operational programs and would require little additional data gathering.

Appendix A: References for Reliability and Validity of Dimension Ratings

American Airlines, 1976
Bentz, 1971
Bray and Grant, 1966
Clingenpeel, 1979
Hall, 1976
Grossner, 1974
Hinrichs and Haanpera, 1974
Hinrichs and Haanpera, 1976
Huck, 1974
Huck and Bray, 1976
Huett, 1974
McConnell, 1973

McConnell and Parker, 1972
Mitchel, 1975
Moses, 1972
Moses, 1973b
Moses and Boehm, 1975
Neidig and Hall, 1977
Neidig et al., 1978
Sackett and Hakel, 1979
Schmitt, 1977
Slivinski, Grant, Bourgeois, and Pederson, 1977
Wollowick and McNamara, 1969
Worbois, 1975

6
The Assessment Process

In the last two decades a number of serious charges have been made against the field of industrial psychology. Two predominant criticisms have been: (a) industrial practice has often outstripped empirical research evidence; and (b) the field lacks sound theoretical foundations. Chapter 7 will respond to the first charge by reviewing in detail the massive body of predictive-validity evidence which has demonstrated the accuracy of the overall assessment rating in relation to managerial performance and progress. This chapter responds to the second charge. In it we extract a number of principles that underlie the observation, evaluation, and prediction processes in assessment centers. Our analysis of the assessment center process is relevant to a number of problems in person perception, social judgment theory, and psychological assessment.

The judgment processes involved in making assessments of managerial capabilities and in making predictions of managerial success are central in many assessment center programs and will probably remain so. However, it should be recognized that assessment centers serve many functions in organizations. For some of these functions, the accuracy of judgments is less important. For example, in assessment centers whose purposes are to stimulate self-motivation for behavioral change, the accuracy of assessor evaluations is less critical although still important. This chapter is relevant to the understanding of all assessment center procedures, but it is most clearly relevant to those cases where accuracy of dimension ratings and prediction of success are the primary objectives.

Steps in the Assessment Procedure

In this section we describe the process of gathering and integrating the information obtained during an assessment center. The steps covered here are embedded in the three-stage assessment model outlined in Chapter 1. In that earlier discussion we focused on the logistics of matching dimensions to exercises and assessors to exercises and the types of quantified data generated at each stage. In this section we emphasize the *processes* of observing and integrating the information. The first three steps deal with making behavioral observations during the exercises and preparing exercise reports. The next steps describe the process of integrating the information during the assessor discussion of each individual participant. There are many variations on the basic process, but the following sequence is most commonly followed.

FOR EACH EXERCISE

1. *Observation of behavior:* Each assessor observes and records behavior of one or two participants. Assessors are encouraged to record as much detail as possible. They record in objective terms the specific things the participant says and does. To avoid premature conclusions, no interpretations are permitted at this stage. The participant is observed by a different assessor in each exercise. For example, if Participant 1 is observed by Assessor A in the first group exercise, Assessor B is responsible for the observations in a later group exercise. Similar rotation of assignments is carried out for individual exercises. This process ensures that different assessors observe each individual in a variety of settings and tasks. The assignments also ensure that each assessor has exposure to all participants. Assessors watch only for behaviors relevant to dimensions observable in that exercise.

2. *Classification of behavior:* Immediately after the exercise, the assessor sorts and classifies the behavioral observations into the organization's target dimensions. Dimensions are chosen if they are essential to the job and observable in the exercise. They are usually listed on an exercise report form.

3. *Rating behavior:* All of the behavioral evidence for the dimensions is reviewed and ratings of the dimensions are made. A 0-to-5 scale is usually used:

   5   *Much more than acceptable:* Significantly above criteria required for successful job performance

4   *More than acceptable:* Generally exceeds criteria relative to quality and quantity of behavior required

3   *Acceptable:* Meets criteria relative to quality and quantity of behavior required

2   *Less than acceptable:* Generally does not meet criteria relative to quality and quantity of behavior required

1   *Much less than acceptable:* Significantly below criteria required for successful job performance

0   No opportunity existed for the dimension to be shown.

ASSESSOR DISCUSSION

4. *Exercise reports:* During the discussion all information for one participant is reported and integrated before considering the next participant. Each assessor reads the exercise report prepared previously. The report includes a brief narrative of the individual's role in the exercise, ratings on dimensions, and behavior observed relevant to each dimension. In some cases an overall exercise rating is given, but this is usually not appropriate. The order of exercise reports is held constant for all assessees. Often the background interview (if part of the assessment center) is reported first, followed by reports of the group exercises (e.g., leaderless group discussion) and the individual exercises (e.g., analysis problem, interview simulation, and in-basket). There is no standard practice in the order of presentation. Although many organizations save the in-basket report for last because assessors consider it to be such a powerful source of data, using it last also prevents the possibility of the interpretation of other exercise reports from being biased.

5. *Assessors record behavior:* As one assessor reads a report, the other assessors record significant behaviors on a special form and independently rate the participant on each dimension, based on reported behavior. The assessors are permitted to ask clarifying questions but no discussion takes place, nor can the reporter be challenged on an interpretation on ratings at this point. This same process of reporting exercises and rating dimensions continues until all exercises have been covered.

6. *Preliminary dimension ratings:* At this point each assessor independently reviews all data reported for each dimension. Considering the behaviors reported in all the exercises, the assessor gives a preliminary dimension rating, indicating the level of skill demonstrated across all exercises. The assessor must consider that some exercises yield stronger opportunities to observe certain dimensions. For example, the

in-basket is a better measure of Planning and Organizing than the interview simulation. Therefore, the assessor should weigh more heavily the observations from certain exercises when giving an overall dimension rating. It should not be a simple average of dimension ratings from individual exercises.

7. *Preliminary dimension ratings are posted:* The preliminary dimension ratings are posted on a chart listing the dimensions down the left side and the assessors' names across the top. This composite chart provides a quick view of the areas of agreement and disagreement.

8. *Assessor discussion:* The assessors then discuss their ratings on each dimension until a consensus is obtained. In some programs the ratings from the assessors are averaged to provide a final dimension rating. This is usually not done because more insight into the assessee's performance can be obtained from discussing discrepancies. Two assessors will frequently shift their ratings when they hear the third assessor's reasoning based on behavioral data.

9. *Overall assessment rating (OAR):* In most cases an overall assessment is made independently by each assessor; then it is posted and discussed by the group until consensus is reached. The overall assessment rating may be in terms of probability of success if hired, promotability, or likelihood of advancing to middle management. The OAR may also be a summary evaluation of performance in the program or prediction of future success. It takes into account performance across all exercises and dimensions as observed by all assessors.

10. *Other comments:* Depending on the purpose of the program, another discussion may now take place. The assessors may propose developmental suggestions and suggest ways to structure the written and oral feedback to the participant and/or to the participant's manager.

Following the discussion, the administrator or one of the assessors prepares a written report of the assessment and developmental suggestions. Feedback is then given to the participant and appropriate levels of management.

Basic Principles in the Assessment Center Process

The complex assessment procedures carried out in assessment centers will be analyzed in terms of several basic principles. Although not all assessment centers conform to the models we have described or use the exact same steps just listed, there is enough similarity to warrant the following generalizations. Certainly these principles apply to all assessment centers, and it is our contention that when these principles are applied systematically they lead to accuracy of assessment and prediction of managerial performance.

1. Assessment should be based on clearly defined dimensions of managerial behavior.
2. Multiple assessment techniques should be used.
3. A variety of types of job sampling techniques should be used.
4. The assessors should know what it takes to succeed. They should be thoroughly familiar with the job and organization and, if possbile, have experience in the job.
5. The assessors should be thoroughly trained in assessment center procedures.
6. Behavioral data should be observed, recorded, and communicated among the assessor team.
7. Group discussion processes should be used to integrate observations, rate dimensions, and make predictions.
8. The assessment process should be separated into stages that delay the formation of general impressions, evaluations, overall ratings, or final predictions.
9. Assessees should be evaluated against a clearly understood norm—not against each other.
10. Prediction of managerial success must be judgmental.

OVERVIEW OF SOCIAL JUDGMENT THEORY

As we begin to discuss these principles and relate our findings to other research, it will become clear that there is much in common between assessment center procedures and the theories and research in human judgment. Until now, there has been little integration of these two fields. Roose and Doherty (1976) suggested that "it would be fruitful to explore points of contact between judgment and rating literature [p. 247]," and they refer specifically to the assessment methods as a close analogue to judgmental prediction research.

Social judgment research has led to a number of general conclusions:

1. A linear combination of cues can quite accurately predict human judgments in real-world tasks. In some cases, judges make configural judgments using patterns of cues.
2. Individual differences in cue utilization values can be detected (a process called "policy capturing") and studied.
3. Judges use a relatively small number of cues when making

judgments and are unaware that they rely on few cues. Three cues usually account for 80% of the variance in judgment.
4. Judges' stated weights for cues do not always coincide with actual weights used in making judgments. They tend to overestimate the importance they place on minor cues.
5. Cue utilization weights often do not correspond to cue validities. Judges can be trained (a) which cues to use; (b) to use cues more appropriately; and (c) to use combinations and patterns of cues in configured judgment. Of the above, (a) is easier to learn than (b), and (c) is most difficult to learn.
6. Just telling people the accuracy of their judgment (i.e., achievement) is not as helpful as giving them feedback on cue utilization.
7. Once a judge's cue weights are determined, statistical predictions using these weights on a new set of cues are more accurate than the judge's predictions. This is due to the unreliability of human judgment strategies.

Many of the results of social judgment research support the assessment center process whereas others contradict it. As we review the principles of the assessment center methodology, we will high-light the compatible and incompatible principles.

Discussion of Principles and Related Research

ASSESSMENT SHOULD BE BASED ON CLEARLY DEFINED
DIMENSIONS OF BEHAVIOR

Effective assessment center procedures are based on the identification, definition, and evaluation of defined managerial job dimensions. Several important points should be emphasized at the outset.

First, the procedure necessitates a thorough analysis of the job. All other phases of the assessment center, including selection of assessment exercises, training of assessors, observation of participant behavior, and prediction of managerial abilities are predicated on this essential first step. In contrast, other personality assessment approaches begin from the frame of reference of the individual being assessed or from some theory of personality.

Second, the job analysis used in starting an assessment center determines the behavioral dimensions of managerial effectiveness. In contrast, many other management appraisal efforts have focused on outcome criteria of managerial success such as productivity or promotion. Using a distinction set forth by Guion (1965), assessment centers have identified (primary) behaviors rather than (secondary) indices of managerial effectiveness. Korman (1968) made a similar observation when he reviewed techniques for predicting managerial effectiveness. He concluded that judgmental approaches are more effective than psychometric approaches, based partly on different concerns for the criterion. He also reasoned that judgmental approaches are concerned with predicting stable, well known, and psychologically meaningful dimensions of managerial adequacy; whereas psychometric approaches too often focus on complex criteria whose construct validity is unknown.

Third, the assessed dimensions are usually restricted to a select sample of the components of the manager's job. Review of the literature cited in Chapter 4 suggests that managerial jobs have several components including job knowledge and specific skills which are not evaluated in an assessment center. Assessment centers have tended to focus on the managerial components such as administrative skills, leadership, and decision making. They have not attempted to evaluate all components of managerial job success such as technical skills or skills specific to one functional area because these factors can be more adequately judged from on-the-job observations or from interviews. In other areas of industrial psychology, job analysis is often neglected. Job analysis is a lost art no longer receiving its proper attention (McCormick, 1976, 1979). Nevertheless, assessment center programs have reaffirmed the importance of beginning any evaluation procedure with a thorough understanding of job requirements. The better assessment center programs have thoroughly analyzed jobs and have clearly tied the assessment dimensions and exercises to the analyses. Where the dimensions and exercises have been so defined and specified, the programs have been successful. After reviewing a number of the early assessment programs in military organizations, educational settings, and in the field of personality assessment, Taft (1959) concluded that the better programs used some objective methods of analyzing job requirements. For example, Stern et al. (1956) systematically evaluated the job requirements and job demands in educational institutions as they affect teacher effectiveness.

In the context of social judgment research, it has been established that prediction is more accurate when the stimulus variables have high cue validity (Slovic & Lichtenstein, 1973). This condition is met by asking the assessors to observe and evaluate behavior on only dimensions that have emerged from some job analysis procedure, such as the critical incident method, which distinguishes acceptable from unacceptable job performance. As Dawes and Corrigan (1974) have observed, "The whole trick is to decide what variables to look at and then know how to add [p. 105]." Assessors do not have to perform the first part of the "trick" because it has been done for them by the job analysis. (We will explore the second aspect of the "trick" later.)

There is some research that demonstrates that the relative importance of the cues is important to consider in making judgments. But in most assessment centers, assessors are not told in advance the relative importance of dimensions. In many cases it is not possible to determine the correlations of dimensions and a criterion, however the relative importance of dimensions is usually known from the job analyses. Nevertheless assessment center administrators have been reluctant to give assessors numerical weightings, lest the assessors attempt a mathematical integration of data, thus overlooking the interrelationship of the dimensions and overlooking special dimensional weightings for a particular job. In lieu of weighting information, assessors are usually told to use their best judgment in weighting the dimensions. The question arises: How accurate are predictions based on subjective weights? Schmitt (1978) compared the accuracy of prediction when judges used subjectively estimated and objectively determined weights for four test scores when predicting grade point average. Multiple correlations were statistically lower when using subjective weights but the difference was quite small (the correlations were only .03–.05 lower). These findings support the standard practice of advising assessors to weight the information using their best judgment when objective cue validities cannot be provided.

One assessment center study that attempted to account for differences in importance of dimensions was conducted by Worbois (1975). He asked superiors to rate the work performance of subordinate supervisors on 12 abilities and to rate the importance of these abilities. One criterion measure was a multiplicative combination of the rating times the importance (R × I). The results showed a correlation of .79 between the R and R × I variables. In comparison with the simple rating, the R × I combination correlated lower with assessment rating of overall performance and predicted level of management. Worbois (1975) concluded that "the attempt to allow for some abilities being more critical in some kinds of work than in others in the R × I scores appears not to have been very successful [p. 89]."

The preponderance of studies has demonstrated that judges use only a limited number (usually three) of cues (Slovic & Lichtenstein, 1973), however, some research demonstrates more information can be integrated. Slovic (1969) found that expert stockbrokers use up to seven cues in making investment decisions. Phelps and Shanteau (1978) found that livestock judges used 9 to 11 pieces of information when making judgments of breeding quality based on a written list of characteristics, but used only two cues when viewing photographs. The first condition (i.e., having written information) more closely approximates the tasks of assessors in an assessment center. Thus it seems appropriate that a list of assessment center dimensions should have more than three dimensions in it. It seldom seems necessary to include more than 12 or 15 dimensions but some special cases may exist. It should be recognized though that assessors are not likely to use more than a few dimensions when integrating dimension ratings into an overall assessment rating (Sackett & Hakel, 1979).

MULTIPLE ASSESSMENT TECHNIQUES SHOULD BE USED

One of the main features of assessment centers is their reliance on multiple sources of data. A number of errors of measurement can be eliminated by observing an individual in several different exercises designed to measure the same characteristics. Random errors leading to unreliability (e.g., due to unusual sampling of test tasks) can be minimized with multiple observations of the same category of exercise. Redundancy of measurement from several different exercises with demonstrated convergent validity minimizes the potential for method bias.

The argument is not simply "safety in numbers" (Taft, 1959), but rather that the process of seeking confirmation from several exercises leads to more validity of measurement of complex dimensions.

In the last chapter, we cited evidence regarding which dimensions are measured by the various job simulation exercises and showed evidence (Byham & Byham, 1976) that assessors feel that they can make adequate observations of several dimensions in each exercise. Nevertheless, not all exercises are equally appropriate for all dimensions. The game is particularly suitable for assessing the ability to direct others, whereas the case study presentation assesses Oral Communication skill but doesn't give much insight into the assessee's Energy component (working long periods with sustained drive).

Attribution theory (Kelley, 1973) helps us understand the significance of the assessment center technology because assessment centers force us to observe several people in several related situations. Attribution theory (AT) deals with the process by which an observer infers the causes underlying an actor's behaviors. Four possible causes are typically studied: two personal causes—effort and ability—and two external causes—task difficulty and luck. In assessment, we wish to evaluate the individual person on relevant behavioral dimensions. Kelley (1973) explains that the observer attributes success (or failure) to the person when success (or failure) is observed for this person (but not other people) on this task or similar tasks over a period of time. The consistency of behavior over time and tasks and the observation that other people behaved differently allows the observer to eliminate the potential attribution of behavior to external causes or to the "circumstances." Under the conditions described, attribution can accurately be made to the personal characteristics of the actor. Assessment center methodology provides behavioral samples from related exercises and from a number of assessees in standardized conditions.

A VARIETY OF TYPES OF JOB SAMPLING TECHNIQUES
SHOULD BE USED

The last principle emphasized the importance of the *number* of exercises; here we advocate a broad spectrum of *types* of exercises. If properly designed, assessment center exercises can usually mirror 80–90% of the major activities associated with the target job. The major activities and their relative importance are determined and defined through job analysis. Thus, it is possible to measure the degree of coverage provided by a content-valid assessment center. For example, a job analysis may review the following information:

Task	Percentage of time occupied	Assessment center exercise
One-to-one meetings with subordinates on	20	Interview simulation on work habits
Work habits, 5%		
Job performance, 5%		
Absenteeism problems, 2%		
Providing training on new job procedures, 3%		
Other, 5%		
Scheduling subordinates' work	10	Scheduling exercise
Attending meetings as a participant	20	Nonassigned role leaderless group discussion
To gain information		
To distribute finite resources		
To make group decisions		
Attending meetings as a leader	5	Assigned role leaderless group discussion
Diagnose production problems	5	Fact-finding exercise
Plan: material and people	10	In-basket
Administrative decisions, completing forms, reports, etc.	10	In-basket
Other	20	In-basket

As will be noted from above, all of the major components of the job described are covered by assessment center exercises, and even the subject matter of exercises like the interview simulation is derived from the study of the job.

The above information is only a small part of the many pages of the job descriptive information produced by a well-conducted job analysis. The detailed information provided by the job analysis permits the organization to tailor the entire assessment center to job content including each item of the in-basket.

No single test or even battery of tests approaches the intrinsic ability of assessment centers to measure job content. Other tests measure relatively narrow job factors such as intelligence, personality, and other variables.

One of the reasons assessment center exercises can give such a broad coverage of job content is that most assessment center exercises (reviewed in Chapter 5) are designed to measure several managerial abilities (dimensions) at the same time; that is, they are molar rather than molecular in their coverage. This approach is somewhat antithetical to many of the traditional psychometric principles of test construction. The psychometric literature suggests that more effective tests are ones that measure relatively specific, distinct characteristics. It is frequently argued (Cronbach, 1970; Nunnally, 1978) that tests should measure constructs that are uniquely defined and independent: They should measure one, and only one, trait or characteristic.

One cannot argue with these admonitions. Certainly, it is advantageous to narrowly focus many measurement instruments; however, there are many theoretical and practical reasons why assessment center measurements are superior because of omnibus coverage of dimensions:

1. In general, the functions performed by managers are quite complex and interrelated. Thus, to mirror the activity requires a complex test with many interrelated parts, forcing a degree of complication on the measurement system which makes the simultaneous measurement of several dimensions quite efficient.

2. The concept of having a small number of test items all aimed at the same measurement area is quite different from the concept of an assessment center where an entire exercise may lead to only one act of judgment—thus, one opportunity to evaluate that particular dimension. Generally, a dimension such as Judgment must be evaluated in several different places in the assessment center in order to get sufficient reliability of measurement. If only Judgment were evaluated, the process would be very inefficient. As used in assessment centers, several dimensions are

evaluated so that the needed redundancy of observations is maintained while having very efficiently gained additional information.

Does it make a difference to have information from these types of exercises? Research in other human judgment situations suggests that relevant information is used. From research on interviewing at the Life Insurance Agency Management Association, Carlson (1970) concluded that interviewers will use valid information if it is available. Leonard (1973) found that interrater reliability is higher when raters are provided information relevant to the job, and Freeberg (1969) concluded that raters can make valid observations only when the subjects are performing relevant tasks. He showed that ratings obtained when the raters observed the subjects engaging in behavior relevant to the criterion task were more valid than ratings of observed irrelevant behavior.

THE ASSESSORS SHOULD KNOW
WHAT IT TAKES TO SUCCEED

The assessment staff usually consists of managers who are one to three levels above the position for which people are being assessed. Salespeople being assessed for sales manager may be assessed by district or regional managers. Machine operators being considered for first-level supervision may be assessed by second- or third-level managers. In most cases, the assessment is conducted by individuals who have supervised or closely observed persons in the target job. These experiences provide the manager–assessor with an understanding of the types of behaviors associated with successful performance and minimum job requirements in each dimension and an appreciation for organizational demands. In conjunction with assessor training, this background provides a unique combination of knowledge of job requirements and skills for evaluating potential suitability for the position.

In a number of places throughout this book, the limitations of a person's immediate supervisor assessing potential have been pointed out. The immediate supervisor can provide an evaluation of current job performance but not necessarily potential for success on higher level jobs. Having only limited exposure to persons below in the organization hierarchy, the immediate supervisor has limited experience in his or her own job, and is subject to certain biases when asked to evaluate subordinates for promotion. As we have said, the higher level manager is better able to serve as an assessor. With respect to assessors, the standard practice of the assessment centers described in this book differs from the few programs which use representatives of the personnel or training departments or outside professionals (usually psychologists) as assessors.

Basically, psychologists or staff members are probably at least as good as managers in observing, recording, and communicating behavior. They may be poorer in interpreting the meaning of the behavior for a particular job. Their standards of minimally effective Oral Communication may be quite different from the standards of line managers who have seen people with quite poor skills on this dimension succeed on the job. Differences in rating standards would depend on the "outsider's" knowledge of the target job or job level. The more general the target (e.g., "general management" or "executive level"), the less difference one would expect.

Some organizations use combinations of managers and "outside" assessors, assuming that the managers will provide the necessary input on standards. "Outsiders" used in most mixed assessor groups are not outside psychologists or consultants. They are representatives of the organization's personnel or training department. There are definitely situations where it is advisable to use professionals (e.g., at high levels in the organization, or where general management dimensions are required for the target job), but usually the arguments are strongly in favor of using trained managers as assessors because of their greater job knowledge, their greater credibility to the assessees, and the greater acceptance of their conclusions by their fellow managers.

Evidence for the effectiveness of nonprofessional assessors comes from studies by Thomson (1970) and Greenwood and McNamara (1969). Thomson compared the ratings of managers and psychologists using a multitrait–multimethod approach. The means and standard deviations of ratings for managers and psychologists did not differ and the median correlation between the two sets of ratings for 13 scales was .85. The correlation for ratings of managerial potential was .93. In general, he found large amounts of convergent validity for the two groups of assessors. Greenwood and McNamara (1967) found no differences between professional and nonprofessional observers' ratings of participant performance for several groups in three different exercises. With one exception, there were no significant differences among the means and standard deviations. On the basis of these and other considerations (cost, acceptability to participants and higher managers), middle managers are preferable.

Managers being trained as assessors possess different amounts and types of education and training; they have different attitudes and values; and they display different managerial styles and skills. We might wonder what effects these differences will have on their assessments. Such variables have not been researched in assessment centers, but the role of the judge's or observer's personality in social judgments has been investigated extensively by social and personality psychologists. Kaplan

(1975) summarized four potential ways that individual judge's differences can affect social judgment.

First, judges may differ in the value or weight they place on information. In an assessment center, a reported behavior "Bob expressed disagreement with Tim" may be considered positive by one assessor and negative by another assessor, even when both know the task, circumstances, and situation in which the act took place. In the assessor discussion, such differences in values are discussed among the assessor team members. If an interpretation of behavior is idiosyncratic to one assessor, the fact is brought out and it is not used in evaluating a dimension or in the overall assessment rating.

Second, judges may differ in the implicit personality theories (IPT) they use in social judgment. IPT refers to the set of assumptions people have about the relationship among traits. Research in this area has shown that there are some elements common to different people's IPT, judges can be clustered according to common points of view, and there are individual differences in the effects of these IPTs. The important point is that judges may differ in the extent and types of inferences they make when relating known information to additional characteristics about the person. Assessor training attempts to deal with these processes by discussing the definitions and differences among dimensions and by pointing out the analogues of exercise behavior on the job. More importantly, assessors are taught to observe and report behavior in the assessment center and to not get involved in trying to understand the "personality" of the person being involved. In the assessment discussion, the administrator (and other assessors) will challenge an assessor if he or she is making unwarranted inferences from behavior in an exercise.

Third, judges may differ in the way they integrate information when making a judgment. Cognitive styles (e.g., complexity) appear to be related to the ability to integrate inconsistent information and to avoid order-of-presentation effects. Individual differences in the ability to make configured judgments (consideration of the *pattern* of stimulus information) have been noted. More importantly, it has been found that people use configured processing if the task and stimulus conditions permit. In an assessment center, many of these conditions are present. Assessors are provided information from several different independent sources. When formulating dimension ratings, they are presented reports from different observers who watched different exercises. When formulating the overall assessment rating, they are considering information on several dimensions. It is not assumed that the dimensions are completely independent (orthogonal), but they are enough different from each other to provide unique information for a complex decision.

A fourth source of individual differences in judgment is the set of moods, biases, and preconceptions that judges bring to the judgment situation. Both temporary "states" and stable "traits" may affect judgments. These dispositions of the judge seem to be minimized when judges are provided: (a) more information; (b) nonredundant information; (c) relevant information; and (d) information from reliable and confident sources. The assessment center technology meets these criteria in many ways: (a) assessors have access to extensive observations; (b) there are different types of exercises (groups versus individual, verbal versus written, high and low stress, upward and downward communication, etc.); (c) exercises sample job-related behavior and (d) each assessor is a competent manager and thoroughly trained assessor.

In summary, when the assessment center process is considered in relation to the potential problems that the judges may cause in the process of social judgment, many of the negative effects are minimized. Furthermore, the use of multiple managers capitalizes on a number of features of human judgment which can enhance assessment accuracy.

How many assessors are necessary? The typical assessment center program includes three assessors observing six participants. Any one participant is observed, discussed, and rated by all assessors. Although the optimum number has been little studied in assessment center research, support for the number *three* comes from research by Libby and Blashfield (1978). Various numbers of judges were involved in three experimental tasks: (1) prediction of business failure; (2) prediction of graduate school decisions; and (3) differentiation of psychotic from neurotic patients. "In all three tasks, equal-weighted composites of three judges were substantially more accurate than were individual judges . . . . Larger aggregates ($N > 3$) led to only small improvements [Libby & Blashfield, 1978, p. 157]." It should be noted that this was a study of the statistical relationship of composite scores for various groups of judges and did not involve actually varying the size of discussion groups.

THE ASSESSORS SHOULD BE THOROUGHLY TRAINED

Assessor training typically deals with the assessment dimensions, the behavioral observation and rating process, the types of behaviors observable in each exercise, standards for rating behavior in exercises, and the process of integrating information in the assessor discussion. Training usually takes 2–5 days and some organizations provide 2 weeks of training plus the participation in one program as an understudy to an experienced assessor.

Assessment center procedures are effective when members of the staff develop a common understanding of the dimensions being observed and evaluated. Understanding starts with a clear definition of the dimension. A good definition has three parts: (a) the name; (b) the working definition; and (c) examples of behaviors that were classified under the title. Sometimes a fourth component is present in the form of comments to differentiate the dimension from other dimensions. Some sample definitions of dimensions are presented in Appendix B, Chapter 4. Common understanding acquired through formal assessor training and practice in rating participants is sharpened in the assessment discussions. If an assessor misclassifies behavior, it is pointed out. Thus the staff in an assessment center refines its understanding of assessment dimensions by continually discussing meanings and implications.

Acker and Perlson (1970) have shown that assessor training and experience improved the manager's ability to evaluate managerial performance. The amount of disagreement among staff members in rating candidates decreased over four separate assessment center sessions. With experience, the assessors developed more unified standards for evaluating candidates. Acker and Perlson (1970) believe these standards will carry over to future appraisal of subordinates' on-the-job performances. Richards and Jaffee (1972) also found improvements in assessor ratings with training.

The evidence that observation skills can be developed is encouraging. Evidence from human judgment research clearly shows that subjects can learn to use cues that allow accurate prediction. Raters can learn the most appropriate cues to use as well as the shape of the functional relationship between cues and the criterion. Although difficult to master, nonlinear as well as linear relationships between cues and criteria can be learned (Brehmer, 1971; Hammond & Summers, 1965; Ogilvie & Schmitt, 1979). This is important, because assessment center judgments often must be based on nonlinear dimensional relationships in determining managerial success. For example, both low and high standings on a dimension such as Risk Taking may be signs of ineffective management. However, assessor training and experience help the assessor to recognize these nonlinear relationships. Chapter 11 speculates on research opportunities to further enhance assessor capabilities to use complex forms of information.

The effort expended to obtain and maintain consistent standards and the resultant proven consistency of assessment center standards should be contrasted with the frequent lack of such standards in other rating situations. Supervisors on the job, interviewers of job candidates, and clinical psychologists seldom have the opportunity to develop common frames of reference for observing candidates' behavior. Such reference points are important, because it has been found that if observers do not agree they will look for different indicators of future performance.

It is important that training experience be supplemented with further training and guidance, such as that provided in the continuing discussions of candidates in an assessment center.

BEHAVIORAL DATA SHOULD BE OBSERVED, RECORDED, AND COMMUNICATED

As discussed earlier, the entire assessment center process is based on the notion that behavior predicts behavior. The assumption is that if a person does a good job of planning in an assessment center exercise, he or she will do a good job of planning on the job. If a person is insensitive in assessment center exercises, he or she will be insensitive if placed in a job requiring the same kind of sensitivity. Thus, the principal task of an assessor is to observe, record, and communicate the behavior of assigned assessees. Dimensions are only a convenient system of categorizing of those behaviors. The ratings scales used are merely a method of communicating the value of the behaviors in general.

The use of behavior as the foundation of the assessment center process avoids many of the problems inherent in many judgmental processes. As will be discussed later, the judgmental aspects of the assessment center are delayed until the very end of the process where they can be dealt with by a group of people, each giving his or her own judgment.

The emphasis on behavioral observation may explain why managers make such good assessors. Once managers understand the concept of what a behavior is and they have been trained in behavior observation, categorization, rating, and communication, they find assessment relatively easy.

The use of behavior in the assessment center process is critical relative to the exchange of data and the reaching of a consensus. This process will be described later. A good discussion among assessors can be obtained when each contributes his or her behavioral observations. Those observations can be weighed, contrasted, considered, and then a decision can be made concerning their meaning. No real discussion can take place when only judgments are shared. If one person feels an applicant is extremely creative and another assessor feels the person is not creative, they are at an impasse. There is no way for them to settle it. It becomes an issue of which assessor is dominant. But, if assessors are dealing with behavioral data, the weight of evidence decides the issue. If one assessor has many good examples of creative behavior and the other assessor has relatively few examples, the assessor with better examples will usually have more effect on the dimension evaluation.

Accurate observation, recording, and communication of behavior does not come easily. It is a result of the quality of the assessor training provided. A typical assessor training program may have the following components that relate to the issue of observing, recording, and communicating behavior:

1. A definition of *behavior* is given.
2. Assessors participate in specially designed exercises to increase their ability to discriminate between a good example of behavior and a poor example of behavior.
3. Assessors are shown an example of the kinds of notes that must be taken to accurately record behavior.
4. Assessors practice observing behavior in a single exercise and receive feedback on the accuracy of the observation.
5. Assessors practice communicating behavior observed and receive feedback relative to the completeness and meaningfulness of their communication.
6. Steps 4 and 5 are repeated for each exercise in the assessment center.
7. Assessors participate in a mock assessor discussion allowing them to see the importance of behavioral data in the final discussion process.

Videotape replays of participants in assessment center activities demonstrate behaviors which may have been overlooked during the initial observations. Trainees invariably are astonished at the amount of information that they missed; and, ultimately, learn to attend to a greater amount of behavioral data (Byham, 1977b).

During the observation of an assessment center exercise, forms are provided to assessors to guide their attention so that key elements will be observed. These guides are usually in the form of questions that an assessor should keep in mind while observing an exercise.

Finally, because behavioral observations play such a large part in the final assessor discussion, a great deal of reinforcement of good observation technique results. Assessors who do a good job in observing, recording, and reporting behavior are commended by their fellow assessors and those who do a poor job have no trouble recognizing it.

The emphasis on behavioral observation and reporting is designed to overcome the strong halo effects that influence evaluative judgments (Osgood, Suci, & Tannenbaum, 1957). Peabody (1967) has made a clear distinction between descriptive and evaluative aspects of personality perception. Description of personality in terms of behavioral language is important for several functions of person perception, especially when the perceiver is combining traits into an overall evaluation (Peabody, 1970). The task of combining traits is enhanced when the perceiver has independent sources of information. As we have shown, several procedures in an assessment center are designed to keep evaluation to a minimum and to maintain independence across exercises and assessors.

We come to many of the same conclusions as Goldfried and Kent (1972) who reviewed traditional and behavioral personality assessment techniques. The behavioral approach avoids many unsubstantiated assumptions about personality constructs, provides a more direct sampling of criterion behaviors, and is more easily interpretable, more amenable to empirical validation, and potentially more predictive.

That behavioral observation skills can be trained is particularly encouraging. After reviewing over 25 years of research on training observers of behavior in such diverse areas as interviewing, reduction of rater biases, interpersonal perception, and the use of observation as a field research tool, Spool (1978) concluded that "With some exceptions the training programs reviewed were generally effective in increasing the accuracy of observation [p. 879]." In a more recent study, Thornton and Zorich (1980) reported an increase in recall of significant events in a leaderless group discussion after a group had been trained to avoid several systemic errors of observation delineated by Campbell (1958).

GROUP DECISION PROCESSES SHOULD BE USED

Assessment center evaluations are based on judgments from several assessors on the team. They pool their observations, provide feedback to each other on the accuracy of their observations, and help each other interpret the meaning and significance of observations. The joint effort serves as a set of checks and balances on the potential biases of any individual assessor.

The assessment decision is handled in several ways. In some cases the ratings of dimensions and overall ratings must be agreed upon by all staff members, that is they discuss the ratings until there is a consensus. This procedure requires that some assessors must provide substantial observations and arguments in order to convince other assessors to change their ratings. In other cases, the goal of the assessor discussion is a simple majority. For example, among six assessors, four recommending promotion would overrule two recommending no promotion. Most programs strive for consensus by reconciling differences through a discussion of actual observed behaviors.

The group-decision procedure is a critical part of the assessment center process because it exposes many of the foibles to which individual decisions are prone. For example, the requirement of providing behavioral evidence to support ratings exposes biases and stereotyping that may have inflated or deflated ratings. While reading the behavioral backup of a rating, the assessor usually recognizes when the rating is inflated or deflated and corrects it on the spot. If not, the other assessors listening to the report will recognize that the rating has not been substantiated and will tell the assessor. Further, the group of assessors brings to bear a wider background of experience than an individual assessor could. For example, one assessor might be very impressed by a procedure suggested by a participant in an exercise and another assessor might know that the same procedure was standard operating policy in the unit of the organization from where the individual came, thus indicating that the individual may not have conceived the idea. This extra information leads to more accurate interpretation.

Empirical (Lorge, Fox, Davitz, & Brenner, 1958) and theoretical (Einhorn et al., 1977) studies of the quality of group judgment support the efficacy of the assessor discussion. The research findings suggest that a group's judgment is better than the judgments of most individuals in the group. Almost certainly, the average of the individual judgments will be inferior to the group judgment. However, the best individual decision may be superior to the group decision. This sort of effect may be due to dysfunctional aspects of the group discussion and is one argument in support of the nominal group method (Delbecq, Van de Ven, & Gustafson, 1975). The trick in a group discussion is to find the most accurate individual and this is where procedures used in an assessment center assessor discussion come into play. Exercise reports, dimension ratings, and overall assessment ratings must be substantiated by behavioral observations that are consistent and defensible. The best assessor is the one who can cite the most and best behavioral support for evaluations. The assessor discussion usually involves a lively exchange of opposing views. Differences in observations and alternate explanations and interpretations are encouraged. It is hoped that this sort of exchange will enhance understanding and lead to better overall assessment. Cosier (1978) in fact found that a "devil's advocate" approach to the decision-making discussion led to more predictive accuracy than an expert approach or a dialectical inquiry in which a plan and counterplan were presented.

Two common rating biases that are often observed in personnel evaluation are central tendencies and leniency. Both might be thought of as safe strategies that individuals use to avoid confrontation with subordinates or others who may see the ratings. These biases are undesirable to the extent that they overestimate or underestimate the ratee's true ability and fail to differentiate among true ratee differences. In contrast to individual judgments, group judgments are often observed to be more extreme or polarized (Myers & Lamm, 1976). In some cases, the extreme ratings reflect a "risky shift" phenomenon in which group decisions are more risky than an individual's prior to group discussion. In other cases, the extreme rating may be due to the group's tendency to use broader categories in ratings (Vidmar, 1974). For whatever reasons, ratings made by groups tend to be more spread out than those made by individuals and, assuming some validity of ratings, this property is desirable in many situations where we wish to make distinctions among individuals.

Are the assessors likely to be very similar in their initial observations, or highly divergent? What effect does discussion have on the level of assessor agreement? A variety of research, some of which we have reviewed in Chapter 5, suggests the assessors will be in close agreement on their initial ratings and discussion will bring them even closer.

The level of interrater reliability at steps prior to the group discussion of data supports our first contention. Bray and Grant (1966) reported interrater reliabilities of .69 and .75 for evaluation of performance in a manufacturing problem and a group discussion. In a study of performance of several assessor groups in the exercises, Greenwood and McNamara (1967) found a majority of reliabilities in the .70s or .80s, but expressed alarm at finding a few very low levels of agreement. The disagreement did not appear to be located in any single group of assessees, for any one exercise, or for any particular type of assessor.

Two related studies (DeNelsky & McKee, 1969; Dicken & Black, 1965) provide evidence regarding the amount of agreement among assessors who are given the same information upon which to base ratings of managerial dimensions. DeNelsky and McKee presented seven assessors copies of 16 preemployment psychological assessment reports consisting of one- or two-page descriptions of the individual's strengths and weaknesses, based on interviews and a battery of tests. The assessors read them and predicted whether the subject would be rated favorably or unfavorably on each of 25 dimensions in field-fitness evaluation. Analysis of variance reliabilities for single ratings were .63 and .66 for two groups and .92 and .93 for composite ratings. It is important to note that the assessors were working not with original test data or observations but with narrative assessment reports. The results demonstrated substantial agreement of trait ratings on the basis of such data. Dicken and Black's (1965) study was similar in that four assessors were asked to read narrative reports of clinical assessments and rate the subjects on eight rating scales. In one sample, the average reliability was .92 with reliabilities on individual scales varying from .85 to .98. Reliabilities for a second sample were almost identical.

Carlson (1972) reported a study in which interviewers were given a wide variety of information about an applicant including a resume, a 20-page written summary of background information, and a taped 3-hour interview. Each of the 42 assessors was then asked to list all the important factual information, to rate the assessee on 31 descriptive scales, to make predictions of job behavior on 23 job activities, and to make an employment decision. There was substantial agreement among assessors on the important bits of information and only somewhat less agreement on the overall evaluation of the candidate. However, there was considerable disagreement about behavior predictions and employment decisions.

In other studies outside the context of managerial assessment centers, the initial interrater agreement on overall assessment evaluations has been found to be exceptionally high and amenable to improvement with discussion. Goldberg (1966) compared suitability ratings of Peace Corps volunteers by various groups of assessors. The average interrater reliability across groups was .69 prior to discussion, with the lowest agreement between the assessment officer and the host country coordinator (.59); the highest agreement was between the two assessment officers. Postdiscussion agreement averaged .82, with least agreement between Peace Corps Washington personnel and assessment officers (.68), and most agreement between the selection and assessment officers. A replication of the study in a second board yielded very similar levels of reliability.

These studies demonstrate that interrater reliability can be acceptably high. Other studies of selection interviewing suggest the conditions which foster high reliability, namely a structured observation (interview) form, (Carlson, 1972; Mayfield & Carlson, 1966) and simplified judgment task (Carlson, 1972). These conditions have been incorporated into the assessment center procedure.

The most crucial questions concern the effects of the group discussion on validity: What are its benefits and would some averaging of predictions suffice? The Goldberg study (1966) demonstrated that reliabilities increased with discussion, but it said nothing about validity. However, Einhorn (1972) suggested that multiple assessors enhance prediction validity because of "judge-by-assessment-component" interactions. In other words, each assessor, sensitive to different aspects of the assessee's behavior, augments the total picture, making the assessment far more complete and representative.

THE ASSESSMENT PROCESS SHOULD BE SEPARATED INTO STAGES THAT DELAY JUDGMENTS

The assessment center procedure involves a clear separation of (a) the distinct functions of observing behavior, reporting observations to others, rating individual dimensions; and (b) making a final decision. The literature on clinical evaluation, selection interviewing, human judgment, and other areas provides ample illustration that when left to their own intuitive processes, judges mix these phases, use only limited amounts of available information, and introduce systematic biases into their decisions. Assessment centers have set up procedures that require the separation of these functions and delay final decisions as long as possible. Carlson (1972) suggested that this feature of assessment centers may be the most crucial and may offer the best chance for improvement of selection interviewing.

It was previously pointed out that during each assessment exercise, staff members make detailed behavioral observations. Presentation of these observations then occupies a major portion of the assessor discussion time. Beginning with the first assessee, each assessor relates observations of the exercise for which he or she has primary responsibility. For example, Assessor A presents a summary of observations of a simulated problem-solving interview between the assessee and a role player; Assessor B relates observations of the person's performance in the LGD; Assessor C presents the in-basket results; etc. The exercise reports may or may not include dimension ratings based on assessor observations of the individual exercise. (Einhorn, 1972, has presented data that indicate that the common policy of having assessors present a rating of observed dimensions is a good one. He found that the improvement in prediction warrants the minor costs of quantifying the various components involved in the decision.) The assessors discuss the observed behavior and reach a consensus on a rating for each dimension. Then, after all components of assessment have been discussed, final summary judgments are rendered. Although final decision making is handled in different ways in different assessment centers, generally the last step is the easiest one.

Time spent in an assessment discussion is usually broken up as follows: Half of the time is spent reading reports of behavioral observations on assessment exercises, 40% of the time is spent discussing dimensions and coming to agreement on dimension ratings; 5% of the time is spent in reaching an overall decision on promotability or potential; and 5% of the time is devoted to other matters such as developmental recommendations and instruction for the person giving the feedback. The time spent discussing developmental follow-up may be and should be greater in assessment centers with a heavier emphasis on management and personal development.

The problems introduced by hasty decisions are numerous. Springbett (1958) found that not only were decisions made early in the interview, but also that there was a selective process of searching for certain kinds of information, primarily negative, and then stopping the interview. Other studies (Landy & Trumbo, 1980) suggest that interviewers make decisions to hire or not hire by comparing their initial impressions with some stereotype of the acceptable applicant. When this comparison is favorable, the interviewer spends much of the time convincing the candidate to join the organization. When the comparison is negative, the interviewer hastily discontinues the interview. In either case, the biases tend to have the overall effect of limiting the amount of information observed.

In general, the structure and procedures of the assessment discussion are designed to change the psychological set of the assessors. In most selection and promotion decisions, the set is to make a decision. In the assessment center it is to obtain observations of behavior relative to the dimensions. *Only at the end* of the assessment center process is an overall decision made. Because the emphasis in making overall decisions is changed, the assessment process is improved.

ASSESSEES SHOULD BE EVALUATED AGAINST A CLEARLY UNDERSTOOD NORM—NOT AGAINST EACH OTHER

The presence of several assessees together in an assessment center has both advantages and disadvantages. On the one hand, it provides the opportunity to use group exercises and to make the schedule most efficient for the assessors. On the other hand, the assessors may fall prey to inappropriate comparative judgments among assessees. These and other potentially harmful judgment biases are minimized and monitored in the assessment center process.

The biggest advantage of assessment in a group is that it provides the opportunity to place assessees in group exercises which simulate managerial decision making and leadership. Managers get work done through people. They solve problems and make decisions in groups. They must lead subordinates, plan and organize work of others, and exert influence upward to their supervisors. These and many other job activities can be simulated most economically if a number of assessees are assembled for the assessment center.

Assessing several people in a 1–3-day assessment center avoids the problem of sequential contrast effects that plague many judgment tasks. For example, a person may be judged more competent than he or she actually is because he or she is observed after two relatively incompetent persons have been seen, and vice versa. This problem and some of its negative consequences have been substantiated by Hakel, Ohnesorge, and Dunnette (1970). Experimental research in laboratory settings often controls the contrast effect by counterbalancing the order of presentation of stimuli and by repeating evaluations in random order. Suggested solutions to the problem in interviewing are less satisfactory. However, assessment center procedures minimize the effects of contrast by putting all candidates simultaneously through the same evaluation procedures. In individual exercises, order of performance is varied so that a person evaluated first in one exercise, is evaluated later in another. Nonsequential contrast effects are further minimized because no one assessor evaluates all the individuals on one exercise. While Assessor A may conduct the in-basket review with Participants 1 and 2, Assessor B reviews the work of Participants 3 and 4. This continual shifting of responsibility for observation eliminates potential contrast effects. In any event, Cohen and Sands (1978) found that order of participation in exercises did not affect assessment center performance.

The one step of the assessment process which might suffer from potential negative contrast effects is the final assessment discussion. Here each assessee is considered separately, all observations are discussed, and ratings and predictions are made. Although it would be possible for contrast effects to take place, assessment center procedures minimize them. As we have repeatedly emphasized, the focus on behaviors requires that all judgments be based on and substantiated by behavioral observations in assessment exercises rather than subjective impressions. The assessment center administrator must monitor the discussion to prevent comparisons of assessees at the time of integration. Therefore, no individual should suffer from being judged in some particular sequence.

Byham (1981a) investigated potential sequence effects as 18 groups of candidates were processed through an assessment center. He found no systematic difference in average evaluation. The assessee observed first did just as well as the assessee observed last.

Strictly speaking, an assessment center can deal with only one person at a time (assuming no group discussion exercises are required), but there are many advantages to processing several candidates at the same time. However, under all circumstances, evaluations should be made relative to a fixed predetermined standard for the job.

PREDICTION OF MANAGERIAL SUCCESS
MUST BE JUDGMENTAL

With few exceptions, the prediction of managerial success must be based on a judgmental combination of information in an intuitive and clinical manner. There are few situations where a statistical combination of predictor information is possible. Seldom is it possible to develop adequate criterion measures of managerial performance, to obtain an adequate sample of predictor and criterion data, to empirically correlate the two, and to obtain stable regression weights for a statistical combination of information.

In an assessment center, data are integrated judgmentally at two important junctures. First, data from various exercises are combined in a data integration session to form a dimension rating. Since different assessors observe an assessee because they are reporting examples of observed behavior from very different exercises and because it is necessary for them to now compare and contrast the observed behavior, it seems most appropriate to combine information judgmentally. Statistical methodology seems inappropriate and extremely difficult to apply at this stage. Second, data from various dimensions are combined into an overall assessment rating. It is possible that here a statistical combination of data may be more effective than a judgmental combination.

We hasten to emphasize that we are advocating a very special kind of judgmental process which involves all the principles described to this point. The assessment center procedure involves judgmental data gathering and judgmental data integration. In other reviews of assessment procedures, this combination has not been recommended highly. It seems essential then to consider the controversy of clinical versus actuarial prediction and place the assessment center procedure in this context.

Sawyer (1966) reviewed the research studies comparing the relative effectiveness of these two approaches. He contributed much to our understanding this controversy by separating the consideration of data gathering and data combination. Data gathering methods are contrasted as mechanical or clinical; data combination methods are contrasted as statistical or clinical. In the first case, measurement of important psychological variables may require a small or large involvement of the data gatherer. Data collection is mechanical if specific, structured procedures are followed; few judgments are made by the examiner; and there is little interaction between the subject and the examiner. Examples of mechanical measurement include questionnaires, biographical data forms, and traditional paper-and-pencil tests. Data collection is clinical if less structured procedures are used, many judgments are made by the examiner, and the examiner plays a very active role in gathering data. Examples of clinical measurement include interviews, observations, and many performance or situational tests.

In a similar fashion, the methods of data combination can be contrasted. Statistical prediction involves the use of mathematical formulae to combine several separate measures in a weighted composite which maximally correlates with a criterion. The weights for the importance of the variables are empirically determined or derived by studying predictor-criterion correlates for a group of subjects in the situation being studied. Some sources would argue that mechanical prediction includes any case where systematic rules for combining data are used. Clinical prediction, on the other hand, involves the use of inferences and judgments to integrate the data which have been gathered. As with clinical measurement, the individual clinician greatly influences the way in which the data are combined and, presumably, different clinicians would combine the data by different processes.

Subdividing data gathering approaches into clinical, mechanical, and a combination of both and prediction methods into clinical and psychometric approaches yields six methods:

1. *Pure clinical:* Clinically collected data, clinically combined
2. *Trait ratings:* Clinically collected data, mechanically combined
3. *Profile interpretation:* Mechanically collected data, clinically combined
4. *Pure statistical:* Mechanically collected data, mechanically combined
5. *Clinical composite:* Both modes of data, clinically combined
6. *Mechanical composite:* Both modes of data, mechanically combined

Two further approaches include the synthesis of clinical and statistical methods:

7. *Clinical synthesis:* Prediction produced by mechanical combination, treated as a datum, combined clinically with other data
8. *Mechanical synthesis:* Prediction produced by clinical combination, treated as a datum, combined mechanically with other data

After reviewing 45 studies that Sawyer believed provided a good comparison of the clinical versus statistical methodologies, the author concluded that the mechanical method of data combination is always equal or superior to the clinical method regardless of the way in which the data are collected. Sawyer (1966) suggested that both the mechanical and the clinical methods of data gathering contribute to the prediction. More specifically the results suggested:

1. Within each mode of data collection, the mechanical mode of combination is superior.
2. Within each mode of data combination, the clinical mode of collection by itself is inferior.
3. With the exception of a single method, the difference between modes of combination depends very little upon the mode of collection and vice versa.
4. The one exception is the clinical composite—when combination is mechanical, it is better to have both kinds of data than either alone; but when combination is clinical, having both kinds is little better than having only clinically collected data and not as good as having only mechanically collected data.
5. The clinical synthesis surpasses the clinical composite. The mechanical composite, however, is better than either and is *not* improved by adding to it the clinical prediction. Thus, in these studies, neither synthesis appears promising.

In contrast to Sawyer's rather negative picture of the contribution of the clinical approaches, Holt (1970) makes a rather impassioned plea for the recognition of the contributions of clinical judgments. He criticizes many of the studies that are often cited as relevant to the controversy by pointing out many of the common deficiencies: (a) criterion contamination of un-cross-validated formulas; (b) inadequate criterion measures; (c) misleading classification of judges as clinicians; (d) insufficient power to detect differences; and (e) use of quantitative data only. In each case he suggests that clinical methods are unfairly treated in the comparison. For these and other reasons, Holt suggests that the data already collected are not capable of deciding the issue and points out further that clinical judgments are made at various stages prior to any prediction itself and to fairly evaluate the two overall prediction approaches, we must ensure that all of the preliminary steps are the same. Important judgments are made, according to Holt, in the analysis and selection of criteria, the identification of situational and intrapersonal intervening variables, the selection of measuring instruments, the empirical tryout of predictors with a selected sample of subjects, and the choice of method of cross validation. Presumably, Holt is suggesting that approaches that have been previously classified as "clinical" are unduly penalized because they possess an inordinate amount of subjectivity and errors in judgment in the early steps. Therefore, their lack of predictive effectiveness is a result not of inaccurate prediction but of inferior treatment of the preceding problem areas. Both Holt and Sawyer are correct in stating that the controversy has not been settled by the recent surveys of the existing research. Holt is certainly correct in pointing out that judgments are important at various crucial stages of any prediction as well as at the final stages of data gathering and collection.

Data from the management assessment center literature have not been included in these reviews, but several studies of assessor judgments are relevant to the controversy over clinical and psychometric prediction. With regard to methods of data gathering, the evidence strongly supports Sawyer's (1966) conclusion that both mechanical and clinical methods of measurement contribute to prediction. In assessment center studies, both paper-and-pencil tests (measuring intellectual ability and personality characteristics) and judgmental ratings of behavioral dimensions derived from situational exercises contributed to prediction of performance criteria. As indicated in our earlier discussion (Chapter 5) of signs versus samples, neither method shows clear superiority over the other but both measure separate aspects of managerial performance and contribute to the prediction of management success.

With regard to methods of data combination, the evidence is more equivocal. Table 6.1 summarizes the limited amount of empirical data which directly address the question. In support of the clinical method, Huck (1974) and Moses (1973b) found essentially equal predictive validities for the judgmentally derived overall assessment rating and statistical combination of assessment variables. By contrast, Wollowick and McNamara (1969) found that the multiple correlation for all test

Table 6.1
Correlations of Various Combinations of Predictors and Criteria

	Predictor			
Study	Multiple R for tests	Multiple R for dimensions	Multiple R for all variables	Overall assessment rating
Huck (1974)	.24	.42	.42	.42
Blacks	.03	.43	.43	.35
Whites	.26	.45	.45	.41
Moses (1973b)		.461	.463	.44
Wollowick and McNamara (1969)	.45	.41	.62	.37
Mitchel (1975)				
Average correlation			.42	.22
Average "generalized" correlation			.28	

scores and dimension ratings substantially exceeded the correlation of the OAR. Caution is necessary because the multiple R, computed for 94 cases, was not cross validated. The suspicion that this correlation may be an overestimate of the true relationship is reinforced by results in Mitchel's (1975) study at SOHIO. Six sets of predictor and criterion data were analyzed. For Sample A, criterion data were available 1, 3, and 5 years after assessment; for Sample B, 1 and 3 years later; and for Sample C, 1 year later. The average multiple correlation using statistical combination of dimension ratings and test scores was .42, but when the regression equation derived from one set of data was applied to the other five data sets, the predictive accuracy dropped markedly (R = .28). This decrease indicates that a high multiple correlation may be partially due to statistical artifacts. The higher level of accuracy does not generalize when the regression weights are applied to independent samples of criterion data or subjects. The average generalized correlation is still somewhat higher than the average predictive validity of the OAR (R = .22).

The strongest argument for the judgmental integration of dimension ratings comes from the fact that it is seldom possible to empirically derive the appropriate weights because few organizations have conducted the necessary criterion related validity study. To obtain reliable weights, the study must include a large sample, reliable criterion, a relatively homogeneous set of jobs, and a stable job environment. If the weights are to be used for practical decisions, the results should be cross validated.

The empirical research data do not allow any firm conclusions. It is possible that some weighted or unweighted combination of final dimension ratings (and test scores) might show more predictive validity than the OAR. If the statistical and judgmental combination were proven to be equally accurate, it would be more time effective to combine mechanically and allow the assessors to discuss more complex issues such as placement recommendations or developmental suggestions for the individual. A major obstacle to implementing such a procedure would be a negative reaction from assessors. They like the idea of making the final decision and might react negatively to losing this "closure" to the process. More research is needed!

Because the issue is unsettled, the discussion method for integrating the dimension ratings is recommended for several other reasons. Managers (including assessors, participants, and their supervisors) prefer the judgmental approach over statistical–mechanical methods. In addition, the assessor discussion provides an opportunity to develop unique insights into the individual's particular strengths and weaknesses, including the types of situations where the individual has difficulties. Also, assessors or administrators can better select appropriate behavioral examples to make the feedback more acceptable and meaningful.

Summary of Methods of Making Predictions

Prediction of a complex set of managerial behaviors is not a simple task: For years it has defied researchers and practitioners. It cannot be done by means of a simple formula involving a few bits of simple information gathered from one or two sources. By the same token, it cannot be accomplished by a naïve clinical approach to assessment. After reviewing extensive research on human judgment, Holt (1975) concluded: "I believe that one point has been conclusively established: there is no magic in clinical intuition that enables a clinician to predict a criterion about which he knows little, from data the relationship of which to the criterion he has not studied, and to do so better than an actuarial formula based on just such prior study of predictor-criterion relationship [p. 55]."

Similarly, we conclude that managerial success cannot be predicted by any one individual based on limited knowledge of the management job requirements after a scant 1–2 hour interview.

In conclusion, we believe the many years of experience with the assessment center in diverse settings and applications establishes the validity of a special type of "clinical composite" method of making overall assessment decisions described by Sawyer (1966); in other words, we advocate the judgmental combination of data collected by multiple, trained assessors using judgmental and psychometric measurement procedures. We realize that most assessment programs do not use paper-and-pencil tests, and thus in these instances the method is more purely "clinical" (Sawyer, 1966). Organizations often choose not to use tests when the program is operated by nonpsychologists.

Whether or not tests are used, the judgmental aspects of assessment centers are quite different from those in most other "clinical methods." We agree with Holt (1970) that earlier clinical approaches were not fairly compared with psychometric–statistical approaches. When the principles stated in this chapter are applied to prediction of management success, the predictive validity of assessment centers exceeds the validity of purely mechanical or statistical methods. Whether a mechanical or clinical synthesis of dimension ratings emanating from tests and situational exercises has more predictive validity is yet to be determined.

7
Criterion Validity of Overall Assessment Center Judgments

At the beginning of the last chapter we mentioned the criticism that the practice of industrial psychology sometimes goes beyond empirical research support. This chapter is a partial response to that charge with regard to several uses of the assessment center method. It presents and evaluates an extensive body of evidence relevant to the assessment center as a selection and promotion technique. Specifically, we review all available concurrent and predictive validity studies in which an overall assessment rating (OAR) was related to some external criterion of management performance or progress.

Assessment centers started slowly in American industry (Cohen, Moses, & Byham, 1974). During the early industrial application period from 1956 to 1970 only a few large organizations used the method extensively, but each undertook systematic research programs to evaluate the assessment center process. Several studies were reported during this period by each of the following organizations: AT&T, IBM, Sears, SOHIO, and GE. During the general application period, starting in the late 1960s, many other industrial and governmental organizations adopted the procedure and continued the research efforts. Although other organizations have conducted less extensive research efforts, it is our view that the criticism that practice outruns research evidence is incorrect for assessment centers—this technique probably has more research support than any other technique in industrial psychology.

We recognize that not all questions have been answered. For example, we need to know more about how the utility of the assessment center method compares to other methodologies and their role in management development. Many of these research needs are identified at the end of this chapter and in Chapter 11. We also recognize that not all assessment center research has been perfect, even though researchers went to great lengths to design and implement adequate studies in the difficult context of organizational practice. Limitations and methodological weaknesses in the studies will be pointed out.

Overview of the Chapter

To bring order to the large amount of criterion-related validity research in this chapter, the studies will be presented in terms of the research design employed. First, studies using a longitudinal design are described. The better or "purer" studies that allow the most generalization are presented first, then studies with more limitations follow. Next, concurrent validity studies are presented which compare assessment center and job performance of current managers.

Longitudinal designs
    Experimental research
    Studies with no feedback to participants
    Studies with control groups
    Correlational studies with feedback
Concurrent designs

Following the detailed review of validity studies, the evidence is summarized in three ways. First, several methodological issues are examined. Second, evidence is summarized relevant to the effectiveness of assessment centers for various purposes such as selection, promotion, early identification, and management development. Third, studies comparing assessment centers to other methods of evaluating management potential for promotion (e.g., supervisory evaluations and tests) are summarized.

Review of Research Evidence

AN EXPERIMENTAL FIELD STUDY:
THE MANAGEMENT PROGRESS STUDY

In 1956 American Telephone and Telegraph launched the first industrial application of the assessment center approach in the United States as a part of its Management Progress Study (Bray, 1964a; Bray & Grant, 1966, Bray et al., 1974). The MPS, referred to in earlier chapters, was designed to give insight into the developmental patterns of a large group of young men as they progressed in their careers within a large corporation. Individual characteristics (such as background, education, abilities, and personality variables) and organizational experiences (such as type of early job assignment, supervision received, and management progress) were studied. The original goal of the project was to follow the management recruits for a number of years with planned periodic data gathering for both major sets of variables (assessment and criterion data) along the way. Immediate payoff was not the object of the original project, as noted in Chapter 3. This led to several desirable research features. The MPS was initiated to partially fill a major gap in the knowledge of psychological development about working adults (Kappel, 1960) and it has succeeded. Having reached its 20-year goal it is continuing. Many of the important results of the study such as insights into environmental factors that influence early development and progress among the sample (Berlew & Hall, 1966) will not be discussed because these data are reviewed elsewhere (Bray *et al.*, 1974) and are not directly relevant to our present topic.

The portion of the MPS most relevant to our survey is the use of assessment center techniques for gathering data on personal characteristics of the assessees. Assessment centers were designed to measure the abilities, aptitudes, personality traits, values, managerial skills, and behaviors thought to be significant characteristics for this sample. AT&T based its assessment center design largely on the earlier work of Murray (1938) and the Office of Strategic Services (1948). The principles of multiple assessment techniques, performance exercises, and a judgmental process were utilized. Over the first 8 years of the study, 267 subjects were assessed during 1-week programs. The original subjects have been reassessed at least once with an almost identical program and assessed a third time with a vastly different program. In addition, regular periodic interviews have been conducted with the subjects and with their supervisors.

A brief review of the project is in order. The subjects in the MPS were nonsupervisory personnel at the time of initial assessment. Both college ($N = 274$) and noncollege graduates ($N = 144$) were included. The assessment techniques were chosen to measure important characteristics of middle management (third- and fourth-level) positions at AT&T. Among the assessment techniques used were objective tests of intellectual and personality factors, a contemporary affairs test, personal interview, in-basket, leaderless group discussion, business game, personal history questionnaire and biographical essay, and a self-descriptive Q sort. The assessors were largely professional psychologists from inside and outside the company, assisted by a few managers. During each exercise, the assessors recorded their observations and later wrote an "exercise report" summarizing the observations. After the participants had departed, the exercise reports were read and discussed in the assessor meeting. A consensus rating for each dimension was agreed upon and the staff agreed upon a rating predicting whether or not the assessee would reach middle management (levels three to four) within 10 years. Following the discussions, an assessment report was written describing the strengths and weaknesses of each assessee. All of the data were coded and placed in reserve. Neither participants nor management personnel in the operating companies had access to the information.

Criterion data were gathered in 1965 regarding level of management attained and salary progress over approximately 8 years since assessment. The relationships between overall assessment predictions and the criterion of management level attained are presented in the form of expectancy tables summarized in Table 7.1. Predictions by the assessment staff were largely successful. Considering the combined samples, the data show that of the 103 subjects predicted to advance to middle management (levels three to four), 42% had actually done so by 1965. Of the 166 who were judged not to have the qualities for middle management or about whom there was some question, only 7% had advanced to those levels. From another view, the data show that in the sample, 85% (42 out of 49) of those achieving middle management were correctly identified.

The prediction of progress at this stage is equally accurate for combined college and combined noncollege groups, although a smaller proportion of the noncollege subjects had actually advanced to middle management. In the separate subsamples, the relationship of prediction and progress is apparent in all but one group (D) but because of smaller numbers, the results are sometimes not statistically significant.

Table 7.2 summarizes data regarding the relationship of assessment predictors and attainment of middle management from three reports of the MPS. The Bray and Grant (1966) data for 1965 are presented with results from Bray et al. (1974) and Howard (1979). Bray et al. (1974) presented extensive follow-up data for the college sample. Of those predicted to reach middle management in 10 years, 64% had already done so 8 years later, whereas only 32% of the low potential group reached this level. After 16 years, 89% of the top group and 66% of the bottom group had progressed. Howard (1981) reported that the predictive validity coefficient for the college group reached .46 in early years but declined to .33 in the sixteenth year of the study. By contrast, the predictive validity for the noncollege subjects reached the same level, .46, in the early years but remained above .40 into the sixteenth year.

The correlations of OAR and salary progress in 1965 are reported for

Table 7.1

Relationships of Staff Predictions to Management Progress after Approximately Eight Years[a]

Sample[b]		Staff prediction (number that will make middle management)		Percentage attaining management level (6–8 years later)[c]			Significance (p)
				3–4	2	1	
A	College	Yes	33	58	39	3	.02
		No or?	21	19	81	0	
B	Noncollege	Yes	20	30	70	0	.001
		No or?	63	0	21	79	
C_1	College	Yes	11	27	73	0	.17
		No or?	16	6	81	13	
C_2	Noncollege	Yes	13	38	62	0	.03
		No or?	26	8	69	23	
D_1	College	Yes	10	50	50	0	.09
		No or?	9	11	78	11	
D	Noncollege	Yes	8	24	38	38	—
		No or?	14	21	36	43	
E	College	Yes	8	37	63	0	.08
		No or?	17	6	71	23	
Combined college		Yes	62	48	50	2	.001
		No or?	63	11	78	11	
Combined noncollege		Yes	41	32	61	7	.001
		No or?	103	5	35	60	
All samples combined		Yes	103	42	54	4	.001
		No or?	166	7	51	42	

[a] Adapted from "The Assessment Center in the Measurement of Potential for Business Management" by D. W. Bray and D. L. Grant, *Psychological Monographs,* 1966, *80* (17, Whole No. 625). Copyright 1966 by the American Psychological Association. Reprinted by permission.

[b] Separate samples come from different Bell companies participating in the study.

[c] The original assessment center data were collected over a 3-year period thus causing the individuals studied in 1965 to have different amounts of tenure.

four separate groups as shown in Table 7.3. Both zero-order correlations and partial correlations (with test data partialed out) are included. The correlations are moderately large and the partials reveal that the assessment center process is contributing something over and above the objective tests.

In summary, this study affords solid evidence that the assessment process yields valid predictions of the future success of young managers in AT&T. Note that several features of the program are rather unique and may influence generalization of the results. Assessees come from several companies and departments within the Bell System, but they may not be representative of the present group of young managers in the company,

Table 7.2
Assessment Predictions and Attainment of Middle Management at Three Time Periods

Predicted to reach middle management	N[a]	Percentage attaining middle management in		
		1965[b] (8 years or less)	Year 8[c]	Year 16[d]
College				
Yes	62	48	64	89
No or?	63	11	32	66
Noncollege				
Yes	41	32	40	63
No or ?	103	5	9	18

[a] Original sample size; Ns vary from year to year due to attrition.
[b] Bray and Grant (1966).
[c] Bray et al. (1974); Howard (1979).
[d] Howard (1979).

and they may not be representative of managers in other companies. AT&T has launched a longitudinal study of women in the Bell System and a second Management Progress Study called the Management Continuity Study which uses a sample representative of recruits beginning in 1977.

An important feature of this study, in comparison with other AT&T studies, is that the assessors were primarily professional psychologists from outside the company. Bray and Grant (1966) state that a few assessors were managers from the operating companies, but none was in a supervisory capacity over the assessees. Because the current AT&T model (and the one used by most other companies) includes the use of trained management assessors, the predictive validity data of the Management Progress Study is not totally relevant to this latter application. Trained

Table 7.3
Partial Correlations with Salary Progress in Management Progress Study for Subsamples[a]

	A (N = 54)		B (N = 83)		C₁ (N = 27)		C₂ (N = 39)	
	r	Partial r	r	Partial r	r	Partial r	r	Partial r
Staff judgment	.48		.57		.51		.52	
		.32*		.39**		.29		.42**
Ability test	.38		.46		.51		.36	

[a] Adapted from "The Assessment Center in the Measurement of Potential for Business Management" by D. W. Bray and D. L. Grant, *Psychological Monographs*, 1966, 80 (17, Whole No. 625). Copyright 1966 by the American Psychological Association. Reprinted by permission.
* $p < .05$.
** $p < .01$.

management assessors might be more accurate than professional assessors as Cronbach (1970) pointed out, but the MPS does not provide data to affirm these kinds of comparative statements.

Other limitations of the MPS can be noted. Many of the variables assessed in the MPS appear to be personality traits and seem to tap internal motivations, interests, and attitudes. Recent assessment centers have been more focused on managerial and administrative behaviors. The exercises do not include any one-to-one interactions. Finally, the criteria used for follow-up validation have been restricted to indices of management progress. Relationships of assessment data to other measures of job performance would enhance the usefulness of the study.

Summary. As noted earlier, the MPS is a landmark piece of research that has already contributed substantially to our understanding of adult development and to the practical business of selecting managers. The assessment center movement can be traced directly to AT&T's early and continuing research efforts. There can be little doubt that assessment center ratings accurately predict which individuals are likely to advance in the management of the Bell System.

STUDIES WITH NO FEEDBACK TO PARTICIPANTS

In this section we review five longitudinal studies which were conducted to evaluate the assessment center process. In each case the assessment center results were not reported back to participants or to their managers. These conditions virtually eliminate the potential for criterion contamination through knowledge of the predictor data.

AT&T sales recruits. Although this is not strictly a management sample, the study is included because of several unique and strong features. Bray and Campbell (1968) assessed 78 sales recruits (all-male sample) sometime after they had been hired. They were then evaluated on actual field-selling performance. Assessment data were not released to trainers, supervisors, or field performance raters, thus providing uncontaminated criteria as a sound basis for a predictive study. The assessment center activities included some previously untried exercises (i.e., an analysis problem, a fact-finding experience, and an interview simulation) to assess the dimensions of success in the position of communications consultant. A major difference from the MPS was that the salesman center was staffed completely by managers who were familiar with the job.

Salesmen were rated on criteria of selling performance (e.g., preparation, prospecting, recommendations, closing, and implementation). Ratings were provided by trainers, by supervisors (after the salesman had

had 6 months of job experience), and by a special field-review team. These teams were specially trained representatives from the head office who accompanied the salesmen on their calls. The reviewers made as many observations as necessary to provide an accurate rating of on-the-job performance.

Analysis of data showed no correlation between the assessment center rating and either the trainers' or the supervisors' ratings. However, an r of .51 was obtained between assessment center predictions and ratings by the field-review team. By comparison, the multiple correlation of the best combination of four tests was .33, indicating the assessment process was adding something unique (Table 7.4). In terms of expectancy data, Table 7.5 shows that more high-assessed than low-assessed subjects met field review standards.

The positive results for the field review raters as opposed to the lack of significant results for trainers and supervisors points up the criterion problem. From the data in this study alone it is impossible to know which source of performance is more accurate. From other studies, we know that there are serious problems with performance appraisals from un-trained managers who have little opportunity to observe job behavior. From the Bray and Campbell (1968) description we can infer that the trained review team observing actual sales performance provides the better criterion data.

AT&T early identification. Another longitudinal study in which no feedback was given to participants or their superiors was a validation of the Early Identification Assessment program (EIA) at AT&T reported by Moses (1973a, 1973b). The EIA was designed to assess early potential for

Table 7.4

Correlations of Assessment Prediction and Paper-and-Pencil Tests with Field-Performance Ratings[a]

Tests ($N = 78$)	
School and College Aptitude	.25
Critical Thinking	.26
Contemporary Affairs	.28
Abstract Reasoning	.02
Multiple R—four tests	.33
Assessment judgment	.51

[a] Adapted from "Selection of Salesmen by Means of an Assessment Center" by D. W. Bray and R. J. Campbell, *Journal of Applied Psychology,* 1968, *52,* 36–41. Copyright 1968 by the American Psychological Association. Reprinted by permission.

Table 7.5
Validity of Assessment Center for Salesman Recruits[a]

Assessment judgment	No.	Trainers[b]		Supervisors[b]		Field review[c]	
		Higher	Lower	Higher	Lower	Met standards	Did not meet standards
			Percentage receiving ratings by				
More than acceptable or acceptable	41	51	49	57	43	68	32
Less than acceptable or unacceptable	37	55	45	47	53	24	76

[a] Adapted from "Selection of Salesmen by Means of an Assessment Center" by D. W. Bray and R. J. Campbell, *Journal of Applied Psychology*, 1968, *52*, 36–41. Copyright 1968 by the American Psychological Association. Reprinted by permission.
[b] Differences not statistically significant; rs not significant at .05 level.
[c] $\chi^2 = 24.19$; $p < .01$; $r = .51$.

management among recently hired employees. Patterned very closely after the other management assessment programs at AT&T, it used most of the same assessment techniques and the same judgmental procedures. The principal difference was that the EIA took only 1 day rather than the 2.5 days of the regular Personnel Assessment Program (PAP). The shorter time was possible because fewer dimensions were assessed, the exercises were less difficult and complicated, and the assessor note-taking task was simplified.

The sample consisted of 85 individuals who had been assessed in both the EIA and PAP programs. There were approximately equal numbers of blacks and whites, men and women. These subjects were chosen from among 441 employees who had been assessed by EIA but who had not received feedback and who were representative of high, moderate, and low performance groups at the time of initial assessment. Table 7.6 shows the means, standard deviations, and correlations of final ratings for the two programs. It is clear that the correlation is high between the two programs for all groups. In addition to the employees and supervisors not knowing the results of EIA assessment, neither were the results known by the PAP assessors, thus avoiding any possibility of criterion contamination.

Of particular importance is the finding that there were no significant differences in means across the subgroups for either EIA or PAP performance. In other words, the means of the "prediction" and the "criterion" were the same for representatives of all groups. In conjunction with the finding of equal "validities," these results suggest that the abbreviated assessment center does not display differential validity for racial or sex-

Table 7.6

Final (Overall) Ratings Obtained from EIA (1-day assessment center) and PAP (2.5-day assessment center)[a]

Group	N	EIA		PAP		r:EIA–PAP
		X̄	S.D.	X̄	S.D.	
Total group	85	2.81	1.25	2.78	1.26	.73 —
Men	39	2.93	1.23	2.87	1.27	.77
Women	46	2.70	1.28	2.71	1.26	.70
Black	42	2.45	1.21	2.45	1.21	.68
White	43	3.15	1.20	3.11	1.24	.73

[a] From "The Development of an Assessment Center for the Early Identification of Supervisory Potential" by J. L. Moses, Personnel Psychology, 1973, 26, 569–580. Copyright 1973 by Personnel Psychology. Reprinted by permission.

ual subgroups, nor is there potential discrimination in the form of under-prediction of success of any subgroup.

The correlation between ratings of the same management variables for the total sample in the two programs is shown in Table 7.7. These correlations suggest that performance of the participants in the two programs is very similar on several specific behavioral dimensions. Although not shown here, it is relevant that these same-variable correlations are usually higher than the cross-correlations among different variables in the two programs. For example, the EIA rating of Leadership, Forcefulness, Written Skills, and Scholastic Aptitude correlated highest with the corresponding PAP variable. Therefore, there is adequate evidence of convergent and discriminant validity in the dimension ratings.

This study shows considerable agreement between the ratings ob-

Table 7.7

Correlations between Comparable EIA and PAP Variables (N = 85)[a]

Variable	r
Overall	.73
Leadership	.56
Energy	.52
Decision Making	.53
Forcefulness	.62
Oral Skills	.49
Written Skills	.57
Scholastic Aptitude	.72

[a] From "The Development of an Assessment Center for the Early Identification of Supervisory Potential" by J. L. Moses, Personnel Psychology, 1973, 26, 569–580. Copyright 1973 by Personnel Psychology, Reprinted by permission.

tained in a shortened program and those of a longer assessment program. The correlations are substantial and suggest that major similarities in performance existed. Moses (1973b) appears justified in concluding that the EIA program is beneficial in identifying persons with management potential using PAP performance as the criterion.

Only limited conclusions can be drawn from these results. Further validation of the EIA in relation to more appropriate criteria is essential. While the correlations between the EIA and PAP are substantial (e.g., .73 for the OAR in the total group), it does not necessarily follow that the EIA is correlated with subsequent criteria of effectiveness or promotion. In various studies reported in this text, the AT&T assessment center overall ratings correlate around .30 to .40 with various criteria. Cohen et al. (1974) found that the median correlation of all studies reviewed was .37. Elementary statistics demonstrate that approximately 53% of the variance of PAP ratings was accounted for by EIA ratings and approximately 14% of on-the-job criterion variance was being measured by PAP-type assessment processes. Therefore, major portions of variance are not being accounted for: Just because A is related to B and B is related to C, does not mean that A is related to C.

AT&T prehire assessment. In this study (Moses & Wall, 1975), 78 active or recent college recruits were assessed with a 1-day program consisting of a group exercise, an in-basket based in a university setting, a biographical inventory, a background interview, and a mental ability test. The assessment center ratings were not used in making hiring decisions and no feedback was given to the participants. One year after hiring, the individual's supervisor was interviewed to determine actual job performance. The correlation between assessment and job performance ratings was .60. Significantly larger percentages of the high potential group were rated effective performers by their supervisors.

IBM. Another predictive validity study in which the results were not used administratively was reported by Hinrichs (1978). In 1967, 47 marketing recruits being considered for first-level management were assessed with a 2-day program. Attrition and lack of data reduced the sample size to 30. For these individuals the correlation of assessment center predictions and management level attained 8 years after assessment was .46 ($p < .05$) and the partial correlation of the assessment prediction and management level after 8 years (with level of management at time of assessment held constant) was significant ($r = .40, p < .05$). There was not a significant correlation of assessment prediction and *change* in management level. These data show that the assessment center predicts progress over a long period of time.

The obvious limitation of the study is the small sample size. However, this is one of the few studies that affords an uncontaminated criterion. The results confirm the long-range accuracy of predictions found at AT&T. Hinrichs (1978) also found that a review of the individual's personnel folder could accurately predict management progress, raising the question of the proper role of assessment in conjunction with other evaluation procedures. These issues will be discussed later in the chapter.

Public Service Commission of Canada. Slivinski *et al.* (1979) reported a study of 278 middle managers assessed in a special development program within the Canadian government. Information from the program did not go in the personal/personnel files of the participants and no feedback was given to the immediate supervisor. Higher level administrators making promotion decisions did not have direct knowledge of assessment performance, thus the criterion information as a measure of progress was uncontaminated. Slivinski *et al.* (1979) computed the difference between management level at time of assessment and at time of follow-up divided by time since assessment. On the average, 2.5 years of postassessment experience had passed. The OAR correlated .298 with this criterion; the multiple correlation of assessment center and test data was .402.

Summary. The only five studies using this research design are all supportive. Correlations between the assessment center ratings and subsequent criteria were all significant. The results appear to be positive for different types of jobs, subject samples, criteria, and time periods.

STUDIES WITH CONTROL GROUPS

All other validity studies have involved some operational use of the assessment center data; hence, it is possible that validity results are inflated as a consequence of criterion contamination through knowledge of the predictor data. To use operational data for our purposes, procedures that tend to minimize the likelihood of biases must be developed. A number of the following studies have done an admirable job of tracking the potential effects of this sort of criterion contamination. Special types of criteria and innovative research designs have demonstrated the predictive validities are not artificially inflated.

Associated Bell Companies. Three other AT&T studies deserve close study, even though they have fewer desirable features than the ones we have reviewed so far. In each of the studies the results of assessment were used operationally by the management of the company and, in many cases, the results were given to the assessees. The first study was reported by Campbell and Bray (1967). It included 506 employees, 223 of whom had been assessed and were being considered for first-level management jobs and 283 who had not been assessed but who had been promoted to management. The sample of nonassessed subjects included persons promoted both before and after the assessment program was instituted.

Job *performance* of each first-level manager was evaluated in terms of (a) the man's last formal appraisal rating; (b) a rating of job performance; and (c) a ranking of job performance obtained from the man's immediate supervisor in a special interview. These three indices were used to divide the subjects into "above average" and "below average" performers. Evaluation of *potential* was based on (a) the rating of potential made at the last formal appraisal; and (b) a potential ranking made by the supervisor. The two potential measures were combined into a general estimate of potential with the subjects divided into "high potential" and "low potential" groups. The percentage of men already promoted to second level was noted.

The relationship between assessment center staff ratings and the results of the composite performance and potential criteria are shown in Table 7.8. Among the assessed groups, a larger portion of those assessed "acceptable" as opposed to those assessed "not acceptable" (68% versus

Table 7.8

Comparison of Assessment Center Ratings, Ratings of Subsequent Supervisory Performance, and Further Promotions[a]

	Percentage rated "above average"	Percentage rated "high potential" by supervisor	Percentage promoted to second level
Rating by assessment center (N = 223)			
Acceptable	68[b]	50	11
Questionable	65	40	5
Not acceptable	46[c]	31	0
Comparison data not assessed (N = 283)			
Men promoted before assessment	55	28	5
Men promoted after assessment	63	19	5

[a] Adapted from "Assessment Centers: An Aid in Management Selection" by R. J. Campbell and D. W. Bray. *Personnel Administration,* 1967, *30* (2), 6–12. Copyright 1967 by the Personnel Management Association. Reprinted by permission.

[b] Includes 28 persons already promoted to second level.

[c] Seven persons demoted to craft levels were considered poor performers.

46%) were above-average performers. The assessment center rating was also better than the traditional method which had yielded 55% above-average performers. According to Campbell and Bray (1967) the results indicated "that the assessment program has been a definite aid in the selection of better performers at the first level of management [p. 11]." More detailed analyses by the AT&T Personnel Research Staff (1965) show that the correlation between the assessment ratings and the performance criterion is .13. This indicates that the size of the predictor–criterion relationship is very small.

A larger percentage of the group assessed acceptable was considered to have higher *potential* than other groups. The preassessment group was rated high potential in only 28% of the cases, but 50% of the acceptable group was considered high potential. Whereas the expectancy charts look promising, the predictor–criterion correlation was again fairly low, .14.

In terms of promotion to *second*-level management, 11% of the acceptable group, 5% of the questionable group, and none of the not acceptable group had been promoted. Among the nonassessed groups, 5% had been promoted at the time of the study. These results can be considered only preliminary findings due to the small numbers; however, they are somewhat encouraging. It is unlikely that criterion contamination was present at this stage and thus the second promotion would probably provide a better index of individual achievement in the organization. Campbell and Bray (1967) concluded:

> The assessment center method is a valuable technique for the identification of management potential. Promotion of those who achieved a good rating at the assessment center led to an improvement in the quality of management at the first level of supervision, particularly in building a pool of men at the first level who have potential to advance to higher levels . . . . The assessment center produced a moderate, but significant, improvement in performance at the first level . . . . Promotion of men who had never been assessed led to satisfactory results in terms of performance at the first level, but only a small percentage of these men had potential to advance to higher levels of management [pp. 12–13].

The results and conclusions derived from this study must be accepted with reservations because of several problems encountered by the researchers. As stated, three components of performance and two components of potential were considered. By looking at both existing appraisal information and evaluations gathered for research purposes, the criterion data would appear to be fairly accurate. A potential danger existed, however, in that the supervisors had knowledge of (a) whether a subject had been assessed; and (b) if assessed, what the rating was. In the first case, the result might have been that the assessed supervisors received higher criterion ratings simply because of some positive halo surrounding those chosen for assessment. In the second case, the subjects who did well in the assessment center might have been given high criterion ratings because of general faith in the assessment center program.

No evidence is given concerning the comparability of the assessed and nonassessed subjects, but it is possible that other variables (e.g., age and tenure) were related to performance and potential ratings and were not controlled. The information supporting this view comes from Campbell and Bray (1967) who report that the preassessment group averaged 2 years more service than the postassessment comparison group.

Michigan Bell. A second study, using the same type of design but a much smaller sample, yielded essentially the same results (Bray, 1964a). Eighty male vocational employees at Michigan Bell Telephone who had been promoted to management were evaluated for performance and potential. Half of the sample had been assessed and then promoted; the other half had not been assessed. Table 7.9 shows that a larger percentage of the assessed subjects were rated as "better-than-satisfactory" performers. Similarly, a larger percentage of assessed subjects were considered to have potential for advancement. Although there is the possibility of criterion contamination through knowledge of the predictor scores (in fact, feedback was given to line management), the criteria seem adequate in several other regards. Extensive interviews concerning many aspects of the job (Bray, 1964a) were carried out with the supervisor, the supervisor's superior, and with the third-level manager. As with the previous study, no information is available comparing the experimental and the control groups. A major difference between the assessed and control groups is that feedback on assessment center performance was given to the participants and to their supervisors. The evidence on the effects of

Table 7.9
Validity of Assessment Center—Plant Department of Michigan Bell[a]

	Percentage rating of satisfactory performance as foreman	Percentage rating of potential of promotion
Assessed then promoted ($N = 40$)	62.5	67.5
Control (promoted before assessment center) ($N = 40$)	35.0	35.0

[a] From Bray (1964).

feedback on the participants is lacking but it is quite possible that the assessed group was influenced by the feedback coming directly to them and indirectly through the supervisor (e.g., their self-perceptions changed as they took some developmental actions).

A third study, one mentioned briefly by Campbell and Bray (1967), was made at the New England Bell Telephone Company. Performance evaluations showed that the group of managers rated "acceptable" was "definitely superior [p. 9]" to the group rated "not acceptable."

Union Carbide Corporation. The assessment center at the Oak Ridge Gaseous Diffusion Plant of the Union Carbide Corporation (Bender, Calvert, & Jaffee, 1970; Jaffee, *et al.* 1970) included some unique features. Due to the small number of persons assessed, it was not possible to compare on-the-job performance of persons assessed at various levels of acceptability. Therefore, the design included a control group of 13 subjects promoted immediately prior to the initiation of the assessment program and an experimental group of 13 subjects who were assessed and then promoted. Analyses showed that the two groups were comparable on a number of variables, but the experimental group was younger, had less company service, and had been in supervision a shorter period. Criterion information was collected in two areas: *(a)* objective data on the performance of the subject's work group (i.e., absences, grievances, or visits to the infirmary); and *(b)* interview data from supervisors and randomly selected subordinates regarding the adequacy of the subject as supervisor.

No differences in the objective criterion were found between the experimental and control groups. The criterion data were gathered about 1 year after assessment, and "considering the short time in a supervisory capacity for most of the experimental group, it is not at all surprising that these data did not reveal any meaningful differences [Bender *et al.,* 1970, p. 32]."

The interview data showed that more positive than negative comments

Table 7.10
Supervisory Performance of Assessed and Control Groups at Union Carbide[a]

| | Number of comments from | | | |
| | Superiors | | Subordinates | |
	Positive	Negative	Positive	Negative
Assessed group (N = 13)	45	13	105	30
Control group (N = 13)	30	20	72	20

[a] From Jaffee *et al.* (1970).

were made about the performance of members of the experimental group than about the control group. This pattern held for both superiors and subordinates (although the subordinates also made more negative comments regarding assessed subjects). The authors warn that, "These results must certainly be considered carefully and no conclusions of a definite nature may be drawn, but they are certainly indicative of a trend [Bender *et al.,* 1970, p. 33]."

Major limitations of the study, of course, are its small sample size and the potential positive halo surrounding the assessed group.

Caterpillar Tractor Company. The studies reviewed thus far have been generally supportive of the predictive validity of the assessment center technique. By contrast, the Bullard (1969) study was almost wholly negative. It was concerned with (a) the relationship between assessment center predictions and two measures of future managerial behavior; and (b) a comparison of the assessment center and a traditional method of selection and placement.

Caterpillar's assessment center, similar to the ones reviewed thus far, included in its assessment battery a number of situational exercises and leaderless group discussions. Following the 2-day evaluation period, the assessment staff spent the remainder of the week consolidating their observations, rating the individual's performance on 25 dimensions, and deriving one of the following overall ratings for each candidate: more than acceptable, acceptable, not ready now, and low in managerial skill. The dimensions were also used as one of the criterion measures, subsequently evaluated by the general foreman on the job. The dimensions evaluated on the Supervisory Qualification Rating Form (SQRF) included: company attitude, importance of work, inner work standards, motivation, and drive. A brief description of each dimension was given on the criterion evaluation form, followed by a five-point rating scale from low to high. Because no additional descriptors or qualifiers were given for the scale's points, the form may have suffered from lack of clarity and objectivity. Moreover, no data on its reliability were provided. The second criterion, also filled out by the foreman, was the Personal Description Check List (PDCL), a list of 108 specific on-the-job behaviors (e.g., rarely takes chances, cooperates when requested, is too shy to be a leader). However, the assessment center did not use this form, so no direct comparisons can be made.

Criterion data were gathered for 37 experimental (assessed) subjects composed of four groups from different plant locations and for 27 control subjects from the same locations, who had been placed in their jobs by the traditional method of supervisory evaluations. Bullard (1969) stated:

"Absolute control for age, time in supervision, and tenure with the company was difficult in view of the small N [p. 5]." Because the report is unclear about when the experimental and control supervisors were placed in their jobs relative to the institution of the assessment center, several objections can be raised. First, as with the Union Carbide study, if the controls had been on the job for a longer period at the time of criterion measurement, it would be likely that their job performance would be higher. Second, it may have been that the subjects were drawn from different pools of potential supervisors: The controls may have been selected first—the "cream of the crop"—with the experimental group selected from a pool having generally lower abilities. Personal communication with Bullard (1975) indicates this is what happened. Apparently "obviously" superior candidates were promoted without assessment, whereas marginal ones were scheduled to be assessed by the program.

Keeping in mind the question of comparability of subjects, we can examine the mean criterion scores for experimental and control groups shown in Table 7.11. On both the PDCL and the SQRF, the control group scored higher than the experimental group. Analyses for subgroups at the four locations follow the same pattern.

Bullard (1969) interpreted these results "as evidence that if superiority is to be assigned to either group on the basis of mean performance, then it must be assigned to those supervisors constituting the control or 'traditional method' group [p. 12–13]." The second set of analyses was correlations of predictors and criteria, a summary of which is presented in Table 7.12. No significant validities were found. It should be emphasized that major revisions have been made in the assessment center procedure at Caterpillar and this early study is not reflective of the effectiveness of the current program.

Steinberg's. A second study using this design that failed to demonstrate differences was conducted at Steinberg's, a large chain of super-

Table 7.11

Mean Scores for Criterion Variables for Experimental and Control Groups[a]

	Experimental ($N = 37$)	Control ($N = 27$)	Significance of difference
Personal Description Check List	181	195	$p < .01$
Supervisory Qualification Rating Form–job	84	89	$p < .05$

[a] From Bullard (1969).

Table 7.12
Intercorrelations of Predictors and Criteria [a]

Variables	2	3	4
Predictors			
Supervisory Qualification Rating Form–program	.23	.17	.26
Overall rating–program		.19	.12
Criteria			
Supervisory Qualification Rating Form–job			.76*
Personal Description Check List			

[a] From Bullard (1969).
* $p < .01$.

markets in Canada. Grossner (1974) compared the job performance of 24 store managers who were assessed then promoted and 21 managers promoted prior to installation of the assessment program. The assessed group was rated significantly higher on only 1 of 28 work performance ratings. However, on 24 additional variables the assessed group was rated higher, although the differences in the ratings did not reach statistical significance. There were no differences in the promotability ratings for the two groups. Grossner reported differences between the two groups in age, years of experience before promotion, level of advancement before promotion, and amount of formal education. Therefore, the two groups cannot be considered comparable and results of this part of the study are virtually impossible to interpret.

Other companies. In recent years, Wickes has become a major user of the assessment center method at all levels of management. An early report covered two assessment programs for retail lumberyard employees (Ague, 1971). Primarily developmental, the 4-day program for assistant managers enables Wickes to determine when they are ready for promotion. In 5 years, from 1966 to 1971, 184 assistant managers were assessed and 126 had been promoted to manager. The annual turnover rate of assistant managers dropped from 30% prior to the program to 8% after its inception. At the same time, The Wickes Hourly Assessment Program processed 240 hourly employees of whom 129 were promoted to the company's management training program. The annual turnover for these 129 hourly employees, after initial management assignments, has been about 3%. No comparative data for the hourly turnover figure previous to assessment were presented.

The turnover statistics reported by Wickes are a unique criterion that other companies might also use. From the information available, it is impossible to tell whether the reduction in turnover was due to the assessment program, to some other changes in the company, or to changes in the economy as a whole. For example, if the company had launched a broad change in managerial philosophy or if it was experiencing rapid growth and financial success, these would possibly reduce turnover. Certainly more information is needed, but the results are supportive.

Summary. The studies using the comparison group design are generally supportive of the superiority of the assessment center approach over the existing method of selecting managers. In general, the assessed group performs better than a comparison group promoted prior to installation of the assessment procedure. Two of nine comparisons showed no differences in job performance. Summarizing the comparison group studies available at that time, Cohen *et al.* (1974) found that larger percentages of the assessed groups were high in subsequent job performance (.68 versus .59), job potential (.59 versus .28), and progress (.38 versus .08). Notwithstanding the concern over comparability of groups, these studies strongly support the idea that assessment centers are better able to pick candidates who are more likely to be successful than are traditional methods currently being used in these organizations.

CORRELATIONAL STUDIES WITH FEEDBACK

This section covers a series of studies in which assessment center ratings are correlated with subsequent criteria of progress or performance in the organization. Evaluations of operational programs in which feedback is given to participants and line managers are susceptible to inflated validity due to criterion contamination, but some studies use means of avoiding or controlling such biases.

AT&T. Moses (1971, 1972) provided data for the largest sample on record. Over a 10-year period 8885 persons were assessed in two telephone companies. After recently assessed persons were eliminated from consideration (i.e., those assessed within the previous 2 years), the management progress of the remaining employees ($N = 5943$) was noted. Assessment ratings and the criterion of receiving two or more promotions since assessment were compared. Table 7.13 shows that a significantly larger percentage of persons who received high ratings were subsequently promoted. "Individuals assessed as 'more than acceptable' are twice as likely to be promoted two or more times than individuals assessed as 'acceptable,' and are almost ten times as likely to be promoted

Table 7.13
Progress in Management by Assessment Rating at AT&T[a]

Rating	N	Number receiving two or more promotions	Percentage
More than acceptable	410	166	40.5
Acceptable	1466	321	21.9
Questionable	1910	220	11.5
Not acceptable	2157	91	4.2
Total	5943	798	13.4

[a] Adapted from "Assessment Center Performance and Management Progress" by J. L. Moses, *Studies in Personnel Psychology*, 1972, 4 (1), 7–12. Copyright 1972 by Public Service Commission of Canada. Reprinted by permission.
$\chi^2 = 1239, p < .001.$

beyond an entry assignment than those rated 'not acceptable' [Moses, 1972, p. 9,]."

Table 7.14 presents simple and multiple correlations between tests, behavioral ratings from assessment observations, the OAR, and the progress criterion. The validities for the behavioral ratings and the OAR are

Table 7.14
Correlations of Predictors with Management Progress
$(N = 5943)^a$

Predictor variable	r or R
Test scores	
School and College Aptitude Test	
Total	.21
Verbal	.20
Quant	.18
Behavioral assessment variables	
Leadership	.38
Organizing and Planning	.34
Decision Making	.34
Perception	.31
Oral Skills	.27
Written Skills	.25
All behavioral assessment variables	.461
All assessment variables	.463
Final overall assessment rating	.44

[a] Adapted from "Assessment Center Performance and Management Progress" by J. L. Moses, *Studies in Personnel Psychology*, 1972, 4 (1), 7–12. Copyright 1972 by Public Service Commission of Canada. Reprinted by permission.

higher than the test validities. In addition, Moses (1972) points out that the behavioral variables alone account for most of the variation in criterion scores when compared with the combination of behavioral and test variables. The OAR is slightly less predictive than the statistical combination of the assessment variables.

A study answering many questions about previous validation research was reported by Huck (1974) and Huck and Bray (1976). The sample consisted of black and white females and there were analyses to evaluate the effects of criterion contamination through knowledge of the assessment ratings on the part of the supervisors providing job performance ratings. The sample consisted of 91 white women and 35 black women assessed in Michigan Bell's selection program of nonmanagement employees for advancement to first-level supervision. The management assessment team consisted of 35% female and 5% black assessors. Criterion data were gathered 1–5 years after assessment for the sample, of whom all had been promoted. Other data were reported for a supplementary sample of 479 women who had been assessed but not promoted at the time of the study. Performance effectiveness measures, gathered by a member of the company's research staff, included six behaviorally anchored rating scales and ratings of overall effectiveness and potential for advancement. Supervisors were asked to rate all of their immediate subordinates on a confidential basis. At the end of these sessions gathering the appraisal data, the researcher asked each supervisor if he or she knew whether the subordinates had attended an assessment center and, if so, whether they knew the assessment rating.

Table 7.15 shows that the overall assessment rating was quite effective in predicting several criteria of subsequent job effectiveness for both black and white females. The assessment predictions correlated with all six rating scales covering job performance areas for the whites and four of six areas for the blacks. Overall job performance and potential for advancement was predicted equally well for the two samples. Ratings of potential were more accurately predicted than performance ratings, a finding detected in other assessment center studies (Cohen et al., 1974).

Supervisors' knowledge of assessment results did not affect criterion ratings or accuracy of prediction. In 58 (46%) cases, the supervisors stated they knew the subordinates had been assessed and were aware of the assessment rating. Comparisons were made between this group and subjects whose supervisors stated that subordinates had not attended or that they were uncertain. There were no significant differences in the means and standard deviations of the ratings on job performance, potential for advancement, or the overall assessment rating. Furthermore, there were no differences in the correlations of the overall assessment ratings and the performance and potential ratings. Huck and Bray (1976)

Table 7.15

Relationships of OAR and Job Performance for Black and White Females[a]

Job performance ratings	Whites (N = 91)	Blacks (N = 35)
Initiative	.35**	.37*
Interpersonal skills	.29**	.21
Administrative skills	.38**	.37*
Development of subordinates	.35**	.34*
Communications	.28**	.33*
Job knowledge	.39**	.18
Overall job performance	.41**	.35*
Potential for advancement	.59**	.54**

[a] Adapted from "Management Assessment Center Evaluations and Subsequent Job Performance of White and Black Females" by J. R. Huck and D. W. Bray, *Personnel Psychology*, 1976, *29*, 13–30. Copyright 1976 by *Personnel Psychology*. Reprinted by permission.

*$p < .05$.

**$p < .01$.

concluded, "Criterion contamination does not appear to be a factor in the supervisor ratings obtained in this study [p. 24]."

Further evidence of the predictive validity for assessment of women is provided by Moses and Boehm (1975). The relationship of the OAR and promotion rate to first-level management and to second- or higher levels of management are reported in Table 7.16. In terms of first-level promotions, over twice as many of the "more than acceptable group" were promoted than of the "not acceptable" group. Even more striking is the dif-

Table 7.16

Promotion Rates for Women Assessed at AT&T[a]

Assessment level	N	Promoted once N	Promoted once %	Promoted twice or more N	Promoted twice or more %
More than acceptable	294	208	71.4	20	6.9
Acceptable	1364	954	70.4	82	6.1
Questionable	1403	736	52.6	39	2.8
Not acceptable	1785	552	30.9	11	0.6
Total	4846	2,450		152	

[a] Adapted from "Relationship of Assessment Center Performance to Management Progress of Women" by J. L. Moses and V. R. Boehm, *Journal of Applied Psychology*, 1975, *60*, 527–529. Copyright 1975 by the American Psychological Association. Reprinted by permission.

ference for subsequent promotions: Over 10 times as many of the high group were promoted a second or third time. This latter criterion is probably not contaminated by assessment recommendations. The correlation of the OAR and management level was .37 ($p < .01$). These results closely parallel those for men reported by Moses (1971, 1972).

IBM. Several studies at IBM provide evidence of the predictive validity of assessment center judgments and also show in what ways the situational exercises contribute to the evaluations. Support for the assessment center procedure has been produced for several divisions in the United States and foreign countries.

The largest set of validation results for separate jobs involving several criteria was presented by Dodd (1971). Table 7.17 shows that the assessment predictions were valid in at least one sample for salary, salary progress, position level, and change in management level. Assessment centers were most predictive of position level and change in position level.

A study by Wollowick and McNamara (1969) presented evidence for evaluating the relative contribution of various types of assessment pro-

Table 7.17

Summary of Validity Studies at IBM for Overall Assessment Rating[a]

Group	N	Year assessed	Elapsed years to follow-up	Position level at follow-up	Salary at follow-up	Change in position level	Percentage increase in salary
Maintenance service	47	1966	1		.35*		.29*
Financial	44	1967–1968	1	.43*		.18	.06
Maintenance service	47	1965–1966	2		.05		.16
Maintenance service	48	1965	2		.22		.03
Marketing managers	17	1966–1967	2			.52*	
Systems managers	18	1966–1967	2			.51*	
Financial	72	1966–1967	2	.54**		.20	.31**
Financial	42	1967	2	.08		.11	.08
Administrative	31	1965	3	.63**		.36*	
Maintenance service	66	1964–1965	3	.44**		.35**	
Maintenance service	47	1965–1966	4			.30*	

[a] From Dodd (1971).
* $p < .05$.
** $p < .01$.

cedures. They reported a study of 94 lower and middle managers whose progress was followed over a 3-year period after assessment. The criterion, an increase in managerial responsibility, was based on a complex index that included number of persons supervised, complexity of job, financial responsibility, and skill requirements.

The index covered 12 incremental steps and the authors believed it to be a better measure of advancement than position or salary level in the organization. Several results from the study are presented in Table 7.18. The first correlation ($r = .37$) indicates that the overall assessment rating of management potential is a fairly accurate predictor of progress. However, the best combination of psychometric tests correlated .45 with the criterion, suggesting the loss of some predictive efficiency when the judgmental process covers all the assessment data. This higher correlation, using the multiple regression equation, may result from statistical artifacts capitalizing on chance errors. For practical purposes all multiple regression results should be cross-validated when feasible. Of even more significance is the jump from .45 to .62 when tests, ratings on management characteristics, and exercises are statistically combined in the multiple regression analysis. The percentage of predicted-criterion variance increases from 20 to 36%.

Wollowick and McNamara (1969) tentatively concluded that (a) the situational exercises contributed significantly to the assessment of important characteristics related to management success (R increases from .45 to .62); and (b) the mechanical combination of separate sources of data

Table 7.18
Validity of Overall Rating and Three Types of Predictors for Middle Managers at IBM ($N = 94$)[a]

Predictor	R	R^2
Overall rating	.37*	14
Tests	.45*	20
Exercises	.39*	15
Characteristics	.41*	23
Tests and exercises	.54*	29
Characteristics and exercises	.52*	27
Characteristics and tests	.55*	30
Tests, characteristics, and exercises	.62*	38

[a] Adapted from "Relationship of the Components of an Assessment Center to Management Success" by H. B. Wollowick and W. J. McNamara, *Journal of Applied Psychology*, 1969, *53*, 348–352. Copyright 1969 by the American Psychological Association. Reprinted by permission.

* $p < .01$.

gathered in the assessment center may improve predictive effectiveness over and above the subjectively determined overall rating. The first conclusion is similar to others cited in earlier chapters; the second conclusion supports the argument of the superiorty of mechanical over actuarial prediction methods and suggests that some type of systematic weighting of inputs may improve predictions of progress. No other study of assessment centers makes the same comparison as Wollowick and McNamara, but other studies produce related data which will be summarized later in this chapter.

Wollowick and McNamara warn that their results should be cross-validated—always sound advice in multiple regression studies with a large number of variables and a small number of subjects. However, in lieu of actual cross-validation, shrinkage formulas may be used. Although not completely satisfactory, they give an estimate of cross-validation to a new sample (Blum & Naylor, 1968). When this type of analysis is applied to the Wollowick and McNamara data, there is only a slight reduction in multiple correlations and in percentages of criterion variance to be accounted for. Another reason for placing confidence in the results of the Wollowick and McNamara study is the generally accept-

Table 7.19

Assessment Candidates Promoted to Higher Levels after Becoming First-Line Managers at IBM[a]

Assessed potential	Sales[b]		Service[c]		Administration[d]	
	Managers	% promoted	Managers	% promoted	Managers	% promoted
Executive management	12	42	22	30	7	28
Higher management	34	50	26	27	25	12
Second-line management	50	30	35	34	25	12
First-line management	40	15	29	17	19	0
Remain non-management	31	13	29	3	11	0
Overall	167	28	141	23	87	9

[a]From "Validity of an Operational Management Assessment Program" by A. I. Kraut and G. J. Scott, *Journal of Applied Psychology*, 1972, 56, 124–129. Copyright 1972 by the American Psychological Association. Reprinted by permission.

[b]$\chi^2 = 16.18; p < .01.$

[c]$\chi^2 = 10.60; p < .05.$

[d]$\chi^2 = 6.66; p < .16.$

able reliabilities reported for the situational exercises at IBM (Greenwood & McNamara, 1967). Ratings and rankings of the leaderless group discussion, task force committee discussion, and the manufacturing game were shown to have interrater reliabilities predominantly in .70s and .80s. For one group of subjects, the reliabilities were more typically in .60s.

Recognizing that the first-level promotion is influenced by assessment data, Kraut and Scott (1972) provided further data on the validity of assessment center ratings to predict *second-level* promotions at IBM. As shown in Table 7.19, for 167 sales managers and 141 service managers, there is a significant relationship of assessment rating and promotion rate. Insignificant results were found for managers in administration, but only 9% of this entire sample had been promoted at the time of the study, so the effect may not be apparent yet.

Criterion problems plague many research studies in industrial psychology. Hence it is refreshing to see new attempts to measure managerial effectiveness. Kraut and Scott (1972) pointed out that "none of the highest rated group were demoted, and only 6 percent of the second highest rated individuals, compared to about 20 percent of the lowest rated candidates, were demoted [p. 126]." When the two top and two bottom groups are combined, the results approach significance ($p < .07$) as shown in Table 7.20.

Table 7.20
Sales Assessment Candidates Demoted after Becoming First-Line Managers at IBM[a]

	Subsequent movement			
	Full range of ratings[b]		Combined ratings[c]	
Assessed potential	N promoted	% demoted	N demoted	% demoted
Executive management	12	0		
			46[d]	4[d]
Higher management	34	6		
Second-line management	50	14	50	14
First-line management	40	20		
			71[e]	20[e]
Remain nonmanagement	31	19		
Overall	167	14	167	14

[a] From "Validity of an Operational Management Assessment Program" by A. I. Kraut and G. J. Scott, *Journal of Applied Psychology*, 1972, 56, 124–129. Copyright 1972 by the American Psychological Association. Reprinted by permission.
[b] $\chi^2 = 5.82; p < .22$.
[c] $\chi^2 = 5.57; p < .07$.
[d] Calculated for executive management plus higher management.
[e] Calculated for first-line management plus remain nonmanagement.

General Electric. In unpublished research, Meyer (1972) has also reported fewer demotions as the result of installing assessment centers. Prior to using assessment centers to select first-level supervisors, G.E. had a 16% failure (demotion) rate. In the first group of supervisors promoted using the assessment center information, none of the supervisors failed.

Standard Oil (Ohio). The assessment programs of Standard Oil (Ohio) have been studied thoroughly by their corporate staff (Carleton, 1970; Finkle & Jones, 1970; Finley, 1970) and outside researchers (Donaldson, 1969; Mitchel, 1975; Thomson, 1969, 1970). These studies provided evidence of the internal and external validity of assessment data. Of particular interest is the relationship between assessment ratings and on-the-job ratings for the same 13 dimensions. Three different sources (Carleton, 1970; Finley, 1970; Thomson, 1970) provided data relevant to the pre-

Table 7.21

Relationships of Assessments and Supervisory Ratings on Thirteen Traits in Three Standard Oil Studies

	Finley (1970) Assessment versus supervisor committee		Carleton (1970) Assessment versus supervisory committee (N = 122)	Thomson (1970)	
	Sample 1 (N = 109)	Sample 2 (N = 119)		Psychologists versus supervisors (N = 71)	Managers versus supervisors (N = 71)
Amount of Participation	30*	62*	35*	58*	65*
Oral Communication	23*	39*	26*	44*	37*
Personal Acceptability	29*	31*	31*	33*	37*
Impact	20*	36*	24*	50*	47*
Quality of Participation	22*	25*	21*	31*	38*
Personal Breadth	28*	42*	29*	55*	52*
Orientation to Detail	00	19*	01	19	14
Self-Direction	20*	26*	24*	42*	35*
Relationship with Authority	15	31*	12	35*	37*
Originality	29*	43*	28*	45*	45*
Understanding People	17	40*	20*	35*	39*
Drive	26*	21*	29*	12	29
Potential	65*	63*	65*	64*	64*
Median	23	36	26	42	38

* $p < .05$.

dictive validity of assessment ratings for job characteristics some years later. Table 7.21 summarizes these results, and from it one can conclude that assessors can validly predict behavior on several behavioral dimensions as a result of assessment center activities. Most correlations are low to moderate, but "potential" ratings are consistently high (i.e, in the .65 range). Moreover, two dimensions (Orientation to Detail and Relationship to Authority) account for six of the seven nonsignificant correlations. Partial explanation may be offered by the hypothesized curvilinear relationship between these dimensions and success. Carleton (1970) stated that for these dimensions "intermediate ratings were considered more favorable than either high or low [p. 565]."

The criteria in these studies may have been subject to bias and contamination, but distortion of results was probably minimal compared to the distortion inherent in administrative criteria such as promotions and salary data used so frequently in other studies. The rating scales used to gather the criterion ratings seem entirely adequate. Each is labeled, a definition of the dimension is provided, and behavioral descriptions of each of the five-scale points are included (Thomson, 1969).

Several questions might be asked about these data. Since the correlations are only moderately high, is it possible that they are a result only of autocorrelation or method commonality? Why are they not higher? Thomson (1969, 1970) has provided data relevant to these and other questions in a multitrait–multimethod analysis of ratings. The matrix of correlations among 13 traits and three sets of raters (management assessors, psychologist assessors, and supervisors) was examined for convergent and discriminant validity. Table 7.22 provides a summary of the extensive intercorrelations generated by Thomson. The two sets of assessors arrived at a high level of agreement (median r = .85), but each group of assessors was able to predict criterion ratings only moderately well (median r's = .42 and .38). Several indications of discriminant validity were presented. The validities for the two groups of assessors exceeded all other correlations in the psychologist–manager heteromethod block of correlations. (However, a certain percentage (24%) of the off-diagonal correlations in the psychologist–supervisor block and the manager–supervisor block exceeded the validities. Even more severe evidence of lack of discriminant validity was found in the monomethod heterotrait blocks.)

There was general agreement among the pattern of intercorrelations within each of the three sets of ratings. One of the main problems lay in the lack of reliability of the supervisors' ratings. These reliabilities (median = .52) were little more than the average intercorrelation of all the 13 traits (median = .48). By contrast, the reliabilities for the assessors

Table 7.22

Convergent and Discriminant Validity Using Multitrait–Multimethod Correlations in SOHIO
Assessment Ratings $(N = 71)^a$

	Psychologists–managers	Psychologists–supervisors	Managers–supervisors
Convergent validities	.85	.42	.38
(median r for 13 dimensions)			
Discriminant validity			
Percentage heteromethod–heterotrait			
rs which exceeded validities	100	24	17
Rho for patterns of			
monomethod–heterotrait r's	.84	.64	.71
	Psychologist	Manager	Supervisor
Median reliability	.84	.88	.52
versus			
Median monomethod–heterotrait r	.54	.56	.48

^{a} Adapted from "Comparison of Predictor and Criterion Judgments of Managerial Performance Using the Multitrait–Multimethod Approach" by H. A. Thomson, *Journal of Applied Psychology*, 1970, 54, 496–502. Copyright 1970 by the American Psychological Association. Reprinted by permission.

greatly exceeded the corresponding monomethod–heterotrait correlations (.84 > .54; .88 > .56). The supervisors' ratings showed a general halo effect with little differentiation among the 13 traits. Other evidence regarding the quality of the ratings is shown in Table 7.23. It will be seen that the supervisors' ratings are characterized by more leniency, less variance, and lower reliabilities.

Thomson (1970) suggested that "the criterion raters were unable to ar-

Table 7.23

SOHIO Study Data for Two Groups of Assessors and One Group of Supervisors^a

Average on 13 rating scales	Psychologist assessors (P)	Manager assessors (M)	Supervisors on job (S)
Means^b	4.77	4.87	5.39
Standard deviations^c	1.56	1.55	1.30
Reliabilities^d	.85	.89	.52

^{a}Adapted from "Comparison of Predictor and Criterion Judgments of Managerial Performance Using the Multitrait–Multimethod Approach" by H. A Thomson, *Journal of Applied Psychology*, 1970, 54, 496–502. Copyright 1970 by the American Psychological Association. Reprinted by permission.
^{b}P = M; S > P*; S > M*.
^{c}P = M; S < P*; S < M*.
^{d}P = M; S < P**; S < M**.
$^*p < .01$.
$^{**}p < .001$.

rive at a precise and common understanding of the meaning of the different scales and responded to some generalized notion of the goodness or badness of the assessee [p. 501]."

In addition to the 13 behavioral-trait ratings, Carleton's (1970) study involved a composite criterion based on salary growth and promotions over a 4-year period. The correlation of overall assessment committee ratings and the composite criterion was .51. Finkle and Jones (1970) clearly pointed out that the primary purpose at SOHIO was not the early identification of potential, but rather the assessment of specific talents, skills, and characteristics of the highly regarded program nominees. At the same time, the need to differentiate nominees who, in fact, had potential to progress rapidly to high levels was recognized. In view of this, it seems important to investigate the validity of assessed potential in relation to actual progress.

Evidence for the predictive validity of the SOHIO programs was provided by Mitchel (1975). Not only was it established that the overall assessment rating of management potential predicted a criterion of salary progress corrected for initial salary and time on the job, but also the results suggested that the accuracy of prediction increased over time. Mitchel obtained salary data for 95 managers assessed in 1966–1968, 84 in 1969–1970, and 75 in 1971–1972. Salary level was noted 1, 3, and 5 years after assessment for the first group, 1 and 3 years after assessment for the second group, and 1 year after assessment for the third group. Correlations of the dimension ratings and OAR with salary progress are listed in Table 7.24. For the first group assessed, the predictive validity is significant at the first year and increases with time on the job. For the second group, a significant relationship holds only for the third year data. The increase in predictive validity is also noted for most of the individual dimension ratings.

The pattern of improved accuracy of assessment center ratings has been noted elsewhere (Moses, 1973b). Such findings refute the contention that criterion contamination may account for the accuracy of assessment center ratings. It is highly unlikely that subsequent managers will continue to give monetary rewards and promotions to subordinates simply on the basis of high assessment ratings in the absence of effective job performance.

Sears. Klimoski and Strickland (1977) noted that the majority of criterion data for assessment center research has been restricted to indices of job progress such as promotion and salary increase rather than performance measures such as job behaviors. They argue that assessment centers are merely prescient (i.e., they simply record the biases of

Table 7.24

Correlations of Predictors with Criterion of Salary Progress for Three Groups of Managers at SOHIO[a]

	Group A			Group B		Group C
Year:	1	3	5	1	3	1
Potential[b]	.22*	.28*	.32*	.10	.22*	.19
Oral Communication	.32*	.40*	.41*	.12	.13	−.06
Impact	.33*	.43*	.46*	.21	.29*	.17
Drive	.20*	.24*	.25*	.02	.11	.27*
Understanding of People	.25*	.37*	.35*	.18	.18	.02
Originality	.19	.28*	.25*	.13	.17	.10
Personal Acceptability	.25*	.34*	.34*	.13	.17	.20
Relations with Authority[c]	−.11	−.16	−.17	−.27*	−.30*	−.11
Amount of Participation	.26*	.35*	.38*	.24*	.29*	.17
Average	.24	.32	.33	.16	.21	.14

[a] Adapted from "Assessment Center Validity: A Longitudinal Study" by J. O. Mitchel, *Journal of Applied Psychology*, 1975, *60*, 573–579. Copyright 1975 by the American Psychological Association. Reprinted by permission.

[b] Final overall evaluation by assessor.

[c] Negative correlations are the result of the direction of the rating scale.

* $p < .05$.

managers and assessors at an earlier time). Research not covered in the Klimoski and Strickland (1977) review has used job performance data and tends to negate this criticism. A study at Sears (Marquardt, 1976) gathered a variety of criterion data for 329 management trainees after one year in training. Each person was evaluated on nine performance dimensions, three factor scores from a performance evaluation form, three factor scores from a questionnaire (25 items) describing the individual's reactions to problems, seven factors from a semantic differential questionnaire (53 questions) measuring personal effectiveness, and a summary ranking of overall effectiveness. Data were provided by specially prepared training coordinators who monitored the progress of management trainees.

Management applicants were assessed in a 1-day program and rated "no offer," "discuss," and "offer" by the assessment staff. Comparisons (*t* tests) between the job performance for those individuals assessed in the no offer and offer groups revealed significant differences on several performance criteria. Those individuals who were assessed in the high group demonstrated more technical knowledge, better oral communication skills, and aggressiveness on the job; they demonstrated more motivated and alert leadership; and in their approach to problems, they were more creative and independent. They were ranked more effective in overall performance. These data show that the overall assessment center ratings correlate not only with a summary index of perceived effectiveness but also with several separate ratings of on-the-job performance.

American Airlines. Follow-up validity evidence for a group of 59 participants in the American Airlines (1976) assessment center program suggests that dimension ratings can predict salary progress. Twelve of 25 dimension ratings and their sum correlated significantly with base monthly salary and 6 of 25 plus their sum correlated with the amount of the last salary increase. When the participant's age was considered (partial correlations were computed), the correlations increased. When the number of promotions since assessment was partialed out, the correlations between ratings and monthly salary decreased, but still remained statistically significant. These findings suggest that even though management personnel use the assessment results for promotion decisions, a strong relationship between the center results and managerial salary remains. Only three of the dimension ratings correlated with number of promotions since assessment, but the criterion data were collected approximately 1 year after the program. Relatively few promotions were made during this period.

Canadian Public Service Commission. Follow-up validation of two Canadian government programs is provided by Slivinski, Grant, Bourgeois, & Pederson (1977). Criterion data for managers in the Customs and Excise Department and the Department of National Revenue were obtained up to 4.5 years after assessment. Slivinski *et al.* (1977) gathered four different criterion measures: *(a)* salary level achieved, corrected for initial salary; *(b)* position level attained; *(c)* overall job performance evaluation from the standard department appraisal; and *(d)* an anonymous overall performance evaluation for assessment center research purposes. In the Customs and Excise program, data were gathered 1.5, 3, and 4.5 years after assessment. Table 7.25 shows the correlation of the overall assessment evaluation with the various criteria. Although some performance ratings were not obtained, it is clear the assessment center showed consistent validity for these criteria. The accuracy of predicting position level increased over time.

Slivinski *et al.* (1977) formed various combinations of the 4.5-year criterion data using two, three, or all four subcriteria. The predictive validity of the overall assessment rating for these composites was markedly similar, ranging from .42 to .50.

Predictive validities for the Department of National Revenue are reported in Table 7.26. Although statistically significant, these correlations are somewhat lower than for the previous program, especially for

Table 7.25
Relation of Assessment[a] and Four Criterion
Measures of Later Job Success[b]

On-the-job criteria	Overall assessment evaluation at the assessment centre		
	1.5 years	3 years	4.5 years
Career progression			
Salary increase	.42**	.50**	.44**
	41[c]	36	32
Position level	.29*	.35*	.46**
increase	37	36	32
Job performance			
Supervisors' overall	—	.43**	.30*
performance rating		36	31
Departmental	—	—	.41**
appraisal			31

[a] Customs and Excise.
[b] From *Development and Application of a First Level Management Assessment Centre* by L. W. Slivinski, K. W. Grant, R. P. Bourgeois, and L. D. Pederson, Ottawa, Canada: Managerial Assessment and Research Division Personnel Psychology Center, October, 1977. Reprinted by permission.
[c] Number in sample.
*$p < .05$.
**$p < .01$.

the performance criterion at 3.5 years. Correlations for criterion composites are also considerably lower, with a maximum of .36. Slivinski *et al.* (1977) speculated that the difference in validity may be due to different purposes of the second program (staffing versus training) and the different assessee characteristics (older and more experienced managers).

Viewing the total results of the Canadian government programs, we can see the advantages of gathering several types of criterion data at various points in time for different subject samples. In total, the results establish the validity of the assessment program and show that accuracy of predicting management level may increase over longer time periods. The assessment center seems more predictive of measures of progress than of job performance, although the explanation may lie in the qualities of performance ratings as well as the assessment center ratings. The findings that the assessment center predicts two types of overall performance ratings, as well as the finding reported earlier in this chapter that the assessment center predicts several dimension ratings of managerial and personal behavior, dispel many of the earlier criticisms (Klimoski & Strickland, 1977) that assessment centers merely predict management progress criteria and do not assess managerial performance.

Table 7.26
Relation of Assessment[a] and Four Criterion
Measures of Later Job Success[b]

On-the-job criteria	Overall assessment evaluation at the assessment center	
	2 years	3.5 years
Career progression		
Salary increase	.23*	.40**
	65[c]	56
Position level	.24*	.25*
increase	69	56
Job performance		
Supervisors' overall	21*	.16
performance rating	69	57
Departmental	—	.05
appraisal		59

[a] Department of National Revenue.

[b] From *Development and Application of a First Level Management Assessment Centre* by L. W. Slivinski, K. W. Grant, R. P. Bourgeois, and L. D. Pederson, Ottawa, Canada: Managerial Assessment and Research Division, Personnel Psychology Center, October, 1977. Reprinted by permission.

[c] Number in sample.

* $p < .05$.

** $p < .01$.

Summary. The longitudinal studies reviewed in this section support the predictive validity of the assessment center process. The OAR is highly correlated with subsequent measures of a variety of criteria including progress in management level and salary. Initial promotions may be influenced in operational programs where assessment information is disseminated to the person making the promotion decision, but it is unlikely that further promotions are contaminated in this way. Thus, in the studies that used second and third promotions and progress over a period of 3–5 years, the criteria probably reflect uncontaminated job performance. In addition, in the new studies which controlled for knowledge of assessment information, the predictive validity remained high.

Of even more significance is the variety of performance criteria predicted by the assessment center information. Criteria have included ratings of overall performance and potential, increases in management responsibility (job complexity, financial responsibility, and skill requirements), ratings on behavioral scales for performance dimensions, measures of reactions to problems on the job, and measures of personal effectiveness on the job. The sources of these data have been the immediate supervisor, second-level supervisors, specially trained research interviewers, and training-staff members who performed field reviews.

CONCURRENT VALIDITY STUDIES

When an assessment or evaluation procedure is being used to make predictions of management success, the most appropriate validation procedure involves a longitudinal design such as we discussed earlier. Often conditions prevent such research designs, and concurrent studies are substituted in which the evaluation data are correlated with measures of success for a group of employees already on the job. In the latter part of this chapter we discuss the limitations of concurrent studies; for now, we will present the research results.

IBM. Hinrichs (1969) provided further data on the IBM assessment program in a study of 47 marketing recruits being considered for first-level management. The study used as predictors data generated from the assessment center procedure and data gleaned from a careful review of information in each candidate's personnel folder. The question was, "What does the assessment program contribute beyond what is already known about the candidate?" Ratings of behavior during assessment were correlated with (a) an external criterion of salary relative to age peers in the organization; (b) an internal criteria of general management potential evaluation as determined by the 2-day assessment program; and (c) a parallel criterion, the review of the personnel jacket. The correlations among these three criteria and three assessment rating scales are shown in Table 7.27. Hinrichs (1969) focused on the similarity of the relationships between the three assessment variables and both the internal and parallel criteria. His analyses used the overall assessment rating as the variable to be predicted. From this viewpoint it can be seen that there is some overlap of the manager's evaluation of the personnel folder and the assessment information. That the parallel criterion does not give all the information can be seen from the higher correlation for Scale 1 (activity) and from the fact that the correlation of the scales remains significant even after the parallel criterion is partialled out. Based on these results, Hinrichs (1969) concludes; "The data suggest that traditional approaches to the assessment of management potential in the form of careful evaluation of personnel records and employment history (our parallel criteria) can perhaps provide much the same information which evolves from the lengthy and expensive 2-day assessment programs [p. 43]."

The data can be viewed in another way. Rather than looking upon the overall assessment rating as a criterion, it would be preferable to look

Table 7.27
Intercorrelations among Assessment Scales and Criteria in IBM Study[a]

Variable	2	3	4	5	6	Partial correlation[b]
Rating Scale 1—activity[c]	.43*	.37*	.27	.49*	.78*	.72*
Rating Scale 2—administration[d]		.50*	.16	.48*	.50*	.36*
Rating Scale 3—stress resistance[e]			−.15	.26	.25	.15
Relative salary standing (external criterion)				.10	.37*	.37*
Managers' potential evaluation (parallel criterion)					.46*	
Assessment program evaluation (internal criterion)						

[a]From "Comparison of 'Real Life' Assessments of Management Potential with Situation Exercises, Paper-and-Pencil Ability Tests, and Personality Inventories" by J. R. Hinrichs, *Journal of Applied Psychology*, 1969, 53, 425–432. Copyright 1969 by the American Psychological Association. Reprinted by permission.

[b]This column indicates the correlation of the variable and the assessment center evaluation with the manager's potential evaluation held constant.

[c]Rating scales were derived from combinations of the dimensions rated in the assessment center. Activity: Persuasive, Aggressiveness, Energy Level, Interpersonal Contact, Oral Communications, and Self-Confidence.

[d]Administration: Decision Making, Planning and Organization, Written Communication, and Administrative Ability.

[e]Stress resistance: Resistance to Stress and Risk Taking.

*$p < .05$.

upon both the assessment results and the review of the personnel jacket as predictors to be validated against an external criterion. From this frame of reference it can be seen that the assessment program correlated higher (.37) with the external salary criterion than did the managers' evaluation of existing personnel information (.10). It should also be pointed out that current salary is not a completely satisfactory criterion and may be biased in favor of the personnel file predictor. Past salary (as found in the file) is usually a good predictor for future salary.

American Management Association. The studies we have reported thus far were conducted within separate organizations. Positive results can be generalized to other organizations only with certain reservations. However, if a research study uses the same methodology and criteria for the same type of job across several organizations, the basis for generalizing about the results is sounder. Steps in this direction are provided by reports on the effectiveness of an assessment program developed by the American Management Association (AMA). As in the AT&T program, participants are assessed on several management dimensions using individual and group exercises such as an in-basket, leaderless group discussion, and game. McConnell and Parker (1972) provided

Table 7.28.
Concurrent Validity Coeffecients of American Management Association Assessment Center Ratings[a]

Organization	Number of participants	r
Bank	24	.55*
Paper manufacturers	12	.48
Electronics manufacturers	22[b]	.64*
Auto manufacturers	12	.28[c]
Total	70	.57

[a] From "An Assessment Center Program for Multi-Organizational Use" by John J. McConnell and Treadway C. Parker, *Training and Development Journal*, 1972, 26(3), 6–14. Copyright 1972 by the American Society for Training and Development, Inc. Reprinted by permission.

[b] Although 24 participants were assessed, 2 were not included in the validity study.

[c] Although 75% were correctly identified, the r was reduced by severe restriction of range in performance ratings.

* $p < .01$.

evidence of the concurrent validity of overall assessment ratings in four organizations by correlating the results with job performance ratings. Table 7.28 shows that the overall assessment rating was significant for two of the four groups and for the total combined group. Although the subsample sizes were relatively small, the authors found the results encouraging. Some indication of the practical significance of the assess-

Table 7.29
Accuracy of American Management Association Assessment Program in Identifying Job Performance Ratings[a]

Organization	Number of participants	Correct identifications		Misses ± 1 scale point		Misses ± 2 scale points	
		Number	Percentage	Number	Percentage	Number	Percentage
Bank	24	12/24	50	10/24	42	2/24	8
Paper manufacturers	12	6/12	50	5/12	42	1/12	8
Electronics manufacturers	22	14/22	64	7/22	32	1/22	4
Auto manufacturers	12	9/12	75	3/12	24	—	—
Total	70	41/70	59	25/70	36	4/70	5

[a] From "An Assessment Center Program for Multi-Organizational Use" by John J. McConnell and Treadway C. Parker, *Training and Development Journal*, 1972, 26 (3), 6–14. Copyright 1972 by the American Society for Training and Development, Inc. Reprinted by permission.

ment ratings is shown in Table 7.29 where the assessment procedure correctly identified 50 to 75% of the job-performance ratings.

A study of 23 first-level supervisors in the Metro Transit Authority of New York also used the AMA assessment program (Metro Transit, 1972). Job performance evaluations were gathered from the participants' immediate supervisors using a scale comparable to the assessment ratings. The correlation of the overall assessment rating and the criterion performance ratings was .71. On a nine-point scale, 12 of 23 participants (52%) were rated the same by both methods and an additional 10 of 23 (43%) were over- or under-rated by only one score point.

Worbois (1975) reported on the validity of the AMA program at Detroit Edison. Two final assessment ratings were generated for the 48 assessees: (a) overall potential for successful supervision; and (b) an estimate of the level in the management hierarchy the person was expected to attain. Several criterion ratings were obtained from job supervisors: (a) ratings on seven behavioral scales; (b) ratings on 12 dimensions assessed in the program; and (c) an overall rating of demonstrated performance and potential. Table 7.30 shows that the assessment variables correlated significantly with all criteria. There is some indication that the dimension ratings and overall ratings of performance and potential were more accurately predicted than the behavioral ratings. Ratings of the *importance* of the dimension multiplied by the supervisory ratings did not yield any higher validity coefficients, possibly because all dimensions were considered extremely important.

Table 7.30
Predictive Validity of Two Overall Assessment Ratings in Relation to Job Performance Criteria[a]

| | Overall assessment ratings | |
Criteria	Overall potential	Expected level of attainment
Sum of behavioral scales	.29*	.34*
Sum of ability ratings	.46*	.44**
Overall rating	.47**	.45**

[a] Adapted from "Validation of Externally Developed Assessment Procedures for Identification of Supervisory Potential" by G. M. Worbois, *Personnel Psychology*, 1975, *28*, 77–91. Copyright 1975 by *Personnel Psychology*. Reprinted by permission.
*$p < .05$.
**$p < .01$.

In summary, Worbois (1975) concluded that the results demonstrated utility of the externally developed assessment procedure applied to this organization. Furthermore, he believed the program can be of real value in appointing new supervisors.

A summary of data for 280 participants assessed in various AMA programs through 1978 revealed somewhat lower, yet still significant, correlations between assessment center ratings and job performance ratings (Parker, 1980).

Internal Revenue Service. Although the assessment center approach has been used most frequently in industrial settings, it has also gained wide acceptance in government organizations (Byham & Wettengel, 1974). Relatively little data exist on the criterion validity of assessment centers in these settings, but the IRS carried out a small-scale evaluation project (DiCostanzo & Andretta, 1970) involving the assessment of 142 persons from 11 IRS offices. In comparing the results with traditional evaluation information, the authors noted that "there was no correlation between relative strengths and weaknesses shown on [supervisory] evaluations and the corresponding areas in the assessment center reports . . . . [However] feedback from local management officials who used the reports indicates that in many cases they probed deeper with the supervisor and satisfied themselves that the assessment center findings were correct [DiCostanzo & Andretta, 1970, p. 14]."

Criterion contamination may well have existed in the IRS situation. Prior to obtaining managerial evaluations, the managers attended a three session, 2-day assessment center workshop which introduced them to the history and theory of assessment centers and to details of the program. Further, the managers were put through a miniature assessment program (DiCostanzo & Andretta, 1970). The purpose of this experience was to create a favorable set toward the assessment process.

Tennessee Valley Authority. The TVA initiated a pilot assessment center program for managers in the divisions of engineering design and construction, water control, forestry, and navigation (Erpenbach, 1971). The standard types of exercises were used and the assessors were higher-level managers. Independent judgments were made by the assessors on each candidate for 15 managerial skills. Erpenbach (1971) concluded. "The MSAP [Management Skills Appraisal Program] was judged to have been highly successful by the experimenters. They found a high degree of relationship between the appraisers' ratings and the ratings of the appraised employees' supervisors [p. 2]."

Federal Aviation Administration. In a study of a small sample of 25 finalists (among 111 candidates assessed) for an upward-mobility program in the Federal Aviation Administration, Alexander *et al.* (1975) found a correlation of .23 between the assessment center ratings and a sum of ratings from the current and former supervisor. The researchers questioned the adequacy of the supervisory ratings due to their low reliability and high leniency.

American Airlines. Other concurrent validity evidence is presented by American Airlines (1976) for 59 managers. The criteria included the individual's two most recent performance appraisal ratings of potential in the organization. Six of 25 dimensions correlated significantly with the most recent rating and 10 of 25 dimensions plus their sum correlated with the prior performance criterion. Consistent validity was found for Impact, Creativity, Career Ambition, Salesmanship, and Initiative. It would appear from these results that the high-potential managers in this organization are seen as highly assertive and upwardly mobile individuals. The results more clearly reflect the difficulty of obtaining on-the-job observations of most of the dimensions targeted to the higher level job.

Ezaki Gliko Company, Ltd. In a study (Fujie, 1980) of second-level managers of an ice cream and candy manufacturing company in Osaka, Japan, a significant relationship between assessment center ratings and on-the-job performance ratings was obtained. In a concurrent validity study, second-level managers were rated by their bosses using a one-to-five scale. They were then put through an assessment center where the assessors had no knowledge of their current job performance. Since the major purpose of the assessment center was developmental, no overall rating was obtained. However, it was possible to add up the dimensional ratings to group the candidates. The results of the study are presented in Table 7.31.

State of Massachusetts. One other concurrent validity study is worth noting even though it does not deal with the prediction of management potential. The Vocational Rehabilitation Department of the State of Massachusetts has reported the results of a study of the accuracy of their assessment center program used to select vocational rehabilitation counselors (Goldberg *et al.,* 1980). Current counselors, whose performance was known, were assessed by managers who had no knowledge of their job performance. Table 7.32 shows that the program had a high "hit rate" and produced significant results in spite of the small sample.

Table 7.31
Performance by Sum of Dimension Ratings—Validity Study
from Japan[a]

Sum of dimension ratings (five-point scale)	On-the-job ratings				
	5 (high)	4	3	2	1 (low)
45+	1	1			
40–44	1	2			
35–39	2	16	5		
30–34	1	11	23	7	
25–29		1	15	19	3
0–24			1	4	2

[a] From Fujie, 1980. Reprinted by permission.

Summary. The results of the concurrent validity studies are mixed. In some cases significant correlations with performance criteria are found, in others, they are not. The lack of significant results is not surprising because many conditions can contribute to these low correlations. Managers who provide the criterion information often have very different standards of "acceptable" performance, and they are seldom in positions to fully and consistently observe subordinates demonstrate the behaviors and skills being measured by the assessment center. For example, very few managers ever observe a subordinate supervisor conduct a disciplinary interview or performance appraisal interview with one of their subordinates. With these limitations in mind, we can conclude that none of the studies demonstrates that the assessment center is ineffective or less effective than other methods.

Table 7.32
Selection of Vocational Rehabilitation Counselors[a]

Overall assessor rating	Supervisor's performance rating	
	Unacceptable	Acceptable
Acceptable	0	12
Unacceptable	7	4

[a] From Goldberg et al., 1980. Reprinted with permission.

Methodological Critique of
Validation Research

This section reviews the validity studies in terms of several methodological considerations. Questions of sampling of subject populations, criterion measures for evaluating effectiveness of assessment centers, and experimental and research designs are analyzed in some detail. In addition, a number of other considerations such as kinds of organizations, levels and types of jobs, and kinds of assessors are dealt with briefly. While we will attempt to point out the limitations in the various research designs in various studies, we do this with the full recognition of the great difficulty of conducting research in the "real world" using employees and middle-level assessors and being faced with constraints of time, expense, and management cooperation. While the reviewed studies are far from perfect, many are far superior to the average selection research study and as a whole they are better than the norm. It is our observation that organizations have been far more willing to conduct and publish research in this area than in other approaches to managerial prediction such as supervisory predictions, consultant evaluations, or paper-and-pencil tests.

VALIDATION SAMPLE

The assessment process is time consuming (varying from two to five days for assessors) and is expensive, especially since the assessment staff is usually composed of managerial personnel two levels above the participants. In view of this, it is not surprising that many studies involve relatively small sample sizes. Sample size in existing research reports, however, range from 12 to 5943! The median was 55 and most studies used 40 to 50 subjects, but a few studies had over 100 subjects.

The principal criticism of the research has been directed at the lack of representative validation samples. In the reported studies, participants are usually recommended by their supervisors as persons having potential for advancement. Subsequent assessment center performance and performance on the job provide insight into the likelihood of false positives (i.e., the supervisory nominees who assess poorly and those highly assessed who do poorly on the job after promotion). There is little evidence about how many potentially effective supervisors are unrecognized because their supervisors do not recommend them for assessment. The matter is becoming an increasingly moot point as self-nomination rapidly replaces supervisory nomination as the common entree to an assessment center. When self-nomination is used, generally the success rate goes down, as one unpublished set of data (Michigan Bell, 1969) indicates. Among a group of 454 self-nominees, 19% were assessed acceptable or above, compared with 27% of the participants chosen by their supervisors for assessment. In the subsequent three years, 62% of the highly assessed self-nominees were promoted.

Another criticism concerns the use of concurrent validity designs with groups of persons currently holding the target job. Such designs attempt to see if the assessment center can differentiate between good and poor performances on the job. Supervisors in training (Bentz, 1971), experienced supervisors (Hinrichs, 1969; McConnell & Parker, 1972; Worbois, 1975), and middle-level managers (DiCostanzo & Andretta, 1970) were the subjects in studies evaluating the effectiveness of assessment centers for those same respective levels of employees. To the extent that the motivation of aspirants to the position differs from the motivation of incumbents, and to the extent that any learning or growth has taken place on the job, incumbents are probably not an appropriate group for validating selection or promotion procedures. More appropriate for assessment would be a sample of persons on the lower level job and subsequent measurement of their effectiveness on the higher level job. This type of follow-up study should always be conducted, if feasible.

A third criticism focuses on the matching of the experimental group and the control group. In some studies, the performance of an experimental group of subjects who are assessed, then placed on the job, is compared with the performance of a control group placed on the basis of a traditional method—usually supervisors' recommendations. Random assignment to the decision-making procedure is very difficult in this type of study. Matching has been attempted in different ways without total success. The most frequently used procedure has been to compare the performance of the last set of supervisors promoted before introduction of assessment with the performance of the same number of supervisors promoted after assessment. A number of potential flaws are apparent (e.g., the pool of high-potential supervisors may be promoted prior to assessment, thus the remaining pool of nominees may be generally weaker). However, supervisors nominating subordinates for attendance at the center may deliberately recommend only their best people for assessment. Campbell and Bray (1967) reported that despite careful attempts to match subjects, the control group promoted before the start of assessment had, on the average, two years more experience in management than the assessed group. Jaffee, Bender, & Calvert (1970) also found that the control subjects were older, longer tenured, and more experienced as supervisors. He hypothesized that in his sample the control supervisors were perceived as not as effective as the younger, more dynamic men who were evaluated and promoted by the "modern" method. Other studies (Bray, 1964a; Bullard, 1969) reported that the experimental and control groups were not matched, but gave no data on their comparability.

Accuracy for minorities and women. Another criticism of early assessment center research is that the effect of subject characteristics is seldom evaluated in validation studies. For example, ethnic and sex composition of the sample was seldom researched. Jaffee *et al.* (1972) demonstrated that assessment techniques can be applied to disadvantaged groups, but presented no validation data against job performance. Bray (1971a) described the use of assessment at AT&T to identify women with management potential, but again provided no research data. The lack of minority and female subjects is understandable, because unfortunately until the early 1970s most managers and nominees for promotion were white males. With the rising concern over the potential discrimination against minorities and women, there has been more assessment of these groups and concomitant research.

Investigation of sex and race variables has focused on the following questions: (a) Are assessment centers equally valid and fair for different subgroups of participants? (b) Does the sex and race composition of the group affect assessor, self, and peer ratings? (c) What effect does sex or race of the assessor have on assessment ratings?

Moses (1973b) showed that the validity of a 1-day early identification program was equally valid for black and white men and women using a longer assessment program as a criterion. While this is unique and stimulates interesting research ideas, it is not completely satisfactory for the evaluation of job-related validity. Better data come from other comparative validities studies at AT&T and elsewhere. Huck and Bray (1976) found equal validities for black and white females in relation to two global criteria of overall job performance and potential for advancement. Moses and Boehm (1975) found validities of the OAR in relation to management progress for women comparable to the validities for men (Moses, 1971, 1972). Marquardt (1976) found various components of the Sears selection program for recruits valid for black and white males and females.

Age of the assessee should also be considered. Burroughs, Rollins, and Hopkins (1973) found a correlation of $-.34$ between OAR and age among 117 middle managers in a telephone company, and Neidig *et al.* (1978) found a correlation of $-.12$ for 260 FBI agents being considered for first-level management. Both correlations were statistically significant but the second is quite low. No relationship of age and OAR was found by Hall

(1976) in an upward mobility program in the Bureau of Engraving and Printing, by Quarles (1980) among candidates for managerial positions in the Mississippi Bureau of Narcotics, or by Parker (1980) among AMA assessees. We are aware of other unpublished research studies showing a strong relationship between age and overall assessment rating. In one study, age was a better predictor than any single dimension. Age differences are usually much stronger in programs for first-level supervision.

Several explanations are plausible, including the possibility that the assessment exercises are unfair to older subjects. The more likely explanation is that the correlation results from preassessment selection. "High potential" candidates get selected for the assessment center early in their careers. "Marginal" candidates get selected a little later. "Poor" candidates (in the eyes of their boss) either do not get selected or get to go to the assessment center as a "consolation prize" late in their careers. A supervisor tends to say to himself or herself, "Old Joe deserves a try at the assessment center even though there is little chance he will do very well." Evidence of this hypothesis comes from the fact that age bias is lessened dramatically if a self-nomination procedure is used. Further research is clearly needed on this topic.

In addition to the predictive validity of the OAR (i.e., correlation with subsequent performance criteria), the level and distribution of ratings must be considered. The assessment center may have adverse impact if minorities or women get evaluated lower in the program. Whites were rated higher than blacks in Jaffee et al. (1972), Moses (1973b), Huck (1974), Huck and Bray (1976), and Clingenpeel (1979). No differences in ratings were obtained in studies by Alexander (1975) and Russell (1975). In the Sears recruiting study (Marquardt, 1976), larger proportions of blacks than whites received job offers. Byham (1981) reviewed all the published research findings and many unpublished findings and concluded that differences in mean scores for blacks and whites seem to be mainly evident among candidates for first-level supervisory positions. About one-third of the first-level supervisory assessment centers he surveyed showed significant differences between blacks and whites. These data must be viewed quite cautiously. Organizations have been under great pressure to promote blacks and, in the spirit of affirmative action, they may be screening larger groups of minorities including unqualified candidates who pull down the average assessment ratings. A supervisor may hesitate to send a marginal white subordinate to the organization's assessment center but may send a marginally performing black candidate hoping that he or she will work out. The average tenure of black candidates prior to assessment is often lower than for whites because of management's pressure to quickly move blacks into management positions.

An organization's recruiting policy and the image of the job held in the community also affect the pool of candidates available for assessment. In the past, an organization may have tended to hire whites with "management potential" and blacks with the expectation that they would not be advanced. To the degree the selection decisions were accurate, this difference will be reflected in the quality of candidates available for assessment and ultimately in assessment center scores.

The numbers of individuals being promoted now in comparison with previously is more important. Probably one-half of the first-level supervisory assessment centers have been put in for affirmative action purposes. There seems to be no question that more minorities have been promoted as the result.

Regional differences in assessed performance were found by Friedman (1980) using data obtained in a series of assessment centers conducted by the Tennessee Valley Authority to select first-level supervisors.

The data for sex comparisons clearly show no difference in assessment results for men and women (Alexander, 1975; Clingenpeel, 1979; Hall, 1976; Marquardt, 1976; Moses, 1973b; Moses & Boehm, 1975).

The composition of the assessee group has been systematically investigated in only two studies. Schmitt and Hill (1977) studied the effects of sex and race composition of 54 assessee groups on self, peer, and assessor ratings. Sufficient data were available to conduct analyses for black females, white females, and white males. The results clearly showed that group composition had little effect and even though some isolated relationships were found, the authors concluded "It should be stressed that the results were of marginal statistical and practical significance [p. 263]."

Because of the importance of potential adverse consequences, Schmitt & Hill warned that the few significant findings should be recognized. For example, black females were rated lower in forcefulness when in groups with larger numbers of white males and lower in written communications when they were assessed with larger numbers of white females. Both assessor and peer ratings of group performance were adversely affected in a few instances. However, the overall assessment rating (the summary rating which would affect promotion possibilities) did not correlate with any group composition index for the black females or for the other groups.

In a study involving candidates for a high government position (N = 104), Byham (1981a) were able to systematically look into differences between races and sexes for participants and for assessors and the interactions between the two. He found no sex or race differences in ratings given by male and female assessors or by white and black assessors across 17 dimensions. Multivariate analysis of variance revealed no differences among white, black, and Hispanic ratees or between male and female ratees. Furthermore, there were no interactions for ratee sex and race. Detailed analyses of dimension ratings within each exercise revealed no significant differences either. In summary, these results suggest that assessment center ratings on performance dimensions are not affected by the race or sex of the assessor or assessee.

No other reported studies have investigated the question of whether race, sex, or age of assessors affects assessment center ratings received by the participants. Related evidence comes from a study at the FBI by Neidig et al. (1978) who found no effect on rating characteristics due to amount of time since assessor training, repetition as an assessor, or being a member of the headquarters staff or field staff.

CRITERIA

Measuring effective work performance has plagued industrial psychologists for decades and assessment center research is similarly beset. Obtaining reliable and objective indices of performance for significant, relevant segments of on-the-job behavior is an elusive goal for any job and is especially difficult for managerial positions. Assessment center researchers have not solved the problem, but have circumvented it by utilizing a wide variety of criteria, all of which are admittedly limited in some respect.

The predominant criterion for the validation research in this body of literature has been supervisory ratings of both performance and potential. Virtually every study has used ratings, even when more objective data were also gathered, such as salary progress (American Airlines, 1976; Bray & Grant, 1966; Dodd, 1971; Slivinski et al., 1977), progress in management (Bray & Grant, 1966; Carleton, 1970; Dodd, 1971; Hinrichs, 1978; Kraut & Scott, 1972; Michigan Bell, 1969; Moses, 1972; Slivinski, 1979b), absenteeism of subordinates (Jaffee et al., 1970), turnover (Ague, 1971), field observations of performance (Bray & Campbell, 1968; Moses & Wall, 1975), and field interview data (Campbell & Bray, 1967; Huck & Bray, 1976; Jaffee et al., 1970).

Problems with supervisors' ratings are legion. Leniency, halo, and restrictions-in-range biases may occur. Bullard (1969) found 88% of the experimental group and 93% of the control were rated as acceptable or above by supervisors. Thomson (1970) found lack of convergent and discriminant validity among supervisors' ratings. Bray and Campbell (1968) speculated in their study of salesmen that the lack of predictability of supervisors' ratings was due to lack of knowledge of the salesmen's performance.

Table 7.33 presents a summary of the validity findings by type of criterion and outcome of the research. A word of explanation is necessary regarding the entries. Each relationship between an overall assessment rating and a criterion was considered a separate piece of data; therefore, within a single study, job ratings of both performance and potential may be included. In cases where several assessment rating scales were correlated with several comparable criterion scales, the mean or median of those scale validities was used as a piece of data.

While it may appear at first glance that assessment centers are more predictive of one type of criterion than another, a chi-square analysis of the data revealed no such association ($\chi^2 = 4.09$, $df = 4$, $p < .30$). This finding is somewhat different from Cohen, Moses, and Byham's (1974 conclusion that assessment centers are more valid for ratings of potential than performance. They considered the magnitude of predictive accuracy, but did not test the significance of differences they noted.

Table 7.33 suggests a majority of positive results, but it is an aggregate of uncontaminated studies and studies with some probability of contamination of the criteria from both exposure to and use of the assessment results. Ratings of performance and potential and actual progress in management level and salary are all susceptible to this problem. Because the assessment center is usually an expensive program, it must be "sold" to many important persons, resulting in company-wide publicity. Many organizations have extensive orientation programs to describe the nature

Table 7.33.
Summary of Validity Findings by Type of Criterion[a]

Type of criterion	Validity findings[c]		
	Significant results	Nonsignificant results	Total
Ratings or rankings of performance[b]	20	4	24
Ratings or rankings of potential	5	1	6
Objective indices of progress	24	11	35
Objective indices of salary	14	8	22
Miscellaneous: turnover, resignations	3	3	6
Total	66	27	93

[a] Each entry represents a separate correlation of an assessment rating and a criterion measure; several entries might be found in one research report.

[b] Two studies could not be classified because there was only vague reference to the results (Erpenbach, 1971) or because the small number of significant correlations among the large number of correlations computed may have been due to chance alone (Bentz, 1971).

[c] $\chi^2 = 4.09$, $df = 4$, $p < .30$.

and results of the assessment center. Furthermore, the results of assessment are often fed back to the supervisor of the participant or to that supervisor's supervisor. It is highly probable that in the climate of support for the program, these results were given major attention. When subsequent decisions regarding promotion to supervisory level were made, or when ratings of supervisory effectiveness and potential were gathered, it is hard to imagine that the assessment feedback is not one of the factors affecting the judgments of raters. To further complicate the matter, assessors themselves made the criterion ratings in some cases.

It is necessary to precisely delineate the type of feedback and the potential contamination. When assessment results are given only to managers two or more levels above the incumbent, ratings of job performance and potential for advancement obtained from the immediate supervisor may be less susceptible to contamination. But promotion decisions may be highly contaminated if the higher level managers who reviewed the assessment results were, in fact, the most influential in awarding promotions. Similarly, when assessment results are given to the immediate supervisor, contamination of performance and potential ratings and actual job progress can be expected.

Among the studies finding positive results for performance and potential ratings, the following can be considered relatively free from such contamination: Bray (1964a), Bray and Campbell (1968), Campbell and Bray (1967), Hinrichs (1969), Huck and Bray (1976), Marquardt (1976), Mather (1964), McConnell and Parker (1972), and Slivinski et al. (1977). Contamination-free studies using objective indices of progress and salary include Bray and Grant (1966), Bray et al. (1974), Dodd (1971), Hinrichs (1978), Howard (1979), Kraut and Scott (1972), Moses (1971, 1972), Moses and Boehm (1975), Slivinski (1979), and Slivinski et al. (1977). In other words, of the 35 research reports reviewed in this chapter, 28 included positive results and among these, 18 used uncontaminated criteria. (A single program of research, for example MPS, might be covered in more than one report.)

In summary, a large number of studies have been done; many have demonstrated criterion validity; uncontaminated criteria have been used; and the assessment center is equally effective in predicting several types of criteria.

TIME OF CRITERION MEASUREMENT

The time at which criterion measures are taken can also influence validation results. For assessment centers, some evidence supports the contention that the overall assessment rating is more predictive over a longer period of time. Studies have shown that assessment centers are more accurate predictors of promotion to the third and fourth levels of management than of the initial promotion (Moses, 1972), of salary level 8 years postassessment than of 1 year later (Mitchel, 1975), and of management level attained after 8 years than 1 year postassessment (Hinrichs, 1978).

Two exceptions to this trend are seen in data reported by Finley (1970) and Slivinski et al. (1977). For two samples of managers at SOHIO, assessment center ratings of potential were about equally correlated (r's = .63 and .65) with supervisors' ratings gathered 9–29 months and 30–62 months after assessment. Mixed results were found in two groups in the Canadian government. Slivinski et al. (1977) found an increase in predictive validity over time for a criterion of increase in position level for one group (but not the second group) and a higher validity for salary in the second group (but not in the first). In personal correspondence, Slivinski attributes this to the ups and downs of government staff and salary budgets. During tight times, the poorer performers tend to catch up with the better performers; during times when jobs are opening up and more discretionary salary increases are possible, the better people jump ahead. His research indicates that the timing of the criterion measurement is all important.

Preliminary research over a period of 16 years with the Management Progress Study is producing quite mixed results (Howard, 1979). For the college sample, predictive validities topped out at .45 around the sixth to eighth year, and now have dropped off somewhat to about .30. This may be a result of the generally large number of promotions to middle management that occurred during that time period. Validities of a middle-management reassessment of the college sample (after they have had 8 years with the company) have shown a steady upward increase over 12 years (Howard, 1981). The validities for the noncollege sample have remained high and stable through the sixteenth year of the study.

We feel certain that the time period in which criterion information is obtained is an important variable worthy of considerable research. The dynamic qualities of the organizations in which the criteria are collected must be considered.

An Evaluation of Assessment Centers for Various Purposes

SELECTION

To demonstrate the effectiveness of a selection technique, it is appropriate to have evidence of predictive validity (American Psychological Association, American Educational Research Association, & National

Council on Measurement in Education, 1974). Predictive validity can be established by correlating predictor scores, obtained prior to hiring, with criterion measures, obtained sometime after hiring, for a representative sample of the applicant population. The criterion data should be free from contamination and should give reliable and relevant measures of significant aspects of on-the-job performance. Evidence should show that the proposed selection device adds something different from other currently used or more economical techniques. As a minimum, the predictor should correlate significantly with the criterion and, preferably, should have practical significance in improving levels of work performance. The selection device should not be differentially valid for or discriminate against racial or sex subgroups.

Three studies in the assessment center literature approximate this type of study. As described previously, Bray and Campbell (1968) reported on 78 sales personnel who were assessed soon after hiring. No relationship was found between overall assessment performance ratings by the staff at a training school or by supervisors on the job, but there were significant correlations against predictions by a staff of trained observers based on field observations of sales behavior. Although criteria were uncontaminated by assessment results, we do not know whether the assessees were representative of the applicant group. Furthermore, the motivation of applicants in an actual selection situation may differ from that of a group already hired.

The Sears assessment program for college recruits has been evaluated for internal reliability and validity by Kohls (1970). Marquardt (1976) demonstrated that assessment center ratings were predictive against a wide variety of performance ratings made at the end of the probationary training period, including behavioral scales and final ranking by a coordinator assigned to oversee the trainee's first year in an assigned store. One concern about this criterion is its supposed relationship with subsequent job performance. As Marquardt (1976) warns, follow-up studies of on-the-job performance are needed, although it must be recognized that the training period is critical and failure here will preclude later success.

Moses and Wall (1975) reported on the external selection program of management recruits at AT&T. The OAR from a 1-day program correlated .60 with job performance ratings prepared by special interviewers following a field review of performance 1 year after assessment.

EARLY IDENTIFICATION OF POTENTIAL

Within any organization it is essential to be able to identify individuals with potential for growth and advancement. These individuals must be encouraged to remain with the organization in order to retain the high-level talent necessary for effective operation in the future. They must be given special training and development opportunities to prepare them for higher job responsibilities. No organization has the resources to prepare everyone at a particular job level for higher assignments. It is usually not the lack of funds for training and development but the scarcity of the number of "developmental assignments" available that provide early opportunity for decision making and responsibility. An organization must identify potential early in the developmental process if these assignments are to be effectively distributed and not squandered through chance assignment of personnel. Similarly, formal training and development should be provided to those individuals with high probability for advancement.

As an organization becomes more complex, more and more preparation for higher job assignments is required prior to advancement, thus an earlier decision on "potential for advancement" is required in order to effectively provide the training development experiences. This has led many organizations to develop formal programs aimed at early identification of management potential. A secondary, but important, motivation in this area is the need to provide special encouragement to individuals with high potential in order to motivate them to stay with the organization. Highly motivated "high potential" individuals may seek jobs outside of the organization unless they receive some kind of tangible indication that their chances for advancement are higher than the average. Actually providing special assignments, training opportunities, and recognition of potential are effective ways of providing recognition without a formal promise of promotion. Providing these kinds of encouragements requires a more accurate method of identification of early management potential than is typically available in organizations and for this reason, many organizations have turned to the assessment center method.

The problem of early identification of potential among minorities and women is particularly difficult for many organizations. Essentially these persons have not experienced progress comparable to whites. Recent equal employment demands and affirmative action programs have necessitated an acceleration in the advancement of minorities and women. In order to achieve parity of assignments throughout job levels, organizations have been forced to promote minorities and women in greater numbers. This has caused a diminution of available manpower in lower level positions since able minorities and women are advanced into higher positions. Many times an organization finds itself in a situation where its affirmative action plan calls for advancement of five minorities to second-level supervisory positions when there are not even five minorities currently in first-level supervisory positions. The only obvious solution is to "fast track" representatives of minorities and women into the first-level position so they can be more quickly prepared to achieve the second-level position. To do this, some form of "early identification" is necessary and such programs have been initiated by a number of organizations in the United States.

AT&T has devised two similar programs for early identification of potential which use the assesment center for making predictions of potential for minorities and women. In one case, a miniature assessment center is used to assess supervisory potential; in the other case an assessment program is used to predict engineering potential. The rationale of both programs is that special attention should be paid to the development of new nonmanagement employees who have the general administrative skills to handle a more advanced job. Once individuals with these general skills are identified, the organization can provide them with opportunities to acquire job information and knowledge needed to successfully carry out higher level jobs. The training can focus on the areas of weakness for each individual. This tailor-made development program increases effectiveness of training efforts.

The Early Identification Assessment program (EIA) at AT&T (Moses, 1973b) was designed to assess early potential for management among short-service employees. The EIA is patterned very closely after other management assessment programs at AT&T—most of the same assessment techniques and judgmental predictions are involved. The main difference is that the EIA is only 1 day long and more common AT&T assessment programs take 2 days. In 1 day of assessment, a leaderless group discussion, an in-basket, a personal interview, a written exercise, and a general mental ability test are administered to six candidates. Four staff members rate the participants on eight management dimensions such as Leadership, Forcefulness, Energy, etc., and give an overall rating of potential to assume supervisory management assignments. Feedback is given to the participants by a separate staff of experienced counselors who work with the individual and the department to outline developmental opportunities. Moses (1973b) describes a study to evaluate the effectiveness of the judgments of the EIA by using the assessment judgments from the more extensive 2-day assessments provided by the Personnel Assessment Program (PAP). The results were described earlier.

According to Moses (1973a) the 1-day engineering assessment process is the first of its kind because of the unique qualities assessed and the special simulation exercises which were developed. Thorough job analysis of the AT&T engineers revealed that the following qualities were important: calculating skills, ability to interpret information, problem-solving skills, and economic judgment. The assessment techniques developed include individual and group problem-solving situations. In one simulation, the individual has three hours to review material on a high priority engineering project and to prepare forms and make estimates of work that needs to be accomplished. Assessors are concerned with the way the participant attends to detail, goes about solving the problem, and presents findings. Other assessment techniques were devised to evaluate special job-related skills.

The engineering program was evaluated by comparing assessment ratings with criterion ratings for groups of currently employed engineers in two companies. From among 275 engineers rated with a set of behaviorally anchored rating scales, 59 who were high or low performers were identified. Moses (1972) reports, "Of those that the assessment staff saw as having good potential, 75% were also seen as above average engineers on the job, while only 39% of the assessment low-rated engineers were good performers [p. 119]."

Moses concluded that the early results are encouraging and the program was helpful in identifying this type of managerial potential among engineers.

Other early identification programs have been instituted at the Federal Aviation Administration (Alexander, Buck, & McCarthy, 1975), the Bureau of Printing and Engraving (Hall, 1976; Hall & Baker, 1975), and Bendix (Alexander, 1975). No predictive validities have been reported for these programs but the assessment center activities allegedly aid in the identification of worthy candidates beyond the information available from existing job records.

PROMOTION

A technique for aiding promotion decisions should be validated in a way similar to that used in validating a selection technique. A decision to promote is essentially a decision to select from within an organization those most likely to succeed on a higher level job. Many of the same research considerations apply. Promotion decisions for an unrestricted sample of employees on a lower level job should be compared with subsequent measures of success on a higher level job; the criteria should be uncontaminated and relevant; and the proposed prediction technique should contribute something different from that contributed by traditional techniques (e.g., supervisory evaluations of potential or test information).

Most literature on assessment centers is related to promotion decisions. Because detailed descriptions of the results of many of the validation studies are reported in earlier sections of this chapter, they will only be summarized here: Validity has been reported for promotion to first-level supervision and middle level management; no validity studies for higher level executives have been reported.

There has been no more thorough body of predictive validity research generated to support the accuracy of an industrial psychology practice than the evidence on assessment centers. While criticisms have been raised about other aspects of assessment centers, even the critics agree that the process accurately identifies persons who, if promoted, are most likely to experience success as a manager. We can recommend the use of assessment centers for promotion purposes with few reservations.

TRAINING AND DEVELOPMENT

Assessment centers are used for various developmental purposes: (a) identification of training needs; (b) development of self-insights and stimulation of self-improvement; and (c) as a training experience. Relevant to the first purpose, we need evidence that the assessment procedure possesses sufficient validity to measure a set of separate, differentiated aspects of managerial ability. The evidence presented in Chapter 5 suggests that assessment centers measure three or four broad characteristics, namely Administrative Skills, Interpersonal Relations Ability, Decision-making Skills, and Activity Level–Impact. Reliable ratings on more specific dimensions have also been found in a number of studies.

No evidence has been published that assessment centers develop self-insights or lead to management development, although learning and training principles would suggest that these programs should lead to management development. In Chapter 8 we explore the relationships between assessment centers and management development.

Comparisons with Other Methods

In this section we summarize studies that provide a direct comparison of assessment centers with other evaluation methods. We should make our biases clear from the outset. We believe that several different methods are necessary for the complete assessment of managerial abilities in any practical organizational setting. Each of the methods with which assessment centers have been compared can provide unique insights into managerial potential or competence.

COMPARISON WITH SUPERVISORY EVALUATIONS

In an earlier section we discussed several studies which compared managerial effectiveness of experimental groups of assessed/promoted subjects with the performance of a control group promoted on the basis of current methods in operation at the organization. These studies found that the experimental group had a larger percentage of satisfactory supervisors and a larger percentage of above-average performers and high-potential supervisors. Furthermore, the experimental groups tended to receive more positive and fewer negative evaluative comments by supervisors and subordinates and to evidence less turnover after installation of an assessment center program. In an earlier review of this literature, Cohen et al (1974) concluded "median percentages of successes tabulated for both groups indicate the assessed group higher in subsequent job performance (.68/.59), job potential (.59/.28), and progress (.38/.08) [p. 30]."

The generally positive results of the above studies support the contention that judgments based on assessment center observations are more accurate than supervisory judgements. An alternative explanation, mentioned previously, is that the assessment center experience may be acting as a treatment variable and that as a result of exposure to assessment, some learning or development occurs. This possibility is supported by the fact that assessees get feedback on their performance during assessment. However, if attendance at a center (and receiving feedback) is having such an effect, it would be an extremely rare example of a program causing behavioral change at management levels. Thus, this explanation is very unlikely. These problems, compounded by the lack of matching of subjects in the experimental and control groups, leave us with inconclusive evidence regarding the relative merits of assessment center versus traditional promotion methods, but the weight of evidence is on the side of assessment centers.

Another set of data that illustrates that assessment centers and supervisory evaluations provide unique evaluation of management talent comes from an examination of the distribution of overall assessment ratings. In numerous studies, about one-third of assessees are considered promotable, one-third questionable, and one-third not promotable. (Of course, the OAR may be in terms of level of potential, likelihood of advancement, or quality of performance in assessment, but the same general distribution holds.) When we realize that most programs where data were available did some initial screening of candidates for assessment by relying on supervisory nominations or review and approval from a second-level manager, we can see that the assessment center process adds unique insights into the management potential of individuals already rated highly by their managers.

A study of assessment center ratings and performance appraisal ratings on a large number of federal employees found that assessment center ratings, unlike performance appraisal ratings, used much more of the rating scale and did not cluster at the high end of the scale. The study showed that when a selection panel is given performance appraisal data and assessment center data, it tends to place much more weight on the assessment center data (Hall, 1979). This observation coincides with our observations over a large number of situations. Assessment center data are usually more objective and are usually better supported by examples.

A cautionary note has been sounded by Klimoski and Strickland (1981) who present evidence that preassessment ratings of performance and potential can produce higher correlations with subsequent ratings of performance and potential (on higher jobs) than the assessment center method. The assessment center method was a better predictor of organizational grade obtained and grade changes.

A "NATURALISTIC" METHOD

The most serious question raised about the relative effectiveness of assessment centers and alternative evaluation methods has been raised by Hinrichs (1969, 1978). Hinrichs experimented with a naturalistic method in which two management representatives evaluated management potential using the personnel files of individuals. The assessees were 47 college educated males in various marketing positions throughout IBM. Their average age was 30 and average tenure 7.3 years at the time of assessment. Some had managerial experience and others were nonmanagers. Two experienced managers, assistants to district marketing managers, reviewed the personnel records of the assessees. This task was similiar to the frequent evaluation of candidate qualifications normally conducted in the organization. The two managers were instructed to distill all information and predict long-range potential (10–15 years). Information included material normally in the personnel jacket (i.e., education and experience, performance appraisals, sales records, rate of salary growth, place on promotion lists, etc.). In addition, the judges could talk with the immediate supervisor or any other knowledgeable people, but this was actually done in only one or two cases.

As noted earlier, the assessment center ratings were significantly correlated with management level 1 and 8 years after assessment. Although *change* in management level from year one to year eight was not predicted by assessment, a significant partial correlation of the assessment prediction and criterion indicated that the long-term validity was not simply a function of initial differences in management level among assessees.

Questions of utility of the assessment center were raised because the naturalistic method correlated more highly with the criteria. The correlations for the manager's prediction with actual level was higher than the correlations of the assessment center ratings and the same criterion in the first year (.32 versus .26) and in the eighth year (.55 versus .46). Furthermore, the partial correlation of the manager's prediction (holding initial level constant) was also higher (.49 versus .40). However, neither method predicted *change* in management level.

Hinrichs (1978) also examined objective tests as another method of prediction. Again, significant relationships with the criteria were found. Specifically, management level at both the first and the eighth years were predictable from the Gordon Personal Profile (ascendency), the School and College Aptitude Test (quantitative), and the Self-Description Inventory (occupational level).

Hinrichs (1978) warned that organizations may not need to use an elaborate assessment center if their sole goal is to predict management advancement and "they should question whether simpler and less expensive techniques are available for predicting the promotion system as it operates over time in the organization. It makes little sense to use a sledgehammer to swat a fly [p. 600]."

Several observations about the study and conclusions are in order. First, the comparative effectiveness of tests is unusual. Other studies to be reviewed later demonstrate that assessment centers are more predictive than tests. Within the Hinrichs (1978) study, many tests are not valid. The small sample and lack of cross-validation make it questionable to generalize from a few significant correlations. Second, the subjects in this study were experienced middle managers (Hinrichs, 1969) who had substantial background information in their records. The personnel file of less experienced individuals in nonsupervisory positions might be less informative. Third, organizations are seldom concerned only with prediction of advancement, especially when assessing middle managers. Information is desired about relative strengths and weaknesses, diagnosis of developmental needs, and placement information for matching individuals to management positions.

Management assessment is seldom as trivial as swatting a fly. To attack the more weighty problems of identifying management potential requires an arsenal of weapons. One finding supports our contention that multiple methods are necessary: The shrunken multiple correlation for both predictors was .58, suggesting that both sources of information make unique contributions.

Hinrichs has provided some intriguing data on a small sample of managers. The real value of the study may lie in its heuristic use to stimulate research into alternative methods. If subsequent research supports the validity of this naturalistic method, some real contributions will be made. A similar approach to assessment has been taken by Dailey

(1971) in his humanistic model for the assessment of lives. Dailey proposed that the assessment process should examine the life-long biography of each individual to identify the objective events and subjective patterns discernible in the individual's life. Research with over 1400 subjects demonstrated the predictive accuracy of method for some subject groups, but no consistency or cross-validation was apparent.

COMPARISON WITH TESTS

Another area of research has compared the predictive accuracy of assessment centers with psychometric tests. Major studies of tests have found validities in the .30s, .40s, and occasionally as high as .70 for paper-and-pencil devices ranging from tests of abilities to biographical inventories (Campbell *et al.*, 1970; Dunnette, 1967; Guion, 1965; Korman, 1968). The better the research design, the higher the attained validities. Validities for well-designed-and-executed assessment centers cover this same range with about the same pattern of distribution. This sort of informal and unsystematic comparison is unsatisfactory but it does point out that high validity is attainable by both methods. Direct comparisons of assessment centers and tests have been made in a number of the studies previously cited.

Data from AT&T's Management Progress Study (Bray & Grant, 1966) provide some clear evidence that assessment center predictions are more accurate than test results. Table 7.34 summarizes some comparisons. The overall assessment rating, factor scores of assessment variables, and

Table 7.34

Comparison of Predictive Validity of Management Progress Study Variables with Salary Progress for Four Samples [a]

	College		Noncollege	
Variable	A ($N = 54$)	C_1 ($N = 27$)	B ($N = 83$)	C_2 ($N = 39$)
Overall rating	.48*	.51*	.57*	.52*
Assessment variables [b]	.33*	.32	.29*	.33*
Situational exercises [b]	.27*	.41*	.37*	.28
Ability tests [b]	.26	.32	.44*	.28
Scales on personality tests [b]	.09	.08	.08	.07

[a] Adapted from "The Assessment Center in the Measurement of Potential for Business Management" by D. W. Bray and D. L. Grant, *Psychological Monographs*, 1966, *80* (17, Whole No. 625). Copyright 1966 by the American Psychological Association. Reprinted by permission.

[b] median r.

*$p < .05$.

situational tests are consistently more predictive than ability or personality tests for both college and noncollege samples. It appears that the ability tests are fairly accurate predictors of salary progress, especially among the noncollege graduates. To further study the relative contribution of ability tests and the overall assessment rating, Bray and Grant (1966) identified the ability test that correlated highest with salary progress and computed partial correlations between the staff judgment and the criterion with the ability test partialed out. Significant relationships remained for three of four samples. Bray and Grant (1966) concluded, "The results thus indicate that the assessment process does contribute more than can be gained by the simple administration of paper-and-pencil ability measurement [p. 20]."

In another study at AT&T, Bray and Campbell (1968) found the assessment rating more predictive than tests. The overall assessment rating correlated .51 with a special rating of field performance among a group of salesmen six months after assessment, whereas the multiple correlation of the School and College Aptitude Test, Critical Thinking Test, the Contemporary Affairs Test, and an abstract reasoning test was .33.

Moses' (1971, 1972) study of nearly 6000 male managers at AT&T provides clear evidence of the superiority of behavioral assessment data over paper-and-pencil mental ability tests. Table 7.35 shows that the final assessment rating accounts for nearly five times the criterion variance as the mental tests (19% versus 4%). The median correlation of dimension ratings exceeds the test validities and addition of test results to the multiple regression equation yields a trivial increase in predictive accuracy (.461 to .463). Moses (1971) aptly concludes:

> This study clearly shows the importance of the behavioral information generated by the assessment process, as well as indicating the overall robustness of the final global assessment rating. These aspects are what makes the assessment center process unique. For example, questions concerning the contribution of assessment information relative to information obtained by more traditional sources have been raised by several authors. It can be seen that in this study, ratings generated from behavioral simulations such as group exercises and an in-basket exercise are much more strongly related to success in management than test information of mental ability [p. 11].

Similar results were obtained for a sample of 4846 women studied by Moses and Boehm (1975). The OAR is substantially more predictive than the ability tests alone.

Two studies of IBM's assessment center provide some comparative data. Wollowick and McNamara (1969) reported simple and multiple cor-

Table 7.35

Comparison of Predictive Validity of Tests and Assessment Ratings for 5943 Male and 4846 Female Managers at AT & T[a]

	Correlation with management level	
Predictor	Male	Female
Overall assessment rating	.44	.37
Dimension ratings		
Median r	.32	.25
R	.461	Not reported
Mental ability tests		
School and College Aptitude Test		
Total	.21	.25
Verbal	.20	.23
Quantitative	.18	.20
Multiple correlation for all variables	.463	Not reported

[a] Adapted from "Assessment Center Performance and Management Progress" by J. L. Moses, Studies in Personnel Psychology, 1972, 4(1), 7–12. Copyright 1972 by Public Service Commission of Canada. Reprinted by permission.

Also adapted from "Relationship of Assessment Center Performance to Management Progress of Women" by J. L. Moses and V. R. Boehm, Journal of Applied Psychology, 1975, 60, 527–529. Copyright 1975 by the American Psychological Association. Reprinted by permission.

relations between tests, situational exercises, the OAR, and the criterion of increase in managerial responsibility three years after assessment. Table 7.36 shows that the OAR is more predictive than the typical test score. However, the multiple correlation of all tests ($R = .45$) exceeds the predictive validity of the OAR ($r = .37$). The value of the assessment center activities is shown in the increase of criterion variance accounted for when exercise ratings and assessment variables are added to test results (i.e., R^2 increases from .20 to .38).

The fact that the statistical combination of data yielded a higher correlation ($R = .62$) than the subjective integration ($r = .37$) may indicate that the assessors are inappropriately weighting the information or that the higher validity is simply a statistical artifact.

Support for the latter interpretation was found by Mitchel (1975). Similar to the findings of Wollowick and McNamara (1969), the average multiple correlation of all assessment variables ($R = .42$) was higher than the correlation of the overall assessment rating of management potential ($r = .22$) in relation to a criterion of salary progress taken 1, 3, and 5 years after assessment for three samples. However, when regression equations were applied to data from a different sample and/or from a different time

Table 7.36
Comparison of Predictive Validity of Variables in IBM
Assessment Program[a]

Variable	Median r	R	R^2
Overall rating[b]	.37**		.14
Characteristics (assessment variables)	.23*	.41	.23
Situational exercises	.22*	.39	.15
Ability tests	.09		
Scales on personality tests	.14		
All tests		.45	.20
Tests and exercises		.54	.29
Characteristics and exercises		.52	.27
Characteristics and tests		.55	.30
Tests, characteristics, and exercises		.62	.38

[a] Adapted from "Relationship of the Components of an Assessment Center to Management Success" by H. B. Wollowick and W. J. McNamara, *Journal of Applied Psychology*, 1969, *53*, 348–352. Copyright 1969 by the American Psychological Association. Reprinted by permission.

[b] Single correlation and r^2.

* $p < .05$.

** $p < .01$.

period, the correlations are substantially lower. The average generalized correlation was .28, not much different than overall assessment rating. Many of the correlations for equations applied to other samples or years were nil, leading to the conclusion that the overall assessment rating is a more stable predictor than one combination of variables identified by statistical means. By contrast, Wollowick and McNamara (1969) did no cross-validation, so it is difficult to evaluate the stability of their findings. In summary, ratings on assessment dimensions and test scores can all contribute to the prediction of progress, but the process of integrating the material in the assessment discussion may not be optimal.

In another follow-up study at IBM, Hinrichs (1978) found that the overall assessment rating was correlated with managerial level 1 and 8 years after assessment ($r = .26$ and $.46; p < .05$). Some scales of the Allport–Vernon Study of Values, the Gordon Personal Profile, and Ghiselli's Self-description Inventory were also predictive but the median correlations for all personality scales was .24 at the first year and .28 at the eighth year. The Quantitative score on the School and College Ability Test was significantly correlated with progress but in a *negative* direction ($r = -.32$ at both times), and the Concept Mastery Test was not predictive. The inconsistent pattern of test validities suggests that the overall assessment rating is a more reliable predictor of management progress at IBM.

For two samples of middle managers at SOHIO, Finley (1970) compared the predictive validity of projective test results and assessment
committee ratings with supervisory ratings taken 3–5 years (Sample 1) or
1–2 years (Sample 2) after assessment. Criterion ratings were obtained for
overall potential and for 12 dimensions. Table 7.37 shows that the assessment ratings are more predictive of overall potential and dimensions
ratings.

In a more recent study, Mitchel (1975) reported that paper-and-pencil
tests do not exhibit much validity one, three, and five years post assessment ($\overline{X} = .08$), although for one sample the Watson-Glaser Critical
Thinking Appraisal Test and for another sample the Consideration score
on the Leadership Opinion Questionnaire added to the multiple prediction of salary progress. Since the same variables did not appear in the
regression equations for the different samples, it would appear that the
overall assessment rating of potential is a more stable predictor than any
one test scale (or assessment dimension).

Worbois (1975) also found that a set of human relation tests were not
related to either the criterion or assessment ratings. The results are not
conclusive because the test data were available on only a small ($N = 32$)
and unrepresentative sample.

A more balanced view of the contributions of assessment centers is
presented by Slivinski et al. (1979). In two related studies, assessment
centers are compared with other methods of assessment. The strength of
these studies lies in several design features. Slivinski et al. (1979) noted
the following limitations of previous comparative studies: criterion con-

Table 7.37
Comparison of Validities for Projective Tests and Assessment Ratings at SOHIO
for Two Samples[a]

	Predictors			
	Assessment committee		Projective tests	
Criteria	1 ($N = 109$)	2 ($N = 119$)	1 ($N = 109$)	2 ($N = 119$)
Potential rating	.65*	.63*	[b]	39*
12 dimension ratings, number significant r's	9	12	3	6
Median r	.23*	.34*	.12	.18

[a] From Finley (1970).
[b] Correlation not reported.
* $p < .05$.

tamination, small samples, concurrent designs, method contamination (e.g., test data were available to assessors), inadequate statistical analyses, and unfair comparison of methods (e.g., brief tests compared to 2 day's worth of assessment center activities). The following studies improve on some of these limitations.

In Study A, 278 middle managers in the Canadian Federal Public Service were assessed by (a) simulation exercises including individual, group, and written activities; and (b) three paper-and-pencil tests including measures of personality, general intelligence, and administrative judgment. The two sets of predictor data were independent: The assessors had no knowledge of how the individuals did on the tests or of anything about the individual's background or work experiences. There were no background interviews conducted at the assessment center. Since this was a developmental program, no feedback of assessment results was given to middle managers who made subsequent promotion decisions. Thus, the criterion measure, increase in management level 2.5 years after assessment, was uncontaminated.

Both methods predicted the criterion equally well and when combined with the other method resulted in an equally valid combination. Table 7.38 shows the results. Slivinski et al. (1979) concluded that "the assessment centre does not eliminate the need for paper-and-pencil testing and vice versa; and both together do 'a better job' [p. 3]."

Study B used the same data base but added analyses of biographical information including education, age, type of management experience, and tenure in public service. The results indicated that (a) each set of predictors (tests, simulations, bio-data) predicted the criterion; (b) no one set was a more accurate predictor; and (c) each method adds significantly to the predictive validity of all other methods. The multiple correlation for the three sets of information equaled .483 ($p < .01$).

A third study addressed a slightly different question in that no follow-

Table 7.38
Comparison of Two Methods of Predicting Progress in
Canadian Government[a]

Method	Separate correlation	Multiple correlation
Paper-and-pencil tests	.250*	.402*
Simulation	.298*	.402*

[a] From Slivinski et al. (1979). Reprinted by permission.
* $p < .05$.

up data were gathered. Dimension ratings from an assessment center and from a panel interview process were compared. Although six of eleven correlations were statistically significant, the highest was only .49 (median = .33). Slivinski et al. (1979) concluded that "the two techniques are measuring a substantial amount of something different. Therefore, you can't substitute one technique for the other [p. 10]."

Using data from a mid-level assessment center collected over a 5-year period, Klimoski and Strickland (1981) found that some scales from the 16 Personality Factor test achieved significant correlations with criteria such as salary grade obtained, salary grade progress, number of salary changes, and recent potential ratings. Aptitude measures did less well with various tests showing a significant relationship with, at the most, one criterion. The interesting point from Klimoski and Strickland's point of view is the fact that a combination of test scores and performance and potential ratings made prior to assessment could predict the various criteria almost as well by themselves as they could with the addition of assessment center data. Thus, they argue, the inclusion of the assessment center may not be cost effective. These data are very interesting and certainly deserve reflection. It should be noted, however, that the assessment center from which they obtained these data was relatively unusual: three group exercises and one presentation exercise. It seems to have lacked the breadth of evaluation common to most mid-level centers.

SUMMARY

Although there are some mixed results in the studies cited, it appears that data generated in assessment centers can yield more accurate predictions of managerial success than paper-and-pencil tests alone. In most cases the overall assessment rating is more accurate than the typical ability or personality test scores. Situational exercises and dimension ratings by assessors are more valid than single test scores. In some research, multiple correlations of test scores exceed the correlation for the overall assessment rating, but lack of cross-validation and the potential shrinkage in multiple regression analyses (especially with small sample sizes which typify assessment center research) make the reliability of these findings suspect. The literature reviewed in this section suggests that the validities of the overall assessment rating are more stable over time and over samples. Slivinski et al. (1979) have shown that well-designed studies may reveal more nearly equal effectiveness among the various methods and lead to the notion of a need for a selection or promotion "system" that integrates multiple sources of applicant information (Byham, 1979a).

Utility

Our review of the criterion-related validity has shown that assessment centers can accurately predict management performance and progress. A positive validity coefficient indicates that, on average, persons with higher assessment ratings will perform more adequately on the job than those who are assessed poorly. But this valuable evidence does not tell the whole story. Other factors besides the test–criterion relationship must be considered in the overall evaluation of effectiveness of a selection procedure, and it is helpful to translate the validity information into monetary information.

Utility analysis provides estimates of payoffs from instituting a new selection procedure when several external factors are considered. Cascio and Silbey (1979) provided a unique illustration of utility analysis applied to the assessment center process. In this theoretical study of a hypothetical organization, six factors were considered: the validity and cost of the assessment center, the validity of the ordinary procedure, the selection ratio (i.e, the proportion of applicants selected), the standard deviation in dollars of the criterion of management effectiveness, and the number of programs run. The payoff in terms of total gain in utility from using an assessment center was compared to an ordinary selection procedure (a multiple interview procedure) and random selection.

The method of obtaining the various cost and benefit estimates is quite complicated and will not be explained here. In summary, Cascio and Silbey (1979) used standard information available in the assessment center literature, reasonable cost estimates for expenses, and some innovative methods of estimating monetary payoffs from management performance. More important, each of the factors mentioned above was varied systematically to account for different organizational circumstances.

The relative importance of the factors was evaluated by comparing the percentage of change in the payoff to the percentage of change in the factor. For example, wide differences in the number of assessment centers conducted (7–11 or about 50% change) resulted in only a 5.6% change in payoff. Similarly, cost of the assessment center was insignificant. This may seem surprising, but it is understandable when the effects of performance variation are considered. Analysis for this factor showed that assessment centers can make the greatest impact when individual differences in managerial performance are large. In other words, when a manager's decisions can have different monetary effects, then relatively small increases in validity can have a significant payoff. Cascio and Silbey (1979) point out that:

When one stops to consider that for many jobs the standard deviation of criterion outcomes can be as high as $15,000 to $20,000 in the first year (and
$65,000 to $87,000 over a 5-year period), the increased cost of a more highly
valid selection procedure may be a small price to pay for the long-term payoff
that procedure may provide [p. 116].

The other factors, including selection ratio and validities of the ordinary and assessment center methods, also had a significant impact on
utility. With all other factors held constant, the organization will benefit
in a practical way from a lower selection ratio (i.e., selecting a small
percentage of candidates) and an assessment center which is even
slightly more valid than its current method. The improved validity need
not be very large to realize worthwhile cost payoffs. Using a survey
technique, Cohen (1980) asked 82 assessment center users to evaluate the
costs of their program. Analyses revealed an average return on investment of 313%.

Recapitulation

At the beginning of this chapter, we raised the criticism that the practice of industrial psychology often outstrips its empirical research support. The studies in this chapter certainly refute criticism with respect to
assessment centers. The early research on applications in selected
organizations preceded the later widespread adoption in other companies. As research continues, the evidence becomes even stronger. The
most methodologically sound studies demonstrate the clearest validity.
The longitudinal research shows validity increases over time.

After careful review of this research, it appears that many studies
meeting the minimal standards of validation research have been conducted in several organizations. Four organizations have conducted
systematic, programmatic research; several others have carried out individual studies. AT&T has conducted research with large samples,
multiple and unbiased criterion measures, and longitudinal designs.
Detailed analyses of internal and external validity were demonstrated for
several levels of personnel from salespersons to middle managers. IBM
conducted large sample studies for multiple divisions and jobs and for
unique and multiple criteria. Unfortunately, criterion contamination was
not as well controlled as in the AT&T studies. Comparisons with other
measurement methods failed to clearly show the superiority of assessment centers. SOHIO demonstrated the validity of its assessment program with a thorough analysis of behavioral criteria and its generalized,

predictive validity. Research at Sears shows the assessment center procedure has predictive validity for external applicants and internal promotions in relation to a variety of performance and behavioral criteria. In addition, the AMA assessment program has been validated in isolated areas in several different organizations. Only one study provided data regarding assessment for training, development, organization development, or other purported uses for which assessment centers are recommended.

Assessment center research, like most personnel research in field settings, has flaws. In some studies subjects are probably unrepresentative of the pool of potential candidates for promotion; research designs often allow contamination from operational use of assessment data; and, most seriously, there is heavy reliance on supervisors' ratings as criteria. This is particularly disheartening since assessment centers have been developed largely because of dissatisfaction with the ability of supervisors to correctly identify potential among subordinates.

Can generalizations from the current organizations be extrapolated to other organizations of different size, management climate, personnel requirements, and job and environmental demands? Surely as research moves to a general-application stage, the opportunity to replicate studies, extend the findings, and try out new methods of evaluation will occur so that over-generalization is unnecessary. The prospects seem positive.

Moreover, the need for further validation efforts becomes even more apparent when one considers the variety of assessment center procedures (Alexander, 1979; Bender, 1973; Byham, 1978a, b). Bender (1973) sent questionnaires to 38 organizations known to have operational assessment centers and received responses from 29 industrial companies and 4 government agencies. The survey revealed similarities in the content, administration, and use of results, but he concluded that a typical assessment center does not exist. Furthermore, there is no standardization of content in assessment centers or of the way they are administered, and there is no uniform method of treating the performance evaluation data generated by assessment centers (Bender, 1973, p. 56).

Given the variety of existing practices, each of the following variables must be considered parameters for research investigation:

1. *Types of evaluation devices:* In-basket, game, group decision, films, tests
2. *Operating procedures:* Nomination of assessees, direction of the center, composition of assessee group, rotation of assessors among assessees, opportunity for reassessment, site of assessment center

3. *Relation of assessees and assessors:* Ratio of assessees to assessors, level of assessees, number of days of center, amount of training for assessors
4. *Evaluation of observed dimensions.* How many and which dimensions (e.g., Impact, Energy, Forcefulness, Perception)?
5. *Process of integrating information:* Time devoted to integration, order of presentation of information, value of peer evaluations
6. *Uses made of performance data:* Immediate or delayed feedback, oral and/or written feedback, who gives and gets feedback, development plans
7. *Purposes of assessment:* Selection, training, early identification, etc.
8. *Types of criteria:* Performance, potential, advancement.

It is necessary to augment our research knowledge and we should capitalize on the opportunities to do so. When positive results are found in an area so intractable as management appraisal, it is essential that this area of research be pursued. We should avoid the error of reasoning that deficiencies (even as major as the ones pointed out here) are such that no credence should be placed on positive results. However, in dealing with such a burgeoning adoption of assessment centers, it would be a mistake to assume that all the answers are known—they are not. Major weaknesses in the research exist. It is our purpose in this book to identify these weaknesses so that, we hope, answers may be found by research efforts in the many organizations implementing mulitple assessment procedures.

8
Contributions to
Management Development

In previous chapters we have referred to *developmental assessment centers* but actually the term is a misnomer. Assessment centers do not develop people or change behavior—they contribute to developmental efforts aimed at changing behavior. This contribution usually takes the following forms:

1. Selection of better candidates
2. Early identification of management talent
3. Diagnosis of training needs
4. Facilitation of self-diagnosis

An important collateral benefit an organization derives from using the assessment center method is the positive impact of assessor training on managers. Many organizations see this as so important that far more managers are trained to be assessors than can ever be used in the organization's assessment center program. Assessment center technology also benefits other personnel activities and the organization as a whole. Each of the four contribution of assessment centers to behavior change will be discussed in the first part of this chapter. The latter part discusses why assessor skills are transferable to the job and the impact of an assessment center on an organization.

But first let us discuss a fundamental question: *Can organizations change people?* Review of the training literature reveals very little evidence that in-house or external training programs are effective in changing behavior. Campbell has lamented the sad state of this aspect of training research in the United States in his review of training in the 1971 *Annual Review of Psychology.* He found only 84 studies of training-program effectiveness published in the prior 20 years, and few of them met any kind of standards of statistical or scientific research. Hinrichs (1976) and Goldstein (1980) arrived at similar conclusions in more recent reviews of the training literature.

More hope is usually held out for internally organized management development programs such as supervisory coaching, understudy, task force, and controlled assignments. It is often said that managers are "made" through these experiences. Little evidence exists to show the effectiveness of these efforts and at best one would expect their effectiveness to be spotty.

The AT&T Management Progress Study (Bray, Campbell, & Grant, 1974) described in Chapter 2, contains some very convincing evidence on the lack of training effectiveness. When the college graduates in the study were reassessed after 8 years on the job, the researchers found no difference in their average administrative skill from that found in the first assessment, even though the Telephone Company had implemented an organized program of development through a variety of work assignments, special projects, etc.

Surprisingly, the assessed interpersonal skills of the executives decreased over the 8 years. Bray *et al.* speculate that this loss may result from a diminishing concern for group harmony as one goes through the early adult years rather than from actual loss in ability. The finding is certainly contrary to what most managers would expect to happen to their management personnel during their formative years in business.

One should not interpret the AT&T data to mean that the young managers did not change over these 8 years. Although no data are available, it is expected that major changes occurred in their knowledge of the technical aspects of their work, of company systems and procedures, of the particular likes and dislikes of their higher managers, and most important, their knowledge of past practices and procedures of the organization. All of this knowledge helps the individual function better and contribute more. What seems static are the basic management skills such as face-to-face leadership, planning, organizing, logical reasoning, and communicating effectively.

Other organizations, by accident or occasionally by a policy decision, have assessed employees twice. The studies are unpublished and based on small numbers of individuals, but they provide further proof of the reliability of the assessment center process over time and, incidentally the lack of behavior change over time when managers are simply allowed to develop in an unsystematic way.

Improved Selection Results in Better Candidates

A logical response to the lack of demonstration of effectiveness of training programs is to avoid both training and development and concentrate on getting the best people into the organization. Few people would argue with the notion of filling positions with the best people available. Even if training and development programs work, it makes sense to start off with the best raw materials (except for situations where affirmative action plans or other special considerations intervene). The timing of the first promotion is also of critical importance in determining managerial success (Dodd, 1970). Improving the precision of early promotion decisions seems to be the approach suggested by the AT&T Management Progress Study.

Most assessment centers for entry level management positions (e.g., supervisor) have selection as their main interest. The center is used as a finer screen for those candidates nominated by their supervisors or by some other procedure. The usual strategy is to create a pool of qualified candidates equal to the organization's need for new supervisors for a period of approximately six months.

Developmental insights stemming from the assessment center may be passed on to the manager to whom the new supervisor will report but little or no development is provided either for those who are judged to have no potential or for those assessees recommended for advancement.

Early Identification of Management Talent

Early identification of supervisory or management potential provides an organization with a much greater period of time for development prior to putting a person in a position—as much as 6 to 8 years. The best trainer in the world can do little if information on the individuals to be trained is received just before they are to be promoted. If information is received well in advance, an organized and, it is hoped, effective training and developmental effort can be initiated. At the least, individuals can be started on a series of rotational assignments and/or special projects that will provide them with the appropriate knowledge and experience base.

In recent years, the pressure for early identification at the lower levels in U.S. organizations has come mainly from affirmative action programs to which organizations have become committed. In these programs, an organization submits a plan to a government agency and sets goals for the employment of women and minorities at each organizational level. However, a company often does not have enough women and minorities with appropriate experience to place in target levels. Therefore, companies find that they must rapidly advance women and minority candidates (i.e., put them on a fast-track program to provide them with the relevant exposure and experience) (Robison, 1978).

The other important use of early identification programs is to identify candidates for middle- and top-level positions early enough so that management can give them the developmental exposure necessary to perform increasingly complicated top management functions. The United States (Baker & Martin, 1974) and Canadian Civil Service Commissions (Slivinski et al., 1977) and the United States Social Security Administration (Byham & Wettengal, 1974) programs are good examples of this use. The 1978 Civil Service Reform Act (PL95-454) mandates the identification and development of promising candidates for senior civil service jobs. This has caused all government agencies to develop some sort of early identification program. Many are based on assessment center technology.

When organizations take a hard look at their manpower needs, they usually determine that individuals who will occupy middle- and top-level positions should have a long list of development experiences to optimally prepare them. Exposure to the different parts of the line-and-staff operation is needed. Experience with different product lines may be necessary. Perhaps an overseas assignment to provide insight into the organization's foreign operations would be beneficial. A combination of early line or staff experiences and responsibilities is often desirable. These exposures do not happen by chance very often. Thus, some organizations use assessment centers to identify people early enough to ensure that they are given the necessary developmental experiences.

An important objective of early identification programs is to guide the utilization of development resources. In any organization, there are certain jobs at each level that are excellent developmental experiences in that they give the incumbents a broad view of the organization, early responsibility, or certain critical exposures that are extremely advantageous for a higher manager to have at an early point in his or her career. These positions are one of the most valuable resources in an organization and yet they are often filled on a first-come/first-served basis rather than on a basis of identifying the people in the organization with the most developmental potential and putting them in the developmental positions. When a planned early identification program of some kind is not used to fill the key developmental positions, they eventually get filled by dead-end people whose presence in the position deprives the organization of one of its most important resources.

The best known and most researched early identification program is the Early Identification Assessment (Moses, 1973b) run by Bell System Companies. After 1 year of employment with the company, individuals have the option of nominating themselves for participation in the 1-day early identification supervisory assessment center. If they do well at the center, they are then put into a special program to prepare them to be supervisors. The program consists of a series of developmental assignments aimed at providing the wide exposure to company operations deemed important to first-level supervisors. It is anticipated that an individual in the fast track system will be ready for a supervisory assignment in 3 or 4 years rather than the usual 8 to 10 years. It must be pointed out that success in the early identification program does not ensure advancement to supervisory positions. The employee must succeed at each stage in the development cycle. All that success in the assessment center provides is a specialized, more organized learning experience.

Failure to show management potential in the Bell System early identification program does not mean that the person has lost his or her only chance of advancing into management. When the individual becomes eligible for the regular "selection" assessment center, he or she can participate without prejudice. It will just take longer to get to the selection assessment center.

Early identification programs targeted at first- or second-level supervisors usually resemble selection programs very closely. They have the same ultimate goal (identification of success at the target level of supervision), similar dimensions, and similar exercises. The principal difference is in when they are offered. Early identification programs are offered early in a person's career, years prior to a final selection decision; selection programs are offered later in the career, immediately prior to a selection decision.

There are also some structural differences between early identification programs and selection programs. The AT&T early identification program (Moses, 1973b) is shorter than the selection program. This reflects the state of assessment technology during the development of the programs more than a planned difference. However, there is good rationale for early identification centers to be shorter and, therefore, slightly less reliable. The way most programs work, candidates who do poorly in the early identification assessment center program have a second chance later in a selection assessment center program. Thus, the negative effect of misclassification error is lessened. A person falsely thought not to have potential is only slowed, not stopped, in his or her development.

Early identification programs at higher levels of management almost always have as an equal goal the diagnosis of individual strengths and weaknesses. These will be described in the next section.

Early identification programs are particularly appealing because of their humanistic value. Many people spend their careers in jobs for which they are ill suited and to which they have not adapted psychologically. By giving an individual accurate, informed feedback early in the person's career concerning his or her chance of achieving career goals, much more freedom of action is given to the individual. He or she can choose to take other routes to success within that company, or to go to another company. Contrast an individual who after 1 year is assessed for supervisory skills and is found to be wanting with a person who after 8 years is assessed for supervisory skills and is found to be wanting. After 8 years a person may be tied into retirement plans, seniority, and other benefits. His or her freedom to respond is severely limited. The 1-year person can switch directions or even organizations much more easily and, in that way, has a much better chance of finding a good match with abilities and interests. Boehm and Hoyle (1977) make a number of other points in support of the individual and organizational benefits of early identification programs.

The basic intent of early identification strategies is to put the identified individuals on a standardized (not individualized) development route. The programs are not designed to develop more appropriate behavior as much as they are designed to develop new knowledge regarding different products, systems, and personnel in the organization.

Organizations take many routes to identifying the development steps that should follow early identification. At lower levels in the organization where the end result is more clearly defined (e.g., a first-level supervisory position), the learning and experience requirements are fairly easily defined. The task becomes much more difficult when individuals are being identified for higher management positions which might be in many different areas or departments of the organization. In the former instance, standard job analysis and training needs analysis procedures work well. In addition to the specific technical knowledge which the supervisor must know, many organizations make a study of the interpersonal relationships required (e.g., interactions with foremen from other departments, maintenance, quality control) and the kinds of problems a supervisor will face immediately upon taking the job, and include training in these areas. Such areas as "gaining acceptance as a new supervisor" are often included in such programs.

Organizations attempting to define the training and development needs of individuals for higher management positions usually go about the task through brainstorming sessions with a lot of discussion. The first task is to define the knowledge, experiences, and skills needed to adequately perform in a target position. Anticipated changes in the job and the organization must also be considered. The next task is to define learning situations that will provide desired knowledge. The decision about which parts of a development program are formal and which are informal is often based on the possibility of controlling the exposure. Generally, the best experiences are those that have a high probability of producing the desired learning and which form a natural salary and developmental progression for individuals.

It is not uncommon to find that an organization can materially decrease development time by organizing the input of learning experiences. It is also possible to save travel and relocation expenses through more systematic transfer of personnel.

Diagnosis of Training Needs

Another response to the need to develop better supervisors and managers is to use assessment technology to overcome many of the problems inherent in most training and development activities.

We would not think very highly of a physician who prescribed pills to us without asking us anything about where we felt ill or without conducting an examination. Nor would we think very highly of an individual who tried to cure himself or herself by taking medicine on a random basis or by relying on only the claims made by the manufacturer. Most people would agree that, before any medication should be administered, proper diagnosis is necessary. Yet, this is similar to what is lacking in most management training and development programs. Often training specialists do not have a good understanding of the individuals who are being trained; therefore, even if they have the proper tools, they cannot use them appropriately. Without insight into the needs of the people being trained, it is difficult to achieve effective training. The result of poor diagnosis is that programs very often train the wrong people about the wrong things at the wrong times.

Many training programs have been absolutely wasted or even counterproductive because the wrong person went through the program, he or she was trained in the wrong thing, or the training came too late or too early in the individual's career to be used effectively. There are even recorded cases of sending people to management training a few weeks before they were to retire.

People are trained in the wrong things when they are trained in skills which are not related to their current job or to expected future jobs, when they are put in programs to develop strengths they already have, and when they are not put in programs for which they have developmental needs. Some people need a long program to develop a useful job skill; others can get all they need from a short program.

Recognizing these problems, one organization has set a policy that no individual is admitted to a training program unless there is a documented development need. Furthermore, for each need identified and where training is provided, there must be some follow-up action planned and implemented within a specified period.

AIR FORCE SQUADRON OFFICER SCHOOL

In a unique study, the Air Force evaluated the effects of feedback of assessment results on the subsequent performance of students in the Squadron Officer School (Barber, 1980). Several criteria were used, including the final overall centile rating of class performance based on all leadership and academic performance over the 11-week program. After assessment in the first week of training, some participants were provided feedback and others were not. Furthermore, some participants volunteered for special development work on one to three self-selected dimensions observed in the assessment center. The results indicated that the group who received feedback of assessment center results (but no special development) performed somewhat better than the group who received neither feedback or development. More important, the group who received both feedback and special development performed significantly better than all other comparison groups. In other experimental groups, it was found that groups who chose to engage in developmental follow-up performed higher than groups who did not receive special development, and these effects were observed whether or not feedback was given. In still other comparison studies, it was found that the "no-feedback" group had the lowest final class centile among 14 different experimental treatment conditions. In summary, it appears that special development centered on the dimensions leads to improved performance and when such development is done in conjunction with assessment center feedback, the improvement is enhanced even further. It should be noted that the conclusions are tentative because of the nonrandom (i.e., voluntary) assignment of participants to follow-up conditions.

CHARACTERISTICS OF A DIAGNOSTIC
ASSESSMENT CENTER

Assessment centers designed to produce diagnostic insights are usually longer and more complex than centers that provide only a single decision predicting potential. Their increased length and complexity are caused by a number of structural characteristics that must be present if accurate diagnosis is to be achieved.

Diagnostic assessment centers typically have more dimensions. The need to accurately "diagnose" each manager's unique needs demands that the individual's strengths and weaknesses be determined in the most specific manner possible so a highly specific developmental prescription can be developed. Table 8.1 contrasts dimensions that might be sought in an assessment center aimed at selection purposes with dimensions in a center aimed at diagnosis.

A training expert or a manager attempting to prescribe appropriate training and development activities would certainly do a much better job using information from a diagnostic center. For example, one might treat a person proved to be low in Problem Analysis and high in Judgment much differently from a person high on Problem Analysis and low on Judgment. Much different training and development activities would be provided for a person diagnosed as being too decisive as opposed to having poor judgment.

In general, an organization choosing dimensions for a diagnostic assessment center should make those dimensions as specific as possible, consistent with the developmental and training possibilities available. For example, most organizations have available, either internally or externally, remedial programs dealing with general communication and other programs dealing with formal speech making. The programs are

Table 8.1
Contrast of Dimensions for Selection and Development

Selection	Development
Decision Making	Analysis Judgment Decisiveness
Leadership	Individual Leadership Group Leadership Negotiation Behavioral Flexibility
Judgment	Creativity Organizational Sensitivity Extraorganizational Sensitivity Risk Taking
Analysis	Financial Analysis Organizational Awareness Extraorganizational Awareness Oral Fact-finding Recognition of Employee Safety Needs

quite different in content and purpose. Thus, it behooves an organization to break out the dimension Oral Presentation from Oral Communication so proper assignments to these programs can be made when the finer dimensions are job relevant. We disagree with those who claim that job analysis is not necessary for development purposes (Quick *et al.,* 1980).

Sometimes an organization adds a dimension for the sole purpose of determining who should go to a specific training program. Many organizations feel that it is important to teach basic accounting principles to executives who reach a certain level in the organization. A wide variety of external courses are available and many organizations have internal courses. One alternative is to assign all executives to attend the course—whether needed or not. Another is to add the dimension Understanding of Accounting Principles to a diagnostic assessment center and send only the people who need the course.

A second major structural characteristic of diagnostic assessment centers is the use of a larger number of exercises. The expanded list of dimensions found in diagnostic centers would, in itself, demand more exercises so information on all the dimensions could be obtained; but, more importantly, diagnostic centers demand a change in measurement philosophy.

The end result of selection or early identification assessment centers is a final go–no go decision. It is on that decision that the validity of the assessment center stands and it is on that decision that reliability of assessor judgment is most important. In reality, the dimension ratings that precede the final judgments are just steps in the decision process. They are a way of forcing the assessor to consider all important aspects of a person before making a final decision. In a selection center, it's the final decision that counts.

Quite different measurement characteristics are involved in diagnostic centers. The final overall decision is far less important, and in many organizations having "pure" diagnostic centers, no overall decision is made. In a diagnostic center, each dimension must be measured with a high degree of reliability and validity because decisions are being made on each dimension. The practical significance of this change in emphasis on assessment center design is that each dimension must be seen in at least two and, it is hoped, more exercises in order to ensure adequate reliability of measurement. The more important the dimension, the greater the need for redundancy of observation to provide greater reliability. In designing assessment centers, administrators try to make the number of observations of each dimension directly proportional to the importance of the dimension in the selection or developmental decision. Thus, it is arranged that particularly important dimensions are seen many times in an assessment center and less important dimensions may be seen only twice. The evidence reviewed in Chapter 5 demonstrates that assessment centers can give reliable and valid measures of numerous dimensions.

Another feature causing developmental assessment centers to be longer is that more variety in the exercises is demanded in order to provide increased developmental insight. One is not satisfied with merely getting an evaluation of the dimension Leadership. Knowing the research which indicates that Leadership is situational (Stogdill, 1974; Vroom, 1976), one would like to determine how a person handles various kinds of leadership situations. In a diagnostic assessment center, it is possible to look at Leadership in a variety of ways by observing Leadership in situations where the individual is in a peer situation, in a superior situation, in a subordinate situation, in a small group, in a large group, where preparation time is given, where there is considerable stress, where there is no stress, etc. The more variations and permutations of situations in which a dimension is observed, the greater the diagnostic insights. Providing the opportunity for this variety of insight calls for more exercises, increased center length, and greater center complexity.

Thus, for a combination of reasons, developmental assessment centers are usually 2 or 3 days in length while some assessment centers aimed at making only a selection decision are 1 day in length.

DIAGNOSTIC ASSESSMENT CENTER REPORTS

A diagnostic report coming from an assessment center has the same three basic parts as most assessment center reports, namely, summary, behavior by dimensions, and developmental suggestions; but its length and specificity are quite different. It is not uncommon for a selection report to be 2 or 3 pages long; developmental reports often are 16 to 20 pages long. The difference primarily is in the number of dimensions that must be covered in the report and the explicitness of the behavior cited under the dimensions. Because developmental assessment centers have more exercises, more behavior is produced. This, plus the need to help the individual being assessed to completely understand the basis on which assessment was made, forces administrators to provide a great deal of supportive material for all dimensions, particularly those where the individual did not do well. Excerpts from a developmental assessment report are included on the following pages. It should be noted that the report assumes a certain familiarity with the exercises in the assessment center. All recipients of the report either would be trained assessors, would have been assessed in an assessment center, or would be given extensive orientation in the assessment center procedures. In addition, a supplemental description of each of the exercises and their intent, plus descriptions of the dimensions with their definitions, is usually attached to these reports as it is in the following model.

EXAMPLES OF PORTIONS OF AN ASSESSMENT CENTER REPORT
SUMMARIZING THE CONSENSUS JUDGMENTS OF THE ASSESSORS

PLUM–LYNE, INC.
Participant: Pat Urn
Date: November 7–9, 1983

SUMMARY

Ms. Urn was something of an enigma to the assessors. In group exercises, which required no complex preparation, she showed a lot of initiative, was very assertive, and was willing to accept the responsibility for the group's accomplishing its task. In these situations, Ms. Urn was seen as showing a great deal of behavior on the required dimensions. However, in exercises that required analysis and deliberation prior to accomplishing them, her performance fell precipitously. Perhaps one of the most obvious examples of this situation occurred in the in-basket exercise. Here, in contrast to her behavior in spontaneous group situations, she was very tentative and seemed unsure of herself. This exercise, plus others that required analysis and deliberation in complex managerial situations, led the assessors to believe that although Ms. Urn has good "street sense," she needs to pay a considerable amount of attention to management principles and techniques in analyses and administrative situations.

Ms. Urn threw herself into the exercises in a very deliberate and aggressive manner. This resulted in the assessors being able to generate a considerable amount of data on her performance. They were, therefore, quite confident in their analysis of the rather complex behavioral pattern which emerged.

Listening: Use of information extracted from oral communications
Above Average

Ms. Urn was very intent on the detailed content of almost all of the exercises. In the Management Problems Exercise, she frequently clarified statements made by others, restating them in a manner which not only made them easier for others to understand, but indicated that she understood the intent of their thoughts. She also asked a number of questions of people. These questions were very appropriate in terms of the discussion content and indicated that she was following the details of the conversation very carefully. In the City Council Exercise, she grasped the important points of other peoples' presentations very quickly and responded to them. She also corrected a miscalculation of the requested dollar amounts made by another participant. In the Sales Strategy Exercise, she again clarified questions of other group members. Often she asked for restatements of positions in what seemed to be an attempt to uncover the specific rationale used by others in assuming a stance on an issue.

She was also seen as quite effective in this dimension in the Interview

Simulation. She seemed to understand exactly what the role player was telling her, both in terms of overt content and in the subtle meanings in the verbiage. Only in the Fact-finding Exercise did she seem to fall down slightly in this dimension. It was estimated that Ms. Urn missed perhaps half of the cues which were given by the resource person. Many of these cues were obvious. However, it should be pointed out that she often responded to very subtle ones. Her listening skill in this exercise seemed somewhat contaminated by the fact that she appeared to have developed a hypothesis and was seeking data to confirm it, causing her to ignore other input.

Problem Analysis: Identifying problems, securing relevant information, relating data from sources, and identifying possible causes of problems
Above Average—spontaneous situations.
Below Average—less spontaneous, analytical situations.

In a general sense, Ms. Urn was quite effective in analyzing problems that arose unexpectedly. When the problems required a greater in-depth analysis and some deliberation, her performance deteriorated. In the City Council, Management Problems, and Interview Simulation Exercises, her analytical skills were quite acceptable. In the City Council Exercise she quickly understood the interrelationships among the departments and saw the benefit of establishing coalitions. In the Management Problems Exercise, she was quick to understand the details of the various problems and some of the implications which surrounded them. She was also very effective in trying to uncover underlying problems in the situations and she pointed out to the group that they should deal with basic problems and not just symptoms. In the Interview Simulation, she asked very good, probing questions, trying to determine the problems involved in selling the new lines of products. However, it should be pointed out that she often did not follow up on a lot of these questions.

Her performance in the In-basket Exercise and Sales Strategy Exercise did not reflect the standards set in the group situations. She missed many of the implications of the different memos in the In-basket Exercise and she perceived each memo as independent of the others. She seemed to be simplifying many of the problems and to be dealing only with the obvious things which "stood out" in the items. In the Sales Strategy Exercise, she made a number of unwarranted assumptions in the data (the older sales people have very little knowledge and their motivation is the key to increased sales). She also did not understand the detail of one of the participant's suggestions which would have split the sales of the A and B lathes between wholesale distributors and the AMOCO salesmen.

She also seemed to be rather shallow in this dimension in the Fact-finding Exercise. In areas that interested her (such as competition), she went into considerable depth and asked a large number of good, revealing questions. However, she ignored many other areas of importance which could have had a significant impact on the decision. When given cues or data on some of these areas, she seemed to ignore them as if they did not fit into a hypothesis she was trying to confirm. It should be pointed out, however, that her questioning technique was solid as she asked a variety of both open-and closed-ended questions.

Judgment: Making decisions based on logical assumptions that reflect the factual information available
Below Average

There seemed to be a very strong association between Ms. Urn's attempt to deal with data (particularly complex data) and the quality of her decision-making process. The only situations where she was given good evaluations in this dimension occurred in the Management Problems Exercise. (It should be remembered that this exercise does not require a great deal of in-depth problem analysis.) The solutions she offered in this exercise were generally based on the facts and information that appeared in the problems. However, in the In-basket Exercise she gave very poor directions to her subordinates and put off many critical items. This action in itself would have caused considerable problems within the organization.

In the Sales Strategy Exercise, many of her recommendations were based upon unwarranted assumptions. An example of a questionable decision was her suggestion to increase the interval between the time when a customer's bill was overdue and when the salesman would have to collect it. In making this decision, she seemed to ignore the potential cash-flow problem which could result.

In the Interview Simulation, she did not confront the situation as directly as she could have and seemed to "beat around the bush." She seemed to look upon this exercise as mostly a fact-finding situation and tried to "sell" the role player instead of lead him. The role player's real problem was never spelled out specifically; and if it had been a real situation, the subordinate would have left the interview not realizing that he was in danger of losing his job.

Her rather shallow problem analysis in the Fact-finding Exercise also seemed to influence her judgment. It must be remembered that she questioned only a few areas which could have impacted the decision. Her decision was to not recommend the job to the woman because of the competitiveness of the situation and because she was a female with no experience. These arguments were rather successfully rebutted by the resource person; yet, she hung on to his original decision although it was no longer based on facts but primarily on emotion.

Planning and Organizing: Establishing a course of action for self and/or others to accomplish a specific goal; planning proper assignments of personnel and appropriate use of resources
Below Average

In the In-basket, Ms. Urn either did not assign priorities to items or, when she did, seemed to underestimate things. Many of the items she held could have been handled by her subordinates or other support personnel. She also did not use her subordinates to collect information for her so that she would be ready to act on situations she would be confronting when she returned. For instance, on the memo regarding the meeting with Longstreet, she answered with just a "yes." There was no direction for preparation or collection of information which would help her in the meeting. There was also no preparation for Hardwood's visit. The vice president's meeting seemed to be planned in only a very basic way. Although her plans were followed, they were generally rather skimpy.

Management Control: Establishing procedures to monitor or to regulate processes, tasks, or activities of subordinates and job activities and responsibilities; taking action to monitor the results of delegated assignments and projects

Below Average

In the In-basket Exercise, Ms. Urn did not use any standard control procedures. She set up no tickler file, on only two occasions assigned due dates to items that she delegated, and was often unspecific in what she wanted her subordinates to do with items. In the Interview Simulation, no time goals were set for a follow-up and no behavioral objectives were given.

OVERALL EVALUATION

Based on behavior relevant to the supervisory dimensions determined to be important in the position, Ms. Urn's present level of potential as a District Sales Manager could best be described as marginal. Major development in a number of critical managerial dimensions is necessary before satisfactory performance could be expected.

Some reports end in developmental recommendations. These recommendations are of a fairly general nature and are written more as extra comments made by the assessors than as official recommendations. This format is necessitated by the need to avoid having it appear that the assessors are promising organizational responses to the assessed needs which the participant's manager cannot meet.

Management development must come from the individual's immediate supervisor and higher management. *The role of the assessment center is to diagnose. The role of higher management and the training department is to provide opportunities for development. The individual must take advantage of this opportunity and do the development.*

APPLICATION OF DIAGNOSTIC ASSESSMENT CENTERS

The decision about whether to design an assessment center to provide diagnostic insights really boils down to two questions: Can people change? and Is it worth the cost? In spite of the lack of research and in spite of the many problems in changing behavior noted at the beginning of this chapter, we would answer the first with a "Yes" followed by the clause "if subjected to a major developmental effort targeted to the individual's particular and specific needs."

The answer to the second question depends on who is being assessed and for what purpose. At each level of management, an organization must make a decision about whether its limited resources can best be expended on changing and developing new skills or on getting people with the necessary skills into the jobs in the first place. Ideally, it would be nice

if everyone could be developed, but few organizations have the resources, the will, or even the opportunity because of the nature of their
operation (e.g., an assembly line or a restrictive union contract).

Diagnosis is usually not appropriate as part of a selection program for
first-line supervision (e.g., laborer to foreman). There are several good,
practical reasons for this seemingly hard-hearted statement.

1. Development prescriptions, based on diagnostic insights, are often
   severely limited by the characteristics of the participant's job and
   union agreements. If people cannot be treated different on the job,
   then there is no purpose in performing a diagnosis.
2. There are more people to assess in assessment centers targeted at
   first-level supervisors, so efficiency of operation is particularly important. There is a direct relationship between costs and degree of
   emphasis put on obtaining diagnostic insights in an assessment
   center.
3. The diagnosis will not help the participant in his or her current job.

A laborer receiving feedback after going through a diagnostic center
receives relatively little information that would help in performing his or
her current job, because the entire center is designed to produce information on dimensions that differentiate that job from a supervisor's job.

This is far less true when supervisors are being assessed for higher-
level management positions or middle managers for higher-level positions. In those cases, because the individuals are already supervisors or
managers, there is a considerable overlap between the dimensions sought
for the higher target level and dimensions needed for success in their current job. Thus, the feedback provided to them can be more of an aid in
their current jobs.

Investment in a diagnostic assessment center can also be considered
from a cost–benefit perspective. An organization that spends $1000
assessing 12 laborers for a foreman's position and gets 4 viable candidates has spent $250 for each candidate. Another organization that is
assessing supervisors for middle management might spend $2400 on
assessing 12 candidates but would, in addition to identifying 4 individuals who might be advanced, obtain in-depth insight into the
strengths and weaknesses of all 12 individuals which may materially affect their current job performance. Thus it would be appropriate to divide
the cost by 12 rather than 4 because the center has a positive impact on all
12 of the participants. This makes the cost per individual $200. This is
another argument for restricting diagnostic programs to higher level
assessments where everyone assessed benefits.

Some organizations have attempted to accomplish this same economy in assessment centers aimed at first-level supervisory positions—particularly sales management positions. Two organizations have designed their assessment centers so the centers look for both dimensions of sales management success and dimensions of sales success. In structuring the assessment center in this way, all participants gain from the experience and some of the potential problems of deciding who should come to the assessment centers are eliminated. Everyone benefits from the feedback on the sales dimensions.

In these organizations, all sales people at a certain point in their careers are assessed, with the results of the assessment center aiding them and the organization in determining whether the individual should head toward the well-paying route of a career salesperson or should be moved onto the management ladder at a point in their career before they are making so much money that they can no longer be moved.

PURE DIAGNOSTIC ASSESSMENT CENTER PROGRAMS

Most organizations use their assessment programs for both selection and development, but there are increasing applications of the technique for developmental purposes only. A good example was an assessment center program run by the Social Security Administration for executives designated for a high-level two-year management rotation program. Individuals were selected for this program through supervisory and departmental nomination and were put through an intensive nine-exercise, 3-day assessment program during the first week of the 2-year program. The results of this assessment made by professionals were given only to the individual and to a representative of the SSA training department who helped the individual fashion training and developmental goals and strategies over the 2-year program. No data were put in the individual's files or in any way given to the management of the organization.

Other departments in the government and many large and small corporations have had outside assessors aid in the diagnosis of development needs. The data are then processed by professionals, and a report is provided on a confidential basis to the individual.

In these examples of "pure" developmental assessment centers, it should be noted that outside professionals are used as assessors. It appears that the use of outside assessors or the use of self-assessment (see following section) are the only ways that leakage of the data can be avoided and programs kept purely developmental.

Organizations fear that management assessors cannot hold themselves back from using the assessment center results, if they have them, for selection purposes. It is felt that they will use the data subconsciously, if not consciously, in making decisions about individuals even though the intent of the assessment center was for diagnostic purposes.

FACILITATION OF SELF–DIAGNOSIS

Administrators and assessors in most assessment centers go out of their way to minimize evaluative feedback to participants *during* the assessment center process. They feel that any feedback resulting from performance on an exercise may be disruptive of later performance on other exercises—a participant may get discouraged from poor performance in one exercise and this may affect performance in another exercise; or a participant may overreact to feedback about a group exercise and act exactly the opposite in the next group exercise. Assessors are told to be noncommital and supportive, but not evaluative. They are particularly told not to answer any questions from assessees relative to the assessees' performance. They are instructed to tell assessees that they should talk to the administrator and that the proper time to receive feedback is after all of the results are in and the assessors have been able to compare and contrast those results in order to come to a final decision.

However, certain developmentally oriented or career planning assessment centers do combine self-evaluation with the assessment center process itself. This is especially appropriate in diagnostic centers where the individual is there only for his or her benefit and there is a greater level of trust and openness.

Providing self-evaluation insights during or immediately after the assessment center can markedly ease the task of assessment center feedback because the individual is made ready for the feedback based on the insights he or she has already received. Thus, the feedback discussion is more of a general discussion of what went on and the planning of developmental responses rather than a "telling, explaining" discussion.

Heightened self-insight into performance may be obtained in the following ways:

1. Give participants a list of the dimensions to be assessed in the assessment center along with the definitions so that they can get a better feel for the areas in which they will be evaluated.
2. Arrange for more substantive peer feedback after group exercises. In most assessment centers, there is no peer discussion subsequent to group exercises. The participants fill out a "Participant Report Form" that often includes a peer rating, but those data are never shared. It is possible to distribute specially built forms to obtain insights from the group members into group effectiveness. This form is then shared and is the subject of a group discussion.

3. Allow individuals to see each other's presentations on videotape in order to make comparisons of possible ways of handling the situation with which they were presented.
4. Give exercise materials back to small groups of participants to allow participants to compare ways of handling items. This is particularly effective in providing insights into handling the in-basket exercise where participants are put in groups of four and given a new copy of the in-basket. They go through the in-basket item by item, sharing with the others how they handled the items.

The effect of these and other methods is to markedly increase the possibilities of accurate self-evaluation coming from participation in the assessment center without regard to the subsequent assessment feedback from the administrator based on the assessors' findings. However, to not contaminate the diagnostic insights from the assessment center, most of the above extra procedures are arranged to follow the last example of a category of exercises. For example, self-insight into performance in group exercises is not provided until all of the group exercises have been concluded.

An effective means of getting the positive effects of increased self-awareness from assessment center exercises while prohibiting any contamination of assessment results coming from increased awareness, is to have the awareness portions follow immediately after the assessment center portions of the program. For example, it is increasingly common for an organization to have 2 days of assessment followed by 2 days of self-awareness activities based on assessment exercises culminating in the feedback of the assessors' conclusions to the participants on the fifth day. This makes a very nice 5-day package which is particularly appealing to organizations which have to bring their assessors or participants considerable distances. The returns on the travel time investment are maximized.

During the self-awareness sessions (third and fourth days), the participants may watch selected assessment center exercises on videotape, study a variety of training materials (e.g., time management film) to start them toward improvement in their weak areas, or complete self-evaluation and peer evaluation forms and share the information. They often start preparing their own development plans even before they get the official assessment center feedback on the last day.

Obviously, it would be better to foster self-awareness insights after formal feedback, but that is not the usual procedure due to time and organizational constraints. Occasionally it can be done. Some organizations provide the training sequence after the formal assessment feedback.

They are able to do this because they include the assessment program as the first 2 days of a 2-week training program. Feedback is provided at the end of the first week, leaving the participants 1 week to view themselves on videotape participating in several exercises and to participate in group discussions of their roles in the exercises and how portions of the in-basket and other exercises can be handled. No comparative data exist, but this idea seems very good because the formal assessor feedback often raises many issues and questions in the minds of participants which can be resolved through looking back at the exercises on which the assessment report was based. The procedure also allows time for formalized development planning.

Does it help to enhance an individual's self-awareness of developmental needs? Attitude surveys (Dodd, 1977) confirm that a majority of participants believe the assessment center provides valuable information, but whether these new insights lead to development is as yet unconfirmed. As we have discussed, managerial development is hard to accomplish. Self-awareness does not necessarily lead to development for most areas, especially for cognitive skills such as problem analysis, judgment, or planning and organizing. Personal awareness may be enough to lead to improvement in some intrapersonal characteristics such as the willingness (not skill) to delegate, amount of participation in group meetings, risk taking, or initiative.

Assessor Training as a Learning Experience

The content and techniques of assessor training are too complicated to describe in detail here, but can be found in other sources (Byham, 1977b; Finkle & Jones, 1970; Moses, 1979). In summary, most assessor training programs focus on the following key skills:

1. *Understanding the organization's dimensions:* Assessors review job analysis results and definitions, and discuss on-the-job examples and behavior in each exercise illustrating each dimension.
2. *Observation of behavior in exercises:* Assessors learn the meaning of *behavior* in contrast to general traits, classificatory statements, and interpretations; then they practice observing and recording behavior in each exercise.
3. *Categorization of behavior:* For each dimension, the staff practices observing and classifying behavior presented on videotape or by live, mock participants.
4. *Rating behavior by dimensions:* The assessors develop a common

frame of reference by discussing the types of behaviors needed to achieve various levels of ratings on each dimension.

5. *Processing information from various exercises:* Reporting observed behavior, assessors discuss differences in observations and practice defending evaluations.

6. *Determining overall judgments:* Where called for, the assessors practice deriving an overall assessment rating, first independently and then via consensus discussion.

These skills are generalizable to many personnel management and supervisory tasks. Managers usually report that the techniques and approaches they learn in assessor training and then sharpen with experience as assessors have many payoffs for subsequent job duties. As indicated earlier, assessor experience helps the manager carry out developmental activities for his or her own subordinates who have been assessed.

A few organizations such as Steinberg's, Bendix, Public Service Commission of Canada, and IBM have collected questionnaire responses to measure perceived effects of assessor training. For example, Pederson, Slivinski, and Bourgeois (1974) reported that 92 % of the assessors in the Canadian Public Service Commission program said that the assessor training was beneficial to their job-related duties (e.g., appraisal, identifying training needs, and formulating career plans for subordinates). The problem with these kinds of evaluations is that after most training programs, managers do not tend to be very discriminating and some very poor programs have passed the test of trainee evaluation.

A slight improvement on the typical self-evaluation technique was used by Byham and Thoresen (1976) in their study of various assessor training techniques and procedures. They administered a 20-item managerial skill evaluation form to different groups of assessors before assessor training, immediately after assessor training, and after participation as an assessor in an assessment center. This procedure has the advantages of being more systematic than approaches asking for general posttraining evaluations and of being able to tie down the training to specific managerial skills. Several interesting findings came from this research. They are:

1. Managers' perceptions of their own skills go down markedly between the beginning and end of an assessor training program. That is, the effect of an assessor training program is to show the individuals being trained that their skills in many areas were not nearly as good as they had perceived them to be. Most participants start out by checking the top (i.e., 7, 8, and 9) portion of the scale. When asked after the assessment center to evaluate their skill *prior* to the assessment center, the average participant

dropped back two points on the scale. These results are probably an example of "beta change" resulting from a change in perception of the range of ability possible in the skill being measured on the item.

2. Managers feel that assessor training has increased their abilities on many dimensions when compared with their posttraining assessment of their pretraining skill level.

3. The major skills learned by assessors involve their ability to observe and record behavior. Since these skills are the heart of the assessment center process, it would certainly be expected that managers in an assessor training program would improve in these areas.

Based on the research evidence and postprogram interviews with assessors conducted by Byham & Thoreson, these general observations can be made. Assessor training is usually seen by participants to improve their skills in the following areas:

1. *Appraisal interviewing:* It is felt that the new skills in observing and recording behavior will help the manager conduct more meaningful behaviorally based interviews with subordinates. Rather than making generalized statements about performance, the manager is much more apt to have a list of specific behaviors to cite relative to each of the appraisal areas. Skills in feeding back interview information are thought to be enhanced by the manager's increased sensitivity to interpersonal interactions. Improved skills in this area are particularly enhanced when the popular interview simulation exercise is a part of the assessment center. Then a significant portion of the assessor training is devoted specifically to the feedback of performance data. Assessors have the opportunity to compare procedures and discuss various techniques and are often provided with a model. Their sensitivity about what to do and what not to do is greatly heightened.

2. *Handling of administrative detail:* Going over each item in a complicated in-basket and comparing ways that each item can be handled increases one's sensitivity to the need for handling administrative details and the multiple possibilities for such handling. Particularly, areas such as Effective Delegation and Management Control are thought to be enhanced through training on the use of the in-basket exercise. These effects have been observed elsewhere (Carrigan, 1976).

Quantitative evidence that assessor training and experience has an effect on judgments can be found in a few studies. Acker and Perlson (1970) found that over the course of several assessment programs, assessors evidenced more agreement in their ratings of participant behavior. The standard deviation in ratings went from .42, .36, .28, to .26 (using a four-point scale) in four successive assessment programs. In another study, McConnell and Parker (1972) asked 12 assessors to listen to an actual taped report of a participant's performance in an assessment center and evaluate several management abilities and overall performance. Ratings were gathered before and after a 24–28 hour training program. The range of ratings on a nine-point scale diminished from eight to three and the standard deviation diminished from 1.84 to .76.

Our own observations strongly support the meager research that is available. The development of observation, classification, and rating skills are clearly obvious during an assessor training program.

The Impact of Assessment Center Methodology on the Organization

In addition to the direct affects on individual managers being assessed, assessment center activities and follow-up activities have indirect and broader affects on the organization as a whole (Alon, 1973, 1977). Because of their high cost and visibility, assessment centers have drawn attention to the organization's entire system of human-resource utilization. To be successful, a developmental assessment center must be embedded within a carefully planned program of management selection, training, evaluation, and development.

Assessment centers affect broader organizational problems of human resource utilization in a number of ways:

1. The identification and definition of dimensions to be assessed may be the first way the organization has articulated job requirements at the supervisory or management level.
2. Assessment activities are clearly intertwined with other programs of performance review, affirmative action, management by objectives, and training and development.
3. Assessment and subsequent development planning give upper management a framework for monitoring the development responsibilities of lower level management.
4. Assessment centers reveal the need for and create the opportunity for new training and development programs (e.g., reveal the lack of coaching skills among supervisors of assessed personnel).
5. The history of assessment and cumulated results reveal management deficits in various departments and the organization as a whole. One organization learned over time that the appreciation for and use of management control techniques was deficient throughout most of the company.

Can People Be Developed?

A frequent interpretation of the AT&T Management Progress Study is that it shows that adults cannot be changed relative to the dimensions assessed in the study. This interpretation evolved because the men in the study changed relatively little between the assessment taken at their intake into first-level management and the assessment conducted 8 years later.

What the study actually shows is that individuals left to their own devices and exposed only to generalized training and development procedures will not change. The very characteristics that make the Management Progress Study such an excellent research study work against the change taking place. One must remember that the participants in the Management Progress Study were given no feedback whatsoever about their performances in the first assessment center.

Therefore, self-development actions were precluded. One might argue that because the data indicate that people's self-perception of their performances in assessment centers is fairly related to their actual performance in assessment centers, the assessment center without feedback would have acted as a developmental stimulant. This is, of course, a possibility, but the obvious experimental nature of the Management Progress Study would probably rule that out. Throughout the assessment procedure, the assessees were told that it was an experimental procedure and that it would have nothing to do with their career within the company. No reports of individual performance were given to management in the Management Progress Study. Thus, there was no organizational or individual response to the findings in the form of changing jobs, learning situations, etc. At the time of the first assessment, it was a new procedure for the company and it is fairly safe to assume that most people would not have taken their performance in the program too seriously as it related to their careers.

So, we can definitely *not* say that people cannot change their behavior and develop new or improved methods of coping with job responsibilities. We believe that through the complicated and widespread training responses that often follow assessment center programs (Byham, 1977), that change can be accomplished.

We still know far too little about the impact of training and development activities. But we are sure of one thing: Change can be accomplished only through a combination of self-insight and massive organizational effort.

9

Unique Uses of
Assessment Center
Methodology

In theory, assessment center methodology can be used to predict potential for any kind of position. In practice, however, the great majority of applications have involved the selection or promotion of supervisors and managers in business and government. About 95 % of the more than 1000 assessment centers we know of fall into this category.

But things seem to be changing. During the 1970s, several nontraditional uses of assessment center methodology emerged and it is likely that this activity will increase. At the beginning of 1980, the use of assessment centers for purposes other than the identification of supervisory–managerial potential was at about the same place in its acceptance and use as was the assessment center method for the purpose of supervisory and managerial selection and development at the beginning of 1970. By 1980, there was considerable knowledge of the usefulness of the technique—articles were starting to appear, and research results were starting to be reported. We anticipate a marked increase in applications of the assessment center method to nontraditional settings in the future.

Nontraditional assessment centers fall into five broad categories:

1. A criterion for personnel research
2. A criterion for the evaluation of professional competency
3. For career planning
4. For nonsupervisory, nonmanagement selection
5. For nontraditional (unusual) management evaluation

Assessment Centers as a Research Criterion

For as long as industrial psychologists have published, they have lamented the absence of reliable and valid criteria to use in their research. The assessment center method shows considerable promise in helping to solve this problem. Research has been conducted using assessment center results as a criterion for both training and selection studies.

TRAINING CRITERION

The evaluation of training program effectiveness has long been a challenge for trainers and researchers. Many people have written about the need for more research (Campbell, 1971; Goldstein, 1980) but still there have been relatively few scientifically conducted training evaluation studies.

The first reported use of assessment center results as a training criterion was by the Metropolitan Transit Authority of New York City (MTA) in 1972. Two groups of 12 supervisors were matched in terms of age, service, supervisory experience, education, and performance ratings. Both groups were assessed on 12 dimensions as they participated in assessment center exercises. An overall performance rating was obtained on each.

Then one group of 12 supervisors participated in a supervisory training program while the other served as a control group. Both groups were then reassessed using the same assessment center exercises used in the original assessment. Assessors who had assessed one group of 12 supervisors during the pretraining application evaluated the other group of 12 during the post training application so there would be no carry-over in expectations of participant performance between the two applications of the assessment center method. However, it is likely that the assessors knew who had been trained and who was in the control group and some biases may have resulted. An additional complication in evaluating the results of the study is the unexplained loss of the data on two of the experimental subjects in the reported results.

Comparisons of the overall score between the first and second applications of the assessment center showed only a slight improvement in score for the control group (.05 on a nine-point scale) but almost a full point improvement for the trained group (.90 on a nine-point scale). The change in ratings for the experimental group was significant at the .05 level.

Real movement in the use of assessment centers as a training criterion started with the adoption of behavior modeling training by many organizations. The objective of behavior modeling is to change behavior through presenting trainees with a step-by-step approach to accomplish a goal, a positive model of the use of those steps, and the opportunity to practice and receive feedback in using the steps (Byham & Robinson, 1976). The first use of assessment center technology to evaluate the effectiveness of behavior modeling training was by AT&T for its first-level line supervisory training program (Moses & Ritchie, 1975).

A large and representative group of first-level line supervisors was identified in two telephone companies. Two groups matched by sex, age, department, length of service, and number of subordinates were randomly selected from the total group. One group received behavior modeling training; the other group did not receive training.

In each telephone company, a special evaluation assessment center was established. The assessors received training in behavioral observation and use of rating scales specially constituted for the evaluation process. The staff did not know anything specific about the modeling program, nor did they know which supervisors had attended the course.

The study took place 4–7 weeks after the trained supervisors completed the program. All supervisors, trained and untrained, were given a series of simulated problem-solving exercises to be role-played with a real employee. Following each discussion the evaluation staff independently completed a rating scale designed to evaluate the quality of the discussion. The results indicated that the overall performance of the trained supervisors was dramatically superior to that of the untrained supervisors (Table 9.1).

A second study, following a very similar experimental design, was conducted by Lukens Steel (King & Arlinghaus, 1976). The number of participants was smaller, but the results also showed the effectiveness of behavior modeling training.

Both the AT&T and the Lukens Steel studies used assessment center technology, but did not conduct a "complete" assessment center. Both used assessor training technology to train managers as evaluators. Assessment-center-type rating scales were used. Most important, ratings

Table 9.1

Percentage Distribution of Overall Judgment Ratings[a]

Overall judgment	Trained	Untrained
Exceptionally well or above average	84	33
Average	10	34
Below average or poor	6	33

[a]From Moses & Ritchie (1975). Reprinted by permission.

on the effectiveness of handling interactions were obtained from raters independently, and then the evaluators shared their ratings in an assessment-center-like data integration session. But, there was only one type of exercise (four interview simulations). There were no dimensional ratings.

A more complete use of assessment center methodology was used by Central Telephone to evaluate its behavior modeling program. They put individuals through an assessment center and videotaped their performance in five exercises (including a standard interview simulation). The group was then trained and again assessed with their performance being recorded on videotape. No assessors were present for either assessment activity. There was no control group.

The videotapes were sent to an operating assessment center in another part of the country and the individuals were assessed on 12 assessment center dimensions. An overall evaluation of potential was also obtained. The assessors did not know which tapes were made before or after training. The results can be found in Table 9.2.

The largest training evaluation study using assessment center methodology that has ever been designed is being contemplated by the American Assembly of the Collegiate Schools of Business. They have contracted with Development Dimensions International to devise a program to measure the output of schools of business. A random sample of students going into a school of business (undergraduate or graduate) and a random sample of students about to leave the same school would be assessed. Differences in their assessed skills, knowledge, and abilities would be a measure of the "value added" by that school. The Assembly has defined a list of competencies appropriate for a business school graduate and an assessment center program utilizing extensive videotape technology has been designed to tap the managerial–interactive skills.

Table 9.2

Overall Percentage Ratings of Trained Supervisors' Effectiveness in Simulated Situations[a]

Rating	Before[b]	After[c]
Excellent	0	17
Above average	22	25
Average	39	58
Below average	17	0
Poor	22	0

[a]From King & Arlinghaus (1976). Reprinted by permission.

[b]Eighteen supervisors.

[c]Twelve supervisors.

Basically, a single administrator would go to a campus and would put a representative sample of individuals through assessment center exercises, collecting their behavior in written form or on videotape. The data would then be returned to the Pittsburgh office of Development Dimensions International, where a team of specially trained assessors would evaluate it without knowing whether the person was starting or ending business training and without knowing about the school he or she was attending. The project is currently seeking funding for an experimental application.

The use of assessment center methodology as a criterion for evaluating training effectiveness seems like such a good idea that one must wonder why more organizations have not used it. Of course, performance in an assessment center is not the ultimate criterion of training effectiveness. It does not indicate whether an individual actually uses the skills on the job; but it is an excellent indication of new behavior acquisition, which is certainly a considerable step beyond more traditional training evaluations which deal with knowledge acquisition or participant attitude change.

Thus far, the use of assessment center methodology in training evaluation has been fairly limited in the types of training programs evaluated and in the experimental designs used. A very promising area would be the use of assessment center methodology to follow up on the effectiveness of training prescribed from a diagnosis of training needs obtained from an assessment center. Many organizations have implemented training programs to follow up diagnoses derived from an assessment center. It seems quite logical that in certain instances an assessment center might be an appropriate technique to evaluate such training to see if it worked (see section on a systems approach to personnel in Chapter 11).

SELECTION CRITERION

Just as assessment centers have been used as a training criterion, they have also been used as a criterion against which to evaluate cheaper or easier methods of selection. Assuming the validity of assessment center methodology and recognizing the relatively high cost of assessment center operation, it is natural that an organization would look for ways to obtain the same level of predictive accuracy at less expense.

An early example of the application of assessment center methodology as a selection criterion was reported by Grant & Bray (1970) at the American Telephone and Telegraph Company. They developed an elaborate series of work samples simulating the kinds of learning required of a newly hired technician as he or she progressed up the technical ranks within the telephone company. They used scores derived from observing participants in the simulation as a criterion against which to validate various paper-and-pencil tests. The use of the simulations allowed the conduct of a quasi-predictive validity study to be conducted in a fraction of the time a true predictive validity study would have taken.

In another telephone company study, Moses (1973a) used predictions of managerial potential in a 2-day assessment center as a criterion against which to validate a 1-day assessment center. Because the 2-day assessment center had been shown in previous research to be valid, it seemed like an appropriate criterion. Significant correlations in the .70s were obtained indicating that the shorter assessment center could be effectively used as a substitute for the longer, more expensive center.

Researchers at IBM (Dodd & Kraut, 1970) correlated three personality inventories (the Survey of Interpersonal Values, the Gordon Personal Inventory, and the Gordon Personal Profile) with assessment center results obtained 4–5 years later. Only the Ascendancy score was significantly related ($r = .27$).

As part of the same study, it was found that instructor ratings in basic sales training programs did not relate to later assessments of managerial potential, but ratings in an advanced training program did correlate ($r = .32$) in spite of a considerable restriction of range.

The possible use of biographical data and personality tests as an assessment center prescreening device was investigated by Ritchie and Boehm (1980) using AT&T subjects. Eighty candidates were asked to complete a biographical questionnaire, the Gordon Personal Profile, and the Gordon Personal Inventory. Seven of the ten resulting scores were found to be significantly correlated with the final assessment center ratings. The authors developed a composite scoring procedure and applied it to the research sample to estimate the impact on the assessment center passing rate that could be expected from the use of the pretest. The rate was raised from 44 to 48.5 %—an estimated savings of $80,000 a year for AT&T for that style of assessment center operation, assuming 600 candidates over a 1-year period of time.

Assessment Centers as a Competency Criterion

Assessment centers have been used by some organizations as a means to evaluate incumbents on various managerial dimensions, but this use is comparatively rare and usually results from some major organizational upheaval such as new management, a drastic change in competition or products, or the need for a reduction in work force. The use of assessment center information to evaluate the competency of a person in his or her present job is much more common in government than in private industry and much more common at higher levels in an organization.

The use of assessment center information rather than performance appraisal data is not usually recommended as a means to evaluate a person for the job he or she presently occupies. Certainly, one's actual performance on the job is a better measure than the relatively short and relatively unrealistic behavior obtained in an assessment center. The only justification for use of an assessment center to evaluate an incumbent for his or her present job is the lack of reliable and accurate performance information. This may occur when an individual operates in a very isolated situation, when a new manager has no faith in the evaluations made by previous managers, or when there has been a physical or mental change in the individual which would make past performance no longer predictive of future behavior.

PROFESSIONAL COMPETENCE (LICENSING)

A new and extremely promising application of assessment center methodology in competency evaluation is in the area of professional licensing. Professional competency evaluation procedures are becoming more important as licensing is required in an increasing number of occupations from beauticians to undertakers. The maintenance and updating of competency is also becoming more important as states require the periodic recertification of competency.

Coincidental with the expansion of licensing requirements is increasing public and professional unhappiness with the present methodology employed to certify competency. Traditional methods of evaluation (principally paper-and-pencil, multiple-choice tests) are increasingly thought to be limited in their ability to cover important job requirement areas. They are also thought by some people to be unfair because of their reliance on writing skills and memory when these factors may not be primary job requirements. Individual and group interviews which have also traditionally been part of many professional evaluation programs are seen to be too subjective and lacking reliability.

Simulations, but not as part of an assessment center in terms of the use of dimensions and a data integration session, have been used experimentally as part of several competency evaluation programs. Some of these are the evaluation of physicians in interpersonal skills, diagnosis, therapeutic intervention, and patient treatment (Samph, 1978); the evaluation of the competency of behavior therapists (Brockway, 1978); and the self-assessment of pediatricians, psychiatrists, dentists, and radiologic technicians (Friedman, 1978).

A true assessment center program to assess professional competency is in experimental use by the American Board of Professional Psychology (ABPP) as part of the certification of diplomates in clinical psychology.

Under the direction of Douglas Bray, a task force from ABPP developed an assessment center for the position of clinical psychologists (Riess, 1978). Using job analysis techniques, a list of dimensions was developed; subsequently, special exercises were constructed and assessors were trained. The program is currently running in parts of the United States as an alternative to the standard ABPP procedures.

The problem with the ABPP examination is that it is too time consuming for the volunteer assessors used by the organization. The assessors must spend a day in observing behavior and approximately one-half day in data integration for each candidate. A solution to this has been proposed by Byham (1978) involving the use of videotape technology to materially cut down the costs of certification. This is further discussed in the last chapter of this book.

A program to assess the professional competence of pharmacists has been developed by the College of Pharmacy at the University of Minnesota (Hellervik, 1978). Recognizing the inadequacy of typical licensure testing, college and professional representatives designed an assessment center to evaluate competencies to practice in the field (Cyrs, 1978). Grossing (1978) described the job analysis methods used in the competencies identified (e.g., evaluating a product, preparing a product, maintaining drug information). Assessment exercises simulated such job aspects as one-to-one relationships with patients, evaluation of prescriptions and patient medication profiles for accuracy, and supervision of subprofessionals (Silzer, 1978).

ACADEMIC COMPETENCE

Criterion-based learning is a popular concept in educational circles. However, the use of only paper-and-pencil tests as a measurement criterion materially limits the possible applications of criterion-based learning.

An innovative attempt to go beyond paper-and-pencil methodologies to establish educational competence has been promulgated by Alverno College Faculty (1979) of Milwaukee, Wisconsin. Alverno has adopted a set of competencies that must be achieved by the undergraduate students. Some of these competencies are:

1. Effective communications ability
2. Analytical capability
3. Problem-solving ability
4. Valuing in a decision-making context
5. Effective social interaction
6. Effectiveness in individual–environment relationships

7. Responsible involvement in the contemporary world
8. Aesthetic responsiveness

Some of the knowledge competencies are evaluated by means of paper-and-pencil tests but the majority of the competencies are evaluated by means of assessment-center-like exercises. In fact, some of the exercises are very similar to those used in management assessment centers. For example, Alverno uses assigned-role group exercises to evaluate social interaction and an in-basket exercise is used to evaluate decision-making skills. Alverno has developed over 25 simulations. They use their own faculty supplemented by volunteers from the local business community as assessors.

The Alverno program has achieved wide acceptance among its faculty members, students, and the community at large. The experiment has attracted national attention and Alverno has been awarded federal grants to record their experiences and to inform other colleges of the possibility of using this methodology. Several descriptions of their programs have been published and the sponsors feel that the methodology can be applied to colleges of all sizes (Read, 1975). As of 1981, no other college had adopted the method as a total philosophy.

The only other college to make significant use of assessment center methodology as an educational criterion is Nova University in Fort Lauderdale, Florida. It offers an extension program in which individuals holding management positions in school systems can earn an EdD by attending several days of classes once a month for several years. From 1974 to 1976, the university operated an elaborate assessment center program to assess the Leadership skills of their students. Because the program was aimed at preparing individuals for senior school administrative roles, all assessment center exercises were built around the position of an "Area Administrator" in a school district. After an extensive job analysis, 20 dimensions were defined. They were very similar to the dimensions used in middle-management programs in industry.

The unique part of the Nova assessment center program was its use of videotape and paper-and-pencil technology to capture the assessment center data. Because the students were spread geographically over much of the United states, it would have been very difficult and extremely expensive to send assessors to the class locations. The solution to this problem was to design exercises where the behavioral data from the assessment center could either be captured on videotape or by means of paper-and-pencil exercises. For example, a unique fact-finding exercise was developed so that the exercise could be objectively scored relative to breadth and depth of Fact-finding skill.

Another unique exercise developed for this assessment center evaluated Educational Creativity. A scoring methodology was developed for this exercise in which output and quality of ideas could be objectively evaluated.

If an exercise could not be adapted to a paper-and-pencil format, then the behavioral data were collected on videotape. The videotapes were evaluated by trained educators at a central location. Data from all the exercises were integrated in an assessor discussion operated exactly like any other assessor integration discussion and a final report was written. Nova reported a high degree of face validity and acceptance by the participants in the program. The program was particularly useful in providing developmental insights for the participants.

In 1976, Nova reformulated the assessment center program into a regular 3-month study module. Participants self-evaluate themselves on a dimension and then take part in academic and on-the-job development activity to strengthen the dimension if needed. The Nova assessment center program was also used by a few school districts as part of selection and development programs.

Career Planning

The late 1970s and early 1980s have seen an increasing emphasis on career planning. Organizations want to make better use of their personnel resources and employees are no longer satisfied with a boring or unfulfilling job. Students want to avoid jobs where there is little opportunity for advancement. Given this setting, it is not surprising that assessment center technology would be tried as a way of improving planning accuracy.

CAREER PLANNING IN COLLEGE

Colleges have been relatively slow in utilizing assessment center technology for career planning, and the few applications that have been tried have lasted only a short period of time. Cost, administrative complexity, and the difficulty of obtaining assessors seem to be the major deterrents.

The longest running program is aimed at providing self-development and career planning insights to 12 MBA students per year in the Hankamer School of Business at Baylor University (Williams, 1977; Williams & Longenecker, 1976). Twenty to twenty-five dimensions chosen for their relationship with managerial success are evaluated by an in-basket exercise, a series of group exercises, an analysis and presentation exercise, and paper-and-pencil tests. The dimensions and the evaluation instruments have been modified from year to year. The assessment center is conducted at a site away from the university and faculty members serve as assessors. Program participants are given detailed feedback on the results of the assessment center. They then participate in a seminar and personal counseling program involving self-analysis, development of personal goals, information on career plans, and behavior modification where appropriate.

In 1977, J. Clifton Williams, who heads the program, evaluated its effectiveness in this way:

> The effectiveness of the program in achieving its objectives has not been established experimentally, but the reactions of the students have been favorable. Demand for the course is high and participants, including those who have graduated and now see it from the perspective of the work environment, believe they are profiting from the experience. Thus, the course has been validated in essentially the same way as most other university courses. To date a problem with experimental validation has been that the seminar content has changed significantly each year. Once it stabilizes, the program's validity will be quantitatively measured.
>
> One interesting aspect of the program has been its acceptance by the business community. To practicing managers who are sensitive to the fact that a university's best students do not always make the best managers, the program has a refreshing aura of realism about it [p. 6, Williams, 1977].

In late 1981, Williams reported that the program died because of the amount of time required of the professors who participated in the program (Williams, 1981). Thus, the Baylor program joined a well-known program that ran in the Graduate School of Business at Stanford University for 5 years. Thomas Harrell offered a career planning program for second year MBA students. Students participated in assessment center exercises and then were trained to evaluate each other. They also took paper-and-pencil tests and other measures to help decide on their appropriate career orientation. That program was dropped when Harrell retired.

Two large-scale academic programs are being conducted at Brigham Young University. They offer a 2.5-day elective assessment center program for MBA students for career planning and self-development planning. Assessors are second-year students in organizational behavior and local business managers.

Brigham Young also requires all students in the University's Masters in Public Administration Program to go through an assessment center for career development. Local government agency representatives serve as assessors.

A highly unique career planning program was operated in 1978 by the Graduate School of Business of New York University as part of a program to provide individuals with PhDs in nonbusiness areas with enough business expertise to get a job in industry. In the first program, the assessment center was used as a diagnostic instrument for the 50 program participants. A standard list of managerial dimensions was used and the assessors all came from AT&T.

The assessment center was very well received and preliminary results indicated a relationship between assessment center overall results and job placement. It was decided to use the assessment center as a screening device as well as a career planning device. Unfortunately, New York University had trouble recruiting trained assessors and did not repeat the assessment center portion of the program.

On two occasions (1972 and 1979) the graduate program in industrial–organizational psychology at Colorado State University conducted an assessment center to evaluate students in the program. In the first application (Thornton & McCambridge, 1974), faculty served as assessors; in the second, both faculty and students served as assessors. On both occasions nonacademic, job-relevant dimensions were assessed and developmental planning activities were included.

Other universities (e.g., Virginia Polytechnic Institute) are starting programs (Hamilton, 1980), but they can report no real progress as yet.

CAREER PLANNING IN INDUSTRY

Although only beginning to be popular in the United States, assessment center methodology is increasingly being used in Europe and Japan for career planning. More than 500 managers from International Computers Limited (ICL) throughout the world have gone through a self-assessment program as part of an overall career planning program. The supervisors and managers first participate in standard management assessment center activities for 2 days. Videotape is used to record data during the exercise-taking portion of the program (Van Oudtshoorn, 1979). Then participants are trained as assessors and they assess themselves and each other. The resultant profile of managerial strengths and weaknesses is used as an input into career planning decisions.

More than 300 Japanese managers from 25 organizations have participated in similar self-assessment activities. The participants report great satisfaction with the insights provided by the program (Shudo, 1979).

Self-assessment is just starting to become popular in the United States. In 1981 several organizations started programs as part of career planning endeavors. Results appear to be promising. Participants report important self-insights, and management reports that participants seem to take action on their insights. In the American version of the program, the assessment center insight on the dimension is supported by data from supervisors, peers, and subordinates.

Self-assessment (and peer assessment) seems to be a very popular methodology for use in career planning because it is less expensive than normal assessment methodology (higher-level managers are not used as assessors) and worries about the security of the data are overcome. In a normal assessment center where managers serve as assessors there is always the chance that the data will be used for or against an individual even if the purpose of the center is only self-insight for the participant. It is very difficult for managers to put data obtained from an assessment center out of their minds, thus knowledge obtained in the assessment center possibly might affect future decisions about the individual. Even if this does not happen, the participant always has the feeling that it will. Self-assessment eliminates this possibility.

A second methodology that overcomes the confidentiality worry, but not the cost issue, is the use of assessors from outside the organization. There are no available data on the accuracy of outside assessors versus the accuracy of self-assessment, but we would expect that outside assessors would be more accurate. It is always difficult to observe and evaluate oneself and, for that reason alone, we would expect an outside team of assessors to be more accurate—given the same degree of training. Usually, outside assessors are much more highly trained than individuals who would assess themselves.

Assessment for career planning purposes is offered by two consulting groups (Development Dimensions International and Personnel Predictions, Inc.) in the United States. In addition, many private and governmental organizations have conducted special career planning assessment centers totally staffed by individuals from outside their organization.

There are two problems arising from the use of outside assessors. One is that assessors are unfamiliar with the jobs in the organization to which the individual might be aspiring (this becomes less important when career planning is thought of in a broad view which may cover many jobs within and outside a particular organization), and the other is that "out-of-pocket" costs of using outside assessors are high. Graduate students and other individuals who have little job experience cannot adequately assess middle managers. A considerable amount of experience in the "real world" is necessary. It is usually expensive to hire this kind of individual as an assessor. Actually, it is probably not any more costly than using inside assessors, but the use of inside assessors is not an "out-of-pocket" expense—the organization gives up the time of very valuable individuals which, if costed out, might be more valuable than the payment to outsiders. It just does not show up on the books.

All selection assessment centers have an element of career planning in them. By going through many of the actual activities that will be encountered on the job, the applicant is provided with excellent insights into the job. This orientation feature may partially explain the decrease in employee turnover reported when an assessment center is installed—more people who would later quit, select themselves out after getting a better feel for the job.

Some organizations have elected to increase the career orientation effect of their selection assessment center programs. They have done this through calling attention to career planning issues and through their choice of exercises.

Some organizations force the participant to consider his or her career choice after an assessment center by asking the participant to fill out a form or make a special application to continue in the selection process. Thus, anyone wishing to drop out of the process can elect this option by doing nothing. They must make an overt action to continue.

All assessment centers should be simulations of a job, but the choice of the particular simulation may prove especially important in the context of career orientation. This is especially important in the use of an interview simulation exercise. Many good employees have never experienced a negative interview with a supervisor, thus they may underestimate the difficulty of conducting such an interview. As a result, some organizations have chosen to use as the stimulus in an interview simulation a particularly difficult subordinate interaction. This choice is made not only to simulate an important aspect of the job, but also to acquaint the applicants with what they may perceive to be a negative portion of the job. After experiencing the simulation, they can decide if they want to conduct such interviews as a supervisor.

Nonsupervisory and Nonmanagement Assessment Center Programs

It seems so rational that assessment center methodology would be applied to nonsupervisory–managerial positions that one can only wonder why it has taken so long. More than 10 years ago Bray and Campbell (1968) showed that an assessment center could accurately predict sales potential; yet relatively few organizations use the method for this purpose. In fact, it has been only in the last 5 years that there has been a significant growth in this area.

Some of the positions where assessment center methodology has been applied are salesperson, engineer, personnel trainer, police officer, rehabilitation counselor, and commercial attachés.

Salespersons. The first and largest user of assessment center methodology for the selection of salespersons is AT&T (Bray & Campbell, 1968). An assessment center with good predictive validity was established and used as a formal entity in the mid 1960s. Then the technology was incorporated into the normal selection and development system and is still in use. For example, Ritchie (1980) found a highly significant relationship between overall assessment performance ratings and two criteria of training and field performance for commission salespersons. Furthermore, turnover among hirees rated acceptable was approximately one-half the rate for those rated less than acceptable.

Another long-running sales assessment center has been conducted by Johnson's Wax for the selection of salespeople to service supermarkets and other stores that sell their products. Their assessment center uses six dimensions and two simulations (plus an interview). Results of the assessment center application have not been published but executives feel that a substantial decrease in turnover and an increase in productivity have resulted (Shankster, 1979).

Development Dimensions International has made extensive use of assessment center methodology to select salespeople for the last 6 years. Thirteen dimensions were identified in extensive job analyses and are assessed through three targeted interviews plus an in-basket, analysis exercise, and presentation exercise. Assessment center methodology has also been applied in the selection of salespeople for optometry departments in Sears stores, of Allstate insurance agents, of interior decorator–salespeople in Ethan Allen stores, and Xerox salespersons.

Two unusual sales positions have benefited from assessment center methodology. Merrill Lynch Pierce Fenner & Smith make use of an integrated simulation exercise, incorporating many assessment center principles, in selecting stockbrokers. Telephone and in-person interactions and in-basket materials are integrated into a 3-hour exercise in which the applicant assumes the role of a stockbroker. The result of using this method for 2 years is that turnover among "recommended" applicants has dropped by 42% (Hollenbeck, 1980).

The other position in which a representative must sell over the phone is that of an employment agency representative. Representatives must sell their organization's services to their applicants and to business and government clients who are seeking people. An assessment center simulating the job requirements of this sales position was developed for an Indianapolis employment agency and is reported to have significantly improved the caliber of representatives hired. The major exercise is an "interactive in-basket." While the applicant is working on some administrative sales problems, he or she must also use the telephone for fact finding and to make sales calls. The calls are made and received by assessors who are playing various roles. In addition, the participant must prepare for and conduct a face-to-face sales call with a "customer" who is also playing a closely defined role. All exercises are recorded on audio or videotape. Research indicates that behavior elicited and observed in the assessment center has a very high correlation to behavior observed on the job (.85). The correlation between assessment center performance and dollar production is also very high at .88 (Butz, 1980).

Engineers. Several Bell companies are filling some first-level, nonprofessional engineering jobs with employees they have identified through an assessment program (Assessment & Development, 1973). The program, begun in 1973, is designed to find people who have the potential to handle first-level engineering jobs in central office equipment, PBX, or outside plant. This program was called the Engineering Selection Program and it was developed through the joint efforts of the AT&T Human Resources Development and Engineering Departments, Michigan Bell, and Chesapeake & Potomac Telephone Companies.

The program seeks to provide a better way to identify employees who have a talent for engineering early in their careers. It uses a special assessment center developed by intensive analysis of the basic engineering jobs. Candidates may enter the program either through a recommendation from their supervisors or by nominating themselves. It is open to all men and women from any department who have been in their present jobs for at least 18 months and are performing satisfactorily. The assessment lasts for 1 day. A team of specially trained engineers evaluates how well the candidates do a number of assignments and judges basic abilities for engineering jobs. Then the team gives the participant an overall rating on his or her engineering potential.

Instructors. The Federal Aviation Administration uses assessment center methodology to evaluate candidates for instructor positions (Price, 1978).

Development Dimensions International, a Pittsburgh firm that provides training methodology to clients, has used assessment center exercises for some time to select trainers–consultants. The 24 dimensions are assessed through the use of three targeted interviews, an in-basket, and an oral presentation exercise.

Westinghouse has made limited use of assessment center technology to select "facilitators" for its Quality Circle program. A facilitator coordinates a group of QCs, plans meetings, provides training inputs, follows up on special Circle needs, etc. Seven dimensions were evaluated in six exercises (DiCola, 1980).

Scientists. The Canadian Civil Service Commission studied the prediction of advancement of scientists by means of an in-basket. They looked at the progression at 2.5 years, 5.5 years, and 6.5 years and found many positive correlations (Pederson, 1980).

Police recruits. For the last 15 years, the selection of police recruits has been the subject of much litigation throughout the United States. Courts have consistently found that most paper-and-pencil tests used for selection purposes do not meet the EEOC Guidelines. However, because of the expense, assessment centers have been used by relatively few cities for this purpose.

On a small scale, Ft. Collins, Colorado used assessment center exercises to select police officers (Hamilton & Gavin, 1974). A series of three situational exercises was developed to examine applicant behaviors in simulated police situations. The applicants were given a brief description of the necessary information and put in a room with a confederate who played the role of a citizen. The problems covered typical situations encountered, such as illegal parking, marital disputes, etc.

The City of Chicago tried assessment center methodology on a larger scale. They collected predictive validation information using as criteria the completion of the police academy training program and ratings by superior officer in the field. Recruits on entering the Police Academy were put through a series of exercises each of which was evaluated by two assessors, one civilian and one police officer. These evaluations were done on a behavior checklist with supplemental written comments and observations by dimension. The two reports from each person from each exercise were put together and placed into a central file for each candidate. Integration of the file information was done by a team of trained police officers who were convened to review all the data in each applicant's file and to make predictions about the person's performance as a police officer. No validity data are available.

Commercial attachés. Commercial attachés are government employees who represent one country's business interest in another country.

Their job is to help businesses from their country to spot and exploit markets in the country to which they are assigned. They also attempt to aid visiting business representatives from their country in making business and government contacts and in understanding the laws and regulations of the assigned country.

In 1980 the Philippine government wanted to upgrade, develop, and reorganize their more than 200 attachés and used the assessment center method to obtain information on the skills of the incumbents. Two specially devised background interviews and two assessment center exercises were used. A team of five assessors traveled to five sites around the world to conduct the assessments. Dimensions of particular interest were Entrepreneurship, Initiative, and Business Creativity.

Foreign service officer. Since 1978, the U.S. State Department has been a major user of assessment center methodology as part of their selection program for entry-level foreign service positions (Crooks, 1980). In 1979, 2200 candidates were assessed in 14 cities. First candidates take a paper-and-pencil test—less than 20% pass. Those that pass go through the assessment center. Seventeen dimensions are assessed by means of a panel interview, a presentation, an in-basket, a writing sample, and an LGD. Assessors are middle- and senior-level foreign service officers. The total system has a selection ratio of 1–2 out of 100 because 21% of candidates pass the assessment center.

Rehabilitation counselors. The Commonwealth of Massachusetts has made a unique use of assessment centers in the identification of vocational rehabilitation counselors. The counselors deal with physically and psychologically disabled clients such as hearing-impaired individuals, quadriplegics, and the mentally retarded. Both counseling and coaching skills are required. Counselors must provide information and psychological support to clients and they are responsible for the clients' progression toward employment. Counselors must maintain relations with other health care providers and agencies, and must recruit organizations to hire their clients.

Twelve dimensions were identified in a comprehensive job analysis program. Three exercises were developed to elicit the dimensions and a concurrent validity study that showed the effectiveness of the assessment center was undertaken (Goldberg *et al.*, 1980). See the discussion of concurrent validity studies in Chapter 7 for more information.

Administrative judges. Administrative judges are federal judges who adjudicate contract disputes between government agencies and their clients or contractors. There are around 200 in the federal service.

In 1980, it was decided to use a combination of assessment center and targeted behavior interviewing technology to select candidates for these positions. After a detailed job analysis was conducted, a selection system was developed that had a number of unique elements including a dimensionalized applicant screening process.

Nontraditional Management Assessment Centers

After the success of assessment centers for predicting management potential in industrial and government organizations, it was natural that the methodology would be applied to other situations where managerial dimensions are required. Some of these include mine supervisors, chief pilots, matrix managers, school managers (principals, assistant principals), managers of police activities, and military officers.

Mine supervisors. Operating in an underground or above-ground mining situation is substantially different from most supervisory jobs because of the heavy safety emphasis on the job. Mines operated by organizations such as U.S. Steel, Standard Oil of Ohio, Standard Oil (Indiana), and Union Carbide have all used assessment center methodology to select mine supervisors. Special exercises have been developed that stress the safety and health considerations of the job.

Chief pilots. The Tenneco Oil Company has over 150 pilots, and they have used assessment center methodology to select managers from among the subordinate pilots (Jaffee, 1980).

Matrix managers. In matrix management an individual is given a project leadership assignment, but no responsibility for personnel or general administrative duties. This form of management is becoming increasingly popular in space and high technology situations. An individual may be a matrix leader in one project and a contributing member of another matrix team. The job of a matrix manager requires the normal supervisory dimensions but with a different emphasis. Planning and organization skills as well as analytical skills are required to a particularly high degree, while the ability to handle personnel matters such as absenteeism or performance problems is not important since these are the responsibilities of an employee's direct supervisor rather than the matrix manager. In response to these changes in emphasis, some changes in the assessment center design are required; for example, the assessment center for matrix managers at American Express uses two analysis exercises, no interview simulation, and only one group exercise. Planning rather than administration is the focus of the in-basket.

School principals and assistant principals. The assessment of individuals who are being considered for principal and assistant principal positions in schools is increasingly popular. Five school districts in Virginia and Florida have developed assessment center programs with the aid of the National Association of Secondary School Principals (Hersey, 1977; Moses, 1977b; Jeswald, 1977b). The same 12 dimensions and three exercises (leaderless group discussion, fact finding, and in-basket) are used in all programs.

The largest use of assessment center methodology within a school system was conducted by the City of New York in 1980. As a result of a landmark case on June 1, 1972, *Chance v. Board of Examiners* (Byham, 1979b), the Board of Examiners, which is responsible for certifying the competence of all the Board of Education professional employees, was mandated to develop innovative selection techniques that were not discriminatory against protected classes. After reviewing all alternative methodologies, they chose the assessment center method. The first application of the methodology was for the selection of junior-high-school principals. A comprehensive job analysis was conducted to define the target dimensions and to define the exercises used.

British military. As described in Chapter 2, many of the early innovations and research in assessment center technology came from military applications. While the German army did not continue in its use of assessment center exercises to select officers, the British army continues to be a major user. With a few exceptions, entry into the officer corps is determined by the Army's Regular Commission Boards (RCB) which evaluates about 1500 candidates each year. Its major procedures, originally patterned after early work done by the German army, have gone virtually unchanged for 35 years although many minor modifications have been made. Nineteen dimensions are evaluated. They have been divided into three groups: "intellectual," "practical," and "personality and character." Some of the dimensions included under "personality and character" are Coolness, Sense of Urgency, Military Compatibility, and Maturity.

The selection board is designed to evaluate 48 candidates divided into six groups of eight. A Major General heads the board and high ranking regimental officers serve as assessors. The only nonmilitary member of the board is the Education Advisor who interprets test results to estimate the training potential of each candidate.

Four days of activities are involved, but a substantial period of time is spent administering paper-and-pencil tests and in waiting for the next exercise to begin. Some of the exercises in addition to these tests are LGDs, an individual problem-solving exercise, a planning exercise, a presentation exercise, and command opportunity tasks. The command tasks are conducted outdoors and require a group of individuals to solve a problem, usually the crossing of a barrier by using a number of physical aids such as ropes and planks.

There are several interesting features in how behavior observation is organized. Three board members observe each exercise. One has read the candidate's file; one has interviewed the candidate in-depth but has not seen the file; and one knows nothing about the candidate. It is believed that each will bring to the observation a different orientation, and, thus, the combined decision will be more accurate.

Another interesting feature is the use of "pre-board conferences" where initial classifications of the candidates' potential are made. Although board members are required to reach a conclusion and assess each assigned candidate independently of the others prior to the consensus meeting, the system allows for two short pre-board conferences designed to draw the assessors' attention to those candidates who are likely to be difficult to assess and whose performance may be the subject of considerable debate.

In addition to spotlighting certain candidates for special observation, the final event of the assessment program can be manipulated to allow a more complete and wider observation of behavior of those candidates who fall between the obviously qualified and obviously unqualified categories of overall evaluation.

In 1979, the Adjutant General commissioned a review of the Regular Commissions Board which covered the acceptability, consistency, and validity of the procedure (Adjutant General, 1979). The report concluded that the procedure was highly regarded among Headmasters and Career Masters who recommend candidates and by the candidates themselves. However, there have been some critical technical reports including one that argues that "an unconscious class bias influences the outcome of procedures which are, on the surface, neutral as far as class cultural characteristics are concerned [Salaman & Thompson, 1978]."

Consistency (reliability) of the RCB was measured by having individuals go through several different assessment centers and by having two boards observe a single set of candidates as they went through a single assessment center. The first study conducted in the early 1960s found an 80% agreement among boards. A recent study (1978) used the "shadow board" technique where 16 candidates were evaluated by a board while a second board watched every event. Then the two boards switched roles and a second group of 16 candidates were evaluated.

Twenty-eight of the 32 candidates received the same OAR by the two boards (87% level of agreement). All of the remaining four, although accepted in fact by the real board, were failed by the "shadow board."

In the reliability study, the major cause of variance was found to be "a rather wide range of expertise on the part of the interviewers." Not only did both the content and length of the interview vary, but in some cases the ability to interpret information and react to it appropriately was lacking (Adjutant General, 1979). Over 40% of participants found unnecessary repetition between interviews, and many commented on a possible "generation gap" between interviewer and interviewee.

Predictive validity evidence is sparse because of the difficulty in obtaining an accurate criterion and restriction in range of predictor scores due to the use of the RCB reports in making all decisions. It is rare for someone who does poorly to become an officer or to get special training. In the first of several planned studies, the board's OAR for 61 candidates was compared to grades in advanced officer training programs. A correlation of .30 was obtained. With correction for restriction of range, this increased to .50.

According to Richard Wellins (1980), United States Army TRADOC, who has made a survey of British officer selection procedures, the British navy and air force use techniques similar to those of the RCB for selecting their officers. The navy has a shorter assessment program and relies heavily on interviews. The air force includes several aptitude, psychometric, and instrument comprehension tests in their selection system.

United States military. While the OSS was an early user of assessment center methodology in the United States, the U.S. military forces made little use of the technique until the mid 1970s. At that time, a number of experimental applications of assessment centers were conducted. The U.S. military programs are

1. *Army Test Criterion Study (1962–1964):* Nine hundred officers were evaluated as they went through simulations. The data were used as a criterion for the development of paper-and-pencil tests.

2. *Army Leadership Development Program (1972–continuing on and off):* Thirty-two brigadier general designates (as of March 1980) went through the Leadership Development Training Program at the Center for Creative Leadership. Part of the program included assessment-center-like exercises to aid in their diagnosis of development needs.

3. *Army Assessment Center Evaluation Program (1973–1974):* About 500 army personnel from ROTC cadets to captains were assessed in a major evaluation of the assessment center method for predicting performance in army schools and early assignments and to test the value of

assessment feedback as a personal and career development aid. The assessment center lasted 3.5 days. Although the assessment center was seen by participants as a valuable experience and very acceptable levels of reliability were obtained, validity research was not encouraging. Assessment ratings did not correlate with later job performance criteria. In fact, some of the paper-and-pencil tests were better predictors of job performance. The poor validity findings could be due to inadequate performance criteria (i.e., peer and supervisor ratings). It is interesting to note that the assessment center ratings did correlate with some course grades.

4. *Air Force Diagnostic Assessment Center Program tied to Squadron Officer School (1975–continuing):* Incoming students to the SOS program at Maxwell Air Force Base, Alabama, are assessed to determine their leadership strengths and weaknesses. SOS is a leadership school concerned with educating air force lieutenants and captains to meet leadership needs during their current and future assignments. Approximately 600 students are assessed in each class, of which there are four a year. The assessment takes place during the first week of the SOS course.

The program was carefully developed and pilot tested before implementation. Interrater reliability studies yielded a coefficient of .86. Student reactions to the program, as evaluated by a questionnaire, were extremely positive. There are some inconsistent findings on the influence of the assessment experience on course grade. The predictive validity of the assessment center has not yet been investigated. The positive impact of the feedback of assessment center results on program results is discussed in Chapter 8.

5. *Army Diagnostic Assessment Center Program tied to the Fort Carson Leadership Center (1979–continuing):* In 2 days, incoming company commanders, primarily captains, are assessed to diagnose their management and leadership skills. Participants indicated that they gain confidence in their leadership and management skills. Assessors gain benefits from observer training sessions.

6. *Army Diagnostic Assessment Center Program tied to Adjutant General Officer Advance Course (December 1979–continuing):* Captains enrolled in the Adjutant General Officer Advance Course are assessed to diagnose individual leadership–management behavior, provide personalized feedback to the individual, and direct individuals to prescribed skill training. The program lasts 3 days.

7. *Army Recruiter Selection Program (1980–continuing):* The army has developed, but has not put into use, a 2-day assessment center to identify prospective recruiters. Dimensions include prospecting activities (identifying and contacting qualified prospects), publicizing the army

(building a positive army image in the community), selling the army, and administrative activities. Exercises include cold calls, prepared interviews, interview with a wary parent, in-basket, 4- to 5-min speech about the army, and a structured interview. A composite of assessment ratings yielded corrected validities of .50 in a pretest of the methodology (Borman, 1981).

8. *Army Lt. Selection Program (1980–continuing):* In 1980, the army developed an assessment center procedure for determining likely candidates for the officer corps. The program was designed to aid ROTC and OCS selection decisions. Reliability and validity studies were conducted but the results were not in by September 1981. Initial student reaction was extremely positive.

Police and fire management. Probably the fastest growing use of assessment centers outside of traditional uses is for the selection of sergeants, lieutenants, captains, and chiefs in police and fire departments. At least 65 municipalities and state agencies have made use of assessment centers for this purpose (Quaintance, 1980). The New York City Police Department was very active in applying assessment center methodology for selection of captains and higher officers for a period of years but, due to budget problems, the promotional opportunities within the police department diminished and the assessment center program was dissolved.

One of the greatest commitments to management assessment is by the Federal Bureau of Investigation. In their relatively flat organization structure, the first two promotional decisions are based largely on assessment center data.

The Royal Canadian National Mounted Police uses assessment centers as part of the selection process for first-level supervisory positions (inspectors).

Even chiefs of police have been selected by means of assessment center methodology. Very small cities, such as the City of Sewickley, Pennsylvania, and larger cities such as Jersey City, New Jersey, have used the methodology.

Although a few municipalities have done a good job in installing assessment centers, many have done quite a poor job as illustrated by several court cases dealing with this use of assessment center data in police and fire departments (Byham, 1979b). The City of Omaha's use of assessment centers for the selection of deputy police chiefs and the City of Richmond's use of assessment centers to select fire and police lieutenants was upheld by courts. However, the use of assessment center technology for the selection of fire captains by the City of St. Louis was overturned partly because of inappropriate assessment center exercises. An assessment center developed for the City of Evanston's police department was overturned because of inadequacies in the job analysis. Two other cities have had their assessment centers as the subject of court cases (City of Athens, Georgia, and the City of Flint, Michigan). The cases were decided against the cities on grounds other than the assessment center per se and no ruling regarding the validity of assessment centers was made.

All this court activity indicates that the assessment center is being used and is being closely looked at by EEOC and other organizations concerned with civil rights issues. The agencies and courts that are telling municipalities to use assessment centers because content validity can be established and because of its history of racial and sexual fairness are the very agencies and courts that are checking to see if the assessment center is properly designed and run. The City of Omaha's case indicates that if appropriate planning and administration is put into the assessment center, it can be accepted as appropriate and legal. However, if the assessment center design or administration is left to chance or done haphazardly, as in the other cases, it will not be upheld. These and other cases are discussed in more depth in the next chapter.

It appears that many municipalities have, in their frustration, turned to the assessment center as some kind of panacea, not realizing the commitment of time and effort needed to organize and implement a proper program. Many of the city-operated assessment centers that we have observed would fail to meet both the EEOC standards and the most minimal standards of professional competency. There seems to be a much higher rate of poor assessment centers being conducted by cities than by any other employer group.

Conclusion

The purpose of this chapter was not to provide a comprehensive listing of all unusual assessment center applications, but rather to illustrate the flexibility and adaptability of the methodology. Some of the centers described are just applications of the same old technique applied to a new group of managers (e.g., principals, police captains). Others employ significant new ideas such as self-assessment and the use of videotape to capture assessee behavior. The extension of these techniques back into the industrial selection of managers is already taking place.

One concern must be underlined. Of all the court cases dealing with the utilization of assessment centers, 90% have involved the selection of police and fire-fighting employees. All of the negative findings have been in these areas. Even granting a history of litigiousness in these jobs, there still seems to be something wrong. We believe many cities and states are not taking the methodology seriously. They are not spending the money necessary to install and run an assessment center correctly. Instead they are spending much larger sums of money on lawyers in trying to defend selection decisions after the fact.

Individuals and organizations considering the extension of assessment centers to other jobs and settings should attend to the lesson being learned in police and fire departments. Proper steps must be taken to ensure the accuracy of the assessment center method with each new application. In part this requires adequate job analyses, careful selection of relevant dimensions, the development of job-related exercises, adequate assessor training, and constant monitoring of the administration of the program.

10
Assessment Centers
and the Courts

In today's world, personnel administration and personnel practices must face the close scrutiny of administrative, quasi-legal, and judiciary systems. Personnel decision making, in general, and decisions about selection, promotion, and assignment to training programs, in particular, must meet various standards and guidelines of equal employment opportunity compliance agencies. Suits brought by individual parties and the Equal Employment Opportunity Commission have been heard in various levels of state and federal courts. Both statutory (Civil Rights Acts) and Constitutional issues have been raised. The United States Supreme Court has rendered several decisions regarding the use of tests and other personnel evaluation techniques in personnel decisions. Abstracts of these cases are readily accessible in several excellent sources (Byham, 1980; Horstman, 1977; Psychological Corporation, 1978; United States Office of Personnel Management, 1979).

The results of these cases are clear in many regards. If adverse impact[1] is present, the organization must show that it followed the *Uniform Guidelines* (Task Force, 1980) in the development, validation, and use of decision-making procedures. The organization must be able to provide documented evidence that substantiates the validity and fairness of the

---

[1] Adverse impact is defined in the *Uniform Guidelines* (EEOC et al., 1978) as "A selection rate for a race, sex, or ethnic group which is less than four-fifths (4/5) (or 80 percent) of the rate for the group with the higest rate . . . [Section 3D]."

procedures being used. Such evidence must demonstrate the use of professionally sound practices including adequate job analyses, criterion measures, samples of subjects, statistical analyses, and conditions for gathering research data. On the positive side, the courts have affirmed repeatedly that properly validated tests can aid in the effective utilization of human resources and organizations have the right to use those tests. Numerous examples of acceptable testing programs have been observed. Many testing programs have been scrutinized and found acceptable by compliance agencies; furthermore, they constitute an integral part of many affirmative action programs.

There can be little question that the federal government has become a powerful force in matters of testing in industry. Symposia at recent conventions of the American Psychological Association, the Academy of Management, the American Society of Personnel Administration, and other personnel administration associations have explored the government's impact on personnel practices and the profession of industrial psychology.

The use of the assessment center methodology is covered by the testing guidelines and has been the subject of administrative and judicial review. How have assessment centers fared? Quite well (Byham, 1980). Although such matters are in flux at the time of this writing, what evidence there is clearly indicates that assessment centers will be defensible to compliance agencies and the courts. Several lines of thinking lead to this conclusion. The research evidence clearly supports the predictive and concurrent validity and the fairness of assessment centers. Assessment centers can be validated using straightforward, easy-to-understand job analysis procedures. No industrial assessment center application has ever been found illegal and there are very few court cases (Byham, 1979b). In EEOC and court cases involving alleged discrimination from the use of tests and other promotion practices, the assessment center has been accepted as an alternative method of screening. In addition, the EEOC itself has used an assessment center as one part of a reorganization program in the agency.

In the remainder of this chapter we describe types of evidence supporting the validity and fairness of the method. However, a warning is in order. Past research and experience with assessment centers does not ensure that all future applications will be valid and fair. In each new program the user must consider very carefully the appropriateness of an assessment center, conduct a thorough job analysis, design and implement the right type of program, and investigate its predictive or concurrent validity where feasible. A lot is known about assessment centers, but that knowledge must be applied carefully to new settings.

Research Support

The large volume of assessment center research provides a firm basis for defense of a well-designed and well-run assessment center. Each organization must conduct its own research to answer unique questions, but it can also take direction from previous research findings if the job and assessment activities are comparable. While not all questions have been answered, many of the major issues involved in employment discrimination cases have been addressed by assessment center research.

Little adverse impact. Data relevant to adverse impact are difficult to interpret. According to the *Uniform Guidelines* (EEOC *et al.,* 1978), adverse impact exists when a selection procedure leads to the rejection of significantly more minorities or women than majorities or men. More specifically, "A selection rate for any race, sex, or ethnic group which is less than four-fifths (4/5) (or 80 percent) of the rate for the group with the highest rate will generally be regarded as evidence of adverse impact [Section 3D]." For example, if 50 of 100 white applicants are selected, then at least 40 of 100 black applicants (80% of 50) must be selected or adverse impact exists.

For these comparisons to be meaningful, though, the two groups must be comparable. For a variety of reasons, the groups may not be comparable. Real differences in managerial skills may be present at the time of assessment. Because of education or experience differences, one group may not possess the assessed dimensions and this fact might be revealed by the assessment center procedure. The organization might need to respond by dealing with these differences rather than by discontinuing the use of the assessment center.

Adverse impact statistics can be manipulated if an organization wishes to do so. For example, evidence for no adverse impact could be created by nominating only the best blacks to be assessed along with average whites, of whom some will do well and some will do poorly.

Alternatively, the numbers may look "bad" when the organization is, in fact, advancing the employment opportunities for minorities by assessing larger numbers and a wider range of talent. Consider an instance in which 75% of the whites but only 50% of the blacks are recommended for promotion to first-level supervision. This may have resulted from an affirmative action effort to seek high potential black candidates among individuals with less experience and maturity. The problem can become further complicated when an organization allows self-nominations. Many unqualified blacks may opt to be assessed and then do poorly in the program.

The *Uniform Guidelines* make provision for conflicts in adverse impact and affirmative action goals. Section 4E states that "the general posture" of the organization with respect to equal employment opportunity will be considered. Selection programs can consider the race, color, sex, or ethnic origin of candidates and also the ability to do the work. From this can be inferred that adverse impact statistics will be considered in the context of the organization's overall equal opportunity efforts.

Data on the adverse impact resulting from assessment centers are mixed. Some studies (Clingenpeel, 1979; Huck & Bray, 1976; Jaffee *et al.*, 1972; Moses, 1973b; Russell & Byham, 1980) have found a statistically significant difference in dimension ratings or the overall assessment rating between blacks and whites. Other studies (Alexander, 1975; Byham, 1981a; Hall, 1976; Moses & Boehm, 1975; Russell, 1975) found no differences or results which favored blacks (Marquardt, 1976). Byham (1981a) found no differences in dimension ratings for individual exercises or for the consensus ratings across exercises for males or females or for whites, blacks, or Hispanic assessees in a program for high-level administrators in a government agency.

Byham (1981b), who researched all published studies and a number of unpublished studies, notes that about 50% of the studies involving assessment centers for the selection of first-level supervisors have found adverse impact against blacks. Only one study involving middle- and top-level managers reported adverse impact. Women generally do as well as (or better than) men in most studies.

The assessment center findings are supported by research on other types of work sample tests. Schmidt, Greenthal, Hunter, Berner, and Seaton (1977) found less adverse impact from a peformance test of metal trades skill than from a written test. Brugnoli, Campion, and Basen (1979) found no race-linked bias on a behavioral evaluation of performance on a maintenance mechanic's task, although a global rating of performance was significantly lower for blacks. Similar bias on a global rating of performance of a grocery store stocking task had been found by Hamner, Kim, Baird, and Bigoness (1974). The Brugnoli study shows again the importance of insisting on behavioral observation and ratings.

Job analysis. If an organization must defend the use of its assessment center, the job analysis procedures will be examined. This has been a real strength of most assessment center installations. Reports of the better assessment center programs emphasize that extensive job analyses were done to determine the tasks, responsibilities, and skills necessary for successful performance in the positions. Usually the critical incident method, interviews, and observations are used. Incumbents, supervisors of incumbents, and higher level managers are typically involved. Neidig *et al.* (1977) illustrated such a procedure for managers and Neidig (1977) reported high levels of reliability and convergent and discriminant validity using a multimethod–multievaluation approach to job analysis.

Criterion validity. The amount of validity data for assessment centers is impressive. Every major review of the literature (Byham, 1970; Cohen *et al.,* 1974; Dunnette, 1971; Finkle, 1976; Howard, 1974; Huck, 1973a; Norton, 1977) has concluded that assessment centers accurately predict management performance and progress. The numerous studies reviewed in Chapter 7 substantiate that the OAR is predictive of various criterion measures for diverse samples of managers. Organizations setting up an assessment center face a difficult decision. Should they attempt to conduct a criterion-related validity study or should they rely on results from other companies? A satisfactory study is difficult to do: It requires an adequate criterion, large samples, the chance to observe performance of subjects some time after assessment, and the organizational conditions (e.g., a stable job) in which the research is likely to yield unambiguous results. Each organization must consider very carefully whether a criterion-related validity study is feasible before undertaking such a project. Advice in the Division of Industrial/Organizational Psychology (Division 14, 1980) *Principles for Validiation and Use of Personnel Selection Procedures* should be heeded: "Anyone contemplating a criterion-related validity study must first determine whether such a study is feasible. It is not always possible to conduct a well-designed or even reasonably competent study and a poor study is *not* better than none [p. 5]."

Many organizations find that a criterion study is not feasible and opt for the other legitimate strategy—content validation.

Content validity. Although less quantifiable, the content-validity evidence is also impressive. The first question to confront here is whether content validation is an appropriate strategy for validating assessment centers. Content validity is the degree to which test performance is an adequate sample of performance in a broader universe of situations that the test is intended to represent. For employment testing, content validity is composed of evidence, some judgmental and some statistical, demonstrating that the test procedure is representative of an operationally defined job domain and that test responses are a representative sample of responses required for effective job performance. The content-validation process for a paper-and-pencil test requires:

1. A careful definition of important domains from the job universe
2. A clear description of the testing situation including instructions, stimuli conditions, and the tasks presented to the respondent

3. Specification of the responses to be counted or features of the test product to be evaluated
4. Agreement among qualified judges that test stimulus material and test responses are representative samples of the job domain
5. Demonstration that test responses or products can be rated with adequate interjudge agreement

Requirements for establishing the content validity of an assessment center differ somewhat from those of a paper-and-pencil test, although they parallel the major concepts. Such a process requires:

1. A description of the job
2. A description of how the job analysis samples were drawn (how many people were involved in the job analysis and how they were chosen)
3. Most common and important behaviors obtained from each portion of the job analysis
4. Examples of behaviors classified under each dimension (a dimension is a description under which behavior can be reliably classified and thus the task of a job analysis is to show how all the important behaviors associated with the job can be clustered under dimensional titles by the job analyst—the reliability of the process should also be noted)
5. Statistical evidence derived from ratings or rankings of the dimensions by job-content experts
6. Results of studies showing the most common job activities
7. A table showing how the common job activities have been translated into assessment center exercises and how assessment center exercises account for a large proportion of the total job activities
8. A table showing the coverage of dimensions by the exercises; the table should illustrate that all dimensions will be observed and that the most important dimensions could be observed several times
9. A report on efforts to continually monitor assessor reliability of classification of observed behavior by target dimensions

In two major addresses before the Fifth (1977) International Congress on the Assessment Center Method, William A. Gorham of the U.S. Civil Service Commission and James O. Taylor, Jr., of the Equal Employment Opportunity Commission discussed how the testing guidelines relate to content validation of assessment centers. Gorham (1978a) made the strongest statement in support of the assessment center method. He stated that content validation is appropriate, legitimate, and necessary to the method and argued against doing criterion-related studies with inadequate sample sizes and criteria. He warned that content validation is not easy and noted that the user must have a thorough job analysis, behaviorally defined dimensions, extensive documentation of observations, reconstructable assessment processes, and a thoroughly trained staff.

He felt an assessment center with high professional standards is taking the right approach to measuring appropriate job behaviors. Subsequent revisions and refinements to the *Uniform Guidelines* were made and the final version was approved in August, 1978. Gorham (1978b) reaffirmed his stance at the next congress.

Taylor (1978) expressed more reservations. He maintained that although content validity is an appropriate interim step in validation, if a test is used to predict future performance, the user must accumulate predictive validity evidence for later study. With regard to assessment centers, Taylor emphasized the need to perform thorough job analyses of the job in question and to develop tests to simulate the important tasks and activities. He warned against the use of assessment devices developed for other jobs or situations. Like Gorham, he argued that thorough assessor training is essential.

At the 1979 Congress, Barrett (1979) asked several questions derived from the *Uniform Guidelines* as a method of evaluating assessment center applications. He dealt mainly with content validity issues and concerns over the administrative use of assessment centers. For the most part, he expressed confidence in the method to provide answers to the essential questions. For example, he stated that content validation is an appropriate strategy for assessment centers when applicants are expected to bring well-developed management skills to the positions they might be assuming. Job analysis efforts in assessment centers have appropriately focused on behaviors rather than traits.

Barrett felt there is more need to establish the relationship of assessment center activities to job descriptions. Another area of needed documentation is the reliability of behavior in different situations. In other words, even though we know that interrater agreement is high, we need to know more about the stability of people's behavior in different assessment and job activities.

According to Barrett, the assessment center method adequately meets several other psychometric standards. Behavior responses are observable; responses illustrative of high, medium, and low performance on dimensions can be specified; assessment behavior is likely to be reflective of real behavior; the reliability of ratings on dimensions is adequate. In some other testing areas, Barrett urged more caution. He warned that exercises should not be made unnecessarily difficult and we must ensure that the test taker perceives the question as it was intended. Where cutoff scores are used, there must be a clear rationale.

Barrett (1979) warned that even the most proven procedure must be applied adequately in conjunction with other selection procedures. He implied that when used as a part of a multiple measurement system, the assessment center can make a valuable contribution to personnel management.

Although the *Uniform Guidelines* clearly state that content validation is a legitimate approach for employment tests, although experts agree that it is appropriate for validating assessment centers, and although the preponderance of research evidence suggests that well-designed assessment centers possess content validity, it does not necessarily follow that content validity evidence will stand up in a court suit over an assessment center. Kleiman and Faley (1978) reviewed 31 cases involving content validity issues and concluded that courts fail to consistently apply professional standards for validating personnel selection procedures. Some judges consider little more than the rational relationship of the test and job. Other judges look for evidence (usually only judgmental) that the test and job domains overlap. The most sophisticated judges require job analysis information, careful test construction procedures, and some psychometric information (e.g., item discrimination and difficulty level).

Despite the lack of consistent standards used by the courts and the lack of direction given for what job analysis and validation evidence to present, Kleiman and Faley (1978) believe that content-validated tests can be defended in court and they advise that "an employer should make every effort to follow professionally developed standards [p. 711]."

Our earlier warning must be repeated: Not all assessment centers are valid. But, in Chapter 5 it was shown that there is a close correspondence between the dimensions observable in assessment centers and the behavioral dimensions of management. Assessors are able to make highly reliable ratings of performance on many dimensions. Our conclusion at this point is that the preponderance of well-designed assessment centers measures a broad sample of managerial behaviors. With adequate documentation, we believe the content validity of assessment centers can be defended.

Construct validity. Assessment center users have not attempted to use construct-validation approaches. The reasons for this avoidance are clear: (a) behavior observation and reporting have been stressed; (b) the assessors are usually managers, not psychologists; and (c) except for the Management Progress Study, the goals of assessment have been quite practical: diagnosis of training needs and prediction of success. More construct validity research is needed to enhance our understanding of the personal constructs (traits, attributes, etc.) which underlie assessment center performance, but such studies are not needed to defend assessment centers for personnel decision making.

No differential validity. From the existing research it appears that assessment centers are equally valid for blacks and whites (Moses, 1973b; Marquardt, 1976), men and women (Huck & Bray, 1976; Moses, 1973b; Moses & Boehm, 1975: Marquardt, 1976), and older and younger candidates (Hall, 1976; Neidig et al., 1978). See a discussion of this research in the methodological critique of validation research in Chapter 7.

Administrative consistency. A selection procedure must be administered in a fair and consistent manner or it may not attain the reliability and validity it has demonstrated under research conditions.

For this reason, there has been much emphasis on ensuring standardized practice among the programs in an organization. Several presentations at the 1978 and 1981 International Congresses on the Assessment Center Method dealt with issues of standardization and quality assurance (Cohen, 1978; Hoyle, 1978; Russell, 1981; Morrison, 1981; Rosenow, 1981). Byham (1978) outlined a number of steps for performing an audit of an organization's assessment center procedure.

Some parameters of assessment center operation have been investigated. Cohen and Sands (1978) found that the order in which participants went through five assessment exercises (in-basket, two leaderless group discussions, problem analysis–presentation, and a leadership problem in which the assessee is assigned two role players to guide) did not affect nine dimension ratings, five exercise ratings, or an overall rating of managerial skill.

Jaffee and Michaels (1978) found that college students coached in how to handle an in-basket by peers who had already completed an in-basket did no better than an uncoached group. The subjects were similar to college graduates who might be candidates in a management selection program. The authors concluded that "the effects of coaching that cannot be controlled in an assessment center process would be expected to have minimal influence on the overall validity of the decisions made at the center [p. 17]."

Russell and Byham (1980) showed that the order in which assessees are discussed by the assessors is not important. Some people had felt that assessors might become more lenient or more tough as they develop their own group standards and group cohesiveness, but no evidence of any change was found. In addition, they found high reliabilities among almost all of the assessors studied and found no significant relationships between dimension ratings and either the sex and race of assessors or the sex and race of assessees. An equally important finding was that assessee ratings were no different for the two administrators who conducted approximately equal numbers of assessment center programs in this installation.

Ilgen, Campbell, and Peters (1976) found some evidence that assessee's perceptions of the importance of dimensions in exercises were related to the assessment center ratings they received in the program. One hundred twenty-seven assessees were asked to rate the importance of eight dimensions after they had completed the exercises. Three clusters of people were identified on the basis of these importance ratings. The first group placed high emphasis on Decisiveness and Initiative (but *low* importance on Interpersonal Relations) in the in-basket. By contrast, in the group exercises they placed high emphasis on Interpersonal Relations and Planning–Organizing (but *low* emphasis on Initiative). This group was rated lower by the assessors on three of eight dimensions: Initiative, Planning–Organizing, and Leadership. Ilgen *et al.* (1976) concluded that "Performance ratings alone are not capable of assessing whether the individual lacks the skills in question, is unable to recognize the skills being called for in a given setting, or both [p. 5]."

The results must be interpreted cautiously. They do not prove that performance ratings are more a function of assessee understanding than skill, because the assessor ratings are not always the lowest on the dimensions rated unimportant. Furthermore assuming that participants have some self-insights into how well they did on the exercise, the low importance rating may have been a self-protective mechanism resulting from poor performance on the exercise.

For selection purposes (when the candidate must bring well-developed skills to the job) it is unimportant whether the candidate lacks the ability to discern what skills are necessary or how to apply them. Quite properly, Ilgen *et al.* (1976) focused attention on the implications of the study for developmental feedback and planning. For example, it may be important to know that an individual does not perceive that interpersonal relations are important in the memos he or she writes in response to the items in the in-basket.

The study also implied that all assessees should be given a list of dimensions to be assessed in the program and clear instructions for each exercise. The program description and orientation should eliminate any gross differences in the participants' perceptions of assessment center requirements.

Another administrative concern is the matching of assessors and assessees. It is standard practice to assemble a mixture of assessors from different aeas of the organzation and to avoid assigning an assessor to someone from his or her department or division. Neidig *et al.* (1978) investigated other assessor-related issues and found that amount or recentness of assessor experience or whether or not the assessor was from the headquarters or field staff did not affect ratings. More importantly, Neidig & Martin (1979) and the preponderance of research (e.g., Sackett & Hackel, 1979) show high levels of interrater reliability on dimension ratings. Therefore, it does not appear that any individual participant will be penalized by "easy" or "hard" raters.

AT&T CONSENT DECREE

Another support for assessment centers comes from the AT&T consent decree. In 1973 AT&T entered into a massive agreement with the Department of Labor (Landmark Agreement, 1973) to make special payments to certain women hired during the period July 1963–December 1971 and to give them special opportunities to participate in management development programs. Of particular significance was the provision in the agreement that AT&T could use the assessment center method to identify among the affected women those who were most likely to have the potential for middle management success (Landmark AT&T-EEOC Consent Agreement). Thus a special assessment center program was designed and set in operation in three regional locations. During 15 months ending August 1974, 1634 management women were assessed (Hoyle, 1975; Boehm & Hoyle, 1977). The assessment results along with other information were used in a thorough career planning program. The assessment center results played an integral role in the program and participants recommended as having potential for third-level management are monitored by the program coordinator until they have advanced to this level.

Court Cases

Another line of evidence supporting the assessment center comes from actual court decisions. All court cases dealing with assessment centers have been reviewed by Byham (1980). In some cases, alleged discrimination from use of the assessment centers was reviewed by the court. In others, the court approved the use of an assessment center as a means of alleviating discrimination from past practices. The more important cases will be discussed here.

City of Omaha Police Department.[2] In *Berry* v. *City of Omaha* (Mendenhall, 1976) unsuccessful candidates for the position of Deputy Police

[2]*Berry, B., Stokes, E. L., and Laut, K. E. Plaintiffs v the City of Omaha and Wervel.* L.H. No. 31 (Doc. 695). November 1975, District Court of Douglas County, Nebraska.

Chief charged that the assessment center method was not properly conducted and was unfair.

This case is particularly important because it was the first time the assessment center method had been challenged in court. The suit raised several questions about assessor competency and the administration of the program and was decided on the basis of these issues. The case is also important because the judge relied heavily on testimony from expert witnesses and on the *Standards of Ethical Considerations for Assessment Center Operations* (Task Force, 1975). (The current revision of the *Standards* is summarized later in this chapter.)

The suit dealt with several issues (Mendenhall, 1977) regarding the standardization and fairness of the assessment center:

1. Whether the training of the assessors was adequate
2. Whether the number of exercises used (namely, leaderless group discussion, in-basket, and background interview) was adequate
3. Whether different volunteers should have been used as practice subjects in each of the three assessor training programs
4. Whether assessors who knew some candidates should have been used
5. Whether the fact that several days elapsed between the administration of the in-basket and the in-basket interview affected the final results
6. Whether the fact that some assessors had prior assessment experience affected the final results

A major issue was the standards held by the assessors. The plaintiff charged that the three assessor groups had different standards and, thus, some individuals were evaluated against higher standards than others. The possible causes of potential subjectivity were narrowed down to assessor training and assessment center administration. Other things that could have contributed, such as poor job analysis and inappropriate exercises, were not contested. The City of Omaha's practices were reviewed and a determination of reliability of the assessors was made. Written data, including the in-basket, assessor reports on the group exercise, and notes from the background interview, were evaluated by an independent group of trained assessors who were not familiar with the final results of the Omaha assessors. Ten of the top 15 finalists (four from the first assessment session, three from the second session, and three from the third session) were evaluated and rank ordered by the independent judges. A comparison of the Omaha ranking and the subsequent independent ranking showed a very high agreement: the Spearman rank-order correlation was

.84 and the top four candidates were the same on both lists. The results showed high reliability among the Omaha and outside assessor groups and also suggested that the three groups of Omaha assessors had a high level of reliability among themselves. After hearing expert witnesses for both sides and city personnel, the judge ruled that the assessment center met adequate standards for assessment center development and administration.

The case illustrates the importance of systematic development and documentation of the assessment center process. Members of the city personnel department were able to refer to reports of job analysis, assessor training, and assessment center procedures and results. The case also illustrates the benefits which can be derived from a concise set of guidelines for the court judgment.

Richmond Police and Fire Departments.[3, 4] A combination of paper-and-pencil tests of job knowledge and an assessment center to measure managerial skills was approved for the promotional examination for supervisory positions in the City of Richmond, Virginia. The cases began in 1975 when the court found that the paper-and-pencil tests used in the civil service examinations for police sergeant, lieutenant, captain, and major were discriminatory. The court approved the city's plan to use a combination of tests and assessment centers.

These procedures were instituted in the police and fire departments and challenged as discriminatory in a subsequent suit by fire-fighters. Table 10.1 presents the statistics for the sequence of promotion examinations and decisions. Using the 80% rule of thumb, the court found that there was no adverse impact in deciding who was eligible to be examined, who was certified by the assessment program, and who was actually promoted to lieutenant. The pass rate on the written examination was substantially lower for the blacks than the whites but the court considered that it was the entire selection procedure, not any part of it, that must be examined under the law.

Therefore, the entire system had no racial bias. The court ruled that the city could continue to use the combination of paper-and-pencil tests and the assessment center procedure.

[3] *The Richmond Black Police Officers' Association* et al. v. *the City of Richmond* et al.; Civil Action No. 74-0267, U.S. District Court for the Eastern District of Virginia (Richmond Division), September 22, 1975.

[4] *Roscoe Friend* et al. v. *William Leidinger* et al. (City of Richmond). Civil Action No. 74-0327, U.S. District Court, Eastern District of Virginia (Richmond Division) October 3, 1977; May 1, 1978.

Table 10.1
Adverse Impact Statistics in City of Richmond Case

	Number	Percent	Percentage comparison of black and white rates
Firefighters			
White	347		
Black	134		
Took the written test			
White	209	60.2	
Black	67	50.0	81.3
Passed the written test			
White	75	35.9	
Black	14	20.9	58.2
Certified after assessment			
White	16	21.3	
Black	3	21.4	100
Promoted			
White	11	68.8	(ratio in favor of
Black	3	100.0	blacks)
Promotions compared to number examined			
White	11 of 209	5.3	
Black	3 of 67	4.5	84.9

The court reviewed revisions of the procedure in 1978 and again ruled that the city could proceed with further assessment centers and written tests for promotions to the supervisory positions. A significant revision was the use of behavioral scientists from local universities instead of trained city personnel as assessors. Over 200 candidates were assessed in 35 programs over a two-month period (Purdy, 1979a & 1979b).

Michigan Civil Service Commission.[5] The use of an assessment center was also contested in a case involving promotions to Captain of the Michigan Department of State Police. Michigan law states that promotions must be based on a consideration of merit (length and quality of service), efficiency (effective performance of tasks and positions), and fitness (ability to fulfill physical and skill requirements). Since the assessment center dealt only with the management skills (i.e., fitness) and the promotion procedure did not consider merit or efficiency, the court ruled that the promotion list was not compiled in compliance with Michigan

[5]*Richie Davis* v. *Michigan Civil Service Commission.* Circuit Court for Ingham County, June 16, 1978, File No. 78-21743-AZ.

law. The judge declared it unnecessary to rule on other matters (e.g., the appropriateness of the assessment center).

The case illustrates the importance of developing a total personnel selection system. No matter how effective one component is, the entire system must be well integrated or it may be struck down. The case is also instructive because of the arguments presented against the assessment center method. Although the judge did not decide the case based on this testimony, the comments of the expert witness show potential points of weakness and some misconceptions about the method. The witness was correct in stating that high face validity of the assessment center does not ensure actual validity but was wrong in his claim that there are no studies comparing the predictive validity of assessment centers and written or oral examinations. (In Chapters 5 and 7 this literature is reviewed.) The witness correctly warned that generalization from prior validity research is difficult, but it seems too restrictive to state "Even if there were good evidence of comparable validity of assessment centers and examinations, one could *not* infer *anything* about the validity of a *given* assessment program in a *given* setting [p. 5]." The *Uniform Guidelines* clearly make provisions for validity generalization based on appropriate comparisons of job analysis and testing procedures.

Of more interest are the types of criticisms made against the assessment center procedures themselves. Although adequate counterarguments can be made to many points, the criticisms are offered for the insights they provide. The job analysis was criticized because it did not document the process of extracting dimensions from job information (the reason why the final dimensions were chosen in contrast to other dimensions) or the linkage of job duties to assessment exercises. The exercises were seen as unrealistic (e.g., it is unreasonable to allocate a $10 million budget in 1.5 hours). The witness questioned the comparability of the exercises because of differences in assessee groups. Subjectivity of scoring and differences in assessor teams were also questioned.

The most serious concerns in the testimony were indications of shifting standards for assessment over time and uncontrolled differences in the harshness of some raters. A continual increase in the average overall assessment rating was noted over six assessment centers spanning a 5-month period. In addition, the three raters who assessed the plaintiff in the case tended to give significantly lower ratings than the other eleven raters. These problems point up the importance of maintaining adequate quality control over an ongoing assessment program. Procedures for dealing with assessor differences have been addressed by Neidig and Hall (1977). The expert witness concluded that the assessment procedure was not accurate for the plaintiff in this case.

St. Louis Fire Department.[6] In a series of court cases dealing with the promotion practices for Captains in the St. Louis Fire Department, the need to take a "systems approach" to making selection decisions was made clear. The first case in the series dealt with the validity of written job knowledge tests for promotional procedures. The circuit court ruled that the written job knowledge tests did not adequately cover the job requirements and recommended consideration of an assessment center. It was noted that the Kansas City Fire Department was using assessment centers for selection of fire captains and that St. Louis has used the methodology for the selection of deputy fire chief.

The city then developed and administered an assessment center and job knowledge test and used the combined score to determine a promotion list. The test and the assessment center were challenged and after having been upheld by a district court, were struck down by the circuit court. Basically, the judge found that the assessment center portion of the selection procedure was adequate (with some definite problems) but found that the written portion of the examination did not meet EEOC guidelines. Most importantly, the combination of the two did not meet EEOC guidelines. The case has been appealed to the United States Supreme Court (Byham, 1980).

This case is important because it shows that a selection procedure must cover all parts of the job (as defined as important by a job analysis) and that all parts of the selection system must meet EEO guidelines.

Another important aspect of the case involved the response modality of one of the assessment center exercises. The city showed the applicants slides of a developing building fire and asked them to write out "orders." Because orders would normally have been shouted orally, the judge felt the exercise was inappropriate.

Other cases. In several cases of alleged discrimination from paper-and-pencil tests, the assessment center method has been suggested as a more appropriate means of evaluating candidates for promotion. In some cases the parties agreed to implement assessment centers, in others the court has mandated their use.

In a series of cases[7] in the City of New York, the examination pro-

---

[6]*U.S.* v. *City of St. Louis.* U.S. District Court, Eastern District of Missouri, nos. 74-2006(4) and 74-30c(4), April 9, 1976.
Firefighters Institute for Racial Equality v. *City of St. Louis.* U.S. Court of Appeals, Eight Circuit, nos. 76-1507, 76-1663, February 2, 1977.

[7]*Chance* v. *Board of Examiners.* U.S. District Court, Southern District of New York, July 14, 1971, Index No. 70, Div. 4141.
Chance v. *Board of Examiners.* U.S. Court of Appeals, Second Circuit (New York), April 5, 1972 No. 458 F2d 1167; June 1, 1972; August, 1977.

cedures for selecting supervisors in the public schools have been challenged. Starting in 1971, the court found that the existing tests examined only a portion of the relevant duties of school supervisors and had a disproportionate impact on minority groups. It issued an injunction against using the tests to form eligibility lists for promotion. In 1972 the New York Court of Appeals approved the use of an assessment center to examine supervisory personnel. An examination having many of the characteristics of an assessment center (although not an actual assessment center) was completed in 1981.

In *James* v *Stockham Valves and Fittings*[8] the broad personnel practices of a company were challenged as racially discriminatory. The trial court and circuit court concluded that the general practices were racially neutral but that underrepresentation of blacks in supervisory positions and subjective appraisal systems may indicate discriminatory practices. Under court direction to set up new supervisory selection and development programs, the company decided to implement and evaluate an assessment center along with other affirmative action programs.

In a suit[9] over underrepresentation of blacks in management positions in the police department, the City of Evanston agreed to use an assessment center for future examinations. An assessment center was set up but, when it was challenged, the results were thrown out because of a faulty job analysis. The city tried again and followed a much more comprehensive job analysis and assessment center approach.

A final case to be mentioned involves selection and promotion of patrol officers in the City of Chicago Police Department.[10] The court enjoined the use of nonvalidated tests for selection and the city developed and validated an assessment center for patrol officers. The court will not rule on the acceptability of the center until the validity results are submitted.

Assessment Centers in the EEOC

One final bit of evidence suggesting the stature of the assessment center method comes from the recent adoption of the method by the EEOC itself. The agency used an assessment center as part of a complete

[8]*James* v. *Stockham Valves & Fittings.* Case No. 75-2176, Fifth Circuit Court of Appeals, September 19, 1977.
[9]*James C. Edwards* et al. v. *City of Evanston* et al. Civil Action No. 74C2686, August 25, 1975.
[10]*U.S.* v. *City of Chicago.* U.S. District Court, Northern District of Illinois, January 5, 1976.

reorganization of its middle-level administrative positions (Rogers, 1979).

In 1977 Eleanor Holmes Norton, chairperson of the EEOC, launched a reorganization of the structure and operation of the agency in order to improve several functions. Three model offices were set up to test the new processes, and assessment centers were developed to help select executives for the top three levels of these offices: district director, deputy district director, and regional attorney. Nontraditional job analyses were used because the positions did not already exist. Therefore, modified group interview and critical incident methods were used. Several common dimensions for government executives were identified plus others which emphasized unique concerns (e.g., Sensitivity to EEO Principles, Oral Fact Finding, and Organizational Sensitivity).

After an evaluation of the success of the pilot offices and of the procedures used to staff them, the EEOC decided to convert all offices to the new organizational configuration and to fill the top post in each office using a selection system in which an assessment center was a key ingredient (Rogers, 1979). The important thing to note about the EEOC's assessment center application is its "systems approach" to selection. Each part of the selection system was built around the job-related dimensions identified in the job analysis. Special pains were taken in developing screening procedures. These included a screening process that used multiple judges and dimensionally oriented, supplemental applicant information forms. Reference checks and interviews that were built around the target dimensions supplemented the assessment center findings. Assessors in the assessment center were specialists in applying the assessment center method.

Assessment Center Standards

After reviewing many court cases on judicial decisions regarding test validation, Kleiman and Faley (1978) concluded:

> The failure of the courts to act consistently or uniformly can be traced, in part, to the psychologist's failure to develop specific and unambiguous guidelines on many of the issues involved in the establishment of content validity . . . the importance of these standards must be communicated to the courts [p. 711].

An illustration of the payoff from such efforts came in *Berry v City of Omaha*. Standards for assessment centers were available, were supported by the expert witnesses for both sides, and were given great weight in the judge's decision.

In this section we summarize the major principles incorporated in the 1978 revision of *Standards and Ethical Considerations for Assessment Center Operations.* The purpose of the document is to establish minimum professional standards for assessment centers and to aid future application, but not to prescribe specific practices or techniques.

A key section deals with the definition of what an assessment center *is* and what it *is not.* To be considered an assessment center by the *Standards,* the approach must include the following elements: multiple assessment techniques including one job-related simulation exercise, multiple assessors who receive training, pooled judgments from multiple assessors and techniques, a separation in time of the behavioral observation and overall evaluation, dimensions of performance identified by job analysis, and exercises designed to provide information on the dimensions. Appraisal activities which are *not* assessment centers include panel interviews, any single assessment technique, paper-and-pencil tests, individual assessment by a single person, any procedure that does not include pooled judgments, or a physical location called "an assessment center."

Assessors must receive adequate training including knowledge of the dimensions, techniques, procedures, and policies of the program, and skills to observe, record, classify, and integrate behavior observed. The length of the training may vary but some provision should be made to ensure that assessors have met stated standards for competence to function as an assessor.

The *Standards* also require that the organization have a written policy statement about participation in the program and how the information will be used. Issues of informed consent, protection of privacy, and security of records must be covered.

Although the *Standards* do not require validation by each new adopter, they warn that prior research does not guarantee validity in a new setting. Thorough documentation of the development process is stressed.

Prospects for the Future

No one has a crystal ball in the area of employment litigation, but the future is likely to be more stable than the past. After years of conflicting sets of testing guidelines and numerous drafts of joint agency regulations, the *Uniform Guidelines* were finally issued in 1978. This document will probably not be revised in the near future (Barrett, 1979) and, thus, organizations know the standards that will be used in evaluating selection procedures. The technology of content validation of employment testing is in its infancy, but the *Uniform Guidelines* consider it an appropriate strategy under certain conditions.

The revised assessment center *Standards* provide another set of guidelines for developing and defending a program. Many of the major technological questions have been researched thoroughly and proven concepts are available. Not all research questions have been answered, as the next chapter attests, but organizations have clear guidance to standard applications.

We believe it is safe to predict that a carefully developed assessment program, incorporating the principles outlined in the *Standards* and in this book, will be a valuable aid in personnel decision making and stand a good chance of being in compliance with professional practice and government guidelines for employment selection procedures.

11
Past, Present, and Future

The Past: What Has Been Learned

The experience with assessment centers over the past 25 years has increased our knowledge of management and assessment processes. Beginning with the AT&T Management Progress Study and continuing to the most recent applications in diverse jobs and organizational settings, the assessment center method has become established as a valuable research technique and a practical personnel assessment tool. Development and use of the method has advanced our understanding of the components of managerial work, the characteristics of effective assessment techniques, and the elements of an effective process of interpersonal judgment.

There is also a lesson to be learned from the high professional standards evidenced by assessment center proponents. The assessment center method has been subjected to more research and professional scrutiny than any other personnel practice. Because of high quality research and generally positive results, the development of standards for assessment center operations, and widespread self-monitoring to ensure compliance with proven practices, there are good prospects for continued validity of the method. In this section we summarize some of the lessons which have been learned.

NEED TO VIEW ASSESSMENT CENTERS AS PART OF A TOTAL SELECTION OR PROMOTION SYSTEM

The use of assessment centers has moved many organizations toward a systems approach to selection or promotion decisions. In such diverse

391

fields as space research, information processing, economics, medicine, and law enforcement, specialists have discovered that results are increased when they consider an entire system of interrelated and coordinated elements rather than deal with single elements independently. Yet few organizations have applied a "systems approach" to personnel activities. It is not uncommon to find training programs that encourage action in one direction and a compensation system that encourages action in another. Different sets of criteria are used for appraisals than are used for selection into the same job. The organization's training programs are unrelated to job requirements as defined by the performance appraisal system.

A systems approach to personnel activities offers far more effective programs at less cost to the organization. Programs that are part of a system reinforce each other—each is made better by the contribution of the others—needless overlaps or contradictions in goals or procedures are eliminated. Development and training costs are minimized because all parts of the system are built on common elements.

To be effective, a personnel system must be job related. It must be built around elements that are important to job success. In the United States a system must meet the job-relatedness (validity) requirements of the Equal Employment Opportunity Commission (EEOC) in terms of methodology and documentation.

THE ASSESSMENT CENTER IS PART OF A SYSTEM

When an assessment center is used to make promotion decisions or identify supervisory–managerial potential, the results of the assessment center are usually combined with interviews conducted by management and data obtained from performance appraisals. When used to make hiring decisions, the data from an assessment center are usually combined with information from reference checks, medical checks, and multiple interviews. In both cases, the assessment center is part of a complete decision-making system.

Many organizations failing to recognize that most selection–promotion decisions result from the effective use of a system, fail to monitor the accuracy of the system as a whole. Those organizations fail to recognize that the system is only as strong as its weakest part. An organization can have the best assessment center possible but if the procedures for selecting candidates into the assessment center are biased in some way, the system will produce biased data. This often occurs when supervisory nominations are used as the basis for selecting candidates for an assessment center program. If supervisors fail to nominate members of a protected class, the system will have an adverse impact no matter how good the assessment center is.

A more common error occurs when organizations combine precise, behaviorally documented assessment center data with quite imprecise, vague performance appraisal data or interview data in making an overall decision. Very often the dimensions for the job considered by the various sources and the rating scales are different, and the individual (or individuals) who combine the pieces of data have no training in this task and may have little understanding of one or more of the data sources.

The best way to organize a selection–promotion system is to build it around job-related dimensions. Such a system is shown in Table 3.4. Note that different parts of the system are targeted to different dimensions.

Decisions regarding the appropriate dimensions to which a system component is targeted are based on an understanding of the reliability and validity of that component. Assessment centers are effective in obtaining information on certain dimensions, background interviews on others, and performance appraisals on still others. One should note that there is considerable overlap on some dimensions. This provides a repetition of observation that allows for comparing and contrasting the various sources of information on the dimensions.

The ratings produced from each system component must be combined to first evaluate an individual relative to each dimension and ultimately to develop an overall evaluation of the individual. This final data integration can be done by an individual or a team, depending on the purposes of the selection–promotion system. A group–team approach is preferred because it promotes comparison and contrast of the behavioral information collected from each system component, it minimizes the impact of biases by forcing team members to support all decisions made with data, and it maximizes the choice of accurate decisions by combining several opinions on the data.

An ideal system is based on a set of well-defined dimensions, uses a consistent and well-defined rating scale, and is applied by trained individuals. Most assessment centers meet these criteria but often the other components of the system do not. To be effectively integrated, psychological test data or reports from clinical psychologists used to aid in the selection decision must be made consistent with the output of the assessment center. Interviewers must be trained to focus questions on dimensional areas, collect examples of past behavior (comparable to examples of observed behavior obtained in an assessment center), categorize the behavior by dimensions, and rate the dimension using the predetermined rating scale. Supervisors must be trained to categorize on-the-job behavior by the target dimension and apply the rating scale. An organization cannot have a valid (or legal) selection–promotion system until all parts of a system reach the level and accuracy of the assessment center. In each court case that has dealt with the need for a total selection system the court has found that the mere presence of one strong element, such as an assessment center, in a system does not overcome deficiencies in other elements (Byham, 1980).

DEFINITION OF MANAGEMENT JOBS

A significant contribution of the assessment center method has been the defining of management jobs in terms of clusters of observable behaviors. In contrast to task-oriented or trait-oriented approaches to managerial job analysis, assessment center dimensions are merely labels for clusters of demonstrated actions or statements. The labels for these dimensions often appear to be similar to classic management tasks (e.g., planning) or personality traits (e.g., flexibility), but assessment center dimensions are different in that they consist of behaviors identifiable on the job and in simulation exercises.

The development of an assessment center begins with a careful study of the target job. Using observation, individual interviews, group critical-incidents meetings (Flanagan, 1954), and questionnaire techniques, management jobs are scrutinized to identify the behaviors needed for successful job performance. Examples of effective and ineffective performance are examined and clusters of similar behaviors are identified. For the most part, these behavioral job analysis efforts have not been quantitative or statistical (although there is a trend in that direction). The test of the efficacy of a job dimension title and definition has been the reliability with which job analysts and assessors can use the name and definition in classifying behavior. The ultimate test has been the dimension's ability to withstand the rigors of use in an assessment center program. For example, the dimension Analysis consists of identifiable behaviors such as asking questions to seek information, comparing bits of information to determine the cause of a performance deficit, or analyzing data. These behaviors are different from behaviors that are classified under the dimension Decision Making (e.g., suggesting alternative solutions to the problems, listing costs and benefits of alternatives, and making a choice). Similar differences can be seen in the behavior subsumed under other dimensions such as Leadership, Sensitivity, and Aggressiveness.

Assessors must be able to identify relevant behaviors in the exercises, distinguish among dimensions, and reliably rate performance on the dimensions. The dimensions must relate to the overall assessment rating and be predictive of job behavior. Finally, they must also be understandable to assessees and managers who receive feedback.

A large number of dimensions have withstood these tests and have advanced our understanding of managerial performance. Byham (1981b) has described the most common dimensions. It should be emphasized that *all* dimensions are not relevant to *every* management job. Quite the contrary. The experience with assessment centers has shown that management jobs consist of different dimensions and different manifestations of dimensions depending on organizational level, function, and settings.

The assessment center experience would suggest quite strongly that the two-dimensional view of managerial or supervisory behavior is far too simple. Numerous research studies in the 1950s and current management development programs posit a task–production–initiating structure orientation versus a person–human relations–consideration orientation. Management jobs are more complex than this. Whether for selection or developmental purposes, the assessment must be done on a larger set of dimensions.

The data presented in Chapter 5 demonstrated that assessment centers, on the one hand, can provide reliable ratings on numerous dimensions describing the administrative, supervisory, decision-making, and interpersonal aspects of managerial work. On the other hand, when integrating information to form an overall assessment rating, the assessors appear to rely on only about three dimensions. These findings do not argue that management jobs consist of only three dimensions or that assessors should be asked to observe only three dimensions. The assessment of more dimensions aids in formulating a complete picture of the applicant for a job and provides diagnostic information useful for formulating an individualized training and development program.

CONSTRUCTION OF ASSESSMENT TECHNIQUES

Assessment centers are the embodiment of the behavioral consistency (Wernimont & Campbell, 1968) notion of assessment. The exercises are designed to elicit a sample of behaviors relevant to the behavioral domain of the target job in contrast to paper-and-pencil tests which are usually only signs or signals of that domain. Assessment center measurement makes the assumption that behavior demonstrated in the exercises is indicative of behavior that would be demonstrated on the job. For this assumption to hold, the exercises must be carefully constructed to simulate important aspects of the job. Herein lies the difficult task and the unique contribution of assessment center technology.

Assessment center exercises have been built to elicit behaviors relevant to dimensions in the target job and to simulate the important and time-consuming job requirements. However, exact fidelity of the exercise to the job is not advised. The exercise should simulate important job parameters, but should not consist of technical tasks or require technical information unique to a specific job which might give certain candidates undue advantage. For example, an in-basket for first-level supervisors in a city government organization should be set in a civil service setting and should include realistic problems such as business procedures, personnel problems, political pressures, dealings with the public, and limited budgets. Furthermore, it could elicit behaviors relevant to problem analysis, communications, and employee supervision. It should not be a replica of any specific job such as a personnel specialist, the librarian in charge of periodicals, or a supervisor of tax auditors. More properly, a plausible but nonexistent position could be used. For example, a hypothetical department of environmental protection could be depicted with a supervisor of full-time and part-time employees who take readings from air and water quality monitoring stations.

INTERPERSONAL JUDGMENT PROCESSES

The assessment center experience has shown that if careful, standardized, and systematic procedures are followed, highly valid predictions of managerial success can be made from observational data integrated in a judgmental manner. The level of accuracy does not come cheaply, but utility analyses demonstrate the value of this information beyond its cost (Cascio & Silbey, 1979).

The process of interpersonal judgment built into assessment center activities is complex and contains several vital ingredients. A detailed review of these assessment components is presented in Chapter 6. In summary, judgments are made by multiple, trained assessors who are familiar with both job requirements and assessment processes. Assessors are provided opportunities to observe assessees in several situations that simulate relevant aspects of the manager's job. Procedures are followed that clearly separate behavioral observation, reporting, sharing, and comparing from judgments and evaluations of the individual's effectiveness and final predictions of future performance.

The assessment model incorporated in assessment centers is applicable to numerous other situations where interpersonal judgments must be made. Improvements in performance appraisal, personnel interviewing, clinical diagnosis, assessment of educational and training needs, evaluation of professional competence, and standardized measurement of performance in complex interpersonal situations have been obtained or can be envisioned by incorporating these principles.

PROFESSIONAL SELF–MONITORING

Proponents of assessment centers have recognized the potential dangers from misuse of the process and have responded with several self-governing mechanisms. *Guidelines for the Ethical Use of Assessment Centers* were written by a group of leading assessment center researchers and practitioners, then revised and adopted in 1975 by a broader complement of professionals at the Annual International Congress on the Assessment Center Method. In 1978 the *Guidelines* were revised and approved in 1979 by an even more diverse sample of professionals.

Other examples of quality assurance are evident. Tighter controls of assessment center materials have been recommended and instituted. Provision has been made to certify assessment center programs. Assessment center "auditing" procedures have been published (Byham, 1978). Large companies such as AT&T and Westinghouse periodically review the operations of programs in divisions to ensure their compliance with corporate standards.

A sign of maturity is an ability to critically examine one's own actions. Questions and concerns about assessment centers have been raised by many of its leading proponents. A series of articles by Kraut (1972, 1973; also Boche, 1978) raised numerous questions of ethics and morality; Neidig (1978) and Hinrichs and Haanpera (1976) have published data questioning the discriminant validity and utility of assessment center ratings; and Thornton (1979) has warned that selection programs are quite different from development programs and users must be able to satisfy their different assumptions before a program can be used effectively. Many of these concerns are elaborated upon in the next section.

The surest sign of professional responsibility is the extensive research conducted on the assessment center process. As stated earlier, in our estimation, more research has been conducted on assessment centers than on any other personnel practice. The assessment center experience is an exemplary case of responsible integration of empirical research and careful professional application.

The Present: Issues Being Faced

In this section a number of issues surrounding the current use of assessment centers are examined. Research has shown that well-designed assessment centers *can* be effective but there is no assurance that every application will be appropriate. Therefore, it is important to explore the limits of research evidence, articulate the implicit assumptions of various types of assessment centers, and discuss professional and ethical issues raised by assessment center proponents and critics. In this way, current limitations can be overcome and inappropriate criticisms can be answered.

There are two characteristics of this section: It is highly critical of the limitations and potential abuses of assessment centers, and it is a highly subjective account of our concerns about the assessment center process.

THE NEED FOR CRITICAL SELF-EXAMINATION

The assessment center method has matured. Its growth has been documented and its impact on organizations is widely acknowledged (Finkle, 1976; MacKinnon, 1975; Moses & Byham, 1977). Because assessment centers have probably undergone more research than any other personnel technique, the need for further critical examination may not be apparent. Beginning with the Management Progress Study (Bray & Grant, 1966; Bray et al., 1974) and subsequent evaluation of operational programs (Campbell & Bray, 1967; Moses, 1972), AT&T has conducted numerous high-quality studies. Validation research by other large corporations followed. Previous summaries of this research (Cohen, et al., 1974; Howard, 1974; Huck, 1973a; MacKinnon, 1975) have concluded, as we have, that assessment centers show high predictive validity for criteria such as salary, managerial level, and performance ratings. Furthermore, validities for men and women and for whites and blacks are essentially the same (Byham, 1980; Huck & Bray, 1976).

Some warning notes have already been sounded (Boche, 1977; Kraut, 1972, 1973). Why then is there a further need for self-examination? First, not all relevant questions were raised nor have they been answered. Second, personnel procedures are coming under closer scrutiny as a function of equal employment opportunity pressures and the growth of a concern for humanistic philosophy in organizations. Third, the rapid growth of assessment centers may lead to "faddish" adoption of the procedure in situations where it is inappropriate. Failures in such specific cases will reflect poorly on the method in general. Fourth, there is still room for improvement in approach and technology.

General issues.   The assessment center method, as it is most commonly applied, tends to perpetuate the current mode of operation in an organization. Like many other personnel psychology practices, it presumes a rather static model of organizational performance (Argyris, 1976; Schein, 1965). For example, to identify dimensions to be assessed, standard job analysis methods examine the behavior of currently employed individuals who are used as models for effective performance. Such procedures assume that the job is static (i.e., current methods of job accomplishment are appropriate now and will be appropriate in the future). It is assumed that effective job performance can be explained by a set of 10–20 measurable personal characteristics. In some cases these assumptions hold; in others they may not. The validity of these assumptions should be questioned on the basis of what we know about the dynamic nature of jobs, organizations, and their environments; the need for organizations to be responsive to their environments; literature demonstrating the multidimensionality of criteria over time and individuals; and the diversity of means people use to accomplish job objectives (Tyler, 1973; Yan & Slivinski, 1976). Some of these assumptions have already been questioned in the legal and quasi-legal arena.

Different job analysis techniques are already being practiced by many organizations when it is not appropriate to define job requirements exclusively on the basis of job incumbent behavior. In such cases we need to know how the job will change in the future and what characteristics will be needed. Current approaches to this sort of job analysis are more speculative and there is less evidence of the accuracy of these methods.

The standard assessment center practice of using middle managers as assessors may also be problematic. On the one hand, middle managers are probably in the best position to interpret the significance of behavior displayed in the program. On the other hand, even with effective training, assessors will selectively observe, record, and rate behavior. This selectivity will be a function of the assessor's own management style, personal preferences, and previous experience in the organization. Furthermore, the middle manager is likely to have prior knowledge of the assessee. In very few organizations can assessors be totally matched with candidates they do not know. Thus, an individual's evaluation will be a function of the unique biases, idiosyncrasies, and inadequacies of assessors. Assessor training (Byham, 1977b), team balancing (Neidig & Hall, 1977), and the process of the integration discussion (Holmes, 1977) are designed to overcome the limited view of the assessor team, but evidence suggests that assessment ratings are largely determined by only two or three dimensions (Hinrichs & Haanpera, 1976; Sackett & Hakel, 1979; Schmitt, 1977).

The types of assessment techniques are also a mixed blessing. The rationale and evidence for performance and situational tests is quite sound. But, for some people behavior in job simulation activities under close scrutiny by organizational superiors may be cautious at best and conforming, unimaginative, or "showboating" at worst. The crucial point is that there may be individual differences in assessee response to evaluation apprehension.

The method of integrating information in the assessment discussion may also be a mixture of advantages and disadvantages. On the "plus" side, the format encourages an objective discussion of behavior, input from several sources, and postponement of decisions until all information is presented. On the "minus" side, by forcing the assessors to focus only on the data (i.e., behaviors and dimensions,) we may be overlooking valid impressions and ancillary signs of significant problem areas for an individual that are not incorporated in the general set of job requirements. For example, what should be done with a bit of information that the individual is having serious marital problems and may be leaving town?

The use of assessment center data must also be questioned. The actual use may not always match the stated purpose. The most troublesome situation is when the results of a developmental program are used for promotion purposes. It is assumed that higher level managers will not use the diagnostic information in subsequent decision making about an individual. The issue is not whether the information would improve promotion decisions, but whether alternative (unstated) uses of the data are a violation of participants' rights when they were told the program is for development. Here, the written and oral descriptions of the program must be completely honest. Safeguards must be instituted to insure that only those individuals with the "need to know" have access to the results.

A final general concern is the standardization of various specific assessment center programs within a given organization. Variations may appear in setting, instructions given participants, composition of assessee and assessor groups, procedures used in the integration discussion, time devoted to preparation of reports, level and validity of ratings, and quality of feedback given participants and their supervisors.

ISSUES RELATED TO SELECTION

First we must consider whether a selection approach is appropriate to solve the organization's problem. The selection model assumes we can improve organizational effectiveness by better choice of people. A number of other approaches to performance improvement may be equally effective, including improved performance appraisal and feedback, individual career planning, supervisory and management development, organization team building, and organization restructuring. What is critical here is the systematic diagnosis of the organization problem, the

clear statement of organizational objectives, and the careful consideration of alternative personnel programs before the unquestioning adoption of a specific technique such as an assessment center.

Do people change? The evidence is certainly mixed: Adults show
behavioral constancy over time and situations for certain intellectual
functions, cognitive styles, problem-solving strategies, abilities, and
other personal attributes (Bray et al., 1974; Mischel, 1968). But many
social and interpersonal behaviors are less stable (Mischel, 1973) and
adults can acquire knowledge and learn new skills (Knowles, 1973).

The point is that when the assessment center approach is used for
selection, it assumes individuals possess characteristics that will endure
while they are in the target position and that the dimensions being sought
are important to success in that position. For selection, assessment
centers should address only characteristics that meet this criteria. Dimensions that can easily be changed on the job are not appropriate. (This
point is also made in the Uniform Guidelines.)

How then are assessment centers used for both selection and development? The answer is that most assessment centers that purport to fill these
mixed purposes actually are concerned only with development of the
people who are selected for the higher level jobs. That is, individuals who
do poorly in the assessment center are not promoted and receive no further development. Individuals who do well in the assessment center are
promoted but still may not be highly qualified in all the dimensions identified for success in the job. The weaker dimensions then become goals for
development.

This selection–development orientation can be contrasted with the
more pure development orientation of some programs that concentrate
on only dimensions that are trainable. It does no good to assess individuals in areas where it is almost impossible for the individuals to improve if the purpose of the assessment center is behavioral change.

We must constantly be aware that assessment centers tap only a
limited spectrum of the determinants of job success. They do not usually
assess technical expertise, credibility on the job, or organizational
knowledge; nor do they deal with personal problems such as neuroses,
alcoholism, marital problems, or other nonjob factors which may influence job success.

Predictive validity evidence has been extensive, but the research has
been carried out mainly in four large organizations, namely, AT&T,
Sears, IBM, and SOHIO and to a lesser degree in other medium-size
organizations. Diverse applications have relied on generalization from
data from these few organizations. Is this warranted? Has there been adequate comparison of jobs, dimensions, skills assessed by various forms of

exercises, to warrant the massive generalization? Only further research will tell.

ISSUES RELATED TO DEVELOPMENT

Assessment centers are used for development in at least three ways: early identification of management potential, diagnosis of development needs, and as development experience per se. One basic assumption is that adults can learn and develop. That is probably reasonable, but the real issue is whether it is economically feasible to attempt to eliminate the weaknesses identified. As indicated earlier, the program should assess only those dimensions that the individual can change. Is the organization committed to the time and resources it may take to develop all the individuals in their developmental needs? In all developmental applications we must ask whether the assessment center raises false expectations for the participants.

Developmental applications of assessment centers further assume that as a result of the diagnosis and some developmental experience, participants will improve in certain skills or knowledge and thus improve on-the-job effectiveness. Recognizing such assumptions, those advocating developmental assessment centers must be able to deal with the preponderance of literature that fails to show training impacts (Hinrichs, 1976). Current training literature would suggest that certain specific communication skills and problem-analysis techniques can be learned. However, there is general agreement that change is quite difficult in personality characteristics such as Cognitive Style or Flexibility. As Boehm and Hoyle (1977) pointed out, the developability of dimensions such as Leadership or Decision-Making ability is more debatable. Furthermore they question the advisability of an organization's attempting to change such areas as Motivation to Work or Need for Achievement and Status.

Recent work using behavior modeling training techniques offers the best hope that assessment center ratings can be changed as the result of training. Byham and Robinson (1976) report four studies where behavior modeling training produced measurable changes. Dimensions such as Leadership, Sensitivity, Management Control, and Oral Communications show the most change.

In early identification programs we make several additional assumptions. First, we assume that the assessment center measures behaviors which will be stable over a relatively long period of time. Early identification programs often are used to identify individuals for promotions to positions in 5–7 years. A second assumption of early identification programs is that at any one point in time, all candidates' potentials can be measured with the same degree of accuracy. This implies that all individuals have similar patterns of development; in reality individuals show vastly different patterns (e.g., "early spurters" and "late bloomers"). Third, with early identification programs, utility of our decisions becomes extremely important because of the long-range implications. Both false positives and false negatives are possible and if they occurred would be quite costly. For this reason, most organizations using early identification have not made the early identification decision the last decision prior to promotion. If an individual does well in early identification, that individual's career is facilitated through special assignments and special developmental opportunities; however, the final decision of whether to promote the person usually comes as a result of the individual's performance on the last assignment, a second assessment center, or by other organizational methods. Thus there is definitely another check to minimize false positives. In the same way, individuals who do poorly in an early identification assessment center usually have the opportunity to be reassessed after 2 or 3 years and almost always have an opportunity to be reevaluated at the "normal" time for promotion. Thus the impact of the early identification program is to speed decisions but not necessarily to make final decisions.

A critical issue in diagnostic applications is the capability of the assessment center to evaluate accurately each person's level of skill on separate dimensions. Differential diagnosis is a special measurement problem requiring high levels of reliability, evidence of construct validity to measure trainable dimensions, and low correlations among dimension ratings. Research (Byham, 1981a; Hinrichs & Haanpera, 1976; Neidig, 1978; Sackett & Hakel, 1979; Schmitt, 1977) suggests that assessment center ratings may not possess these psychometric properties. High intercorrelations among dimension ratings and the presence of general rating factors pose serious problems for differential diagnosis.

A more complex issue involves the readiness of the organization to respond to the individual's needs for developmental follow-up activities. Diagnostic applications assume that the organization has developed systematic procedures to help the individual lessen his or her areas of weakness. Whether through internal or external courses, special assignments, or other on-the-job experiences, there must be an opportunity for the person to improve. If not, the experience may be dysfunctional. The candidate's immediate supervisor plays a critical role in many follow-up efforts. He or she must understand the results and not be threatened by them. The results must not be used in performance appraisal, but should be used to identify developmental opportunities and to guide daily coaching. All this assumes the higher level managers have the skills and motivation to use the assessment center results properly.

More broadly, developmental programs require a systematic procedure for incorporating assessment center results into human resource planning. There must be a clear statement of how the assessment data will be used in conjunction with performance appraisals, management development activities, career planning, long-range corporate planning, etc. If not, the use of assessment centers will only raise false expectations. Because of their costs and visibility, assessment centers, more than other techniques, must be clearly integrated with other personnel functions.

What evidence exists that assessment centers lead to growth and development as a result of the experience itself? As far as we know, there is only one study (Barber, 1980) that provides research evidence. Some programs emphasize that individual self-insight leads to development. Has this been tested? Again, to our knowledge it has not.

SUMMARY

Several themes run through this critique. First, assessment center technology, ranging from job analysis to assessment procedures and the assessor discussion, often assumes a static model of job performance and tends to perpetuate the status quo unless specific steps are taken to overcome the problem.

Second, assessment centers are used for various purposes and each application makes a different set of assumptions. These assumptions must be recognized and examined in light of existing research data and the circumstances of each specific organization. Then the organization must determine that it can meet the assumptions and design an assessment program to do so.

Third, assessment center users should guard against unwarranted claims for the assessment center method. Beyond the evidence that assessment centers predict managerial progress in a few large organizations, the predictive validity data are quite limited. Little evidence of value as a developmental tool has been reported.

Many of the criticisms raised in this section can be appied to other selection and development methods (Argyris, 1976). It would be a real loss if faddish adoption and misuse led to disrepute and disuse of assessment centers as so often has happened with other practices in industrial–organizational psychology. One of the current challenges of the assessment center movement is to avoid such a demise.

The Future: Research Needs

Twenty-five years of research, beginning with the Management Progress Study in the mid-1950s, have established the predictive accuracy of
the assessment center process and contributed much to our understanding of management and assessment. There are many areas that require
additional research. In this section we list research possibilities under
four general areas: the role of assessment centers in the organization's
total system of personnel appraisal, selection, and training; research
designed to explore the limits of the assessment center method and the
reasons why it works; studies of the effects of assessment centers and how
to maximize payoffs; and the application and extension of personality,
social, and judgment theories relevant to management assessment.

Not all of the ideas for needed research are ours. Many of the
unanswered questions are posed at the end of research studies we have
previously discussed. Some of the particularly valuable sources of ideas
include Boehm and Hoyle (1977), Bray (1977a), Huck (1977), and Jeswald
(1971).

Many ideas have come from continual interaction with managers, colleagues, and students involved in assessment processes. Rather than cite
an individual source for each question, we acknowledge the stimulation
we have received from many sources over the years.

THE ROLE OF ASSESSMENT CENTERS IN
PERSONNEL MANAGEMENT SYSTEMS

For many years it has been recognized that an organization's personnel
management activities interact with each other in complex fashion
(Schein, 1965), and human resources utilization models have been proposed (Miner, 1969). The assessment center technology offers an opportunity to accomplish the difficult task of actually developing an integrated systen of personnel management. Research in this area should
focus on the areas that follow.

1. Which dimensions should be evaluated at the time of selection and
   which should be trained after hiring? For promotion, which dimensions should be appraised on the current job, which assessed, and
   which developed subsequently?
2. What are the most effective means of assessing various dimensions?
   When is it most appropriate to use an assessment center, interviews,
   background check, tests, etc.?
3. How should information from various sources be integrated? When

      is it appropriate to use statistical or judgmental approaches for in-
      tegration?

4. Can the basic elements of the assessment center process (e.g., multi-
    ple assessors, simulation exercises) be applied to other personnel
    appraisal techniques such as the selection interview, performance
    appraisal, and evaluation of training effectiveness?

5. How can candidates for assessment centers be screened more effec-
    tively (e.g., by using tests, bio data forms, orientation–counseling,
    imposing self-study requirements)?

6. What additional information is needed to use assessment centers as
    a management placement technique to match individuals and jobs
    more effectively?

RESEARCH ON CONTENT AND PROCESS

Assessees

1. What effects do differences in age, sex, race, and job experiences
    have on assessment center performance?

2. Are there individual differences in evaluation apprehension? Do
    these differences affect assessment center performance? Can ap-
    prehension be alleviated?

3. In what ways do self-nominees differ from management nominees
    in terms of ability, motivation, values, and personality?

Assessors

1. What effects do differences in age, sex, race, and job experiences
    have on assessor performance?

2. What are the behaviors required by the assessor role? Are there dif-
    ferent assessor behaviors required for different types of exercises
    (e.g., in-basket versus group exercises)? Are there different assessor
    behaviors required for different types of programs (e.g., evaluation
    versus developmental programs)?

3. What are the characteristics of "good" assessors and how are they
    measured?

4. How can assessor competence be certified?

5. Does prior experience as an assessee influence subsequent perfor-
    mance as an assessor?

6. What characteristics should be considered when forming teams of
    assessors? Could we identify and match a good "observer of
    details" with a "reliable rater" with an "effective integrator"?

Assessment Techniques

1. What are the parameters or qualities of effective assessment center
    techniques, over and above the traditional psychometric qualities?

2. How can the level of complexity of exercises be ascertained and matched to job complexity?
3. Can exercises be built to accurately elicit the behaviors relevant to dimensions?
4. What are some alternative modes of responding (e.g., written responses in group exercises)?
5. How can the comparability of various in-baskets, group discussion exercises, and games be established?
6. What is the optimal amount of redundancy of exercises?
7. What are the benefits, if any, of developing an integrated set of exercises?

Dimensions
1. What is the best (accurate, reliable, efficient) method of identifying dimensions?
2. What methods (e.g., Delphi) might be used to identify expected future behavior of job incumbents? Can the job analysis procedure be an "OD" technique used to identify dimensions which *should be* present in the organization?
3. What is the appropriate number of dimensions to use in a selection or development program? What is the smallest number to ensure parsimony yet attain program goals?
4. Are there differences in the reliability and validity for judgments of different types (e.g., interpersonal versus administrative) of dimensions?
5. Can level of complexity of dimensions be assessed? Are there identifiable differences in a given dimension (e.g., Planning and Organizing) at different levels of management?
6. Does assessee knowledge of dimensions and definitions affect assessment center performance? On what dimensions?
7. Can and should dimensions to be assessed include descriptions of the context in which behavior is to be performed (e.g., climate, settings, styles of higher management, environmental pressure, and constraints)?

Information Processing
1. What barriers inhibit accurate observation?
2. How can assessors be taught to be better observers?
3. Should assessors share observations before subsequent observations?
4. What "policies" do observers use in combining information across exercises and across dimensions?
5. How can judges be taught to use the right dimensions and the right

number of dimensions when formulating an overall assessment rating?

6. Can and should assessors make configural judgments when integrating dimension ratings?

7. What techniques might be developed to reduce time spent in the assessor discussion (e.g., reporting only dimension ratings, providing photocopies of exercise reports)?

8. What benefits or losses might be experienced by reducing the time spent in the assessor discussion?

9. What are the characteristics of a good team of assessors who can effectively integrate the information?

Reliability

1. How does one measure the reliability of an assessment center? There has been some debate on this in recent court cases *(Firefighters Institute for Racial Equality* v *City of St. Louis,* 1980).

2. What are the determinants of the reliability of assessee behavior? Is there consistency across exercises? Is there consistency from job to exercises?

3. On what dimensions is there interrater agreement of behavioral ratings in various exercises?

4. What is the reliability of overall assessment ratings? How do individuals perform when reassessed after 1, 2, or 3 years?

Content Validity

1. What job analysis approaches (task or behavior oriented) are best for content validity studies?

2. What are the appropriate techniques for demonstrating the correspondence of dimensions and jobs, dimensions and exercises, and exercises and jobs?

3. What are the determinants (e.g., type of judge, judgment question, type of job analysis variable) of content validity judgments?

4. How are cutoff scores established using content validity?

Construct Validity

1. What psychological constructs are measured by the assessment center process? To what extent is assessment center performance a function of management skills, personality variables, knowledge of business procedures, insight into dimensions being measured, etc.?

2. Is an assessment center an "ability test," or "aptitude test"? To what extent does training or coaching affect performance in each exercise?

Criterion Validity
1. Which behavioral criteria are best predicted by the assessment center process?
2. Would accuracy of prediction be improved if the context or organizational climate of management behavior is considered?
3. Would predictive accuracy be improved if better information regarding situational demands and role requirements were provided to assessors and considered in criterion measurement?
4. What is the utility of assessment centers of various lengths, purposes, structures, etc.?

STUDIES OF THE EFFECTS OF ASSESSMENT CENTERS

Feedback
1. What form of feedback (oral or written, quantitative versus verbal) leads to more understanding, retention, and acceptance?
2. How can "negative" feedback be given, especially in promotion programs, without reducing the participants' self-esteem?
3. When giving feedback to the immediate supervisor in a developmental program, how can "positive" feedback be given and not dismissed as self-evident and how can "negative" feedback be given so that appropriate development actions take place?
4. What individual characteristics (agreement with assessment, desire for improvement, or flexibility) influence participant use of feedback?

Effects on Personnel
1. What types and levels of stress do participants experience?
2. What effects are there on a participant's attitudes, self-esteem, motivation, job expectations, perception of organization climate, career development, etc.?
3. What effects are there on an assessor's management skills, supervision of subordinates, ability to do performance appraisal, career development, etc.?
4. What effects are there on the organization morale, manpower planning, organizational climate, accuracy of training needs analysis, etc.?
5. What effects are there on the supervisors of participants? Do they feel threatened, loss of autonomy? Do they believe they have been provided a positive tool for personnel management?
6. What effects are there on nonparticipants? On middle managers not chosen as assessors?

7. What are the long-range effects of being assessed "not pro-motable"?
8. Does participation in an assessment center foster "anticipatory socialization," (i.e., identification with higher level management and consequent reduction of commitment to the current group or peer group)?

Training
1. What dimensions should be assessed in a developmental program? Are there some dimensions which are inappropriate or unethical to assess? What training exists for specific dimensions?
2. Does participation in an assessment center lead to more accurate self-perceptions of abilities? Do these lead to action to strengthen areas that are weak?
3. Does participation develop new skills?
4. Do subordinates of participants perceive change following par-ticipation, feedback, and subsequent training?
5. What are the unique assessor behaviors and skills required for developmental programs? Does the assessor role shift to coun-selor–coach?
6. How can self-assessment be maximized and linked to subsequent developmental planning?

APPLICATION AND EXTENSION OF
PSYCHOLOGICAL THEORIES

The research questions we have posed so far are problem oriented; they emanated from the complex process of designing, conducting, and evaluating assessment centers for the difficult business of identifying, selecting, and training managers. In this section we turn our attention to research areas that are suggested by several psychological theories. The assessment center process provides a rich field setting for applying, ex-tending, and testing a number of personality, social, group-process, and judgmental theories. Such research opportunities exist because of: (a) the high level of control exercised over the observation and evaluation proc-ess in an assessment center; and (b) the emphasis on documentation in most assessment centers.

Two types of benefits are envisioned. First, the process of assessment centers will be improved by providing more thorough and more accurate assessments. Second, the field testing of theory will enhance the reality, generality, and utility of the theory.

Social judgment theory. Theories of human judgment have attempted to understand the determinants and conditions under which individuals learn about and make judgments about their environment, including other people. Hammond, Stewart, Brehmer, and Steinmann (1975) state that "the organism in its normal intercourse with its environment must cope with *numerous, interdependent, multiformal relations* among variables which are *partly relevant* and *partly irrelevant* to its purpose, which carry only a *limited amount of dependability,* and which are *organized in a variety of ways* [p. 272]".

We have previously (Chapter 6) described some regression analyses to study human judgment processes. At this point we need only emphasize that human judgment theory has been applied productively to such diverse fields as attitude change, union-management negotiations, medical diagnoses, evaluation of stock portfolios, and hog judging. We believe practitioners and researchers on assessment centers would benefit from knowledge of this literature, and social judgment theorists could extend and test their principles in the context of assessor judgments.

The human judgment literature is relevant to the process of an assessor formulating a dimension rating after hearing exercise reports and the process of formulating an overall assessment rating after agreement on final dimension ratings. Techniques for enhancing the learning of social cues can be applied and tested in assessor training programs. Policy-capturing techniques could be used to evaluate the effects of assessor training on cue (dimension) utilization and for the certification of assessor competence to combine information. Statistical indices contained in the regression analysis of the lens model applied to assessor judgments could be used to understand the determinants and limits of assessor accuracy, the conditions under which assessors can make configural judgments, and the types of exercises providing the most salient cue (dimension) information.

Attribution theory. Attribution theory (Jones, 1979; Jones & Davis, 1965; Kelley, 1973) deals with the process by which one person (an observer) infers the causes of behavior in another person (the actor). It attempts to explain how observers use available information about the actor's behavior to form conclusions about the reasons for that behavior. Possible causes of action may be grouped as internal (i.e., due to the actor), such as abilities or effort, or as external (i.e., due to the situation), such as task difficulty or luck. The theory also deals with self-attributions that individuals make about their own behavior.

Some of the consistent findings in the research in this area are that observers tend to attribute the behavior of others to internal causes whereas actors tend to attribute their own behavior to external causes. When viewing their own success, individuals believe themselves to be responsible, but attribute failure to external causes. When viewing the complex dynamics of several people involved in different situations over time, observers tend to attribute behavior to internal causes when they see unique behavior from a person that is consistent over time and situations.

Attribution theory has been used in industrial–organizational psychology to study attitudes toward success and failure of women in management (Garland & Price, 1977), assignment of prison terms in criminal offenses (Carroll & Payne, 1977), expectations of task success (Kovenklioglu & Greenhaus, 1978), disciplinary judgments in business (Rosen & Jerdee, 1974), hiring decisions in the employment interview (Tucker & Rowe, 1979), and leader–follower interactions (Green & Mitchell, 1979).

Attribution processes could be studied in the context of assessor training, assessment center judgments, and the process of integrating assessment observations with observations by the immediate supervisor. Inconsistencies between sources in the attribution of success or failure to personal skills or situation factors ("the job" and "the department") could be studied. Self-attribution processes of participants who do well or poorly in assessment could be compared to attributions about job success or failure.

Adult and social learning theory. Knowles (1970) has stressed that adults' learning is different from children's learning. The mature person is independent and self-directed, has a reservoir of knowledge and experience to draw upon, and is ready to learn skills which will help solve immediate problems encountered in current social roles. From these basic premises, Knowles makes several inferences about the types of conditions that will foster adult learning. The person should be involved in self-diagnosis of competencies to perform successfully in life and job responsibilities. The training should emphasize experiential techniques and practical implications. Individuals who face the same types of problems should be trained together in programs emphasizing common sets of practical problems.

Bandura's (1977) theory of social learning emphasizes vicarious, symbolic, and self-regulatory processes of learning. Vicarious learning means that we benefit from observation of others as well as from direct experience. We learn by observing the consequences of the behavior of role models. Observations provide the occasion for human beings to use symbols (words, images, or pictures) to learn what behaviors of others are rewarded or punished, under what conditions we should exhibit or restrain behaviors, and whether we expect ourselves to be personally effective. Social learning theory emphasizes that rewards and punishments need not be externally controlled. People partly guide their own actions by self-regulatory mechanisms. People plan, set standards for themselves, induce themselves to action, and provide self-administered rewards and punishments. In general, Bandura emphasizes that people use cognitive aids in learning.

In the future, assessment centers might call for more participant involvement in the assessment process, including identifying dimensions to be assessed, making observations, comparing behaviors from different exercises, identifying strengths and weaknesses, and comparing assessment and job behaviors. Giving such responsibility to assessees may enhance acceptance, improve accuracy, and lead to greater likelihood of follow-up training activities. Research might explore the conditions in which participants willingly become more involved and benefit from such involvement.

Social learning concepts of modeling and behavioral goals have been incorporated into assessor training. More of this should be done. Assessors might be shown the on-the-job payoffs of increased assessor skills. Similar approaches might enhance the training payoffs from participation in an assessment center. Model in-basket responses or ways of handling an interview simulation could be shown. Behavioral steps for analyzing a financial report might be provided in connection with a written case study. Research might explore what types of vicarious learning take place from peer observations during an assessment center (e.g., do people learn new attitudes, communications skills, managerial skills)?

Theory of tasks. Miller (1966) has provided a framework for understanding job tasks. He distinguishes between a task *description* which is a statement of a work objective to be accomplished and task *analysis* which indicates worker behaviors and functions which accomplish the objectives. We see benefits to be derived for assessment centers from using Miller's framework for describing tasks. For each task activity the following features should be specified:

Task feature	Example
An indicator that provides the cue	Traffic signal
The indication or cue that calls for a response	Appearance of a red light
The control objective to be activated	Automobile brake pedal
The activation or manipulation to be made	Press foot on brake pedal
The indication of response adequacy or feedback	Car stops before intersection

Although the model has been mainly applied to physical tasks, Miller points out that indicators can be in verbal or written form, the indication can be any information that the situation is "out-of-tolerance," and the control object can be a telephone or another person. Thus, cognitive tasks might be described in terms of the theory. Miller's approach accounts for task complexity by specifying the kinds of disturbances and irrelevancies which make an indication difficult to identify and by requiring several activities at one time. Other types of complexity can be envisioned: providing conflicting cues and giving conflicting feedback.

In assessment centers a systematic procedure for describing tasks would be particularly helpful in providing a frame of reference for analyzing job activities (parallel with critical-incident behaviors), building simulation exercises, evaluating the level of complexity (difficulty) of exercises, and comparing exercises and job activities. In addition, content validity, as well as realism, would be enhanced for participants. Assessment centers would benefit from having clearer notions of what behaviors are likely to be elicited from exercises. The theory of task description would be advanced by attempting to incorporate cognitive tasks into the current framework that most clearly applies to physical tasks.

Group decision processes. Assessment centers have typically used one method of integrating the assessment information—presentation of behavioral data followed by group discussion to arrive at consensus. Many other group decision-making processes have been studied in other contexts. The nominal group technique (Delbecq et al., 1975) brings individuals together but structures their verbal discussion. The process includes: (a) a period of silent writing by members; (b) recording ideas on a "flip chart"; (c) discussion of ideas for clarification and evaluation; (d) individual voting on selected alternatives; and (e) a mathematical decision derived from ranks or ratings. The process is designed to avoid problems of interacting groups such as dominance by some members, premature closure, and conformity.

The Delphi technique (Dalkey, 1967) involves a series of questionnaires administered to experts who need not be assembled at one location. The first questionnaire poses a broad question and each subsequent questionnaire reports results and asks for another round of judgments. The decision maker considers his or her own expertise plus the judgments of others. Iterations stop when consensus has been reached.

There are other group decision-making procedures (e.g., parliamentary procedure, force-field analysis, and brain-writing) which offer alternatives to the typical assessor discussion. These and other processes could be tested for efficiency, reliability, effects on the psychometric properties of dimension ratings, predictive validity of the overall assessment rating, and acceptance by assessors.

References

Acker, S. R., & Perlson, M. R. *Can we sharpen our management of human resources?* Stamford, Conn.: Olin Corporation, Corporate Personnel Department, June 1970.

Adams, S., & Fyffe, D. *The corporate promotables.* Houston: Gulf Publishing, 1969.

Adjutant General of British Army. *A Review of the Regular Commissions Board Selection Tests and Procedure,* London, January, 1979.

Ague, K. C. Personal communication, March 16, 1971.

Albrecht, P. A., Glasser, E. M., & Marks, J. Validation of a multiple assessment procedure for managerial personnel. *Journal of Applied Psychology,* 1964, *48,* 351–359.

Albrook, R. C. How to spot executives early. *Fortune,* 1969, *72,*(2), 106–111.

Alexander, H. S., Buck, J. A., & McCarthy, R. J. Usefulness of the assessment center process for selection to upward mobility programs. *Human Resource Management,* 1975, *14,* 10–13.

Alexander, L. D. An exploratory study of the utilization of assessment center results. *Academy of Management Journal,* 1979, *22,* 152–157.

Alexander, S. J. Bendix Corporation establishes early identification program. *Assessment and Development,* 1975, *2*(2), 10.

Alon, A. *The assessment center in organizational development.* Paper presented at the First International Congress on the Assessment Center Method, Williamsburg, June, 1973.

Alon, A. Assessment and organizational development. In J. L. Moses & W. C. Byham (Eds.). *Applying the assessment center method.* New York: Pergamon Press, 1977.

Alverno College Faculty. *Assessment at Alverno College.* Milwaukee, Alverno College, 1979.

American Airlines. *A preliminary report on the validity of the key manager human resources center.* New York, Personnel Resources Department, 1976.

American Airlines. Linda Salokas, Personal communication, June 14, 1980.

American Psychological Association. *Standards for educational and psychological tests and manuals.* Washington, D.C.: American Psychological Association, 1966.

American Psychological Association, American Educational Research Association, and National Council on Measurement in Education. *Standards for educational and psychological tests.* Washington, D.C.: American Psychological Association, 1974.

American Telephone and Telegraph Company, Personnel Research Staff. *Personnel assessment program: Follow-up study.* New York: American Telephone and Telegraph, 1965.

Anderson, N. H. Looking for configurality in clinical judgment. *Psychological Bulletin,* 1972, *78,*(2), 93–102.

Ansbacher, H. L. German military psychology. *Psychological Bulletin,* 1941, *38,* 370–379.

Ansbacher, H. L. German industrial psychology in the fifth year of war. *Psychological Bulletin,* 1944, *41,* 605–614.

Ansbacher, H. L. The history of the leaderless group discussion technique. *Psychological Bulletin,* 1951, *48,* 383–391.

Anstey, E. The civil service administrative class: A follow-up of postwar entrants. *Occupational Psychology,* 1971, *45,* 27–43.

Anstey, E. A 30-year follow-up of the CSSB procedure, with lessons for the future. *Journal of Occupational Psychology,* 1977, *50,* 149–159.

Argyris, C. Problems and new directions for industrial psychology. In M. D. Dunnette (Ed.), *Handbook of industrial and organizational psychology.* Chicago: Rand–McNally, 1976.

Arvey, R. D. Unfair discrimination in the employment interview: Legal and psychological aspects. *Psychological Bulletin,* 1979, *86,* 736–765.

Asher, J. J., & Sciarrino, J. A. Realistic work sample tests: A review. *Personnel Psychology,* 1974, *27,* 519–533.

Assessment applied to engineering jobs. *Assessment and Development,* 1973, *1*(1), 8.

Baker, D. R., & Martin, C. G. *Evaluation of the Federal Executive Development Program.* Washington, D.C.: U.S. Civil Service Commission, Applied Psychology Section, Personnel Research and Development Center, September, 1974.

Balma, M. J. The development of processes for indirect or synthetic validity (a symposium). 1. The concept of synthetic validity. *Personnel Psychology,* 1959, *12,* 395–396.

Bandura, A. *Social learning theory.* Englewood Cliffs, N.J.: Prentice-Hall, 1977.

Barber, R. E. Personal communication, March 28, 1980.

Barrett, R. S. The agreement scale: A preliminary report. *Personnel Psychology,* 1961, *14,* 151–165.

Barrett, R. S. *EEO Guidelines—How they impact on use of assessment centers.* Paper presented at the Seventh International Congress on the Assessment Center Method, New Orleans, June, 1979.

Barron, F. *Personal soundness in university graduate students.* Berkeley: University of California Press, 1954.

Barron, F. Some studies of creativity at the Institute of Personality Assessment and Research. In G. A. Steiner (Ed.), *The creative organization.* Chicago: University of Chicago Press, 1965.

Barron, F. *Creative person and creative process.* Princeton: Van Nostrand, 1968.

Barton, N. P. *The assessment center* (MBA #410 Management Psychology). Chicago: Loyola University, January 12, 1971.

Bass, B. M. *An international study of objective responding in small group exercises as a predictor or managerial rate of advancement.* Paper presented at the Seventh International Congress on the Assessment Center Method, New Orleans, June, 1979.

Bass, B. M. The leaderless group discussion technique. *Personnel Psychology,* 1950, *3,* 17–32.

Bass, B. M. The leaderless group discussion. *Psychological Bulletin,* 1954, *51,* 465–492.

Bass, B. M., & Barrett, G. V. *Man, work, and organization.* Boston: Allyn and Bacon, 1972.

Bass, B. M., & Burger, P. C. *Assessment of managers: An international comparison.* New York: The Free Press, 1979.

Bayroff, A. G., Haggerty, H. R., & Rundquist, E. A. Validity of ratings as related to rating techniques and conditions. *Personnel Psychology,* 1954, *7,* 93–113.

Beck, A. C., Jr., & Hillman, E. D. (Eds.). *A practical approach to organization development through MBO—Selected readings.* Reading, Mass.: Addison–Wesley, 1972.

Beech, C. A. The assessment center: A promising approach to evaluation. *The Canadian Personnel and Industrial Relations Journal,* November 1972, 35–38.

Beer, M., Ruh, R., Dawson, J. A., McCaa, B. B., & Kavanagh, M. J. A performance management system: Research, design, introduction, and evaluation. *Personnel Psychology,* 1978, *31,* 505–535.

Belinsky, B. *Outside consultants to industry:* Strengths, problems, and pitfalls. *Personnel Psychology,* 1964, *17,* 107–114.

Bender, J. M. What is "typical" of assessment centers? *Personnel,* 1973, *50*(4), 50–57.

Bender, J. M., Calvert, O. L., & Jaffee, C. L. *Report on supervisor selection program, Oak Ridge gaseous diffusion plant.* (K-1789). Oak Ridge, Tenn.: Union Carbide Corporation, Nuclear Division, April 17, 1970.

Bentz, V. J. *The Sears experience in the investigation, description, and prediction of executive behavior.* Princeton: Executive Study Conference, Educational Testing Service, 1962.

Bentz, V. J. The Sears experience in the investigation, description, and prediction of executive behavior. In F. R. Wickert & D. E. McFarland (Eds.), *Measuring executive effectiveness.* New York: Appleton–Century–Crofts, 1967, 147–205.

Bentz, V. J. The Sears executive model. In W. C. Byham (Chair), *The assessment center.* Symposium presented at the Executive Study Conference, New York, 1969.

Bentz, V. J. Validity studies at Sears. In W. C. Byham (Chair), *Validities of assessment centers.* Symposium presented at the meeting of the American Psychological Association, Washington, D. C., September, 1971.

Bentz, V. J. *A basic investigation into the nature of managerial styles.* Chicago: Psychological Research and Services National Personnel, Sears, 1974.

Bentz, V. J. *Overview of Sears research with multiple assessment techniques.* Chicago: Unpublished paper, 1980.

Berkwitt, G. J. The big new move to measure managers. *Dun's Review,* 1971, September, 61–64.

Berlew, D. E., & Hall, D. T. The socialization of managers: Effects of expectations on performance. *Administrative Science Quarterly,* 1966, *11,* 207–233.

Biesheuvel, S. *Selection and classification tests for native labour on the gold mines.* South Africa: Council for Scientific and Industrial Research/National Institute for Personnel Research Report, 1948.

Biesheuvel, S. *Aptitude tests for native labour on the Witwatersrand Gold Mines Part 1.* (H16/35), South Africa: National Institute for Personnel Research Report, 1951.

Biesheuvel, S. Personnel selection tests for Africans. *South African Journal of Science.* 1952, *49,* 3–12.

Biesheuvel, S. Personnel selection tests—A means of improving the production of native labour. *Municipal Affairs,* 1953–1954, *19,* 220–221.

Biesheuvel, S., & Hudson, W. *The validation of boss boy selection tests.* South Africa: Council for Scientific and Industrial Research/National Institute for Personnel Research Report, 1950.

Biesheuvel, S., & Hudson, W. *The validity of boss boy selection tests* (3rd Interim Report),

Council for Scientific and Industrial Research/National Institute for Personnel Research, 1952.

Bion, W. R. The leaderless group project. *Bulletin of the Menninger Clinic,* 1946, *10,* 77–81.

Blum, M. L. & Naylor, J. C. *Industrial Psychology* (2nd ed.). New York: Harper and Row, 1968.

Blumenfeld, W. S. Early identification of managerial potential by means of assessment centers. *Atlanta Economic Review,* December, 1971, 35–38.

Boche, A. Management concerns about assessment centers. In J. L. Moses & W. C. Byham (Eds.), *Applying the assessment center method.* New York: Pergamon Press, 1977.

Boehm, V. R., & Hoyle, D. F. Assessment and management development. In J. L. Moses & W. C. Byham (Eds.), *Applying the assessment center method.* New York: Pergamon Press, 1977.

Bolinsky, B. Some experience and problems in appraising executive personnel. *Personnel Psychology,* 1964, *17,* 107–114.

Borman, W. C. *Validity of rival methods for predicting military recruiter training performance: Behavioral assessment versus first impression, structured interview, and paper-and-pencil testing.* Minneapolis: Personnel Decisions Research Institute, 1981.

Bourgeois, R. P., Leim, M. A., Slivinski, L. W., & Grant, K. W. *Evaluation of an assessment centre in terms of its acceptability.* Public Service Commission of Canada, Managerial Assessment and Research Division, March 1973.

Bourgeois, R. P., & Slivinski, L. W. The inter-rater reliability of the consolidated fund in-basket. *Studies in Personnel Psychology,* 1974, *6*(1), 47–52.

Bourgeois, R. P., Slivinski, L. W., & Grant, K. W. *Assessees' reactions to CAP assessment centre 73-2.* Public Service Commission of Canada, Managerial Assessment and Research Division, Career Assignment Program, December 1973.

Bowman, G. W. What helps or harms promotability? *Harvard Business Review,* 1964, *42*(1), 5–26; 184–196.

Brammer, L. M. *The helping relationship: Process and skills* (2nd ed.). Englewood Cliffs, New Jersey: Prentice Hall, 1979.

Bray, D. W. The management progress study. In Educational Testing Service. *Identify Management Talent,* Princeton: The Conference on the Executive Study, December 7–8, 1961.

Bray, D. W. The assessment center method of appraising management potential. In J. W. Blood (Ed.), *The personnel job in a changing world.* New York: American Management Association, 1964, 225–234. (a)

Bray, D. W. The management progress study. *American Psychologist,* 1964, *19,* 419–429. (b)

Bray, D. W. *Three global constructs in the study of the growth of managers.* Paper presented at the 74th annual convention of the American Psychological Association, New York, August, 1966.

Bray, D. W. *Assessment centers.* Paper presented at New York Workshop on Assessment Centers, New York, October, 1969.(a)

Bray, D. W. *In-basket as used in assessment centers.* Paper presented at New York Workshop on Assessment Centers, New York, October, 1969. (b)

Bray, D. W. The assessment center: Opportunities for women. *Personnel Magazine,* 1971, *48,* 30–34. (a)

Bray, D. W. The uses of assessment center methods. *Projector: BNA Monthly Report,* April 1971, 1–3. (b)

Bray, D. W. New data from the Management Process (sic) Study. *Assessment and Development,* 1973, *1*(1), 3.

Bray, D. W. Current trends and future possibilities. In J. L. Moses & W. C. Byham (Eds.), *Applying the assessment center method.* New York: Pergamon Press, 1977.(a)

Bray, D. W. New program assesses technical potential at AT&T. *Assessment and Development,* 1977, 4(2), 14.(b)

Bray, D. W. American Board of Professional Psychology moves to assessment. *Assessment and Development,* 1978, 5(1), 4.

Bray, D. W. Personal communication, April 2, 1981.

Bray, D. W., & Campbell, R. J. Selection of salesmen by means of an assessment center. *Journal of Applied Psychology,* 1968, 52, 36–41.

Bray, D. W., Campbell, R. J., & Grant, D. L. *Formative years in business: A long-term AT&T study of managerial lives.* New York: Wiley, 1974.

Bray, D. W., & Grant, D. L. The assessment center in the measurement of potential for business management. *Psychological Monographs,* 1966, 80 (17, Whole No. 625), pp. 1–27.

Bray, D. W., Grant, D. L., & Campbell, R. J. The study of management careers and the assessment of management ability. In A. J. Morrow (Ed.), *The failure of success.* New York: AMACOM, 1972. pp. 154–169.

Bray, D. W., & Moses, J. L. Personnel selection. In P. H. Mussen & M. R. Rosenzweig (Eds.), *Annual Review of Psychology,* Palo Alto: Annual Reviews, Inc., 1972.

Brehmer, B. Subjects' ability to use functional rules. *Psychonomic Science,* 1971, 24(6), 259–260.

Brockway, B. S. Evaluating the competency of behavior therapists: Methods and issues. Paper presented at the 8th annual meeting of the American Psychological Association, Toronto, Canada, August 29, 1978.

Brugnoli, G. A., Campion, J. E., & Basen, J. A. Racial bias in the use of work samples for personnel selection. *Journal of Applied Psychology,* 1979, 64, 119–123.

Bryant, W. H. *Assessment center evaluation.* Wright-Patterson Air Force Base, Ohio: Headquarters Aeronautical Systems Division, Department of Air Force, September 8, 1974.

Bullard, J. F. *An evaluation of the assessment center approach to selecting supervisors.* Peoria: Caterpillar Tractor Company, May, 1969.

Bullard, J. F. Personal communications with William C. Byham, May, 1975.

Bureau of National Affairs, Bulletin to Management. *Management appraisal: The assessment approach.* Washington, D.C.: BNA, 1972.

Burroughs, W. A., Rollins, J. B., & Hopkins, J. J. Equality of assigned positions in a leaderless group discussion. *Studies in Personnel Psychology,* 1972, 4(4), 13–17.

Burroughs, W. A., Rollins, J. B., & Hopkins, J. J. The effect of age, departmental experience, and prior rater experience on performance in assessment center exercises. *Academy of Management Journal,* 1973, 16, 335–339.

Butz, R. R. Assessment center an effective selection promotion method for the "smaller" company. *Assessment & Development,* 1980, 7(1), 4.

Byham, R. N., & Byham, W. C. Effectiveness of assessment center exercises in producing behavior. *Assessment & Development,* 1976, 3(1), 9–10.

Byham, W. C. *The uses of assessment centers.* Paper presented at the meeting of the Executive Study Conference, April, 1969.

Byham, W. C. Assessment center for spotting future managers. *Harvard Business Review,* 1970, 48(4), 150–160, plus appendix.

Byham, W. C. The assessment center as an aid in management development. *Training and Development Journal,* 1971, 25(12), 10–22.

Byham, W. C. Assessment centers: The place for picking management potential. *European Business,* 1972, 35, 27–36. (a)

Byham, W. C. How a scientific assessment center works. In A. J. Marrow (Ed.), *The failure of success*. New York: AMACOM, 1972. (b)

Byham, W. C. How to spot management potential early enough to do something about it. *Personnel News and Views*. Winter 1972, 7–10. (c)

Byham, W. C. A new way to identify management potential. *European Business*, Autumn, 1972, 27–36. (d)

Byham, W. C. *Validity and differential validity of the assessment center method*. Paper presented at the conference on Alternatives to Paper and Pencil Testing, Graduate School of Business, University of Pittsburgh, May 1972. (e)

Byham, W. C. The "center" is a process, not a place. *Simulation/Gaming/News*, May, 1974, p. 12.

Byham, W. C. Application of the assessment center method. In J. L. Moses & W. C. Byham (Eds.), *Applying the assessment center method*. New York: Pergamon Press, 1977. (a)

Byham, W. C. Assessor selection and training. In J. L. Moses & W. C. Byham (Eds.), *Applying the assessment center method*. New York: Pergamon Press, 1977. (b)

Byham, W. C. How to improve the validity of an assessment center. *Training and Development Journal*, 1978, *32*(11), 4–6. (a)

Byham, W. C. *Intercultural adaptability of the assessment center method*. Paper presented at Nineteenth International Congress of Applied Psychology, Munich, August 1978. (b)

Byham, W. C. Measurement of managerial competence. Paper presented at the 86th annual meeting of the American Psychological Association, August 29, 1978. (c)

Byham, W. C. *Applying assessment center technology to a personnel system*. Paper presented at the meeting of the Seventh International Congress on the Assessment Center Method, New Orleans, June, 1979. (a)

Byham, W. C. Review of legal cases and opinions dealing with assessment centers and content validity. Monograph IV. Pittsburgh, Pennsylvania: Development Dimensions International, 1979. (b)

Byham, W. C. Starting an assessment center the correct way. *The Personnel Administrator*, 1980, *25*, 27–32.

Byham, W. C. (Chair). *What do we know about assessment centers?* Preliminary Report, The Assessment Center Research Group, Pittsburgh: June 1980.

Byham, W. C. *Validation of Government Assessment Center*, Pittsburgh: Development Dimensions International, 1981(a).

Byham, W. C. *Dimensions of managerial success*. Pittsburgh: Development Dimensions International, 1981(b).

Byham, W. C. & Bobin, D. (Eds.). *Alternatives to paper and pencil testing*. Pittsburgh: University of Pittsburgh, 1972.

Byham, W. C., & Bray, D. W. Administering an assessment center. Pittsburgh: Development Dimensions Press, 1973.

Byham, W. C., & Pentecost, R. The assessment center: Identifying tomorrow's managers. *Personnel*, 1970, *47*(5), 17–28.

Byham, W. C., & Robinson, J. C. Interaction modeling: A new concept in supervisory training. *Training and Development*, 1976, *30*, 20–33.

Byham, W. C., & Spitzer, M. E. *The law and personnel testing*. New York: American Management Association, 1971.

Byham, W. C., & Temlock, S. Operational validity—a new concept in personnel testing. *Personnel Journal*, 1972, *51*, 639–647, 654.

Byham, W. C., & Thoresen, J. *Effectiveness of Assessor Training Techniques*. Pittsburgh: Development Dimensions International, June 12, 1976.

Byham, W. C., & Thornton, G. C., III. Assessment centers: A new aid in management selection. *Studies in Personnel Psychology*, 1970, *2*(2), 21–35.

Byham, W. C., & Wettengel, C. Assessment center for identifying and developing management potential in government operations. *Public Personnel Management*, 1974, *3*, 352–364.

California Youth Authority. *Manager assessment selection and training project.* Health & Welfare Agency, Division of Personnel Management, February, 1975.

Campbell, D. T. Systematic errors on the part of human links in communication systems. *Information and Control*, 1958, *1*, 334–369.

Campbell, D. T., & Fiske, D. W. Convergent and discriminant validation by the multitrait–multimethod matrix. *Psychological Bulletin*, 1959, *56*, 81–105.

Campbell, J. P. Personnel training and development. In P. H. Mussen & M. R. Rosenzweig (Eds.), *Annual Review of Psychology.* Palo Alto: Annual Reviews, Inc., 1971.

Campbell, J. P., Dunnette, M. D., Lawler, E. E., III, & Weick, K. E. *Managerial behavior, performance and effectiveness.* New York: McGraw–Hill, 1970.

Campbell, J. T. Assessments of higher level personnel: Background and scope of the research. *Personnel Psychology*, 1962, *15*, 57–73.

Campbell, J. T., Otis, J. L., Liske, R. E., & Prien, E. P. Assessments of higher level personnel: II. Validity of the overall assessment process. *Personnel Psychology*, 1962, *15*, 63–74.

Campbell, R. J., & Bray, D. W. Assessment centers: An aid in management selection. *Personnel Administration*, 1967, *30*(2), 6–13.

Campion, J. E. Work sampling for personnel selection. *Journal of Applied Psychology*, 1972, *56*, 40–44.

Carleton, F. O. *Relationships between follow-up evaluations and information developed in a management assessment center.* Paper presented at the 78th annual convention of the American Psychological Association, Miami Beach, August, 1970.

Carlson, R. E. Selection interview decisions: The effect of interview experience, relative quota situation, and applicant sample on interview decisions. *Personnel Psychology*, 1967, *20*, 259–280. (a)

Carlson, R. E. Selection interview decisions: The relative influence of appearance and factual written information on an interviewer's final rating. *Journal of Applied Psychology*, 1967, *51*, 461–468. (b)

Carlson, R. E. Employment decisions: Effect of mode of applicant presentation on some outcome measures. *Personnel Psychology*, 1968, *21*, 193–207.

Carlson, R. E. Relative influence of a photograph vs. factual written information on an interviewer's employment decision. *Personnel Psychology*, 1969, *22*, 45–56.

Carlson, R. E. Effect of applicant sample on ratings of valid information in an employment setting. *Journal of Applied Psychology*, 1970, 54, 217–222.

Carlson, R. E. Effect of interview information in altering valid impressions. *Journal of Applied Psychology*, 1971, 55, 66–72. (b)

Carlson, R. E. The current status of judgmental techniques in industry. In W. C. Byham & D. Bobin (Eds.), *Alternatives to paper and pencil testing.* Pittsburgh: University of Pittsburgh, 1972.

Carlson, R. E., & Mayfield, E. C. Evaluating interview and employment application data. *Personnel Psychology*, 1967, *20*, 441–460.

Carlson, S. *Executive behavior: A study of the workload and the working methods of managing directors.* Stockholm: Strombergs, 1951.

Carrigan, P. M. Assessors' on-the-job performance affected by assessment center training. *Assessment & Development*, 1976, *3*(2), 6; 8; 11.

Carroll, J. S., & Payne, J. W. Crime seriousness, recidivism risk, and causal attributions in judgments of prison terms by students and experts. *Journal of Applied Psychology,* 1977, *62,* 595–602.

Carter, L. F. Evaluating the performance of individuals as members of small groups. *Personnel Psychology,* 1954, *7,* 477–484.

Cascio, W. F., & Phillips, N. F. Performance testing: A rose among thorns? *Personnel Psychology,* 1979, *32,* 751–766.

Cascio, W. F., & Silbey, V. Utility of the assessment center as a selection device. *Journal of Applied Psychology,* 1979, *64,* 107–118.

Casserly, M. C., Slivinski, L. W., & Bourgeois, R. P. *The assessment centre counselling session: The candidates' reaction.* (CAP 73-2 and CAP 74-1). Public Service Commission of Canada, Managerial Assessment and Research Division, Career Assignment Program, March, 1974.

Clingenpeel, R. *Validity and dynamics of a foreman selection process.* Paper presented at the meeting of the 7th International Congress on the Assessment Center Method, New Orleans, June, 1979.

Cohen, B. M. The assessment center: Whom to develop. *Training in Business and Industry,* 1974, *11*(2). (a)

Cohen, B. M. Increased learning opportunities from the assessment center technique. *Assessment and Development,* 1974, *11*(1), 4. (b)

Cohen, B. M., & Jaffee, C. L. *Assessment centers in government agencies.* Paper presented at the Development Dimensions Conference, Washington, D.C., 1972.

Cohen, B. M., Moses, J. L., & Byham, W. C. *The validity of assessment centers: A literature review.* Monograph II. Pittsburgh: Development Dimensions Press, 1974.

Cohen, S. L. *Standardization of assessment center technology: Some critical concerns.* Presentation at the 6th International Congress on the Assessment Center Method, White Sulphur Springs, West Virginia, April 7, 1978.

Cohen, S. L. The bottom line on assessment center technology. *The Personnel Administrator,* 1980, *25*(2), 50–55.

Cohen, S. L., & Sands, L. The effects of order of exercise presentation on assessment center performance: One standardization concern. *Personnel Psychology,* 1978, *31,* 35–36.

Cook, E. M. The in-basket exercises: For secretarial training? *Training and Development Journal,* 1973, *27*(7), 26–27.

Cosier, R. A. The effects of three potential aids for making strategic decisions on prediction accuracy. *Organizational Behavior and Human Performance,* 1978, *22,* 295–206.

Cowan, J., & Kurtz, M. Internal assessment center: An organization development approach to selecting supervisors. *Public Personnel Management,* 1976, *5,* 15–23.

Craig, R. L. (Ed.). *Training and development handbook* (2nd Ed.). New York: McGraw–Hill, 1976.

Craig, R. L., & Bittel, L. R. (Eds.). *Training and development handbook.* New York: McGraw–Hill, 1967.

Cronbach, L. J. *Essentials of psychological testing.* New York: Harper & Row, 1970.

Crooks, L. A. The selection and development of assessment center techniques. In J. L. Moses & W. C. Byham (Eds.), *Applying the assessment center method.* New York: Pergamon Press, 1977.

Crooks, L. A. *Issues in the development and validation of in-basket exercises for specific objectives.* (Research Memo 68-23). Princeton: Educational Testing Service, 1968. Also in J. Campbell (Chair), *The In-basket exercise—test or technique?* Symposium presented at the 76th annual convention of the American Psychological Association, San Francisco, 1968.

Crooks, L. A. *Research on the foreign service assessment program.* Symposium presented at the 8th International Congress on the Assessment Center Method, Toronto, Canada, August, 1980.

Crooks, L. A., & Slivinski, L. W. *In-basket test score profiles of a CAP group compared with score profiles of three other groups of varied background and experience.* Personnel Assessment and Research Division, Public Service Commission, August, 1971.

Crooks, L. A., & Slivinski, L. W. Comparison of in-basket test score profiles of four managerial groups. *Studies in Personnel Psychology,* 1972, 4(1), 19–30.

Cummings, L. L., & Schwab, D. P. *Performance in organizations: Determinants and appraisal.* Glenview, Ill.: Scott, Foresman, 1973.

Cummings, P. W. All about assessment centers. *Applied Training,* August, 1973, 2–7.

Cummins, P. C. TAT correlates of executive performance. *Journal of Applied Psychology,* 1967, 51, 78–81.

Cyrs, T. E., Jr. Issues in assessment and training for professional competence. In L. W. Hellervik (Chair), *Professional competence: I/O psychology applied to professional education and assessment.* Symposium presented at the meeting of the American Psychological Association, Division of Industrial and Organization Psychology, Toronto, 1978.

Dailey, C. A. *Assessment of lives.* San Francisco: Jossey–Bass, 1971.

Dalkey, N. C. *Delphi.* Los Angeles: Rand Corporation, 1967.

Dapra, R. A. EEOC uses profile assessment center in major reorganization. *Assessment & Development.* 1978, 5(1), 1; 2; 4; 5; 8.

Dapra, R. A., & Byham, W. C. Applying the assessment center method to selection interviewing. *Training and Development Journal,* 1978, 32(4), 44–49.

Dawes, R. M., & Corrigan, B. Linear models in decision making. *Psychological Bulletin,* 1974, 81, 95–106.

Delbecq, A. L., Van de Ven, A. H., & Gustafson, D. H. *Group techniques for program planning.* Glenview, Ill.: Scott, Foresman, 1975.

DeNelsky, G. Y., & McKee, M. G. Prediction of job performance from assessment reports: Use of a modified Q-sort technique to expand prediction and criterion variance. *Journal of Applied Psychology,* 1969, 53, 439–445.

Denning, D. L. *An examination of in-basket scores.* Unpublished doctoral dissertation, University of Georgia, 1980.

Department of Labor, Employment & Training Administration. *Dictionary of Occupational Titles* (3rd ed.). Washington, D.C.: U.S. Government Printing Office, 1977.

Development Dimensions, Inc. Research finds equality for females and blacks in assessment. *Assessment & Development,* 1973, 1(1), 6. (a)

Development Dimensions, Inc. Worldwide spread of assessment seen especially in international organizations. *Assessment & Development,* 1973, 1(1), 5. (b)

Development Dimensions, Inc. Assessment centers without assessors. *Assessment & Development,* 1974, 11(1), 3.

Dicken, C. F., & Black, J. D. Predictive validity of psychometric evaluations of supervisors. *Journal of Applied Psychology,* 1965, 49, 34–37.

DiCola, G. Assessment center used to select Quality Circle facilitators at Westinghouse. *Assessment & Development,* 1980, 7(2), 8.

DiCostanzo, F., & Andretta, T. The supervisory assessment center in the Internal Revenue Service. *Training and Development Journal,* 1970, 24(8), 12–15.

Division of Industrial-Organizational Psychology (Division 14), American Psychological Association. *Principles for the validation and use of personnel selection procedures.* (2nd Ed.) Dayton: The Industrial-Organizational Psychologist, 1980.

Dodd, W. C. Validity studies at IBM. In W. C. Byham (Chair), *Validity of assessment centers.* Symposium presented at the 79th annual convention of the American Psychological Association, Washington, D.C., 1971.

Dodd, W. E. *Two factors related to career progress in IBM: A summary of longitudinal studies in the identification of management potential.* Armonk: IBM, Personnel Research Studies, 1970.

Dodd, W. E. *Will management assessment centers insure selection of the same old types?* Paper presented at the 79th annual convention of the American Psychological Association, Washington, D.C., August, 1971.

Dodd, W. E. Attitudes toward assessment center programs. In J. L. Moses & W. C. Byham (Eds.), *Applying the assessment center method.* New York: Pergamon Press, 1977.

Dodd, W. E., Kraut, A. I. *The prediction of management assessment center performance from earlier measures of personality and sales training in performance: A preliminary report.* Armonk: Corporate Personnel Research, IBM, April 1970.

Dodd, W. E., Kraut, A. I., & Simonetti, S. H. *Selected annotated bibliography on identification and assessment of management talent.* Armonk: IBM, Personnel Research Studies, 1971.

Dodd, W. E., & McNamara, W. J. *The early identification of management talent in field engineering.* Armonk, IBM, Personnel Research Studies, 1968.

Donaldson, R. J. *Validation of the internal characteristics of an industrial assessment center program using the multitrait–multimethod matrix approach.* Unpublished doctoral dissertation, Case Western Reserve University, January 1969.

Dowell, B. E., & Wexley, K. N. Development of a work behavior taxonomy for first-line supervisors. *Journal of Applied Psychology,* 1978, *63,* 563–572.

Dubin, R., & Spray, S. L. Executive behavior and interaction. *Industrial Relations,* 1964, *3,* 99–108.

DuBois, P. H. *A history of psychological testing.* Boston: Allyn and Bacon, 1970.

Dunnette, M. D. Predictors of executive success. In F. R. Wickert & D. E. McFarland (Eds.), *Measuring executive effectiveness.* New York: Appleton–Century–Crofts, 1967.

Dunnette, M. D. Multiple assessment procedures in identifying and developing managerial talent. In P. McReynolds (Ed.), *Advances in psychological assessment* (Vol. 2). Palo Alto: Science and Behavior Books, 1971.

Educational Testing Service, The Executive Study Conference. *The in-basket technique.* Princeton: Educational Testing Service, 1960.

Educational Testing Service, The Executive Study Conference. *Executive decision research.* Princeton: Educational Testing Service, 1963.

Educational Testing Service, The Executive Study Conference. *Management games in selection and development.* Princeton: Educational Testing Service, 1964.

Edwards, A. L. *The social desirability variable in personality assessment and research.* New York: Dryden Press, 1957.

Edwards, A. L., & Abbott, R. D. Measurement of personality traits: Theory and technique. In P. Mussen & M. Rosenzweig (Eds.), *Annual review of psychology.* Palo Alto: Annual Reviews, 1973.

Eeeny, meeny, miney . . .supervisor? *Industry Week,* November 16, 1970, 28–32.

Egan, G. *The skilled helper.* Monterey, Calif.: Brooks/Cole, 1975. (b)

Egan, G. *Exercises in helping skills: A training manual to accompany the skilled helper.* Monterey, Calif.: Brooks/Cole, 1975. (a)

Einhorn, H. J. Expert measurement and mechanical combination. *Organizational Behavior and Human Performance,* 1972, *7,* 86–106.

Einhorn, H. J. Cue definition and residual judgment. *Organizational Behavior and Human Performance*, 1974, *12*, 30–49.

Einhorn, H. J., Hogarth, R. M., & Klempner, E. Quality of group judgment. *Psychological Bulletin*, 1977, *84*, 158–172.

Equal Employment Opportunity Commission, Civil Service Commission, Department of Labor, & Department of Justice. *Uniform Guidelines on Employee Selection Procedures*, Federal Register, *43*(166), Friday, August 25, 1978.

Equal Employment Opportunity Commission, James D. Hodgson, & Secretary of Labor. *United States Department of Labor and United States of America vs. AT&T and various subsidiaries*. In the United States District Court for the Eastern District of Pennsylvania. Civil Action NO. 73-149.

Erpenbach, J. J. Personal communication, March 11, 1971.

Ewing, D. W. The knowledge of an executive. *Harvard Business Review*, 1964, *42*(2), 91–100.

Eysenck, H. J. *Uses and abuses of psychology*. Baltimore: Penguin Books, 1953.

Ezekiel, R. S. The personal future and Peace Corps competence. *Journal of Personality and Social Psychology*, 1968, *8* (Monograph Supplement 2).

Fabian, H. A. *Comment on aptitude testing procedures: A report on a survey of procedures presently used by various mining groups within the Republic of South Africa*. National Institute for Personnel Report, 1963.

Fancher, R. E., Jr. Explicit personality theories and accuracy in person perception. *Journal of Personality*, 1966, *34*, 252–261.

Fancher, R. E., Jr. Accuracy versus validity in person perception. *Journal of Consulting Psychology*, 1967, *31*(3), 264–269.

Farago, L. (Ed.). *German psychological warfare*. New York: G. P. Putnam's Sons, 1942.

Fine, S. A. A structure of worker functions. *Personnel & Guidance Journal*, 1955, *39*, 66–73.

Fine, S. A., & Wiley, W. W. *An introduction to functional job analysis*. Kalamazoo: W. E. Upjohn Institute for Employment Research, 1971.

Finkle, R. B., & Jones, W. S. *Assessing corporate talent: A key to managerial manpower planning*. New York: Wiley–Interscience, 1970.

Finkle, R. B. Managerial assessment centers. In M. D. Dunnette (Ed.), *Handbook of industrial and organizational psychology*. Chicago: Rand McNally, 1976.

Finley, R. M., Jr. *An evaluation of behavior predictions from projective tests given in a management assessment center*. Paper presented at the 78th annual convention of the American Psychological Association, Miami Beach, August, 1970.

First court test of assessment center method. City of Omaha use of assessment center method upheld. *Assessment & Development*, March 1976, 1–2.

Fisher vs. Procter & Gamble Manufacturing Company Nos. 77-2204, 77-2205 and 77-2474, United States Court of Appeals, Fifth Circuit. March 12, 1980. Synopses, Syllabi and Key Number Classification by West Publishing Company, 1980.

Fiske, D. W., & Pearson, P. H. Theory and techniques of personality measurement. In P. H. Mussen & M. R. Rosenzweig, *Annual Review of Psychology*, Palo Alto: Annual Reviews, Inc., 1970.

Fitts, P. M. German applied psychology during World War II. *American Psychologist*, 1946, *1*, 151–161.

Fitz-Enz, J., Hards, K. E., & Savage, G. E. Total development: Selection, assessment and growth. *The Personnel Administrator*, 1980, *25*(2), 58–62.

Flanagan, J. C. Defining the requirements of the executive's job. *Personnel*, 1951, *28*, 28–35.

Flanagan, J. C. The critical incident technique. *Psychological Bulletin*, 1954, 51, 327–349. (a)

Flanagan, J. C. Some considerations in the development of situational tests. *Personnel Psychology*, 1954, 7, 461–464. (b)

Fleishman, E. A. The description of supervisory behavior. *Journal of Applied Psychology*, 1953, *37*(1), 1–6.

Fleishman, E. A. *Manual for Leadership Opinion Questionnaire*. Chicago: Science Research Associates, 1960.

Fleishman, E. A., Harris, E. F., & Burtt, H. E. *Leadership and supervision in industry*. Columbus: Ohio State University, 1955.

Fleming, J. L., & Sells, S. B. *The corporate personnel assessment center: A review and evaluation of potential and performance*. (IBR Report 72-11). Texas Christian University Institute of Behavioral Research, Eastern Airlines Research Training Project, August 4, 1972.

Frederiksen, N. Factors in in-basket performance. *Psychological Monographs*, 1962, 76(22, Whole No. 541).

Frederiksen, N. *Correlates of factors in in-basket performance* (RB-63-12). Princeton: Educational Testing Service, April 1963.

Frederiksen, N. Validation of a simulation technique. *Organizational Behavior and Human Performance*, 1966, *1*, 87–109.

Frederiksen, N., Jensen, O., & Beaton, A. E. Contribution by Bloxom, B. *Prediction of organizational behavior*. Elmsford, NY: Pergamon Press, Inc., 1972.

Frederiksen, N., Saunders, D. R., & Wand, B. The in-basket test. *Psychological Monographs*, 1957, *71*(9 Whole No. 438).

Freeberg, N. E. Relevance of rater–ratee acquaintance in the validity and reliability of ratings. *Journal of Applied Psychology*, 1969, *53*, 518–524.

Friedman, M. J. *Differences in assessment center performance as a function of the race and sex of ratees and the race of assessors*. Unpublished doctoral dissertation, University of Tennessee (Knoxville), 1980.

Friedman, T. B. Self-testing, continued competence, and relicensure. Paper presented at the 8th annual meeting of the American Psychological Association, Toronto, Canada, August 29, 1978.

Fujie, O. *Assessment in a Japanese Organization*. Paper presented at the 1st annual conference of assessment center users, Tokyo, Japan, August 28, 1980.

Garland, H., & Price, K. H. Attitudes toward women in management and attributions for their success and failure in a managerial position. *Journal of Applied Psychology*, 1977, *62*, 29–33.

General Electric Company. *Talent development program (supplement for potential staff members)*. Ossining, N.Y.: GEC, Management Development Institute, 1969.

Ghiselli, E. E. Managerial talent. *American Psychologist*, 1963, *18*, 631–642.

Ghiselli, E. E. *The validity of occupational aptitude tests*. New York: Wiley–Interscience, 1966.

Ghiselli, E. E. *Explorations in management talent*. Pacific Palisades, Calif.: Goodyear Publishing Co., 1971.

Gill, R. W. T. *Achievement versus aptitude measures in assessment centers*. Paper presented at the 7th International Congress on the Assessment Center Method, New Orleans, June, 1979.

Ginsburg, L. R., & Silverman, A. The leaders of tomorrow. Their identification and development. *Personnel Journal*, 1972, *51*, 662–666.

Glaser, R., Schwarz, P. A., & Flanagan, J. C. The contribution of interview and situational procedures to the selection of supervisory personnel. *Journal of Applied Psychology*, 1958, *42*, 69–73.

Glennon, J. R., Albright, L. E., & Owens, W. A. *A catalog of life history items.* The Creativity Research Institute of the Richardson Foundation, American Psychological Association, Division 14, June 1966.

Glaser, E. M. Psychological consultation with executives. *American Psychologist*, 1958, *13*, 486–489.

Glickman, A. S., Hahn, C. P., Fleishman, E. A., & Baxter, B. *Top management development and succession.* New York: Macmillan Company, 1968.

Goldberg, L. R. Reliability of peace corps selection boards: A study of interjudge agreement before and after board discussions. *Journal of Applied Psychology*, 1966, *50*, 400–408.

Goldberg, L. R. Methodological critiques seer over sign. The first "good" example? *Journal of Experimental Research in Personality*, 1968, *3*, 168–171. (a)

Goldberg, L. R. Simple models or simple processes? Some research on clinical judgments. *American Psychologist*, 1968, *23*, 483–495. (b)

Goldberg, L. R. Man versus model of man: A rationale, plus some evidence, for a method of improving on clinical inferences. *Psychological Bulletin*, 1970, *73*, 422–432.

Goldberg, L. R. Man versus model of man: Just how conflicting is that evidence? *Organizational Behavior and Human Performance*, 1976, *16*, 13–22.

Goldberg, R. T., Costello, K., Wiesen, J. P., Popp, A. Use of the assessment center method for external hires: The case of the rehabilitation counselor. *Assessment and Development*, 1980, *7*(2), 4–7.

Goldfried, M. R., & Kent, R. N. Traditional versus behavioral personality assessment: A comparison of methodological and theoretical assumptions. *Psychological Bulletin*, 1972, *77*, 409–420.

Goldstein, I. L. *Training: Program development and evaluation.* Monterey, Calif.: Brooks/Cole, 1974.

Goldstein, I. L. Training in work organizations. In M. R. Rosenzweig & L. W. Porter (Eds.), *Annual Review of Psychology* (Vol. 31). Palo Alto, Calif.: Annual Reviews, Inc., 1980.

A good man is hard to find. *Fortune*, 1946, *33*, 92.

Gordon, L. V. Clinical, psychometric, and work-sample approaches in the prediction of success in Peace Corps training. *Journal of Applied Psychology*, 1967, *51*, 111–119.

Gorham, W. A. Federal executive agency guidelines and their impact on the assessment center method. *Journal of Assessment Center Technology*, 1978, *1*(1), 2–8. (a)

Gorham, W. A. *The uniform guidelines on employee selection procedures: What new impact on the assessment center method.* Speech presented to the Sixth International Congress on the Assessment Center Method, White Sulphur Springs, West Virginia, April 5, 1978. (b)

Graham, T. M. Combining assessment and training in the Peace Corps. In W. C. Byham (Chair), *The assessment center.* Symposium presented at the Executive Study Conference, New York, 1969.

Grant, D. L. *Assessment of management potential. The development and current status of AT&T's assessment center program.* Presented at the Executive Study Conference, New York, 1969.

Grant, D. L., & Bray, D. W. Contributions of the interview to assessment of management potential. *Journal of Applied Psychology*, 1969, *53*, 24–34.

Grant, D. L., & Bray, D. W. Validation of employment tests for telephone company installation and repair occupations. *Journal of Applied Psychology*, 1970, *54*, 7–14.

Grant, D. L., Katkovsky, W., & Bray, D. W. Contributions of projective techniques to assessment of management potential. *Journal of Applied Psychology*, 1967, *51*, 226–232.

Grant, D. L., & Moses, J. L. *Assessment of management potential and the application of assessment centers.* New York: AT&T, Personnel Research, May 1969.

Grant, K. W., & Slivinski, L. W. *The assessment centre approach: A literature review and implications for the federal government.* Public Service Commission of Canada, Personnel Assessment and Research Division, March 1970.

Green, S. G., & Mitchell, T. R. Attributional processes of leaders in leader–member interactions. *Organizational Behavior and Human Performance,* 1979, *23,* 429–458.

Greenwood, J. M. *The personnel assessment program: New exercises and OP and data analysis.* Armonk: IBM, Personnel Research Studies, 1968.

Greenwood, J. M., & McNamara, W. J. Interrater reliability in situational tests. *Journal of Applied Psychology,* 1967, *51,* 101–106.

Greenwood, J. M., & McNamara, W. J. Leadership styles of structure and consideration and managerial effectiveness. *Personnel Psychology,* 1969, *22,* 141–152.

Grossing, P. G. Professional competency: Identification, validation and training implications in pharmacy. In L. W. Hellervik (Chair), *Professional competence: I/O psychology applied to professional education and assessment.* Symposium presented at the 86th meeting of the American Psychological Association, Division of Industrial and Organizational Psychology, Toronto, 1978.

Grossner, C. *The assessment of the assessment center.* Unpublished doctoral dissertation, Sir George Williams University, 1974.

Gruenfeld, E. F. *Promotion: Practices, policies, and affirmative action* (Key Issues Series, No. 17). Ithaca: Cornell University, 1975.

Guilford, J. P. *Psychometric methods.* New York: McGraw–Hill, 1954.

Guion, R. M. *Personnel testing.* New York: McGraw–Hill, 1965.

Guion, R. M., & Gottier, R. F. Validity of personality measures in personnel selection. *Personnel Psychology,* 1965, *18,* 135–164.

Haas, J. S., Porat, A. M., & Vaughan, J. A. Actual vs. ideal time allocations reported by managers: A study of managerial behavior. *Personnel Psychology,* 1969, *22,* 61–75.

Hakel, M. D. Similarity of post–interview trait rating intercorrelations as a contributor to interrater agreement in a structured employment interview. *Journal of Applied Psychology,* 1971, *55,* 443–448.

Hakel, M. D., Dobmeyer, T. W., & Dunnette, M. D. The relative importance of three content dimensions in ratings of job applicant's resume. *Journal of Applied Psychology,* 1970, *54,* 65–71.

Hakel, M. D., Hollman, T. D., & Dunnette, M. D. Accuracy of interviewers, certified public accountants, and students in identifying the interests of accountants. *Journal of Applied Psychology,* 1970, *54,* 115–119.

Hakel, M. D., Ohnesorge, J. P., & Dunnette, M. D. Interviewer evaluations of job applicants' resumes as a function of the qualifications of the immediately preceding applicants—an examination of contrast effects. *Journal of Applied Psychology,* 1970, *54,* 27–30.

Hall, H. L. *An evaluation of the upward mobility assessment center for the Bureau of Engraving and Printing.* (TM 76-6). Washington, D.C.: U.S. Civil Service Commission, July, 1976.

Hall, H. L. *Analysis of an executive-level assessment center: A comparison of assessment center ratings to supervisor ratings and bio-data* (TM 79-1). Washington, D.C.: Personnel Research and Development Center, U.S.A. Office of Personnel Management, Applied Psychology Section, April 1979.

Hall, H. L., & Baker, D. R. *An overview of the upward mobility assessment center for the*

Bureau of Engraving and Printing (TM 75-5). Washington, D.C.: U.S. Civil Service Commission, August 1975.

Hall, H. L., & Baker, D. R. *An overview of the federal executive development program II assessment center* (TM 76-14). Washington, D.C.: U.S. Civil Service Commission, August 1976.

Hamilton, J. W. *Virginia Tech uses assessment centers for graduate training and evaluation.* Blacksburg: Virginia Polytechnic Institute and State University, 1980.

Hamilton, J. W., & Gavin, J. F. Small community police assessment. *Assessment & Development,* 1974, (1), 3.

Hammond, K. R., Stewart, T. R., Brehmer, B., & Steinmann, D. O. Social judgment theory. In M. F. Kaplan, & S. Schwartz (Eds.), *Human judgment and decision processes.* New York: Academic Press, 1975.

Hammond, K. R., & Summers, D. A. Cognitive dependence on linear and nonlinear cues. *Psychological Review,* 1965, *72,* 215–224.

Hamner, C. W., Kim, J. S., Baird, L., & Bigoness, W. J. Race and sex as determinants of ratings by potential employers in a simulated work sample task. *Journal of Applied Psychology,* 1974, *59,* 705–711.

Hardesty, D. L., & Jones, W. S. Characteristics of judged high potential management personnel—The operations of an industrial assessment center. *Personnel Psychology,* 1968, *21,* 85–98.

Harris, H. *The Group approach to leadership testing.* London: Routledge and Paul, 1949.

Haws, W. F. Selecting and training new supervisors. *Modern Casting,* 1969, *55,* 66–68.

Haynes, M. E. *Operations supervisor assessment program—Five-year post program evaluation.* Head Office Employee Relations, Shell Oil Company, March 28, 1978.

Heisler, W. J. Promotion: What does it take to get ahead? *Business Horizons,* April, 1978, 57–63.

Heisler, W. J., & Gremmill, G. R. Executive and MBA student views of corporate promotion practices: A structural comparison. *Academy of Management Journal,* 1978, *21,* 731–737.

Hellervik, L. W. *Professional competence: I/O psychology applied to professional education and assessment.* Symposium presented at the 86th meeting of the American Psychological Association, Division of Industrial and Organizational Psychology, Toronto, 1978.

Hemphill, J. K. Job descriptions for executives. *Harvard Business Review,* 1959, *37*(5), 55–67.

Hemphill, J. K., Griffiths, D. E., & Frederiksen, N. *Administrative performance and personality: A study of the principal in a simulated elementary school.* New York: Teachers College Bureau of Publications, Columbia, 1962.

Hersey, P. W. NASSP's assessment center—From concept to practice. *NASSP Bulletin* (National Association Secondary School Principals), 1977, *61,* 74–76.

Hilton, A. C., Bolin, S. F., Parker, J. W., Jr., Taylor, E. K., & Walker, W. B. The validity of personnel assessments by professional psychologists. *The Journal of Applied Psychology,* 1955, *39,* 287–293.

Hinrichs, J. R. Comparison of "real life" assessments of management potential with situation exercises, paper-and-pencil ability tests, and personality inventories. *Journal of Applied Psychology,* 1969, *53,* 425–432.

Hinrichs, J. R. Two approaches to filling the management gap: Management selection vs. management development. *Personnel Journal,* 1970, *49,* 1008–1014.

Hinrichs, J. R. A cross national evaluation of assessment centers in eight countries. *Assessment & Development*, 1975, *2*(2), 1; 5; 7.

Hinrichs, J. R. Personnel training. In M. D. Dunnette (Ed.), *Handbook of industrial and organizational psychology*. Chicago: Rand–McNally, 1976.

Hinrichs, J. R. An eight-year follow-up of a management assessment center. *Journal of Applied Psychology*, 1978, *63*, 596–601.

Hinrichs, J. R., & Haanpera, S. *A technical research report on management assessment in IBM World Trade Corporation* (Personnel Research Study, No. 18) IBM Europe, March 1974.

Hinrichs, J. R., & Haanpera, S. Reliability of measurement in situational exercises: An assessment of the assessment center method. *Personnel Psychology*, 1976, *29*, 31–40.

Hofstede, G. H. *The validity of staff ratings during management development courses*. IBM, Europe Personnel Research Study, July 1969.

Hogue, J. P., Otis, J. L., & Prien, E. P. Assessments of higher level personnel: Validity of predictions based on projective techniques. *Personnel Psychology*, 1962, *15*, 335–344.

Hollander, E. P., & Julian, J. W. Contemporary trends in the analysis of leadership processes. *Psychological Bulletin*, 1969, *71*, 387–397.

Hollenbeck, G. Personal commmunication, April 13, 1980.

Holmen, M. G. *An assessment program of OCS applicants* (HUMRRO Technical Report No. 26), 1956.

Holmes, D. S. *A report on an evaluation of eleven battalion commanders*. Greensboro, North Carolina: Center for Creative Leadership, February, 1972.

Holmes, D. S. How and why assessment works. In J. L. Moses & W. C. Byham (Eds.), *Applying the assessment center method*. New York: Pergamon Press, 1977.

Holt, R. R. Yet another look at clinical and statistical prediction: Or, is clinical psychology worthwhile? *American Psychologist*, 1970, *25*, 337–349.

Holt, R. R. Clinical and statistical measurement and prediction: How not to survey its literature. *JSAS Catalog of Selected Documents in Psychology*, 1975, *5*, (MS No. 837), 178.

Holt, R. R., & Luborsky, L. *Personality patterns of psychiatrists*. New York: Basic Books, 1958.

Horne, J. H., & Lupton, T. The work attitudes of "middle" managers—An exploratory study. *The Journal of Management Studies*, 1965, *2*, 14–33.

Horstman, D. S. *1975–76 court case compendium: Legal standards for personnel practices*. Washington, D.C.: Applied Psychology Section, Personnel Research and Development Center, United States Civil Service Commission, September 1977.

How to spot the hotshots. *Business Week*. October 8, 1979, 62; 67–68.

Howard, A. An assessment of assessment centers. *Academy of Management Journal*, 1974, *17*, 115–134.

Howard, A. Assessment center predictions sixteen years later. Paper presented at the 7th International Congress on the Assessment Center Method. New Orleans, June 6–8, 1979.

Howard, A. Personnel communication, February 16, 1981.

Hoyle, D. F. AT&T completes assessment of nearly 1700 women under consent agreement. *Assessment & Development*, (1975), *2*(2), 4–5.

Hoyle, D. F. *AT&T field review: How standards are maintained among more than 50 centers*. Paper presented at the 6th International Congress on the Assessment Center Method, White Sulphur Springs, April 6, 1978.

Huck, J. R. Assessment centers: A review of the external and internal validities. *Personnel Psychology*. 1973, *26*(2), 191–212. (a)

Huck, J. R. *The assessment process: Yesterday, today, and tomorrow*. Paper presented at the 1st Annual Industrial and Organizational Psychology Conference, Ohio State University, Columbus, September 1973. (b)

Huck, J. R. *Determinants of assessment center ratings for white and black females and the relationship of these dimensions to subsequent performance effectiveness.* Unpublished doctoral dissertation, Wayne State University, Detroit, Michigan, 1974.

Huck, J. R. The research base. In J. L. Moses & W. C. Byham (Eds.), *Applying the assessment center method.* New York: Pergamon Press, 1977.

Huck, J. R., & Bray, D. W. Management assessment center evaluations and subsequent job performance of black and white females. *Personnel Psychology,* 1976, *29,* 13–30.

Hudson, W. *The occupational classification of Africans.* Unpublished doctoral dissertation, Wits, 1953.

Hudson, W. Psychological research on the African worker. *Civilization,* 1958, *8*(2), 193–203.

Hudson, W., Biesheuvel, S., & Sichel, H. The experimental use of boss boy selection tests at Modderfontein B. Gold Mining Co., *CSIR/NIPR Bulletin,* 1951, *3*(2), 61–62.

Hudson, W., & Kruger, C. F. The selection of African supervisors by leaderless group tests. *Inter African Labour Institute Bulletin,* 1958, *5*(1), 10–27.

Huett, D. L. *The State of Wisconsin's Executive Assessment Center: A pilot investigation of convergent and discriminant validity.* Madison Department of Administration, State of Wisconsin, November 1974.

Huett, D. L. *The structure of final ratings rendered at Wisconsin's Executive Assessment Center.* Madison: State Bureau of Personnel, January, 1975.

Hulin, C. L. The measurement of executive success. *Journal of Applied Psychology,* 1963, *46,* 303–307.

Huse, E. F. Assessments of higher level personnel: The validity of assessment techniques based on systematically varied information. *Personnel Psychology,* 1962, *15,* 195–205.

Huse, E. F. Evaluation by structured interview as compared with quantitative scoring of in-basket test performance. In J. Campbell (Chair), *The in-basket exercise—test or technique?* Symposium presented at the 76th annual convention of the American Psychological Association, San Francisco, 1968.

Hyatt, J. C. More companies use "assessment centers" to gauge employees' managerial abilities. *The Wall Street Journal,* January, 3, 1974. p. 10.

Identifying tomorrow's managers: Edgars builds a top team. *People & profits,* 1973, *1*(2), 26–33; 36.

Ilgen, D. R., Campbell, D. J., & Peters, L. H. Assessees' perception of exercise affect performance during assessment. *Assessment and Development,* 1976, *3*(2), 4–5.

Ivey, A. E., & Authier, J. *Microcounseling: Innovations in interviewing, counseling, psychotherapy, and psychoeducation.* Springfield, Ill.: Thomas, 1978.

Jackson, D. N., Neill, J. A., & Bevan, A. R. Interpersonal judgmental accuracy and bias as a function of degree of acquaintance. *Proceedings of the 77th Annual Convention of the American Psychological Association,* 1969.

Jacobs, G. F. Testing native aptitudes for mining. *Optima,* 1957, *7,* 73–78.

Jaffee, C. L. Assessment centers help find management potential. *Bell Telephone Magazine,* 1965, 44(3), 18–24.

Jaffee, C. L. Managerial assessment: Professional or managerial prerogative. *Personnel Journal,* 1966, 45(3), 162–163.

Jaffee, C. L. A tridimensional approach to management selection. *Personnel,* 1967, *46,* 453–455.

Jaffee, C. L. *Problems in supervision: An in-basket training exercise.* Reading, Mass.: Addison–Wesley, 1968.

Jaffee, C. L. *Effective management selection.* Reading, Mass.: Addison–Wesley, 1971.

Jaffee, C. L. Personal communication, April 24, 1980.

Jaffee, C. L., Bender, J., & Calvert, O. L. The assessment center technique: A validation study. *Management of Personnel Quarterly,* 1970, 9(3), 9–14.

Jaffee, C. L., Cohen, S. L., & Cherry, R. Supervisory selection program for disadvantaged or minority employees. *Training & Development Journal,* 1972, 26(1), 22–28.

Jaffee, C. L., & Michaels, C. E., Jr. Is in-basket performance subject to coaching effects? *Journal of Assessment Center Technology,* 1978, 1(1), 13–17.

Jaffee, C. L., & Sefcik, J. T., Jr. What is an assessment center? *The Personnel Administrator,* 1980, 25(2), 40–43.

Jennings, H. H. Military use of sociometric and situation tests in Great Britain, France, Germany, and the United States. *Sociometry,* 12, 1949, 191–201.

Jeswald, T. A. Research needs in assessment—A brief report of a conference. *The Industrial/Organizational Psychologist,* 1971, 9(1), 12–14.

Jeswald, T. A. Issues in establishing an assessment center. In J. L. Moses & W. C. Byham (Eds.), *Applying the assessment center method.* New York: Pergamon Press, 1977. (a)

Jeswald, T. A. A new approach to identifying administrative talent, *NASSP Bulletin* (National Association Secondary School Principals), 1977, 61, 79–83. (b)

Jolson, M. Criteria for promotion of faculty view. *Academy of Management Journal,* 1974, 17, 149–154.

Jones, E. E. The rocky road from acts to dispositions. *American Psychologist,* 1979, 34, 107–117.

Jones, E. E., & Davis, K. E. From acts to dispositions: The attribution process in person perception. In L. Berkowitz (Ed.), *Advances in experimental social psychology* (Vol. 2). New York: Academic Press, 1965.

Kahneman, D., & Tversky, A. On the psychology of prediction. *Psychological Review,* 1973, 80, 237–251.

Kaplan, M. F. Information integration in social judgment: Interaction of judge and information components. In M. F. Kaplan & S. Schwartz (Eds.), *Human judgment and decision processes.* New York: Academic Press, 1975.

Kaplan, M. F., & Schwartz, S. (Eds.). *Human judgment and decision processes.* New York: Academic Press, 1975.

Kappel, F. R. *Vitality in a business enterprise.* New York: McGraw–Hill, 1960.

Kappel, F. R. From the world of college to the world of work. *Bell Telephone Magazine,* 1962, 41, 3–16.

Katz, D., & Kahn, R. L. *The social psychology of organizations* (2nd ed.). New York: Wiley, 1978.

Katz, R. L. Skills of an effective administrator. *Harvard Business Review,* 1955, 33, 33–43.

Katzell, R. A., Barrett, R. S., Vann, D. H., & Hogan, J. M. Organizational correlates of executive roles. *Journal of Applied Psychology,* 1968, 52, 22–28.

Kavanagh, M. J., MacKinney, A. C., & Wolins, L. Issues in managerial performance: Multitrait–multimethod analyses of ratings. *Psychological Bulletin,* 1971, 75, 34–49.

Kay, B. R. Key factors in effective foreman behavior. *Personnel,* 1959, 36, 25–31.

Kelley, H. H. The processes of causal attribution. *American Psychologist,* 1973, 28, 107–128.

Kellogg, M. S. *Career management.* New York: American Management Association, 1972.

Kelly, E. L. The place of situation tests in evaluating clinical psychologists. *Personnel Psychology,* 1954, 7, 484–492.

Kelly, E. L., & Fiske, D. W. *The prediction of performance in clinical psychology.* Ann Arbor: University of Michigan Press, 1951.

Kelly, E. L., Goldberg, L. R., Fiske, D. W., & Kilkowski, J. M. Twenty-five years later: A follow-up study of the graduate students in clinical psychology assessed in the VA selection research project. *American Psychologist*, 1978, *33*, 746–755.

King, H. D., & Arlinghaus, L. G. Interaction management validated in the steel industry. *Assessment & Development*, 1976, *3*(2), 1–2.

King, L. M., & Boehm, V. R. Assessment center judgment stability across time periods and assessors. Paper presented at the 88th annual convention of the American Psychological Association, Montreal, September, 1980.

Kinslinger, H. J. Application of projective techniques in personnel psychology since 1940. *Psychological Bulletin*, 1966, *66*, 134–149.

Kirchoff, L. L. *Early identification assessment: A survey of participants' reactions.* Detroit, Michigan Bell Telephone, Personnel Research Department, 1972.

Kleiman, L. S., & Faley, R. H. Assessing content validity: Standards set by the court. *Personnel Psychology*, 1978, *31*, 701–713.

Klimoski, R. J., & Strickland, W. J. Assessment centers: Valid or merely prescient. *Personnel Psychology*, 1977, *30*, 353–363.

Klimoski, R. J., & Strickland, W. J. *A comparative view of assessment centers.* Unpublished manuscript, 1981.

Klinefelter, J., & Ship, T. *Assessment center approach: A comprehensive summary.* State of Illinois, Division of Research and Test Development, Department of Personnel, November 1972.

Knowles, M. S. *The modern practice of adult education: Andragogy versus pedagogy.* New York: Association Press, 1970.

Knowles, M. S. *The adult learner: A neglected species.* Houston: Gulf Publishing Co., 1973.

Kohls, J. W. *Evaluation of the assessment center approach to the selection of college recruits in the eastern territory.* Chicago, October 1970, Sears Roebuck & Co., Psychological Research & Services Section.

Korman, A. K. The prediction of managerial performance: A Review. *Personnel Psychology*, 1968, *21*, 295–322.

Kovenklioglu, G., & Greenhaus, J. H. Causal attributions, expectations, and task performance. *Journal of Applied Psychology*, 1978, *63*, 698–705.

Kraut, A. I. Intellectual ability and promotional success among high level managers. *Personnel Psychology*, 1969, *22*, 281–290.

Kraut, A. I. A hard look at management assessment centers and their future. *Personnel Journal*, 1972, *51*, 317–326.

Kraut, A. I. Management assessment in international organizations. *Industrial Relations*, 1973, *12*, 172–182.

Kraut, A. I., & Scott, G. J. Validity of an operational management assessment program. *Journal of Applied Psychology*, 1972, *56*, 124–129.

Landmark AT&T–EEOC consent agreement increases assessment center usage. *Assessment & Development*, 1973, *1*(1), 1–2.

Landy, F. J. The validity of the interview in police officer selection. *Journal of Applied Psychology*, 1976, *61*, 193–198.

Landy, F. J., & Bates, F. Another look at contrast effects in the employment interview. *Journal of Applied Psychology*, 1973, *58*, 141–144.

Landy, F. J., & Trumbo, D. A. *Psychology of work behavior* (2nd ed.). Homewood, Ill.: The Dorsey Press, 1980.

Langdale, J. A., & Weitz, J. Estimating the influence of job information on interviewer agreement. *Journal of Applied Psychology*, 1973, *57*, 23–27.

Laurent, H. Early identification of managers. *Management Records*, May, 1962, pp. 33–38.

Laurent, H. Cross-cultural cross-validation of empirically validated tests. *Journal of Applied Psychology*, 1970, *54*, 417–423.

Lawler, E. E. The multitrait-multirater approach to measuring managerial job performance. *Journal of Applied Psychology*, 1967, *51*, 369–381.

Lawless, J. Promotion: All in a day's work. *Industrial Management*, April, 1973, pp. 28–31.

Leim, M. A., Slivinski, L. W., & Grant, K. W. *Assessors' and assessees' attitudes toward the customs and excise assessment centre*. Public Service Commission of Canada, Managerial Assessment and Research Division, August 1972.

Leonard, R. L., Jr. *Relevance and reliability in interpersonal judgments*. Washington, D.C.: American Institutes for Research, 1973.

Libby, R. Man versus model of man: Some conflicting evidence. *Organizational Behavior and Human Performance*, 1975, *15*, 1–12.

Libby, R. Man versus model of man: The need for a nonlinear model. *Organizational Behavior and Human Performance*, 1976, *16*, 23–26.

Libby, R., & Blashfield, R. K. Performance of a composite as a function of the number of judges. *Organizational Behavior and Human Performance*, 1978, *21*, 121–129.

Loacher, G. Assessment procedures used as educational criterion. *Assessment & Development*, 1974, *2*(1), 5–6.

London, M., & Hakel, M. D. Effects of applicant stereotypes, order, and information on interview impressions. *Journal of Applied Psychology*, 1974, *59*, 157–162.

Lopez, F. M., Jr. *Evaluating executive decision making: The in-basket technique* (AMA Research Study No. 75). New York: American Management Association, 1966.

Lopez, F. M., Jr. The in-basket exercise: Utility and limits. In J. Campbell (Chair)., *The in-basket exercise—test or technique?* Symposium presented at the 76th annual convention of the American Psychological Association, San Francisco, 1968.

Lopez, F. M., Jr. *The making of a manager*. New York: American Management Association, 1970.

Lorge, I., Fox, D., Davitz, J., & Brenner, M. A survey of studies contrasting the quality of group performance and individual performance, 1920–1957. *Psychological Bulletin*, 1958, *55*, 337–372.

Lupton, D. E. Assessing the assessment center—A theory Y approach. *Personnel*, 1973, *50*(6), 15–22.

Lyngen, R. J. *An evaluation of the selection phase of the new supervisory selection and training program*. Peoria: Caterpillar Tractor Company, undated. (Mimeo)

MacKinnon, D. W. An assessment study of Air Force officers. Part V: Summary and applications [WADC Tech. Rep. 58-91 (V)]. Dayton: Wright Air Development Center, 1958.

MacKinnon, D. W. The study of creative persons: A method and some results. In J. Kagan (Ed.), *Creativity and learning*. Boston: Houghton Mifflin, 1967.

MacKinnon, D. W. The identification and development of creative personnel. *Personnel Administration*, 1968, *31*, 9–17.

MacKinnon, D. W. *An Overview of Assessment Centers*. (CCL Tech. Rep. 1). Berkeley: University of California, Center for Creative Leadership, May, 1975.

MacKinnon, D. W. From selecting spies to selecting managers. In J. J. Moses & W. C. Byham (Eds.), *Applying the assessment center method*. New York: Pergamon Press, 1977.

Mahler, W. R. Coaching. In R. L. Craig & L. R. Bittel (Eds.), *Training and development handbook*. New York: McGraw–Hill, 1967.

Mahoney, T. A., Jerdee, T. H., & Carroll, S. J. The job(s) of management. *Industrial Relations*, 1965, *4*, 97–110.

Mandell, M. N. The group oral performance test. In P. J. W. Pigors, C. A. Myers, and F. T.

Malm (Eds.), *Management of human resources.* New York: McGraw–Hill, 1964, pp. 267–268.

Marquardt, L. D. *Follow-up evaluation of the second look approach to the selection of management trainees.* Chicago: Psychological Research and Services, National Personnel Department, Sears, Roebuck and Company, July 1976.

Martin, A. H. Examination of applicants for commissioned rank. In L. Farago & L. F. Gittler (Eds.), *German psychological warfare.* New York: Committee for National Morale, 1941.

Mather, B. E. *Assessment of men: A validity study.* Unpublished masters thesis, Massachusetts Institute of Technology, 1964.

Mauer, K. F. *The African production supervisor in the South African mining industry.* Unpublished masters thesis. University of Natal, Durban, 1953.

Mayfield, E. C. The selection interview—A reevaluation of published research. *Personnel Psychology,* 1964, *17,* 239–260.

Mayfield, E. C., & Carlson, N. E. Selection interview decisions: First results from a long-term research project. *Personnel Psychology,* 1966, *19,* 41–53.

McCall, M. W., Jr., Morrison, A. M., & Hannan, R. L. *Studies of managerial work: Results and methods* (Tech. Rep. 9) Greensboro, North Carolina: Center for Creative Leadership, May, 1978.

McClelland, D. C., Atkinson, J. W., Clark, R. A., & Lowell, E. L. *The achievement motive.* New York: Appleton–Century–Crofts, 1953.

McClelland, D. C., & Boyatzia, R. *The leadership motive pattern and long-term success in management.* McBer and Company, 1980.

McClelland, D. C., & Winter, D. G. *Motivating economic achievement.* New York: Free Press, 1969.

McConnell, J. H. The assessment center in the smaller company. *Personnel,* 1969, *46*(2), 40–46.

McConnell, J. H. The assessment center: A flexible program for supervisors. *Personnel,* 1971, *48*(5), 35–39.

McConnell, J. H. Sizing up assessment centers. *Personnel Management,* October, 1973, pp. 36–38.

McConnell, J. J., & Parker, T. An assessment center program for multiorganizational use. *Training and Development Journal,* 1972, *26*(3), 6–14.

McCormick, E. J. The development of processes for indirect or synthetic validity. III. Application of job analysis to indirect validity. A symposium. *Personnel Psychology,* 1959, *12,* 402–413.

McCormick, E. J. Job and task analysis. In M. D. Dunnette (Ed.), *Handbook of industrial and organizational psychology.* Chicago: Rand McNally, 1976.

McCormick, E. J. *Job Analysis: Methods and applications,* New York: AMACOM, 1979.

McCormick, E. J., Cunningham, J. W., & Thornton, G. C. III. The prediction of job requirements by a structured job analysis procedure. *Personnel Psychology,* 1967, *20,* 431–440.

McCormick, E. J., Jeanneret, P. R., & Mecham, R. C. A study of job characteristics and job dimensions as based on the position analysis questionnaire (PAQ). *Journal of Applied Psychology Monograph,* 1972, *56,* 347–368.

McCormick, E. J., & Tiffin, J. *Industrial Psychology* (6th ed.). Englewood Cliffs, NJ: Prentice–Hall, 1974.

McCowan, W. B., Jr. *An evaluation of the usefulness of the assessment center in personnel selection and promotion.* Thesis submitted to George Washington University, May 1972.

McIntyre, F. M. Unique appraisal program developed by Chevrolet–Sales. *Assessment & Development*, 1975, *2*(2), 3; 6.

Mendenhall, M. D. *A report on an assessment center for the position of Deputy Police Chief*. Omaha: Personnel Department, City of Omaha, Nebraska, 1976.

Metropolitan Transit Authority. *The uses of the assessment center in a government agency's management development program*, June 29, 1972. pp. 1–26.

Meyer, H. D. Comparative validity of dimension ratings based on simulation exercises and tests and interviews, separately and combined. *Assessment & Development*, 1980, *7*(2), 17–19.

Meyer, H. H. The validity of the in-basket test as a measure of managerial performance. *Personnel Psychology*, 1970, *23*, 297–307.

Meyer, H. H. *Assessment centers at General Electric*. Paper presented at the Development Dimensions Conference, San Francisco, 1972.

Michigan Bell. *Personnel research, summary—male promotion study—1958–1968*, December 12, 1969.

Michigan Bell Telephone Company. *Nonmanagement men's assessment program*, Detroit 1/6/69, 12/26/69, 12/31/70, 4/20/71.

Michigan Bell Telephone Company, Personnel Relations Department. *PAP-IBMC Study*, Detroit: October 1970.

Michigan Bell Telephone Company, Personnel Relations Department. *Early identification program*. Detroit: January 1971. (a)

Michigan Bell Telephone Company, Personnel Relations Department. *Personnel assessment-MBT*, Detroit: February 1971. (b)

Michigan Bell Telephone Personnel Assessment Program. Evaluation Study Detroit 1961.

Miller, D. *Assessment centers at Syntex*. Paper presented at the meeting of the Personnel Division of the National Pharmaceutical Assoc., Hot Springs, Va., 1972.

Miller, R. B. Task description and analysis. In R. M. Gagne (Ed.), *Psychological principles in system development*. New York: Holt, Rinehart, & Winston, 1966.

Miner, J. B. *Personnel Psychology*, New York: Macmillan, 1969.

Miner, J. B. Psychological evaluations as predictors of consulting success. *Personnel Psychology*, 1970, *23*, 393–405. (a)

Miner, J. B. Executive and personnel interviews as predictors of consulting success. *Personnel Psychology*, 1970, *23*, 521–538. (b)

Miner, J. B. Personality tests as predictors of consulting success. *Personnel Psychology*, 1971, *24*, 191–204.

Mintzberg, H. *The managerial work*. New York: Harper and Row, 1973.

Mischel, W. *Personality and assessment*. New York: Wiley, 1968.

Mischel, W. Toward a cognitive social learning reconceptualization of personality. *Psychological Review*, 1973, *80*, 252–283.

Mitchel, J. O. Assessment center validity: A longitudinal study. *Journal of Applied Psychology*, 1975, *60*, 573–579.

Moore, B. *Personnel assessment centers in Britain and America*. Sydney, Australia: New South Wales Public Service Board, December 1969. (Mimeo).

Morris, B. S. Officer selection in the British Army, 1942–1945. *Occupational Psychology*, 1949, *23*, 219–234.

Morrison, D. Paper presented at the 9th International Congress on the Assessment Center Method, San Diego: March–April 1981.

Morse, J. J., & Wagner, F. R. Measuring the process of managerial effectiveness. *Academy of Management Journal*, 1978, *21*, 23–35.

Moses, J., & Ritchie, R. Assessment center used to evaluate an interaction modeling program. *Assessment and Development*, 1975, *2*(2), 1–2.

Moses, J., & Wall, S. Pre-hire assessment: A validity study of a new approach for hiring college graduates. *Assessment and Development*, 1975, *2*(2), 11.

Moses, J. L. On the application of clinical method in personnel psychology. Paper presented at the meeting of the New York State Psychological Association, Kiamisha Lake, N.Y., May 1969.

Moses, J. L. Assessment center performance and management progress. In W. C. Byham (Chair), *Validity of assessment centers*. Symposium presented at the 79th annual convention of the American Psychological Association, Washington, D. C., 1971.

Moses, J. L. Assessment center performance and management progress. *Studies in Personnel Psychology*, 1972, *4*(1), 7–12.

Moses, J. L. Assessment center for the early identification of supervisory and technical potential. In W. C. Byham & D. Bobin (Eds.), *Alternatives to paper and pencil testing*. Proceedings of a conference at Graduate School of Business, University of Pittsburgh, May, 1973 (a).

Moses, J. L. The development of an assessment center for the early identification of supervisory potential. *Personnel Psychology*, 1973, *26*, 569–580. (b)

Moses, J. L. The assessment center method. In J. L. Moses & W. C. Byham (Eds.), *Applying the assessment center method*. New York: Pergamon Press, 1977. (a)

Moses, J. L. Developing an assessment center program for school administrators. *NASSP Bulletin* (National Association Secondary School Principals), 1977, *61*, 76–69. (b)

Moses, J. L. Behavior modeling for managers. *Human Factors*, 1978, *20*(2), 225–232.

Moses, J. L. Assessing the assessor: A systems approach to assessor training. Paper presented at the 7th International Congress on the Assessment Center Method, New Orleans, June, 1979.

Moses, J. L., & Byham, W. C. (Eds.). *Applying the assessment center method*. New York: Pergamon Press, 1977.

Moses, J. L., & Boehm, V. R. Relationship of assessment center performance to management progress of women. *Journal of Applied Psychology*, 1975, *60*, 527–529.

Murray, H. *Explorations in personality*. Cambridge: Oxford University Press, 1938.

Myers, D. G., & Lamm, H. The group polarization phenomenon. *Psychological Bulletin*, 1976, *83*, 602–627.

National Institute of Personnel Research. *Final report on the experimental use of boss boy selection tests at Modderfontein B. Gold Mining Co.*, 1951.

National Institute of Personnel Research. *Charts based on validation studies into the use of selection and classification tests for native mine workers* (SACSIR/NIPR) 1955.

National Institute of Personnel Research. Aptitude tests for South African Mine Workers. *Mining Survey*, 1958, *9*(1), 33–37.

Nealey, S. M., & Fiedler, F. E. Leadership functions of middle managers. *Psychological Bulletin*, 1968, *70*, 313–329.

Neidig, R. D. Reliability of determining dimensions from critical incident job analysis data. *Assessment & Development*, 1977, *4*(1), 1.

Neidig, R. D. Assessment center program evaluation. Paper presented at the 6th International Congress on the Assessment Center Method, White Sulphur Springs, West Virginia, April, 1978.

Neidig, R. D., & Hall, H. L. *Assessor team balancing* (TM-77-19). Washington, D.C.: U.S. Civil Service Commission, September 1977.

Neidig, R. D. & Martin, J. C. *The FBI's Management Aptitude Program Assessment Center*

(Report No. 2): An Analysis of Assessors' Ratings. (TM79-2). Washington, D.C.: Applied
    Psychology Section. Personnel Research & Development Center, U.S. Civil Service
    Commission, April, 1979.

Neidig, R. D., Hall, H. L., & Baker, D. R. A job analysis technique for determining job tasks
    and performance skills (TM 77-18). Washington, D.C.: U.S. Civil Service Commission,
    July 1977.

Neidig, R. D., Martin, J. C., & Yates, R. E. The FBI's Management Aptitude Program Assess-
    ment Center: Research Report No. 1 (TM 78-3). Washington, D.C.: Applied Psychology
    Section, Personnel Research & Development Center, U.S. Civil Service Commission,
    April 1978.

Norton, S. D. The empirical and content validity of assessment centers vs. traditional
    methods for predicting managerial success. Academy of Management Review, 1977, 2,
    442–453.

Nova University. Educational leadership appraisal (ELA): A progress report. The
    Gatekeeper's Gazette 7(2), Ft. Lauderdale: Nova University, (Undated).

Nunnally, J. C. Psychometric Theory (2nd ed.) New York: McGraw–Hill, Inc., 1978.

Office of Strategic Services Assessment Staff. Assessment of men: Selection of personnel
    for the Office of Strategic Services. New York: Rinehart, 1948.

Ogilvie, J. R., & Schmitt, N. Situational influences on linear and nonlinear use of informa-
    tion. Organizational Behavior and Human Performance, 1979, 23, 292–306.

O'Leary, L. R., Knowles, E., & Powers, M. Assessment center assists in selecting St. Louis
    fire chief (Personnel Letter No. 278). Chicago: IPMA Personnel Letter, September,
    1975. pp. 3–8.

Olin–Mathison. Supervisor selection program. OM, Corporate Personnel Department, un-
    dated. (Mimeo)

Olmstead, J. A., Cleary, F. K., Lackey, L. L., & Salter, J. A. Development of leadership assess-
    ment simulations (Tech. Rep. 73-21). Arlington, Virginia: Human Resources Research
    Organization, September 1973.

Olmstead, J. A., Cleary, F. K., Lackey, L. L., & Salter, J. A. Development of Leadership As-
    sessment Simulations. (Abstract) JSAS Catalog of Selected Documents in Psychology,
    1975, 5, 212.

Osgood, C. E., Suci, G. J., & Tannenbaum, P. H. The measurement of meaning. Urbana, Ill.:
    University of Illinois Press, 1957.

Otis, J. L., Campbell, J. T., & Prien, E. P. Assessment of higher level personnel: VII. The na-
    ture of assessments. Personnel Psychology, 1962, 15, 441–446.

Owens, W. A., & Henry, E. R. Biographical data in industrial psychology: A review and
    evaluation. The Creativity Research Institute of The Richardson Foundation, Inc.,
    February 1966.

Pacific Telephone and Telegraph Company. The PAR effects study. PT&T, Personnel Rela-
    tions Department, 1968.

Parker, T. C. Assessment centers: A statistical study. The Personnel Administrator, 1980,
    25(2), 65–67.

Peabody, D. Trait inferences: Evaluative and descriptive aspects. Journal of Personality &
    Social Psychology Monograph, 1967, 7(4, Whole No. 644).

Peabody, D. Evaluative and descriptive aspects of personality perception: A reappraisal.
    Journal of Personality and Social Psychology, 1970, 16, 639–646.

Pederson, L. Managerial success for a group of professionals via the in-basket. Symposium
    presented at the 8th International Congress on the Assessment Center Method, To-
    ronto, Canada, April, 1980.

Pederson, L. D., Slivinski, L. W., & Bourgeois, R. P. Assessors' reactions to the career assignment program Assessment centre 74-2 training session. Ottawa, Canada: Managerial Assessment and Research Division, Career Assignment Program, Public Service Commission, December 1974.

Penfield, R. V. Time allocation patterns and effectiveness of managers. Personnel Psychology, 1974, 27, 245–255.

Perlson, M. R. Failure—Focused selection. Unpublished paper, 1979.

Peter, L. F. The Peter Principle. New York: William Morrow, 1970.

Phelps, R. H., & Shanteau, J. Livestock judges: How much information can an expert use. Organizational Behavior and Human Performance, 1978, 21, 209–219.

Pigors, P. Case method. In R. L. Craig (Ed.), Training and development handbook (2nd ed.). New York: McGraw–Hill, 1976.

Pigors, P., & Pigors, F. Case method in human relations: The incident process. New York: McGraw–Hill, 1961.

Pomerleau, R. Identification systems: The key to effective manpower planning. Personnel Journal, June 1973, pp. 434–441; 474.

Porritt, D. Research evaluation and development responsibilities for the personnel assessment center. Sydney, Australia: Public Service Board, C & R Division, 1970.

Price, A. Assessment centers in the Federal Aviation Administration. Paper presented at the 6th International Congress on the Assessment Center Method. White Sulphur Springs: April, 1978.

Prien, E. P. Assessments of higher level personnel: V. An analysis of interviewers' predictions of job performance. Personnel Psychology, 1962, 15, 319–334.

Prien, E. P. Development of a supervisor position description questionnaire. Journal of Applied Psychology, 1963, 47, 10–14.

Prien, E. P., & Liske, R. E. Assessments of higher level personnel: III. Rating criteria: A comparative analysis of supervisor ratings and incumbent self-ratings of job performance. Personnel Psychology, 1962, 15, 187–194.

Prien, E. P., & Ronan, W. W. Job analysis: A review of research findings. Personnel Psychology, 1971, 24, 371–396.

A promising new method for spotting potential: The assessment center. Interpersonal, 1970, 1(19), 1–8.

Psychological Corporation. Summaries of court decisions on employment testing 1968–1977. New York: The Psychological Corporation, April, 1978.

Public Service Commission of Canada. The career assignment program. PSCC, CAP Communique, 1973, 2(1).

Purdy, D. C. Personal communication, including PCI Insights, No. 28 and memo Assessment center program for determining promotions for the fire and police departments in the City of Richmond, January 26, 1979. (a)

Purdy, D. C. Personal communication to George C. Thornton, III. January 26, 1979. (b)

Quaintance, M. K. Search for alternative selection procedures: The assessment center. Address to International Personnel Management Association, Harrisburg, March 13, 1980.

Quarles, C. L. The assessment center as a managerial success predictor in criminal justice. Paper presented to the Society of Police and Criminal Psychology, Atlanta, Georgia, October 24, 1980.

Quick, J. C., Fisher, W. A., Schkade, L. L., & Ayers, G. W. Developing administrative personnel through the assessment center technique. The Personnel Administrator, 1980, 25(2), 44–62.

Rappoport, L., & Summers, D. A. (Eds.). Human judgment and social interaction. New York: Holt, Rinehart, & Winston, 1973.

Rawls, J. R., & Rawls, D. J. Recent trends in management selection. *Personnel Journal,* 1974, *53,* 104–109.

Read, Sister Joel. A degree by any other name: The Alverno program. In F. Hughes & O. Jills (Eds.), *Formulating policy in post-secondary education: The search for alternatives,* Washington: American Council on Education, 1975.

Reeve, E. G. *Validation of selection boards.* London: Academic Press, 1971.

Reliability of the assessment center method. *Assessment & Development,* 1976, *3*(1), 4.

Research Institute of America, Inc. Assessment centers: A technique for finding future managers (14). *Alert,* January 13, 1971.

Research Institute of America, Inc. The "assessment center"—A better way to select supervisors (493). *Alert,* November 14, 1973. (a)

Research Institute of America, Inc. Assessment centers: Helping to get your man. *Marketing for Sales Executives,* October 1973, 4–5. (b)

Rice, B. Measuring executive muscle. *Psychology Today,* December, 1978, pp. 95–110.

Richards, S. A., & Jaffee, C. L. Blacks supervising whites: A study of interracial difficulties in working together in a simulated organization. *Journal of Applied Psychology,* 1972, *56,* 234–240.

Riess, B. F. Measuring professional competence: A challenge to the profession. Paper presented at the 8th annual meeting of the American Psychological Association, Toronto, Canada, August 29, 1978.

Ritchie, R. J. Selecting commission sales people with an assessment center. Paper presented at the 8th International Congress on the Assessment Center Method, Montreal, June 1980.

Ritchie, R., & Boehm, V. *Screening for assessment centers using biographical data and paper-and-pencil tests.* Paper presented at the 7th International Congress on the Assessment Center Method, New Orleans, June 1979.

Ritchie, R., & Boehm, V. Reducing costs by pre-screening assessment center candidates. *Assessment & Development,* 1980, *7*(2), 5.

Robison, D. AT&T women employees making faster strides into middle management. *World of Work Report,* 1978, *3*(1), 1, 6–7.

Rogers, R. EEOC uses systematic appraisal to select district directors, *Assessment and Development,* 1979, *6*(1), 1–3.

Roose, J. E., & Doherty, M. E. Judgment theory applied to the selection of life insurance salesmen. *Organizational Behavior and Human Performance,* 1976, *16,* 231–239.

Rosen, B., & Jerdee, T. H. Factors influencing disciplinary judgments. *Journal of Applied Psychology,* 1974, *59,* 327–331.

Rosenow, R. Paper presented at the 9th International Congress on the Assessment Center Method, San Diego, March–April 1981.

Roskind, W. L. Confidentiality of selection instruments challenged. *Assessment & Development,* 1976, *3*(1), 3–4.

Russell, G. Differences in minority/nonminority assessment center ratings. *Assessment and Development,* 1975, *3*(1), 3; 7; 8.

Russell, P. Paper presented at the 9th International Congress on the Assessment Center Method, San Diego, March–April 1981.

Russell, P., & Byham, W. C. *Reliability and Validity of Assessment in a Small Manufacturing Company.* Pittsburgh: Development Dimensions International, 1980.

Russell, P., & Byham, W. C. *Relationship between item completion and time limits in the in-basket exercise.* Pittsburgh: Development Dimensions International, 1981.

Rustin, Richard E. Merrill Lynch is charged by U.S. agency with widespread bias in job practices. *Wall Street Journal,* September 8, 1975, 1.

Sackett, P. R., & Hakel, M. D. Temporal stability and individual differences in using assessment information to form overall ratings. *Organizational Behavior and Human Performance,* 1979, *23,* 120–137.

Sadoka, J. M. Factor analyses of OSS situation tests. *Journal of Abnormal & Social Psychology,* 1952, *47,* 843–852.

Salaman, C., & Thompson, K. Class culture and the persistence of an elite: The case of army officer selection. *The Sociological Review* 26(2), 283–304.

Salas, R. G. *The WOSB's revisited: An experimental evaluation of the Australian Army version of the War Office Selection Board procedure.* Melbourne: Australian Army Psychological Research Unit, 1970.

Samph, T. Three methodologies for assessing physician competency in interpersonal skills. Paper presented at 8th annual meeting of the American Psychological Association, Toronto, Canada, August 19, 1978.

Sawyer, J. Measurement *and* prediction, clinical *and* statistical. *Psychological Bulletin,* 1966, *66,* 178–200.

Schaffer, A. J. Information about assessment center for ES&D program finalists. Memorandum from Director, Personnel Division, National Office, Washington, D.C.: Internal Revenue Service, September 16, 1970.

Schein, E. H. *Organizational psychology.* Englewood Cliffs, NJ: Prentice–Hall, 1965.

Schmidt, F., Greenthal, A. L., Hunter, J. E., Berner, J. G., & Seaton, F. W. Job sample vs. paper-and-pencil trades and technical tests: Adverse impact and examinee attitudes. *Personnel Psychology,* 1977, *30,* 187–197.

Schmitt, N. Interrater agreement in dimensionality and combination of assessment center judgments. *Journal of Applied Psychology,* 1977, *62,* 171–176.

Schmitt, N. Comparison of subjective and objective weighting strategies in changing task situations. *Organizational Behavior and Human Performance,* 1978, *21,* 171–188.

Schmitt, N., & Hill, T. E. Sex and race composition of assessment center groups as a determinant of peer and assessor ratings. *Journal of Applied Psychology,* 1977, *62,* 261–264.

Schneier, D. B. The impact of EEO legislation on performance appraisals. *Personnel,* 1978, *55,* 24–34.

Schoenfeldt, L. F. *Maximum manpower utilization: Development, implementation, and evaluation of an assessment-classification model.* Paper presented at the 80th annual convention of the American Psychological Association, Honolulu, August, 1972.

Schuh, A. J. Effects of interview rating form content and rater experience on the evaluation of a job applicant. *Personnel Psychology,* 1973, *26,* 251–260.

Schwab, D. P., Heneman, H. H., Ill, & DeCotiis, T. A. Behaviorally anchored rating scales: A review of the literature. *Personnel Psychology,* 1975, *38,* 549–562.

Schwartz, R. Personal communication, November 21, 1980.

Shankster, M. G. Personal communication, June 1, 1979.

Shankster, M. G., & Cordea, D. J. The assessment center at Johnson Wax. *Assessment & Development,* 1976, *3*(1), 7.

Sharf, J. C. Content validity: Whither thou goest? *The Industrial-Organizational Psychologist,* 1980, *17*(3), 8–14.

Shartle, C. L. Leadership and executive performance. *Personnel,* 1949, *25,* 370–380.

Shell Oil Company. *Operations supervisor assessment program five-year post program evaluation Southern E & P Region.* Head Office Employee Relations, March, 1978.

Shinn, J. Fostering talent at General Electric. *International Management,* 1971, *26,* 30–32.

Shipe, T. R. *Assessment center feasibility study. Project summary.* State of Illinois, Division of Recruitment, Research and Test Development, Department of Personnel, October 1973.

Shudo, K. Personal communication, August 8, 1979.

Sichel, H. S. A validation of the boss boy selection procedure. *Bulletin National Institute of Personnel Research.* 1951, 3(2), 20–27.

Silzer, R. F. Competency assessment: Use of performance ratings and assessment center. In L. W. Hellervik (Chair), *Professional competence: I/O psychology applied to professional education and assessment.* Symposium presented at the meeting of the American Psychological Association, Division of Industrial and Organizational Psychology, Toronto, 1978.

Slevin, D. P. The assessment center: Breakthrough in management appraisal and development. *Personnel Journal, 1972, 51,* 255–261.

Slivinski, L. W. *Comparison of different methods of assessment.* Paper presented at the 7th International Congress on the Assessment Center Method, New Orleans, 1979. (a)

Slivinski, L. W. *Identification of senior executive potential: Development and implementation of an assessment centre.* Ottawa, Canada: Public Service Commission, October 1979. (b)

Slivinski, L. W., & Bourgeois, R. P. Feedback of assessment center results. In J. L. Moses & W. C. Byham (Eds.), *Applying the assessment center method.* New York: Pergamon Press, 1977.

Slivinski, L. W., & Ethier, L. *Development of the assessment centre for the career assignment program: Descriptive analysis of the senior executive population.* Public Service Commission of Canada, Managerial Assessment and Research Division, November 1973.

Slivinski, R. W., & Grant, K. W. *Assessment centre proposal.* Personnel Assessment and Research Division, Public Service Commission of Canada, January 1970.

Slivinski, L. W., & Grant, K. W. *Behavioral validation prediction model.* Paper presented to the International Public Personnel Association, San Francisco, November 1971.

Slivinski, L. W., Grant, K. W., Bourgeois, R. P., & Pederson, L. D. *Development and application of a first level management assessment centre.* Ottawa, Canada: Managerial Assessment and Research Division of the Personnel Psychology Centre, October 1977.

Slivinski, L. W., McCloskey, J. L., & Bourgeois, R. P. *Comparison of different methods of assessment.* Paper presented at the 7th International Congress on the Assessment Center Method, New Orleans, June 1979.

Slivinski, L. W., Yan, T. R., Richter, I. L., McDonald, V. S., & Bourgeois, R. P. *Reactions to an assessment centre.* Managerial Assessment and Research Division, Personnel Psychology Centre, Public Service Commission, January 1977.

Sloane, L. Exercise simulates business situations. *New York Times,* Business and Finance Section, November 28, 1971, pp. 3; 8.

Slovic, P. Analyzing the expert judge: A descriptive study of a stockbroker's decision process. *Journal of Applied Psychology, 1969, 53,* 253–263.

Slovic, P., Fischhoff, B., & Lichtenstein, S. Behavioral decision theory. In M. R. Rosenzweig & L. W. Porter (Eds.), *Annual review of psychology* (Vol. 28). Palo Alto: Annual Reviews, Inc., 1977.

Slovic, P., & Lichtenstein, S. Comparison of Bayesian and regression approaches to the study of information processing in judgment. In L. Rappoport & D. A. Summers (Eds.), *Human judgment and social interaction.* New York: Holt, Rinehart, and Winston, 1973.

Social Science Research Division. *Summary report of the early identification of management potential research project in Standard Oil Company (New Jersey) and affiliated companies.* Employee Relations Department, Standard Oil Company (NJ), August 1961.

Social Science Research Division. *Social science research reports. Vol. 5: Individual and organizational development.* New York: Employee Relations Department, Standard Oil Company (NJ), December 1963. (a)

Social Science Research Division. *Social science research reports. Vol. 3: Performance review and evaluation.* New York: Employee Relations Department, Standard Oil Company (NJ), June 1963. (b)

Social Science Research Division. *Social science research reports. Vol. 2: Selection and placement.* New York: Employee Relations Department, Standard Oil Company (NJ), December 1963. (c)

Social Science Research Division. *Social science research reports. Vol. 4: Surveys and inventories.* New York: Employee Relations Department, Standard Oil Company (NJ), August, 1963. (d)

Social Science Research Division. *Social science research reports. Vol. 1: Introduction and review.* Employee Relations Department, Standard Oil Company (NJ), February 1964.

Smith, P. C., & Kendall, L. M. Retranslation of expectations: An approach to the construction of unambiguous anchors for rating scales. *Journal of Applied Psychology*, 1963, *47*, 149–155.

Spool, M. D. Training programs for observers of behavior: A review. *Personnel Psychology*, 1978, *31*, 853–888.

Springbett, B. M. Factors affecting the final decision in the employment interview. *Canadian Journal of Psychology*, 1958, *12*, 13–22.

Stagner, R. Attitudes of corporate executives regarding psychological methods in personnel work. *American Psychologist*, 1946, *1*, 540–541.

Standing, T. E. Assessment and management selection. In J. L. Moses & W. C. Byham (Eds.), *Applying the assessment center method.* New York: Pergamon Press, 1977.

Stern, G. G., Stein, M. I., & Bloom, B. S. *Methods in personality assessment.* Glencoe, Il.: Free Press, 1956.

Stewart, A. M. *The identification of management potential. A brief description and review.* Sussex, England: Institute of Manpower Studies, February 1973. (Mimeo)

Stewart, R. *Managers and their jobs: A study of the similarities and differences in the way managers spend their time.* London: Macmillan, 1967.

Stogdill, R. M. Personal factors associated with leadership. *Journal of Psychology*, 1948, *25*, 35–71.

Stogdill, R. M. *Handbook of leadership: A survey of theory and research.* New York: The Free Press, 1974.

Stogdill, R. M., & Shartle, C. L. *Methods in the study of administrative leadership*, Columbus: Bureau of Business Research, Ohio State University, 1955. (a)

Stogdill, R. M., & Shartle, C. L. (Eds.). *Patterns of administrative performance* (Monograph 81). Columbus: Bureau of Business Research, Ohio State University, 1955. (b)

Story, W. *Assessment centers.* Paper presented at the New York Workshop on Assessment Centers, New York, 1969.

Taft, R. Use of the "group situation observation" method in the selection of trainee executives. *Journal of Applied Psychology*, 1948, *32*, 587–594.

Taft, R. The ability to judge people. *Psychological Bulletin*, 1955, *52*, 1–23.

Taft, R. Multiple methods of personality assessment. *Psychological Bulletin*, 1959, *56*, 333–352.

Task Force on Assessment Center Standards. Standards and ethical considerations for assessment center operations. *The Personnel Administrator*, 1980, *25*(2), 35–38.

Taylor, B., & Lippitt, G. L. (Eds.). *Management development and training handbook.* Maidenhead, Berkshire, England: McGraw–Hill, 1975.

Taylor, E. K., & Nevis, E. C. The use of projective techniques in management selection. *Personnel*, 1957, *33*, 462–474.

Taylor, J. O., Jr. The EEOC guidelines on content validity and their application to the assessment center method. *Journal of Assessment Center Technology*, 1978, *1*(1), 9–12.

Tennessee Valley Authority. *Managerial skills appraisal program—Report of study*. TVA, Division of Personnel, June 26, 1968.

Tennessee Valley Authority. *TVA's experiment in the assessment of managerial potential*, undated.

Thelen, M. H., Varble, D. L., & Johnson, J. Attitudes of academic clinical psychologists toward projective techniques. *American Psychologist*, 1968, *23*, 517–521.

Thigpen, E. A small company approaches assessment one to one. *Assessment & Development*, 1974, *2*(1), 8.

Thigpen, E. Pre-employment assessment—A systematic approach to selecting new employees. *Assessment & Development*, 1977, *4*(1), 7.

Thompson, D. E., Klasson, C. R., & Lubben, G. L. *Performance appraisal and the law: Policy and research implications of court cases*. Presented at the Academy of Management meetings, Atlanta, GA, August 1979.

Thomson, H. A. *Internal and external validation of an industrial assessment program*. Unpublished doctoral dissertation, Case Western Reserve University, 1969.

Thomson, H. A. Comparison of predictor and criterion judgments of managerial performance using the multitrait–multimethod approach. *Journal of Applied Psychology*, 1970, *54*, 496–502.

Thoresen, J. Blue collar assessment at Rohm & Haas Company. *Assessment & Development*, 1974, *2*(1), 2; 6.

Thoresen, J. D., & Jaffee, C. L. A unique assessment center application with some unexpected by-products. *Human Resource Management*, 1973, *12*(1), 3–7.

Thornton, G. C., III. Image of industrial psychology among personnel administrators. *Journal of Applied Psychology*, 1969, *53*, 436–438.

Thornton, G. C., III. Varieties of validity of assessment centers in other companies. In W. C. Byham (Chair), *Validity of assessment centers*. Symposium presented at the 79th annual convention of the American Psychological Association, Washington, D.C., 1971.

Thornton, G. C., III. *Job analysis procedure for Kodak Colorado Division, SSW/CDP Programs*, unpublished manuscript, 1976.

Thornton, G. C., III. Assessor evaluation of assessment center experiences. Unpublished manuscript, 1977.

Thornton, G. C., III. *Research on observer training*. Paper presented at the 7th International Congress on the Assessment Center Method, New Orleans, June, 1979.

Thornton, G. C., III. & McCambridge, J. The use of assessment centers for graduate students. *Professional Psychology*, 1974, *5*, 366–368.

Thornton, G. C., III, & Zorich, S. Training to improve observer accuracy. *Journal of Applied Psychology*, 1980, *64*, 351–354.

Tiffin, J., & McCormick, E. J. *Industrial psychology* (5th ed.). Englewood Cliffs, N.J.: Prentice-Hall, 1965.

Tiffin, J., & Prevratil, W. Industrial psychology in the aircraft industry. *American Psychologist*, 1956, *11*, 246–248.

Tornow, W. W., & Pinto, P. R. The development of a managerial job taxonomy: A system for describing, classifying, and evaluating executive positions. *Journal of Applied Psychology*, 1976, *61*, 410–418.

Trankell, A. The psychologist as an instrument of prediction. *Journal of Applied Psychology*, 1959, *43*, 170–175.

Tucker, D. H. & Rowe, P. M. Relationship between expectancy, causal attributions, and final hiring decisions in the employment interview. *Journal of Applied Psychology*, 1979, *64*, 27–34.

Turner, T. S. A different way to assess management. *Canadian Business*, August, 1973, pp. 54–56.

Tyler, L. E. Design for a hopeful psychology. *American Psychologist*, 1973, *32*, 587–594.

Ulrich, L., & Trumbo, D. The selection interview since 1949. *Psychological Bulletin*, 1965, *63*, 100–116.

United States Office of Personnel Management. *Equal Employment Opportunity court cases* (OIPP 152-46). Washington, D.C.: Office of Intergovernmental Personnel Programs, September 1979.

Van Oudstshoorn, M. Personal communication, October 19, 1979.

Vernon, P. E., & Parry, J. B. *Personnel selection in the British forces.* London: University of London Press, 1949.

Vernon, P. E. The validation of Civil Service Selection Board Procedures. *Occupational Psychology*, 1950, *24*, 75–95.

Vernon, P. E. *Personality tests and assessments.* London: Methuen and Company, 1953.

Vidmar, N. Effects of group discussion on category width judgments. *Journal of Personality and Social Psychology*, 1974, *29*, 187–195.

Vroom, V. H. Leadership. In M. D. Dunnette (Ed.), *Handbook of industrial and organizational psychology.* Chicago: Rand McNally, 1976.

Vroom, V. H., & Yetton, P. W. *Leadership and decision making.* Pittsburgh: University of Pittsburgh Press, 1973.

Ward, L. B. *The business in-basket test* (Research bulletin, RB-59-8). Educational Testing Service, April 1959.

Ward, L. B. Putting executives to the test. *Harvard Business Review*, 1968, *38*, 6–7; 10; 15; 164–180.

Washburn, P. V., & Hakel, M. D. Visual cues and verbal content as influences on impressions after simulated employment interviews. *Journal of Applied Psychology*, 1973, *58*, 137–140.

Wasserman, H. N. A new tool for identifying tomorrow's managers. *Retail Overview*, 1972, *4*(4), 11–17.

Wellins, R. Personal communications, January 15, 1980.

Wernimont, P. F., & Campbell, J. P. Signs, samples, and criteria. *Journal of Applied Psychology*, 1968, *52*, 372–376.

Wexley, K. N., Sanders, R. E., & Yukl, G. A. Training interviewers to eliminate contrast effects in employment interviews. *Journal of Applied Psychology*, 1973, *57*, 233–236.

Wexley, K. N., Yukl, G. A., Kovacs, S. Z., & Sanders, R. E. Importance of contrast effects in employment interviews. *Journal of Applied Psychology*, 1972, *56*, 45–48.

Where they make believe they're the boss. *Business Week*, August 28, 1971, pp. 34–35.

Whisler, T. L., & Harper, S. F. *Performance appraisal.* New York: Holt, Rinehart, and Winston, 1962.

Wickert, F. R., & McFarland, D. E. *Measuring executive effectiveness.* New York: Appleton–Century–Crofts, 1967.

Wickes Corporation. *Management assessment program.* Corporate Personnel Department, 1969. (Mimeo)

Wiggins, J. S. *Personality and prediction: Principles of personality assessment.* Reading, Mass.: Addison–Wesley, 1973.

Wikstrom, W. S. Assessing managerial talent. *The Conference Board Record*, 1967, *4*, 39–44.

Williams, J. C. Systematic career assessment/planning for MBA students. Paper presented at the 37th annual meeting of the Academy of Management, Orlando, August 14–17, 1977.

Williams, J. C. Personal communication, September 14, 1981.

Williams, J. C., & Longenecker, J. G. Non-traditional dimensions of managers of education in academia. National Meeting of Academy of Management, 1976.

Wilson, J. E., & Tatge, W. A. Assessment centers—Further assessment needed? *Personnel Journal*, 1973, *52*, 172–179.

Wofford, J. C. Factor analysis of managerial behavior variables. *Journal of Applied Psychology*, 1970, 54(2), 169–173.

Wollowick, H. B., & McNamara, W. J. Relationship of the components of an assessment center to management success. *Journal of Applied Psychology*, 1969, *53*, 348–352.

Worbois, G. M. Validation of externally developed assessment procedures for identification of supervisory potential. *Personnel Psychology*, 1975, *28*, 77–91.

Wright, O. R., Jr. Summary of research on the selection interview since 1964. *Personnel Psychology*, 1969, *22*, 391–413.

Yan, T. R., & Slivinski, L. W. *A history of the assessment centre method in the military.* Ottawa, Canada: Managerial Assessment and Research Division of the Personnel Psychology Centre, Public Service Commission of Canada, November 1976.

Author Index

Subject Index